Julie C. Hulse
Shallowford. Feb 2007.

OPENINGS IN
FIRST CORINTHIANS

OPENINGS IN FIRST CORINTHIANS

And I, brethren, could not
speak unto you as unto spiritual,
but as unto carnal,
even as unto babes in Christ

I Corinthians 3:1

JOHN METCALFE

THE PUBLISHING TRUST
Church road, Tylers Green, Penn, Buckinghamshire

Printed and Published by the
John Metcalfe Publishing Trust
Church Road, Tylers Green
Penn, Buckinghamshire

—

Distributed by Trust Representatives
and Agents world-wide

In the Far East

Bethany, Orchard Point P.O. Box 0373
Singapore 912313

—

© John Metcalfe Publishing Trust 2002
All Rights Reserved

—

First Published 2002

—

ISBN 1 870039 84 X

—

This work is available at less than the cost of production through subsidies on the part of the John Metcalfe Publishing Trust. The Author waives all royalties in favour of the Trust, a Registered Charity.

CONTENTS

THE BEGINNING	1
THE VISION	3
THE OPENING: THE TESTIMONY OF CHRIST; I CORINTHIANS 1:1-9	18

PART ONE — JUDGMENT CONCERNING THE TESTIMONY, CHAPTERS 1:10-11:6 — 29

JUDGMENT CONCERNING DIVISIONS IN THE ECCLESIA AT CORINTH; I CORINTHIANS 1:10-4:21	31
JUDGMENT CONCERNING THE WICKED; I CORINTHIANS 5:1-13	71
JUDGMENT PERTAINING TO THE SAINTS: WHETHER OF THE WORLD; OF ANGELS; OF BRETHREN; OF UNRIGHTEOUSNESS; OR OF THE BODY AND THE SPIRIT; I CORINTHIANS 6:1-20	73
JUDGMENT CONCERNING QUESTIONS OF MARRIAGE; I CORINTHIANS 7:1-40	93
JUDGMENT CONCERNING MEATS OFFERED TO IDOLS; I CORINTHIANS 8:1-13	98
[PAUL VEHEMENTLY VINDICATES HIS APOSTLESHIP - PARENTHESIS; I CORINTHIANS 9:1-10:13]	100
RESUMPTION OF I CORINTHIANS 8:1-13; JUDGMENT CONCERNING MEATS OFFERED TO IDOLS; I CORINTHIANS 10:14-11:1	105
JUDGMENT CONCERNING HEADSHIP; I CORINTHIANS 11:2-16	108

PART TWO — JUDGMENT CONCERNING ASSEMBLING TOGETHER, CHAPTERS 11:17-15:58 — 115

(1) THE LORD'S SUPPER, CHAPTER 11:18-34	117
(2) THE UNITY OF THE SPIRIT IN THE BODY OF CHRIST, CHAPTERS 12:1-13:13	123
(3) THE MANIFESTATION OF THE GIFTS IN THE ASSEMBLY, CHAPTER 14:1-40	245
(4) THE EVANGELICAL TRUTH OF THE RESURRECTION OF THE DEAD, CHAPTER 15:1-58	271

THE CONCLUSION: I CORINTHIANS 16:1-24	405
ON THE COLLECTION FOR THE SAINTS AT JERUSALEM, VERSES 1-4	405
ON MINISTERING TO THE SAINTS AT CORINTH, VERSES 5-14	407
MINISTRY CONCERNING STEPHANAS, FORTUNATUS, AND ACHAICUS, VERSES 15-18	409
SALUTATIONS; AN ADMONITION; THE BLESSING, VERSES 19-24	412

OPENINGS IN FIRST CORINTHIANS

The Beginning

DEPARTING from Athens, Paul came to Corinth, abiding with Aquila – a Jew – and his wife Priscilla, both of whom were likewise strangers to the city. Paul reasoned in the synagogue every sabbath, persuading the Jews and the Greeks.

The arrival at Corinth of Silas and Timotheus from Macedonia seemed to have stirred Paul, seeing that he had testified in the synagogue sabbath after sabbath without that effect which he so earnestly desired. Perhaps being especially moved by prayer together with his newly arrived brethren, pressed in spirit, Paul was constrained to persuade no longer, but actually to bring to an issue before the Jews the truth that Jesus was Christ.

Under the force of this newly confrontational preaching, the Jews opposed themselves; and blasphemed. At this Paul shook his raiment, declaring their blood to be on their own heads. He was clean: from henceforth he would go to the Gentiles.

He departed thence and entered into the abode of Justus, a man that worshipped God, whose house joined hard by the synagogue. Crispus, the chief ruler of the synagogue, believed on the Lord with all his house; and many of the Corinthians hearing believed and were baptized. This aroused very great fear and controversy, both from the Jew and the Gentile.

Then spake the Lord to Paul in the night by a vision, 'Be not afraid, but speak, and hold not thy peace: for I am with thee, and no man shall set on thee to hurt thee: for I have much people in this city.'

Paul continued in Corinth a year and six months, teaching the word of God among them. Notwithstanding the hatred and enmity stirred up against Paul—particularly by the religious to the authorities—brought about much tumult. But out of it all the Lord delivered Paul.

After this the apostle tarried there yet a good while before he took his leave of the brethren, and sailed thence into Syria, accompanied by Priscilla and Aquila. After a considerable passage of time, Apollos, an eloquent man, and mighty in the scriptures, came to Corinth and mightily convinced the Jews, and that publicly, showing by the scriptures that Jesus was Christ. This helped them much which had believed through grace. All this may be confirmed from Acts 18.

Following these things letters passed between the long absent Paul and the *ecclesia* at Corinth. First from Paul to the Corinthians, warning them not to company with fornicators, I Corinthians 5:9. But if such an elementary exhortation, surely a thing obvious in itself, then into what state had the Corinthians fallen, and into what forgetfulness had they lapsed—Apollos or not—in Paul's absence?

Next the Corinthians wrote to Paul, I Corinthians 7:1, but, once again, concerning things both carnal and rudimentary, hardly evincing evidence of growth in grace in the absence of the apostle.

Thereafter–and perhaps coincidental with the visit to Paul of certain concerned brothers–Paul heard of the state of the brethren at Corinth from those of the household of Chloe, I Corinthians 1:11. Then were there no brethren, to sound the alarm in the *ecclesia*, that this godly sister must perforce send those of her own household? However the coming to Paul of Stephanas, Fortunatus, and Achaicus supplied that which had been lacking, and the apostle became aware through this information of the low–if not appalling–state into which the Corinthians had fallen as an assembly.

Given this intelligence, and upon receiving such ill tidings, Paul wrote the first epistle to the *ecclesia* at Corinth. Nevertheless, mindful of the vision of the Lord, and of the power of God in their beginnings, being confident of the work of the Spirit through the word of the truth of the evangel, far from being full of despondency and gloom, the epistle actually abounds with great assurance, much consolation, being full of grace and of glory.

The Vision

The vision of First Corinthians differs from that of the other epistles. By 'vision' I mean the spiritual enlightenment conveyed in the various books of the new testament concerning the place to which God in Christ has brought–or is bringing–his people. This also entails the revelation of the Father, the Son, and of the Holy Ghost distinctively seen in each epistle respectively.

I repeat, the vision of First Corinthians differs from that seen in the other epistles. This is because the apostle by the Holy Ghost discerns the *spiritual condition* of the people to whom he is writing.

It is not a question of a show of erudition, or of conveying an impressive body of learning: to do so would stumble rather than further the faith of those in need of truth directly applicable to *their own* spiritual growth. This is divinity worth the name: less is beneath contempt.

The vision of the first epistle to the *ecclesia* at Corinth was in fact *limited* by the errors into which that company had fallen. Nevertheless, the light of the glorious evangel radiates throughout, giving so much radiance, that one cannot but be thankful for the truth of God brought forth even though it were through the failure of man and by the occasion of so grievous a list of errors.

Yet how different appears the vision in other epistles: it is not just the matter of the doctrine or the exhortation, it is *the revelation of the Lord, and of the place to which the saints are brought in him*, by which they stand in grace, that is so distinctive.

To illustrate this vital truth, and to give an example of this essential principle—and one quite different from First Corinthians—take the position revealed in the epistle to the Romans.

The following relevant short extract appears in 'Justification by Faith'.

Romans views man in the light of his personal accountability. It takes up the individual. The majority of the epistles deal with the *ecclesia*, having to do with the company. They take up a corporate position, they speak to the assembly, the congregation.

The epistle to the Romans, however, addresses the individual. It is a question of what answers to baptism. That is personal.

Baptism may introduce one into a company, but it, itself, is personal. Baptism is the figure in which one is depicted as buried with Christ, and, having been buried, raised up with him in newness of life.

Everything in Romans is through the death of Christ. It is true that one sees oneself risen with Christ in newness of life, and that the nature of that life stands in freedom from the law of sin and death.

It is also true that—by the mercies of God—the saints find themselves in a company, in one body, with many members.

But these are things glimpsed, these are the consequence; such things show the light of the glory beginning to break, the glorious prospect before those who have been crucified with Christ.

His death is what is central, and their death in him: they have been buried with him. That is the answer to every moral question, to the very judgment itself, in the light of the great white throne: crucified with Christ.

Buried with him by baptism into death.

It is this that brings in the body of Christ. Nothing less and nothing else. Upon the hearing of this by faith, there follows the baptism of the Holy Ghost.

Hence Romans, dealing with the individual in the light of the judgment of God, is the true evangelist's message. Anything else is false. But the true evangel brings, and must bring, the faithful to one body in Christ as a reality.

So that forgiveness, remission, justification, propitiation, reconciliation, redemption, sonship, substitution, sanctification, can neither be preached nor received in isolation from the truth of the company to which these things inevitably lead, and which they bring in.

It is impossible that the true evangel should result in continued individualism and independency.

The gospel unites us and must unite us in one body with many members. Salvation is preached with an end in view. The *ecclesia*–the 'church'–is in view. It is *this* that is the pillar and ground of the truth, nothing else. The 'church'–properly, *ecclesia*–which is his body, the fulness of him that filleth all in all.

This appears at the close of the epistle, Rom. 16:25. It is not expounded but it is indicated. We are brought to a mystery. This mystery is made known by revelation. It is the mystery of the fellowship.

This fellowship is that of the *ecclesia*, the assembly, the house of God not made with hands, indwelt by the Father and the Son, and united in the life and power of one Spirit.

This is what the preaching and teaching of the evangel, the gospel, achieves. This is what evangelism properly so-called achieves. This is what the evangelist who is sent of God achieves.

And it is what the evangel maintains. Death with Christ and in Christ is the basis of the fellowship of the mystery. It is what is depicted by baptism, and set forth in Romans.

The Lord's supper is not mentioned in the epistle to the Romans. The Lord's supper is for the company, it is the communion of the body of Christ.

The epistle in which the supper is mentioned is the first epistle to the Corinthians, which takes another position in Christ altogether.

In Romans, the death of Christ is studied, together with our death in him. By grace in Christ we are judicially slain, and buried, by a death and burial that meets and answers all responsibility through him who loved us, and gave himself for us.

Romans is a book about death, it studies death in Christ. It is a book that studies the death of Christ for the individual, and the individual's death in Christ. Christ died for him, and he died in Christ.

What a wonderful peace this gives, what a tremendous salvation, what assurance this brings to the conscience. How marvellous is the epistle to the Romans!

The book takes up the faith of the individual, it plunges him into the waters of death, it carries him down into the tomb of Christ, it buries him in the depths of the death of Christ.

He has died with Christ, he is buried with Christ. That is the position Romans takes. Buried with him by baptism into death.

That is not Christ dying for him, it is his dying with Christ. It is not Christ being buried for him, it is his being buried with Christ.

But if he is buried, then he is taken out of sight: the man has disappeared from view.

From view of what?

Why, from view of the law, from view of the curse, from view of sins, guilt, rebellion, from view of the old man, of Adam, from view of sin, the world, corruption and death, and from view of the great white throne in the day of judgment.

The saints are dead and buried to it all, they are out of sight in that chamber of death called the tomb, and they cannot be brought back from the sepulchre to face the charges of the accuser, or the sight of that to which they have died, any more, world without end, Amen.

When a man is dead, the law brings no more charges against him, and neither does it require any more from him for ever. It cannot.

The ultimate sanction of the law is death, and when that sanction has been brought into execution, that is the end of any relationship between the law and the man upon whom the death penalty has been executed.

Will they bring him back into court? By this time he stinketh.

It cannot be. He has answered to the grim reaper, and the law has nothing to say, nothing to require, nothing to demand of a corpse. That is the place of all who are 'buried with him by baptism into death'. It is the position of Romans.

However, the vision in the first epistle to the Corinthians is distinct. Here a company is seen. 'Even as the testimony of Christ was confirmed in you.' That is, 'you', plural. Not 'thee', singular. It is the assembled company, plural.

A fellowship is seen, in the wilderness of this present world.

In a figure it is the pilgrim company, passed over the Red sea by faith, now entered into the wilderness, bound for the distant promised land beyond the river Jordan.

However, once separated from Egypt, once entered as a body upon the pilgrim way, the testimony, 'the pattern shown on the mount', comes down, 'even as the testimony of Christ was confirmed in you'.

The Holy Ghost fills the body, Christ above in glory administers the Spirit to the separated company below, gifts are given, guidance obtained, truth ministered, a pillar of cloud and fire, by day and night, goes before.

The Lord's supper shows the people's severance from Egypt in the past, their unity in the wilderness at present, and their entry into the land of promise in future.

The testimony came down in Chapter one, love fills the saints in Chapter thirteen, the descended Spirit from the headship of Christ forms the body and guides the assembly in Chapters twelve and fourteen, and the entire company is raised up to ascend with Christ in his likeness in Chapter fifteen.

Here are special provisions for the time of pilgrimage.

Gifts, prophecies, signs, the principles governing differing ministries, the manifestation of the Spirit, the Spirit himself, the distinction between male and female, the Lord's supper, provision for the ministry and service of women: here is the pillar of cloud, there the pillar of fire.

As many as are led by the Spirit of God, these are the sons of God. The Spirit leads into all truth.

This lowly, pilgrim, sojourning company, meek, submissive to the truth in the love of it, this is the company that the Holy Ghost owns, in which he dwells, and none other. It is the church of God on earth.

In the epistle to the Colossians however the emphasis is otherwise, and so a different position in respect of the union of the saints with Christ is seen.

In Colossians the saints are risen with Christ, that is the opening position, it answers in them to Christ risen from the dead, but seen on earth.

Through his indwelling life they are sustained on earth by him from glory.

There is an interior living union, they live by him who is invisible, above in the heavens. Their life is hidden. But hid with Christ in God.

In Ephesians the position of the saints is not on earth at all, in the counsels of God they are outside of this world.

Everything is dead on earth, the world already judged, all who live before God are ascended with Christ in the heavenly places, the saints are seated with Christ in glory.

Here, their position corresponds with his.

God's eternal purpose has already come in, the saints answer to it even now, eternal things are come to pass, and the light, power, and spirit of them govern the elect, as seen in the faith and love of the saints at Ephesus.

But all—no matter *which* epistle—is *based* on his death. Did Christ die, and was he buried? And was his death and burial for the saints? Then they also died, and they too were buried, with him.

Constantly one must return to the position in Romans. Here all that is to be revealed of death and burial in Christ, is brought to light for faith, the faith of God's elect.

This is a truth that will appear again and again in the openings from First Corinthians.

Neither is it fanciful to conclude that the Corinthian epistle corresponds with Israel in the wilderness: indeed, it is the very language of the apostle in Chapter 10:1-11.

This is hardly being at rest in the inheritance of the land, having passed over Jordan, signifying the present enjoyment of every spiritual blessing in heavenly places in Christ, reposing in everlasting glory.

For the Corinthians, in figure, the land of promise, Canaan, remained a distant and as yet an unrealized dream.

The spiritual consciousness—such as it was—of the Corinthians, the limitation of the vision to which the apostle was reduced to reach their condition, was that of being in the time of pilgrimage through an alien wilderness: the tabernacle passing through a hostile world.

Having left Egypt, yes, but very very far short of Jordan, and with the trial of faith in their sojourning bringing to light the unbelief, carnality, rebellion, and worldliness once latent and hidden in their hearts.

Here is no permanent position: they are marching through the desert on their way to the inheritance. They are in tents, not the city. They bear up the tabernacle, not enter into the temple. But the LORD loveth the gates of Zion more than all the tents of Jacob. Such a figure exactly portrays the Corinthian position.

The epistle envisages the testimony of Christ in his people, separated from the world, in their pilgrimage to the heavenly inheritance. The figure of this was seen in the separation of Israel from Egypt by the waters of the Red sea, and their receiving the tabernacle of witness in which the presence of the LORD should accompany them on their journeyings till they crossed the river of Jordan and entered the promised land.

Provision is made for the wilderness, for their pilgrimage, but all this is temporary: it is what is provided until they reach the promised land of their inheritance. Just so, at the beginning, the testimony of Christ is confirmed in them, chapter 1:4-9, *with a view to their bearing that testimony throughout their pilgrimage.*

In the figure, they *are* the tabernacle in the wilderness. The Spirit dwells in them, not in the world through which they are passing on their way to glory. This journey is not their rest: there *remaineth* a rest for the people of God, and to it they are travelling on their way to Jordan.

Hence the tabernacle was pitched; it was a tent: it was *designed* to be moved, and to be moved nearer and nearer to the land of promise. Till then, the testimony had no resting place: not in this world. There was no floor to the tabernacle. It was pegged, it had no foundations, there was no floor, all was fashioned for pilgrimage, as the people were led ever onwards.

But the temple had a floor: it was the pillar and ground of the truth: it had foundations which were never to be moved. This is beyond the visionary scope of First Corinthians, but the tabernacle of witness is not: it *is* the vision of First Corinthians.

With the descent of 'the testimony of Christ' which was 'confirmed in you', I Corinthians 1:6, the pilgrimage—according to the figure of the tabernacle in the wilderness with Israel—properly begins. The tabernacle must be suitably carried by chosen brethren, and, when the halt is commanded, properly pitched and arranged for the service.

So much the more when that of which the tent in the wilderness was nothing save a visible outward figure, manifesting the inward glory of Christ in reality. For if the sign of the glory was about the tabernacle, the glory itself was *within* the *ecclesia*. That is, in 'you', plural, the entire company.

This is not individual; here, everything is corporate: it is for *worship*. Not what *he* is for us: what *we* are for him.

With the beginning of pilgrimage from this present world to the world to come, separation in its totality was signified by the crossing of the Red sea. Thus in fulfilment the saints were for ever dead to this world, to all this world, and to all this world's religion. For them everything, but everything, was to come from God out of heaven: 'then were all dead': 'old things are passed away; behold, all things are become new.'

Nevertheless thereafter every divine provision *was for the journey, the pilgrimage through this world, alone.* Such things were nothing to do with God's inheritance in the land. It was wholly to do with God's provision to *get* to the land. It was provision *till* the land. Now, *with that* the vision in Corinthians corresponds.

This was depicted by Israel's separation from Egypt: by the pillar of cloud and of fire; by the manna falling from heaven; by the water from the Rock which followed them, 'which Rock was Christ', I Corinthians 10:4. Nor can the terrible judgments which fell upon the unbelieving and rebellious be ignored.

These things being so – continuing with and applying the figure – provision for this short earthly pilgrimage was *temporary*. It was *in passing through this present world*. It did not pertain to the inheritance. None of this was for everlasting. It was not for the city. Nothing of it was for eternity. All was provision *for the wilderness*. Thereafter, it would pass away.

But, given that the glory descended and filled the tabernacle of the testimony, one must enquire, What things were temporary, to last through this journey, till all was caught up to glory at the last?

First, that there was no room for the flesh in the service of God. In a figure, fleshly service and servants were driven out by the smoke from the glory which filled God's dwelling place: his presence, and his service, was fulfilled by the evangel, and if so, in the Spirit of Sonship, and by the place of sons.

God would judge the flesh and its works, whether the carnal mind; proud division or schism; opinionated reasoning; the spirit of the world and of worldliness; covetousness and the love of money; fornication or uncleanness; false worship and idolatry; hypocrisy or legality: whatever was of the flesh *was to be utterly excluded from the dwelling place of God*.

To that end, to the continual remembrance and maintenance of that end, commandments, ordinances, doctrine, and discipline were all laid down for a testimony from the commencement of the journey, and for a continuation till the end of it. The apostles' doctrine; baptism; the cross; the recognition of and submission to the Holy Ghost; sanctification; owning and being subject to the Lord in the word of the truth of the evangel.

Walking together as brethren; judging the flesh; separation from the world; the observation of and correct propriety in the distinction between male and female; the covering of the head of the woman in prayer and prophecy; the Lord's supper; the unity of the body. *One* body.

Gifts of whatever order; the order of the gifts; the administration of the gifts; the dangers of and in the wilderness; the dangers of and in pilgrimage; the necessity of righteous judgment; the imperative of the love of God in Christ; the place of women in relation to the brethren in the order of God and in the meetings of the saints.

Above all, and so much the more as the end approaches, the resurrection *must* be kept constantly before the eye of faith. And since faith cometh by hearing, and hearing by the word of God, by this is meant *the resurrection as it is taught in the apostles' doctrine*.

By the Holy Ghost, in the midst of the *ecclesia*, here is a *constantly reiterated vision* in and at the coming of the Lord. This ends the journey. It concludes the pilgrimage.

So it was with Israel in the figures of the true. For as long as they passed through the wilderness on their pilgrim journey to the river of Jordan and the land of their inheritance, so long they bore the moving tent of witness. So long the water from the Rock followed them. So long the manna fell about the camp. So long the pillar of cloud by day and of fire by night went on before them.

At the beginning, with the *ecclesia*, the assembly, 'the testimony of Christ' had been 'confirmed in them'. Throughout the years of their pilgrimage through the wilderness of this world, in the inward glory, Christ was remembered as present in the Spirit, in his death, till he came.

Here the body of Christ is not seen in heavenly places – or even as united to the Head – but as constituted by, filled with, and led through this present and passing evil world by the Holy Ghost, within *and below*, as descended from the Head on high.

As the tribes were to keep rank and be encamped in due and proper order and station in relation to the one tabernacle, so the saints are to be found united together in the Spirit's unity in the one body gathered in assembly. All the brethren in any given place – say, Corinth – were met, and there met unitedly, each rightly esteeming with all humility the measure and gift of the Spirit in the other.

Brethren deferred one to the other, each esteeming other better than himself, all waiting in the fear of God, and the power of the Spirit, to magnify in order the glory of Christ according to the scriptures. Likewise in their giving forth and singing in psalms and hymns and spiritual songs. Women were to keep silence in such an assembly.

But all this till the land that is very far off was viewed at last, and the King in his beauty, the river crossed over dry shod past the stationary ark of the LORD, held up in priestly strength, and, after so long and arduous a sojourning, possession taken of the inheritance, and the entering into the promised rest.

What a wonderful change will then have been wrought! How old things – albeit divine, still, only for the wilderness – will have passed away; behold: all things are become new! For when that which is perfect is come, then that which is in part shall be done away, I Corinthians 13:10.

At the beginning of the pilgrimage, when 'the testimony of Christ' – having come down from heaven – 'was confirmed in you', thence began the long, afflicting, and persecuted journey, but always, from the very first, 'Waiting for the coming of our Lord Jesus Christ', I Corinthians 1:6,7.

As it were, through fourteen long chapters their travail and weary passage across the face of this wilderness below was recorded. But always, as in a figure, carrying the ark of the testimony let down from heaven. Now no longer. At last, journey's end is reached: the Lord comes, and the resurrection follows. They are changed in a moment, in the twinkling of an eye, and, in the body of glory, caught up into heaven, I Corinthians 15.

The *ecclesia*–united as one in one body–goes up by resurrection, leaving the wilderness, the manna, the water from the Rock, the pillar of cloud and fire; leaving all the temporary provision for the journey.

Baptism, the supper, the covering of the head, all distinction between male and female; yea, rather, this body of corruption, dishonour, weakness, and nature: all is left behind. In a blaze of glory, of honour, of immortality, the spiritual body, like unto his glorious body, 'for ever with the Lord'.

But *now*, amidst the wilderness of this world, on pilgrimage out of it, the apostle having been absent these long months, those things which were ordained for this short time of sojourning here below–to be discarded once entering the inheritance of the land–were being sorely abused–among other things–at Corinth. This brought Paul to tears at the report of it. It also gendered First Corinthians.

But then, it is all important to realize that God's temporal and temporary provisions for the wilderness, *even without abuse*, and given that they are correctly and spiritually preserved, *are not in themselves worship in the essence of it at all.*

Worship properly so-called is not reached nor is it realized but rather is surrounded by the periphery of the things that pertain to the journey through the wilderness. Things such as the Lord's supper; the form of meetings; the provision and exercise of gifts; ordinances, forms, or manifestations; the veil; no: none of these things.

Worship is inward in the Spirit; it is neither external in form nor formal in word. But it is certainly truthful in heart: for God is a Spirit, and they that worship him must worship in spirit and in truth. Indeed, the Father *seeketh* such to worship him.

Worship does not *deny* the outward words or formal ordinances in their place: rather, peripherally, it *requires* them. But that which the Father seeks, owns, and receives as worship lies infinitely beyond *all* outward things.

Nevertheless, outward things, and, in effect, ordinances, occupy the greater part of the matter of First Corinthians. This follows from the limitation of the vision of the book. The Head may be in heaven, but is hardly so seen: it is the body on earth, filled with the Spirit descended from the Head, that most occupies the revelation.

The great watershed of the first epistle to the *ecclesia* at Corinth occurs in chapter 11:18 with the words 'For first of all, when ye come together in the church'. If so, whatever preceded did not concern their 'coming together in the church'. Otherwise what follows, chapter 11:18, could not be described as 'first of all'.

Thus the greater part of the epistle falls into two parts: *before* the watershed of chapter 11:18, *The saints' testimony before the world, as seen without*. *After* the great watershed of chapter 11:18, *The saints' testimony before the Lord, as seen within*. This covers the wilderness journey.

Both phases of the revelation take their rise from *the nature of God, in Father, Son, and Holy Ghost*.

First, what is in accord with his justice and judgment made manifest in the cross of Christ. From this it follows that the saints are to cleanse themselves from all filthiness of the flesh and of the spirit, perfecting holiness in the fear of God, judging by the Holy Ghost according to the word of the truth of the evangel.

Last, to come to what he is in and of himself: not the ordinance, but *he who ordains*. Not gifts, but *the Giver*. *His* nature. Love. What he is *in and of himself*. It is *this* that fills the *ecclesia*; it is *this* that motivates every ministry and administration.

From the love of God, in Father, Son, and Holy Ghost, by one Spirit filling the *ecclesia* in its entirety, radiates a light outshining all: even the blazing revelation of the resurrection from the dead. All other things shall have their day, or pass into the day. But love, eternal, unchanging, everlasting, *is* the day. It is the true light, that now shineth.

'And now abideth faith, hope, and love, these three.' Yes; now. But from eternity to eternity, 'the greatest of these is love', I Corinthians 13:13.

The Opening: The Testimony of Christ; I Corinthians 1:1-9

To be strictly accurate, the opening words of this epistle read,'Paul, a called apostle of Jesus Christ, by [the] will of God, and Sosthenes the brother', I Corinthians 1:1.

Observe that Paul ascribes his sole authority to Jesus Christ in heaven, according to the will of God. Nothing else. Nowhere else. No one else.

Paul had no call from Jesus on earth. He had rejected Jesus on earth. In consequence he 'verily thought with himself that he *ought* to do many things contrary to the name of Jesus of Nazareth', Acts 26:9.

So that Paul had no authority from the Son of man on earth; no authority from the twelve at Jerusalem; no authority from those in the ministry before him; no authority from the *ecclesia*. Nothing on earth and nothing from man at all.

Then how was he 'a called apostle of Jesus Christ'? What? That persecutor? Called? But Jesus Christ was no longer on earth. He was in heaven, in the glory. Then how could Paul—formerly called Saul—possibly have been called by Jesus Christ from such unimaginable heights and dimensions as that?

Let him speak for himself, just as he spoke for himself before king Agrippa: 'Many of the saints did I shut up in prison, having received authority from the chief priests; and when they were put to death, I gave my voice against them.

'And I punished them oft in every synagogue, and compelled them to blaspheme; and being exceedingly mad against them, I persecuted them even unto strange cities. Whereupon as I went to Damascus with authority and commission from the chief priests,

'At midday, O king, I saw in the way a light from heaven, above the brightness of the sun, shining round about me and them which journeyed with me. And when we were all fallen to the earth, I heard a voice speaking unto me, and saying in the Hebrew tongue, Saul, Saul, why persecutest thou me? it is hard for thee to kick against the pricks.

'And I said, Who art thou, Lord? And he said, I am Jesus, whom thou persecutest.

'But rise, and stand upon thy feet: for I have appeared unto thee for this purpose, to make thee a minister and a witness both of these things which thou hast seen, and of those things in the which I will appear unto thee; delivering thee from the people, and from the Gentiles, unto whom now I send thee,

'To open their eyes, and to turn them from darkness to light, and from the power of Satan unto God, that they may receive forgiveness of sins, and inheritance among them which are sanctified by faith that is in me.'

'Whereupon, O king Agrippa, I was not disobedient to the heavenly vision', Acts 26:10-19. The Lord, Jesus, 'appeared unto' Saul? But it was a light above the brightness of the noonday sun, shining from the heavenly glory, that appeared unto him. If so, that brightness—beyond sight to bear—was but the uttermost of the radiant beams that shone from his person who answered from the highest glory, I am Jesus.

'A called apostle of Jesus Christ'? Then, called in 'the heavenly vision' by 'a voice from heaven' sounding out of the unbearable light of the glory. Thus he was called, and hence he was an apostle of Jesus Christ.

It was *thence* that Jesus Christ sent him away 'to open their eyes, to turn them from darkness to light, and from the power of Satan unto God, that they may receive forgiveness of sins, and inheritance among them which are sanctified by faith that is in me', Acts 26:18.

And *that* was how, and *that* was why, Paul came to Corinth: not of his own will, nor of his own coming; but as sent by Jesus Christ from the heavenly glory, and, as he says, 'through the will of God', I Corinthians 1:1. Sent to the Corinthians by the Lord of glory, and in the will of the God of glory. Now, *that* is ministry, and ministry worth the name.

And yet with what touching solicitude of humility the apostle adds immediately, 'and Sosthenes the brother'. Paul ever had the brethren in mind, as saith the Lord, 'Behold I and the children which God hath given me'. 'He is not ashamed to call them brethren', Hebrews 2:13,11.

As it is written, 'Behold, how good and how pleasant it is for brethren to dwell together in unity!', Psalm 133:1. And again, 'Go to my brethren, and say unto them, I ascend unto my Father, and your Father; to my God, and your God', John 20:17. And shall the apostle put himself above this? God forbid! Rather, below it: 'And Sosthenes the brother', I Corinthians 1:1.

'To the *ecclesia* of God which is in Corinth, having been sanctified in Christ Jesus, called saints, with all those in every place calling on the name of our Lord Jesus Christ, both theirs and ours', I Corinthians 1:2.

This accurate rendering of the Greek Text appears in 'The Englishman's Greek New Testament', 1877, perhaps the most faithful translation in existence. Comparison with the Authorized Version should be of considerable help to the reader.

From which it is to be observed that there was but *one* – the one and only – *ecclesia* in Corinth, and if so, in *any* given place, and that the *one ecclesia* was of and for *the one* God. Then, more than one would imply – and *does* imply – pantheism, that being the only logical conclusion from the existence of a *number* of so-called 'churches' in any one given place.

Moreover, that the one *ecclesia* is 'of God' shows that it is not of man. Man has nothing to do with it: he has his own houses, but *this* is the one house of the one God, and, if so, not for man to receive individual blessings, but for God to receive corporate worship.

Likewise, further to the one *ecclesia* in any given locality – as in Corinth – the words 'all in every place' and 'Jesus Christ our Lord, both theirs and ours' show that the unity of *every ecclesia* – and no less – constitutes *the ecclesia* in its full expression.

As to those of whom each and every *ecclesia* was—and, properly, is—constituted, these are described as 'having been sanctified in Christ Jesus'. Now, *that* took place, and at the price of blood, before they were called, as saith the Lord, 'I have much people in this city', Acts 18:10. But *no one knew that, or who they were—least of all themselves—but the Lord who had purchased them before they knew him.*

These are 'called saints', having been called by grace through the evangel in due course. Hence, all the saints were in the one *ecclesia*, not one was outside that *ecclesia*, and, together, they constituted the *ecclesia*. As to anyone else outside of the *ecclesia*, they were not of it: 'of the rest durst no man join himself to them', Acts 5:13.

Wherefore the *ecclesia* was not a sphere of evangelism: it was a sphere of worship. There those having been sanctified in Christ Jesus, called saints, called on the name of our Lord Jesus Christ in one body, and as one body. Unitedly they worshipped the Father in spirit and in truth, and, in truth, the Father sought such to worship him.

No wonder the apostle proclaims to such, 'Grace unto you, and peace, from God our Father, and [the] Lord Jesus Christ', I Corinthians 1:3. Here is the covenant between the Father and the Son in all the effectual consummation of its blessedness to the elect.

The Son having glorified the Father, righteousness of God having been established for his people world without end, rising up from the depths, ascending into the heights, an accomplished blessing is pronounced upon the *ecclesia* from the Father and the Son to everlasting from the heights of heavenly glory.

It is to all the heirs of promise: all the chosen in Christ Jesus: all the elect: the whole *ecclesia*, that is, all the children of the Father, and, if so, all the brethren. The Father and the Son have come out and come down and done all, and the word is 'grace'.

It is eternally established for and upon all the children of the Father, the entire body of Christ.

The effect of this—both to and upon the whole *ecclesia* for evermore—is 'peace'. This has been wrought by the Father and the Son. The Father who chose and begat us in the Son reveals the Son, in which light he shows us his hands, his feet and his side. That is, *from the glory!*

Thence, by the blood of Christ, 'he is our peace'; for abolishing in his flesh the enmity, the law of commandments, he made in himself of twain one new man, 'so making peace'; and came nigh in the Spirit to us who were afar off 'and preached peace'. This is the Peacemaker, and the peace stands on behalf of all the seed between God our Father, and the Lord Jesus Christ.

Thus the Son of God from the glory by the apostles through the Holy Ghost on earth proclaims to the whole *ecclesia*, in the resurrection appearing to them on behalf of us all, declaring with a threefold declaration as he shows them his hands and his feet, breathing upon them, 'Peace be unto you'. 'Receive ye the Holy Ghost.'

THE APOSTLE PAUL GIVES THANKS FOR THE GRACE OF GOD WROUGHT FOR, IN, AND ON BEHALF OF THE *ECCLESIA* AT CORINTH; I CORINTHIANS 1:4-9

Here is thanksgiving for grace given; enrichment bestowed; testimony confirmed; blamelessness assured; calling ratified; and all in the fellowship of God's Son Jesus Christ our Lord.

Not a word of reproach; not a scintilla of doubt; not a question of perseverance: the apostle looks into heaven; he beholds the Lord of glory; he discerns the work of God in Christ: he perceives the covenant: he has room for nothing but thanksgiving for the grace given unto those called into such favour.

Whatever may come later; whatever he may see when he drops his eyes to their present condition; whatever he may behold when his gaze descends to what had been allowed to come in: Whatever! His eyes were fixed on the heavenly grace and glory of the Father and the Son *first and last*.

It is a remarkable fact that in the narrative of the beginnings at Corinth, Acts 18, no record exists of that taking place which caused Paul to give such constant thanks in I Corinthians 1:4-9.

What happened, when it happened, how it happened no one can tell. Only, *that* it happened is certain, and that for it the apostle is wellnigh transported with joy.

'I thank my God always on your behalf, for the grace of God which is given you by Jesus Christ; that in every thing ye are enriched by him, in all utterance, and in all knowledge; even as the testimony of Christ was confirmed in you:

'So that ye come behind in no gift; waiting for the coming of our Lord Jesus Christ: who shall also confirm you unto the end, blameless in the day of our Lord Jesus Christ.

'God is faithful, by whom ye were called unto the fellowship of his Son Jesus Christ our Lord', I Corinthians 1:4-9.

Now *this* describes the *ecclesia* which is *of God*, and describes it *experimentally*. The apostle thanks *his* God – 'I thank *my* God' – and he does so constantly – 'always' – on behalf of the one *ecclesia* gathered in the unity of the body of Christ at Corinth. *His* God? Yes, as a father, and as an apostle, by *him* God had brought *them* into being through his evangel.

He gives thanks always because *God* had done this: man was not in it. It was nothing to do with man: '*of him*' – of *God* – 'are ye in Christ Jesus', I Corinthians 1:30. It was all of grace, but grace through the ministry of the Spirit, of the new testament, administered by the apostle, so that he *witnessed* the grace of

God *as it was being given to them*. What cause of continual thanksgiving this brought to Paul!

It was *all* of God: 'that in *every thing* ye are enriched by him.' They had been utterly penurious. But grace had been poured down from God out of heaven through the ministry of the apostle, and now they were—as a company—*so rich*. 'In all utterance, and in all knowledge.'

All this was etched on the apostle's memory, as he took his leave after something like two years at Corinth.

Then how vivid his remembrance of the time when 'the testimony of Christ was confirmed in you', I Corinthians 1:6.

The testimony of Christ came down from the glory. When Christ ascended into heaven, he went up with the five scars that marked the perfection of his atoning sacrifice on earth: four, when his sufferings began; the fifth when they had ended, and he was dead.

Raised from the dead, *having already redeemed by his blood every last one of his people from the beginning of time to the end of it*, he ascended into heaven to sit at rest on his Father's throne.

Thence, on behalf of his people, he received the promise of the Father, the Holy Ghost, whom he sent to descend into the midst of the *ecclesia*. This was the testimony of Christ, and at that from the glory, and it was 'confirmed in you'.

Notice that: '*in*' you. It was an interior testimony, sent down to the *ecclesia*—the 'you' is plural—on earth. If so, it was the testimony of the Father's total, absolute, and everlasting satisfaction in righteousness with the work of his Son wrought on behalf of his people on the cross.

This testimony was first made known in the *ecclesia* at Jerusalem—'to the Jew first'—'that we should be to the praise of his glory, who *first* trusted in Christ', Ephesians 1:12.

Of this descent of the Holy Ghost, Peter bore witness on the day of Pentecost: 'This Jesus hath God raised up, whereof we all are witnesses', referring to the resurrection of Christ from the dead, Acts 2:32.

Immediately Peter continues: 'Therefore being by the right hand of God exalted, *and having received of the Father the promise of the Holy Ghost*'–referring to the ascension of Christ to the throne of heavenly glory–'*he hath shed forth this, which ye now see and hear*', Acts 2:33.

'He' hath shed? Who? Why, Christ exalted. 'This'? Yes, the Holy Ghost. Then, *that was the testimony of Christ, and it was confirmed in them*. And so it was in the Corinthians, I Corinthians 1:6.

'So that ye come behind in no gift.' How could they come behind in any gift *when the Giver himself filled the whole body?* And with what effect?

Above all to glorify Christ, and set the heart of his saints on his coming again, as pilgrims and strangers on the earth, 'waiting for the coming of our Lord Jesus Christ', I Corinthians 1:7. Now, this marks out those filled with the Spirit!

Now what a glorious affirmation follows, yea, for those very saints at Corinth, chosen of the Father before the world was: redeemed by the blood of his Son before they knew of his existence: and baptized in one Spirit into one body in their own interior experience!

I say, What a glorious affirmation follows of necessity from the ascended Lord of glory to his beloved so far below: 'Who shall'–*shall; shall!*–'shall also confirm you unto the end, blameless'–*blameless; blameless!*–'in the day of our Lord Jesus Christ', I Corinthians 1:8.

At this all heaven resounds and echoes with the triumphant salvation of God, in Father, Son, and Holy Ghost, as the words roll down the steeps of heaven from the heights of glory to be ratified in the heart of his people below:

'God is faithful, by whom ye were called unto the fellowship of his Son Jesus Christ our Lord', I Corinthians 1:9.

Surely these verses—chapter 1:4-9—mark out the *ecclesia* that is *of God*, and mark it out *experimentally*. And so does the verse that follows, whether it be the *ecclesia* in Corinth, or in any other one given place, or the *ecclesia* in its unity as a whole, with every place seen together as one.

PART ONE

JUDGMENT CONCERNING THE TESTIMONY
CHAPTERS 1:10-11:6

Part One

JUDGMENT CONCERNING THE TESTIMONY
chapters 1:10-11:6

Judgment concerning divisions in the ecclesia at Corinth;
I Corinthians 1:10-4:21

'Now I beseech you, brethren, by the name of our Lord Jesus Christ, that ye all speak the same thing'–yes, all of *you*, at Corinth; and the *whole ecclesia*, everywhere, together as one – 'and that there be no divisions among you; but that ye be perfectly'–mark that: *perfectly*–'joined together in the same mind and in the same judgment', I Corinthians 1:10.

However, there *were* divisions at Corinth. That is, *within* the one *ecclesia* at Corinth. For theirs was not the shameless sin of separated denominations divided *from* the one *ecclesia*, to *none* of which independent sects Paul speaks. Nor did they then so much as exist.

But the divisions which the apostle reproves were those *within the one body: the single and only ecclesia at Corinth.*

There were divisions over Paul; Apollos; Cephas; and Christ, as though each had his own particular philosophy or school of thought concerning religion. Parties formed in support of such divisions were the cause of contention, each opting for that which its followers supposed the wiser, I Corinthians 1:11-16.

Paul directs to the preaching of the cross as the corrective. The preaching of the cross defied logic: it set forth divine and supernatural work; it was contrary to reason, and hence was foolishness to the wisdom of the philosophical Greeks.

The preaching of the cross declared a free divine righteousness, imputed by grace through faith; thus it was a stumblingblock to the laborious and continuous works of the law for righteousness on the part of the Jews.

The cross that is preached is miraculous, and the preaching of it divine; hence it is beyond the comprehension of the natural mind. It is to *this* therefore that Paul directs the Corinthians in their contentions for schools of thought under party names, I Corinthians 1:17-25.

In the first epistle to the Corinthians, the first chapter, verses 18-25, the apostle Paul brings home and applies the truth of the cross.

It is not that it is different teaching from that given in the epistle to the Romans concerning the body of sin, but it is a particular application of that teaching.

Here he takes the general truth that 'our old man is crucified with him', and applies it precisely to the state of mind of those at Corinth.

It is not a new truth further to Romans 6:6, but a distinct use of that truth in relation to the Corinthian mentality.

Unlike the epistle to the Romans, which is purely didactic, the epistle to the Corinthians is also corrective.

Certain things had come into the *ecclesia*, which must be corrected by the apostolic doctrine.

It is not a question of correction by exhortation, or admonition. Rather, the premise of the exhortation, the ground of admonition, must be laid down: it is a question of doctrine.

Paul first postulates the doctrine, on the basis of which he then exhorts and admonishes. That is the apostolic method: the truth concerning Christ comes first.

To expose what had come in at Corinth, the apostle reveals the spiritual wickedness of being carnally minded. Because 'the carnal mind is enmity against God.' It fulfils 'the desires of the flesh and of the mind.' Therefore, 'to be carnally minded is death.'

It was true that once they had been 'enemies in their minds by wicked works', but now they knew that in Christ the 'body of sin' had been crucified, and if so, the head had been judged, the old mentality, the carnal mind, condemned on their behalf in their Substitute.

So objectionable to God was this 'mind of the flesh', and the 'minding of earthly things', that, in order to save them from judgment, it had been crucified in Another.

And will they now return to that which had been judged and put away on their behalf?

Yes, they will, and that return to what they had once judged and put away became the occasion of this epistle.

The apostle could not speak unto them as spiritual, but as carnal, as those who had fallen, who with the mind served the law of sin, and walked again in the vanity of their mind, and worse, for now it was mixed with the profession of the gospel of God.

But to be carnally minded was death, no matter how high the Christian profession, and solemn warnings attend the epistle.

Rather, they should be transformed by the renewing of their minds, having their hearts and minds kept by the peace of God through Christ Jesus.

Such was the effect of the apostle Paul's having applied the doctrine of the cross in the first epistle to the Corinthians, that he was able later to give thanks for their recovery in the second letter.

The corruption from which afterwards they were delivered by the cross, had been the work of Satan. 'But I fear, lest by any means, as the serpent beguiled Eve through his subtlety, so your minds should be corrupted from the simplicity that is in Christ.'

How could such a thing come to pass?

'If he that cometh preacheth another gospel', saith Paul, searching out the root of the matter, and finding that they had been seduced by false preachers, full of spiritual-sounding speeches, pleasing to the ear, but devoid of the doctrine of the cross.

It had been reported to Paul by them which were of the household of Chloe, that the brethren at Corinth were divided, and had fallen into contention, one party with another.

This was the carnal mind in its strength, the negation of the truth that the old man, with all his mentality, the whole head, all that pertained to the carnal mind, had been crucified.

If crucified, why were they carnally minded?

If they had been crucified with Christ, if the body of sin had been destroyed, how could they dwell in the mind that pertained to that body?

The Spirit of truth supported the cross: in what spirit, then, were they dwelling?

If they had the mind of Christ, if, in support of this, the Spirit dwelt in them as one body, how could they be divided?

The mind in Adam was divided. But is Christ divided? No he is not. Then in him there can be no division.

Brethren must of necessity put away all carnal mindedness, and, having the mind of Christ, must 'be perfectly joined together in the same mind and in the same judgment'.

But it was not so at Corinth. They all spoke different things, there were divisions among them, they were forming parties on the basis of personality, opinion, and preference. The wisdom of words, intellectual and oratorical, prevailed.

The love of argument, of worldly reasoning, the 'wisdom of the wise', the 'understanding of the prudent', rose up in the pride of life, so that the will of man ruled in the *ecclesia* at Corinth.

The result was disputing, contention, debate, and consequently heated striving and schism. Not one vestige of this was in the mind of Christ. It was all in the mind of Adam.

'Now I beseech you, brethren, by the name of our Lord Jesus Christ, that ye all speak the same thing, and that there be no divisions among you.'

But Paul's entreaty for the unity of brethren in the *ecclesia* bears no relation to the deceptive 'church unity' of today, in which denominations agree to form one 'church'.

That is not church unity in the mind of God.

It is an unauthorized agreement of denominations, in themselves improper, grouped to form a loose subordinate structure that never was nor ever could be the *ecclesia* of God.

No such thing as 'the unity of churches'—by which they mean denominations—was envisaged in the new testament, for the simple reason that churches as such were not then divided into denominational fragments as they are now.

Then, it was a question of the unity of brethren in one *ecclesia* properly so-called.

If those in the denominations, whether Roman, Protestant, or Sectarian, really desire unity, they must, who are of God, who seek his face, come out of their divisions, into the unity of one body.

Being thus rightly gathered by the cross and in the unity of the Spirit, brethren will then be in a position where the new testament teaching on unity applies: within the *ecclesia*. There, all must speak the same thing. There, there must be no divisions.

Why not? Because it is the house of God, where brethren are not in Adam, but in Christ. Where the old man with his carnal mind is seen to have been crucified. Where the saints put on the new man, raised from the dead. Where brethren show forth the mind of Christ.

There, carnal mindedness, which is death, has been put away, the body of sin destroyed, and the mind of the Spirit is life and peace.

At the beginning, abiding in the love of God, led by the Spirit, in communion with Christ, brethren were seen to be dwelling together in unity. All spoke the same thing.

Outside was the mind of the flesh with its contentions. Within, the cross was effective to shut out all that was of the flesh.

The Spirit, the mind of the Spirit, which was life and peace, filled the unity of the body, expressing in one the mind of Christ.

However, false teachers had come in, uncalled and unsent, with their false doctrine, to undermine the cross, and to seduce the brethren from the simplicity which was in Christ.

But Paul knew nothing among them, save 'Jesus Christ, and him crucified'.

Were some following him in the flesh? What flesh, in the body of Christ?

'Was Paul crucified for you?' No he was not, Christ was crucified for them, that they might dwell in him, in one body, by the cross.

Then, Paul brings in the doctrine of the cross again, declaring to the people fallen from grace, 'The preaching of the cross is to them that perish foolishness; but unto us which are saved it is the power of God.'

The cross was foolishness to them that perish. That is, to the world. Why? Because they, the worldly, considered themselves too wise to believe it.

Worldly wisdom, in the eyes of the world, was superior to the cross, and the worldly, in their wisdom, thought that they could see through this foolishness.

But, I Cor. 1:25, 'The foolishness of God is wiser than men.'

As to worldly wisdom, saith God, 'I will destroy the wisdom of the wise, and will bring to nothing the understanding of the prudent.' This destruction, this bringing to nothing, was wrought at the cross.

Why then is the cross foolishness to the world? Because the wisdom of it cannot be seen by the natural eye, it demands faith alone, it evades the senses, it lies outside of the rules of natural intelligence, in a word, as men say, there is no proof. But then, mysteries are beyond 'proof'.

What mysteries are these, that lie beyond proof? First, the mystery of the one who was crucified. The mystery of his Person was hidden from the world, for, 'had they known it, they would not have crucified the Lord of glory.'

The divine Person of the Lord of glory was hidden behind the apparent weakness of his human nature.

No amount of worldly wisdom, natural perception, or human intuition could have penetrated this mystery.

Then why does the world boast of its wisdom? In divine things its wisdom is not only inadequate, it is disastrous.

The mystery of the cross lies beyond all understanding of men to comprehend.

Who could comprehend the eternal, the immortal, the invisible God, smiting the Son of man, the human nature of his own Son?

Who could understand that 'it pleased the LORD to bruise him', when no bruising discoloured his skin?

That 'by his stripes we are healed', when neither whip nor rod appeared, and neither beating nor lashing occurred, as he hung upon the cross?

How can the world, trusting in a wisdom dependent upon natural observation, understand that 'The LORD hath laid on him the iniquity of us all', when nothing whatsoever was seen to have been laid on him during the whole of his passion?

Even the Jews could not believe it, religious as they were, because it was so contrary to reason. 'Unto the Jews a stumbling-block', I Cor. 1:23.

The mystery of God was hidden from human wisdom. Who can understand the mystery of the invisible God?

To the world, it cannot be seen, therefore cannot be proven, ergo, it cannot be. But it is: there is one God in three Persons, and there are three Persons in one God.

The Father did smite the Son, the church of God was purchased with his own blood, God did make him to be sin for us, our old man was crucified with him. All this is the truth, the whole truth, and nothing but the truth.

It is the truth, but, being a divine mystery, it must be received by revelation, and made known by preaching, even the preaching of the cross.

To the wise, who reject what they call uncertain and unproven assertions, this is 'foolishness'.

That is, it is foolishness to 'them that perish', I Cor. 1:18. But what kind of wisdom is this, that causes its advocates to perish?

The mystery of the power of God lies beyond proof also, and hence is denied by human wisdom. What folly! The wisdom of the world denies the power of God, because it cannot be proven.

Since by its wisdom the world rejects the preaching of the cross, and since, I Cor. 1:18, the preaching of the cross is the power of God, how can the world complain of lack of proof?

It denies to itself the only means of proving the power of God, that is, by experience, because it refuses the gospel which brings that experience.

But the world cannot see the power of God. No, it cometh not by observation. It is inward, this power. It is wrought in the interior, it is experienced in the inward man.

It is the power of the Spirit of truth, 'Whom the world cannot receive, because it seeth him not, neither knoweth him: but ye know him; for he dwelleth with you, and shall be in you.'

Hence, 'The world by wisdom knew not God', I Cor. 1:21.

To them that perish the cross is foolishness. The world is too wise, its knowledge too great, its learning too vast, to embark on such vague speculations.

It did not please God by the foolishness of preaching to save the world. But to save them that believe.

The preaching of the cross is insufficient for the religious. They want signs to settle the question, I Cor. 1:22.

Such preaching is also insufficient for the intellectual. He wants tangible proof. 'For after that in the wisdom of God the world by wisdom knew not God, it pleased God by the foolishness of preaching to save them that believe', I Cor. 1:21.

Observe, it is preaching that saves. The preaching of the cross, which, of course, means doctrinal preaching.

It is the preaching of the mystery. 'Unto me, who am less than the least of all saints, is this grace given, that I should preach among the Gentiles the unsearchable riches of Christ; and to make all men see what is the fellowship of the mystery.'

This preaching, by which the mystery is made known and the power of God communicated, is called variously, The preaching of the gospel, I Cor. 1:17; The preaching of the cross, 1:18; The foolishness of preaching, 1:21; and, The preaching of Christ crucified, 1:23.

The preaching of the gospel divides mankind into two. It divides the world and the *ecclesia* of God asunder.

When the preaching of the cross sounds forth, it appears 'foolishness to them that perish', but becomes 'the power of God unto us which are saved', I Cor. 1:18.

The preaching finds out the wise, the scribe, the disputer, the sign-seeker, the mighty, the noble, and the understanding, and it finds them out to be too wise for the gospel, and too knowledgeable for the cross.

The preaching finds out believers also, who are the called, the chosen, the brethren.

These are unwise after the flesh, foolish in the world, the weak things of the world, the base things of the world, the despised, the nothings. Nevertheless, they are saved by the power of God, called by the grace of God, and destined for the glory of God.

When Christ crucified is preached to such poor creatures as these, whom the world despises but whom God chooses, whom the world rejects but whom God calls, God is magnified.

He is glorified because 'no flesh shall glory in his presence'. Since by definition they can do nothing, it is very plain that God has done everything.

The whole work is of himself. The glory is God's alone. In such brethren the evangel is effectual, the cross is saving, power attends the word, revelation accompanies the preaching, and, behold, the fellowship of the mystery is let down from heaven.

They have not chosen him but he has chosen them. God chose them in Christ Jesus, whom he, himself, makes unto them wisdom, both righteousness, sanctification, and redemption.

Yet for all this glorious doctrine and experience, the flesh, and worldly wisdom, had come back again at Corinth.

How could this be? By false teachers, with erroneous doctrines.

Just as at the first the power of God had come in by the preaching of the cross, so now the working of Satan came in by false doctrine.

Thus by fair words and flattering speeches pleasing to the flesh, the cross had been made 'of none effect' in those who embraced the error.

'For if he that cometh preacheth another Jesus, whom we have not preached, or if ye receive another spirit, which ye have not received, or another gospel, which ye have not accepted', why be surprised at the schisms? the heresies? the divisions? 'For such are false apostles, deceitful workers.'

'But', says the apostle Paul, 'though we, or an angel from heaven, preach any other gospel unto you than that which we have preached unto you, let him be accursed.'

Accursed? Yes, because it is by believing the gospel, in the true preaching of it, and believing the gospel alone, that men are saved, just as it is by rejecting the gospel that they shall be lost.

The preaching of the cross therefore stands as the only hope of a fallen world. Accursed indeed let him be who perverts it, denies it, or corrupts it by worldly wisdom or human sentiment.

What will Paul do, now that the carnal mind, and worldly wisdom, had come in at Corinth? The cross is Paul's answer. The preaching of the cross is his antidote.

It was that by which the Spirit had come in, and that by which the flesh had gone out, in the beginning.

At the cross the body of the flesh had been hung up, accursed and execrated. Withal it was the body of sin, Rom. 6:6, and was made sin, II Cor. 5:21.

The cross was the judgment of God upon sin in the flesh, in the body.

It was not a question of the body in terms of outward appearances, the skin that appeared to the eye. It was what appeared to God, inward realities, what lay beneath the skin in the sight of God. That was what was seen in the substitutionary sacrifice on the cross.

It was the whole man, the old man, the body of sin, that had been mysteriously transferred to the Substitute by the work of God.

Then, if the whole man, the head also. And if the head, the fleshly mind. And if the fleshly mind, then carnal wisdom.

Or ever men could be saved, that must be condemned. And it was condemned, in the Saviour on the tree.

How then could brethren at Corinth return to that which God had condemned, to save them? How was it that the carnal mind, and fleshly wisdom, had come in? How did it happen that there were contentions in the flesh, a party spirit?

And if these things were so, what had they to say of the cross? Well, they speculated about the cross, they had their own views, it was a question of opinion, of ideas. 'I am of Paul; and I of Apollos; and I of Cephas; and I of Christ.'

In tears, afar off, Paul took up his pen, once again to apply the cross. 'Is Christ divided? was Paul crucified for you?' Paul had come, and now wrote, preaching the evangel. Not with the wisdom of words, lest the cross of Christ should be made of none effect.

Openings in First Corinthians

Paul did not come, or write, speculating, proposing, pleading, or intellectually discussing. He came preaching, and preaching dogmatically.

Paul preached doctrinally, according to the revelation of the mystery which he had both received and experienced from Jesus Christ. 'How shall they hear without a preacher?' That is, a preacher of this order.

'How shall one preach except he be sent?' But Paul was sent, and came preaching the word of the cross, a savour of life unto life to the saved, and of death unto death to the lost.

The Lord had much people in the city of Corinth, and under the preaching of the gospel, as a savour of life unto life, God revealed the truth to them, calling them and saving them by the washing of regeneration and renewing of the Holy Ghost.

To the rest of the city, it was a savour of death unto death, this preaching: foolishness.

Men mocked at it, or it saved them. It quickened them, or it slew them.

'Go into all the world, and preach the gospel. He that believeth and is baptized shall be saved; and he that believeth not shall be damned.'

Life unto life, or death unto death. Saved or lost, the gospel determined the issue. But it did not ask for man's opinion. It condemned it on the tree.

The preaching of the cross, of the gospel, is not therefore intellectual, or for intellectuals to debate. But that was what had come in at Corinth: as though the *ecclesia* of God, the pillar and ground of the truth, were a debating forum for intellectuals, pulling down the truth from heaven to earth, God to man, in order to pronounce upon it.

They sought wisdom, they were following the academics, debating the cross, airing opinions, discussing the various views. Paul's view and Cephas', the Jesus of the Synoptics and the Johannine Jesus, this historical aspect and that, one tradition and another.

But this whole carnal mind, and how much more all that came from it, stunk in the nostrils of God.

It was a putrid reek that rose up from Corinth, a stinking offence.

But God's goodness and everlasting mercy viewed not the departure but the Saviour. Not the apostasy but the Substitute. Not their debating but his crucifixion. Not carnal wisdom but a crucified Head. Not the offensive reek but the sweet-smelling savour of Christ.

And he freely forgave them all.

Paul preached the cross, and he wrote of the cross, and this brought them back, who had erred and strayed like lost sheep at Corinth.

By the word of the cross they were deeply convicted of their having shamed Christ and his gospel by their departure from the truth.

The Holy Ghost came in again in power, and convinced them of the wickedness of the natural mind, its utter offensiveness to God, of the obnoxious nature of high thoughts to the Almighty.

Oh, every thought was brought into captivity to the obedience of Christ, when the Holy Ghost brought in by the word of the cross the alarming, awakening, convicting, slaying, humbling work that marks out those whom God will bring to repentance.

The saints at Corinth were renewed in the spirit of their minds, transformed by the renewing of their minds, every imagination being cast down, every high thought, as the Holy Ghost subdued and mortified the flesh, bringing in the mind that was in Christ Jesus.

What mind was this? The mind that the Spirit of God had begun to form in them, and would yet bring to completion in the new man.

'Let this mind be in you, which was also in Christ Jesus: who, being in the form of God, thought it not robbery to be equal with God: but made himself of no reputation, and took upon him the form of a servant, and was made in the likeness of men: and being found in fashion as a man, he humbled himself, and became obedient unto death, even the death of the cross.'

This is preaching the cross, and applying the preaching, with a witness.

But with what effect? What real result came from all this doctrinal preaching? All this taking the doctrine of the cross concerning the crucifixion of the old man, and applying it particularly to the carnal mind, the fleshly mentality, that had come in at Corinth, what did it achieve?

What effect? What result? What did it achieve?

'Now', writes the apostle, having sent the first epistle, and having received the report of their response to that letter, 'Now I rejoice, not that ye were made sorry, but that ye sorrowed to repentance: for ye were made sorry after a godly manner, that ye might receive damage by us in nothing.

'For godly sorrow worketh repentance to salvation not to be repented of: but the sorrow of the world worketh death.

'For behold this selfsame thing, that ye sorrowed after a godly sort, what carefulness it wrought in you, yea, what clearing of yourselves, yea, what indignation, yea, what fear, yea, what vehement desire, yea, what zeal, yea, what revenge!

'In all things ye have approved yourselves to be clear in this matter', II Cor. 7:9-11.

And this is called, Preaching the gospel effectually. 'For Christ sent me not to baptize, but to preach the gospel: not with wisdom of words, lest the cross of Christ should be made of none effect.

'For the preaching of the cross is to them that perish foolishness; but unto us which are saved it is the power of God. For it is written, I will destroy the wisdom of the wise, and will bring to nothing the understanding of the prudent', I Corinthians 1:17-19.

If so, the knowledge of God is not—and cannot be—attained by the wisdom of this world, or through the mind of the flesh. To the contrary, it is totally obscured by worldly wisdom, and hidden behind impenetrable darkness from the carnal mind.

'For ye see your calling, brethren, how that not many wise men after the flesh, not many mighty, not many noble, are called:

'But God hath chosen the foolish things of the world to confound the wise; and God hath chosen the weak things of the world to confound the things which are mighty;

'And base things of the world, and things which are despised, hath God chosen, yea, and things which are not, to bring to nought things that are: that no flesh should glory in his presence', I Corinthians 1:26-29.

'But of him are ye in Christ Jesus, who of God is made unto us wisdom, both righteousness, and sanctification, and redemption', I Corinthians 1:30. Here Paul directs us to the very beginning: to the divine initiative: 'Of *him* are ye in Christ Jesus.'

If 'of him'—much more *but* of him—'are ye in Christ Jesus', then not of yourselves. This does not refer to the beginning in terms of their first coming to Christ: it precedes that. It concerns *how* they came to Christ. The original cause of their coming to him. *Before* they came, what preceded, *that* they came?

Paul affirms vehemently for all who ever came, or ever shall come, for the whole *ecclesia* throughout time, '*of him* are ye in Christ Jesus'. It is *all of God*—not only that Christ is all of God—*it is all of God that ye came to him, and are in him.*

Those thus found in Christ, who were brought to him in truth, are designated: 'ye in Christ Jesus.' Who is 'ye'? But Paul has made this clear: 'Ye see your calling, brethren', verse 26. 'Ye' are the 'foolish things'; the 'weak things'; the 'base things'; the 'despised things': in a word, the *nothings*, I Corinthians 1:27,28.

These are called 'chosen of God'; they are the ones 'called of God', and they are designated 'brethren'; the 'ye' who are 'in Christ Jesus'. This is all 'of him'—long before they came—*he* chose; *he* called. Thus they came. And so God has all the glory.

He chose them to get to himself all the glory in their salvation; that Christ should fill them; that the Spirit should fill them; that the word of the truth of the evangel should fill them. And fill them *together as one*. Thus the world would see plainly, this fulness in them must be of God, because these were the sort who had nothing in themselves.

Then it was of God that they were in Christ Jesus, since it was impossible for them to have been in him of themselves. Yes; but how did God bring it about? He brought it about by that interior work, and those exterior providences, which reduced them to inward poverty; bitter mourning; humble meekness; and to pining hunger, Matthew 5.

They wept; they trembled; they feared; they felt the weight of their sins, the inwardness of their sin, the eternity of the wrath to come, in a word, they felt the terror of the Lord. The curse of the law sounded from heaven in their ears and they despaired within themselves of any hope.

But 'blessed'–not 'cursed', as it appeared, and felt within their souls–but 'blessed is the man whom thou chastenest, O LORD, and teachest out of thy law', Psalm 94:12. None but those whom God purposes to bless come to such experimental realities as this.

Though it were the deserved cursing of the law, yet to be given ears to hear it was all of God: it was the beginning of the Father's drawing: nothing but such divine dealings with the soul prepare it to be drawn to Christ. 'No man can come to me, except the Father which hath sent me draw him', John 6:44.

And again, 'It is written in the prophets, And they shall be all taught of God. Every man therefore that hath heard, and hath learned of the Father, cometh unto me', John 6:45. Hence the law was their schoolmaster to bring them to Christ, and by it the Father shut them up to faith against the day of the revelation of the Son of God through the evangel.

God did it, and God did it all. And God did all of it to such as these. Why these? So that they could never glory afterwards, as if they had done either anything of themselves, or had assisted him in the doing of it. Doing of what? Of their coming to Christ.

Or ever they had known him, he knew them. 'When thou wast under the fig tree, I saw thee', John 1:48. The Lord said to Paul, 'I have much people in this city.' But of this, or that they were his, that people was wholly oblivious.

If it was of him that they were in Christ Jesus, it was not of themselves. God had mercy on whom he would have mercy, and whom he would, he hardened. It was not of him that willed, nor of him that ran, but of God that showed mercy, Romans 9:15-18.

That they were in Christ Jesus was not of the will of the flesh, nor of the will of man, but of God, John 1:13. The drawing of the Father, the chastening under the law, the revelation of Jesus Christ, why, these are things God hides from the pride of man, from the wisdom of the wise, and from the understanding of the prudent.

Wherefore Jesus gave thanks to the Father, the Lord of heaven and earth, 'because thou hast hid these things from the wise and prudent, and revealed them unto babes', Matthew 11:25. These things? What things? The Father's drawing to the Son, his chastening under the law, and the glorious shining into the heart through the evangel, at his command, giving the light of the knowledge of the glory of God in the face of Jesus Christ. And this to 'babes'? Which babes? Such as those described in I Corinthians 1:26-31.

This was the work of God from the beginning: the apostles preached, but God wrought, and '*the Lord* added to the *ecclesia* daily such as should be saved.' Thus, 'as many as were ordained to eternal life believed', Acts 2:47; 13:48.

What a difference from modern evangelicalism and evangelism, where everything is of man, of man's persuasion, and of man's methods. What a difference from the modern 'gospel'—as they call it—where all the emphasis is upon what man must do.

'God has taken nine steps' they tell us, 'but you must take the tenth.' 'Jesus is knocking on the door, but the handle is on the inside' we are informed, illustrated by Victorian art.

But, 'Of *him* are ye in Christ Jesus.' Take the tenth step? Who, Lazarus? The impotent man lain paralysed thirty-eight years? Door handle on the inside, helpless Christ standing outside knocking? Tell that to Samson, when they locked and barred the great doors of the city against him, so that it was impossible for him to pass through.

'And Samson lay till midnight, and arose at midnight, and took the doors of the gate of the city, and the two posts, and went away with them, bar and all, and put them upon his shoulders, and carried them up to the top of an hill', Judges 16:3.

O, but today, blinded and deceived, without a sound evangel, without an inward change, without a preparatory work, without any spiritual experience, without the least anxiety, men and women decide for themselves—if they will—when they might choose to call on him.

But in the beginning, *he* chose to call on *them*! 'Blessed is the man whom *thou* choosest, and *causest* to approach to thee', Psalm 65:4. 'Ye see your calling, brethren, how that not many wise men after the flesh, not many mighty, not many noble, are called: *but God hath chosen.*' Where calling is not after man's will, but according to God's grace.

The work stood in the power of God, not the guile of men. God did it: God came down: God wrought. But this has been forsaken today. And men wonder at the shallow carnality, the vain worldliness, the triumph of error?

It was not so at the beginning. It was not so at Corinth: '*Of him* are ye in Christ Jesus', I Corinthians 1:30.

'Who'—continues the apostle—'is made unto us wisdom.' That is, Christ Jesus, he, himself, in his own person, is made unto us wisdom. If so, God did not give them a *book*, that out of it they might display their *own* wisdom.

That is what the Jews did with the dead letter of the scriptures. But all they brought forth was wind. They found nothing in the scriptures. Hence Jesus challenges them, 'Search the scriptures'— go on: *search* them—'for in them ye think ye have eternal life.'

But think what they would in the wisdom of man, which was foolishness with God, they would never find eternal life in the dead letter. No, not in any or all of the books of scripture. Why not? Because there is no eternal life in them.

For, continues Jesus, 'they are they which testify of *me*. And ye will not come to me, that ye might have life', John 5:39,40. 'In *him* was life', John 1:4, nowhere else. 'He that hath the Son hath life; and he that hath not the Son of God hath not life', for all the profession of scripture in the world, I John 5:12.

Said Jesus, '*I* am come that they might have *life*': they already had the scriptures, but they were dead. And out of the dead letter these dead men expected life? Life was—and is—in *him*, and in him alone: 'This is the true God, and eternal life', I John 5:20.

But they thought they had life in the scriptures, and with that, these dead men were content. But they had not God; they crucified his Son; and they blasphemed the Holy Ghost. And all in consequence of their wisdom in the scriptures.

Neither did God give to the Corinthians—or anyone else—four gospels and twenty-three epistles so that out of them they might work out their creeds, statements of 'faith', doctrinal positions, denominational stances, or systems of theology. God gave them *Christ Jesus himself,* just as it was of God that they were found in him.

If so, *that* was to be their wisdom: that God had made Christ Jesus *himself* to be their wisdom: 'who *of God* is made unto us wisdom', I Corinthians 1:30.

Hence in another place the apostle prays 'that the God of our Lord Jesus Christ, the Father of glory, may give unto you the spirit of wisdom and revelation in the knowledge of him: the eyes of your understanding being enlightened', Ephesians 1:17,18. And where is the mind of man, or the wisdom of men, in that?

'For God, who commanded the light to shine out of darkness, hath shined in our hearts, to give the light of the knowledge of the glory of God in the face of Jesus Christ', II Corinthians 4:6. This is to reveal these things–*reveal* them–unto babes, Matthew 11:25.

It is of Christ *himself*, in person, and Christ alone, that it is said 'in whom'–mark that: *in* whom–'are hid'–observe closely: *hid*–'all'–note the totality: *all*–'the treasures of wisdom and knowledge', Colossians 2:3.

Again, the apostle exhorts, 'Let this mind be in you, which was also in Christ Jesus', Philippians 2:5. But how can the mind which was in him, peculiar to himself, be in us, since it is *his* mind, not ours? Clearly, by the Spirit taking of his mind, and filling ours with it. This is called 'a spirit of wisdom and revelation', Ephesians 1:17.

All our knowledge of Christ therefore stems from what God gives to us experimentally and by revelation: 'who of God is made unto us wisdom.' It is not of ourselves, our own wisdom: it is all of God's operation. We do not, you do not, know *anything* of Christ but what God has made him to be to you.

Now, if ever the brethren at Corinth had erred in favour of their carnal minds and natural wisdom, if pride and boasting had come in with those who did run well, thus to be rebuked: What is the case today, with no such auspicious beginnings, but yet with even more assertive pride and conceited presumption?

Where is the being built upon this rock: 'flesh and blood hath not revealed it unto thee, but my Father which is in heaven', Matthew 16:17? Where is the experience of this favour: 'but when it pleased God, who separated me from my mother's womb, and called me by his grace, to reveal his Son in me', Galatians 1:15,16?

But after the flesh man thinks that *he* knows something about religion. Man is going to come at the knowledge of Christ, you see:

his wisdom is adequate. Man is going to get at the gifts, observe: he will draw down the favour of heaven with his own free will, after the working of his own natural desires.

This spirit of the flesh had broken out at Corinth, where, at least, God had wrought so mightily at the beginning. But, after the departure of Paul, *they* would contribute their intellectual supplement; their emotional excitement; their passionate argument. What? To the spiritual knowledge and divine revelation of Christ?

Chaos was the result, and error was the consequence.

Then how much more chaotic, how much greater the error, with the denominated factions professing Christ today? For when last did *God* start the work within living memory? When last did the power of God begin to move upon the people the religious heirs of which now exhibit such confusion and ignorance?

Today, man floats this vain thought, or that empty idea, of what the 'gospel' should be; of how 'evangelism' ought to be conducted; of which of the multitude of 'versions' of the bible he will elect to fancy.

The mind and will of the flesh prevails everywhere in modern Christendom, so that it is accepted as normality for man to apply his ideas; his innovations; his traditions; his flights of fancy; his schemes of 'evangelism'. But this is not the Christian religion properly so-called.

'For *of God* is *Christ* made unto us wisdom', I Corinthians 1:30. This is immutable and abiding. As it was in the beginning; is now; and ever shall be. The whole purpose of God in calling those who are nothing, is that all should be seen to be of God, and nothing of man, that no flesh should glory in his presence.

For such a people, for called saints, for the true *ecclesia*, there is nothing to know but Christ; and none who can reveal Christ to us but God: 'Who of God is made unto us wisdom.'

None can lead us into this spiritual reality but the Holy Ghost, and that by revelation, quickening, and enlightenment, bringing us into union and communion with Christ Jesus. Hence it is written, 'who *of God* is made unto us wisdom', I Corinthians 1:30.

But what is the essence of this spiritual wisdom? What is the sum of the wisdom which God has made Christ Jesus to be to those whom he has called by his grace? Why, Paul tells you plainly: it is 'righteousness, sanctification, and redemption', I Corinthians 1:30.

Now, is that what God has discovered to you, even the hidden treasures of wisdom and knowledge of Christ, you whom he has called to be in him? For the apostle clearly shows that the revealed wisdom of God in Christ stands in these three things.

To Paul, this is the sum of the wisdom hidden in Christ, and, if so, the essence of the evangel of Christ.

Righteousness embraces all that was wrought in the death of Christ. Sanctification encompasses all that Christ administers from the glory. And redemption speaks of all that Christ shall bring to fruition at his coming again.

Briefly—therefore—consider this wisdom brought from the past; revealed at the present; and yet to appear in the future. Consider it, I say, and more: yield to it, this wisdom of God in Christ, yield the obedience of faith, according to the grace given unto you.

First, righteousness. If in the wisdom of God *Christ* is made unto us righteousness, what folly is it in man to suppose that he has any righteousness of his own? If to make Christ unto us righteousness God spared not his own Son from the substitutionary sufferings and death of the cross, of what use is the law for righteousness?

Then, whoso goeth about to establish his own righteousness, frustrates the grace of God. Wherefore Paul declares, 'I do not frustrate the grace of God: for if righteousness come by the law, then Christ is dead in vain', Galatians 2:21.

But his death is not in vain, for, in the wisdom of God, by the substitutionary sacrifice of Christ, he brought in everlasting righteousness to be imputed to the account of all that ever were, are, or shall be justified.

And if the Jews, who sought after righteousness by the law, have not attained unto righteousness, then where shall sinners of the Gentiles appear? 'That every mouth may be stopped, and all the world may become guilty before God', Romans 3:19.

Then, how great is the wisdom of God in bringing in righteousness where no righteousness existed: that is, in another than ourselves—but on our behalf—and on a different principle—namely, by the grace of him who loved us and gave himself for us.

'Even as David also describeth the blessedness of the man, unto whom God imputeth righteousness without works, saying, Blessed are they whose iniquities are forgiven, and whose sins are covered. Blessed is the man to whom the Lord will not impute sin', Romans 4:6-8.

Thus the wisdom of God in his love brought in a righteousness for man when man had none, but stood guilty and condemned under wrath and the curse. But God lay both guilt, wrath, and the curse upon the Saviour on the cross, that by him, in the wisdom of God, sinners might be freely justified through grace.

Then, if God spared not his own Son, gratuitously to provide a righteousness for us who had no righteousness of our own, will he spare those who despise it, and count it foolishness, let alone fail to hunger and thirst after it that it might be imputed unto them?

Here is God's love in the motive, and his wisdom in the method, by which he spared not his own Son, the rather transferring to him on the cross all that we were, and all that we had done, that it might be counted as his to bear before the curse of the law and the justice of God.

Having borne all away, in the wisdom of God he is made righteousness unto us.

If so, it is our wisdom to submit to the righteousness of God in Christ by renouncing our own righteousness as filthy rags, Isaiah 64:6; by confessing the curse of the law sounding against our transgressions; by owning the justice of God in condemning our sin and our sins; by embracing the atonement; and by believing from the heart and confessing with the mouth that the wisdom of God has made Christ our righteousness, and that there is none other.

Second, sanctification. As the word is used here this indicates the whole of sanctification, the sum of it. Not the quality that is imparted, but the entire concept in itself: *it is Christ*. God makes *Christ Jesus* to be our sanctification, I Corinthians 1:30.

Here is wisdom. The hidden wisdom. Christ is that wisdom, and, in the threefold nature of it, that Christ our sanctification is central.

O, the torture of supposing that we have none but what is imparted! But the truth is, it is not in us in its essence, though its essence is communicated to us. But, essentially, Of God *Christ Jesus* is made unto us sanctification. The question is, How?

In the essence of sanctification, in the sum of it, *by his blood*. 'Wherefore Jesus, that he might sanctify the people with his own blood, suffered without the gate', Hebrews 13:12.

Peter describes the called of God in this way: 'Elect according to the foreknowledge of God the Father, through sanctification of the Spirit, unto obedience and sprinkling of the blood of Jesus Christ', I Peter 1:2. Where the elect are sanctified through the Spirit *unto* obedience and sprinkling of the blood of Jesus Christ.

Then, the blood of Jesus Christ is that to which the Spirit leads us – so as to glorify him – in order effectually to inwork our sanctification. Hence it is written, 'We are sanctified through the offering of the body of Jesus Christ once for all', Hebrews 10:10.

And as if that were not enough for confirmation, the apostle of our profession settles the matter for ever a little lower in the same passage: 'For *by one offering* he hath *perfected for ever* them that are sanctified', Hebrews 10:14.

If so, the fulness of the Spirit, the abundance of the glory, from the death of Christ is *assured* to all who are the called of God. Then it is to that body and blood that we must look and believe for sanctification, all strife and warfare over for ever.

Christ is our wisdom for sanctification, as saith the apostle, I Corinthians 1:30, and that sanctification is in his body once offered, and blood once shed, as it is written in Hebrews and by Peter.

In a word, and a word of wisdom at that, Christ Jesus is already – that is, he *has been* – made our sanctification in its entirety, in the wisdom of God in his own dear Son. All else, all that is from the Spirit, *flows from that*. Not without it.

Third, redemption. There are two words in the new testament in connection with redemption. The first is indicative of the payment of a price –'ye are bought with a price'– that is the basis.

The second word declares the consequences of that payment having been made. The redeemed are loosed away, let go, out and from all that had bound them.

Now the apostle declares that Christ Jesus is made unto us wisdom from God, and the end of that wisdom is that the Son of God is our redemption. Not only is he our Redeemer: he, himself, is made our redemption.

That is, redemption from sins. 'In whom we have redemption through his blood'–note the past tense: we *have* it–'the forgiveness of sins', Ephesians 1:7. 'For thou wast slain, and hast redeemed us'—again, mark the tense: *hast* redeemed us—'to God by thy blood', Revelation 5:9.

Again, redemption from all iniquity. That is, from all lawlessness; the intention, the wilfulness, the defiance: 'Who gave himself for us, that he might'—observe the tense: the verb respects our *will*—'redeem us from all iniquity', that is, correctly, lawlessness, Titus 2:14.

Thirdly, redemption from the curse of the law. 'Christ hath'—note that: *hath*. He has already done it—'redeemed us from the curse of the law, being made'—of God, on the cross—'a curse for us', Galatians 3:13.

The law sounded the curse upon us continually from heaven; till he took our place under it, absorbing the curse in his own body. And there was a great calm.

Once more, redemption from the law itself. 'God sent forth his Son, made of a woman, made under the law, to redeem them that were under the law'—this is not the curse of the law; it is the law as an entity, in and of itself, as such—'that we might receive the place of sonship', Galatians 4:4,5.

Fifth, redemption from among men. All mankind was begotten of Adam, under the Fall, conceived in sin, shapen in iniquity, sons of disobedience, children of wrath, born in the man of sin and death. But 'These were redeemed from among men, being the firstfruits unto God and to the Lamb', Revelation 14:4.

And again, redeemed from this body. We which have the firstfruits of the Spirit, 'even we groan within ourselves, waiting for the place of sonship, to wit, the redemption of our body', Romans 8:23.

Seventh, redemption from death. 'He cried with a loud voice, Lazarus, come forth. And he that was dead came forth', John 11:43,44. 'Jesus said unto her, I am the resurrection, and the life', John 11:25.

In a word, as to all those called of God, 'I will ransom them from the power of the grave; I will redeem them from death', Hosea 13:14.

It is this verse from Hosea that caused Paul – in the revelation of it – to cry out in triumph, 'O death, where is thy sting? O grave, where is thy victory?', I Corinthians 15:55.

Likewise the faith of Job rose above all his terrible afflictions and adversities to exclaim, 'I know that my redeemer liveth, and that he shall stand at the latter day upon the earth: and though after my skin worms destroy this body, yet in my flesh shall I see God', Job 19:25,26.

And to bring forth the headstone thereof with shoutings, crying, Grace, grace unto it, this sevenfold redemption in Christ administers a portion for seven, and a portion for eight, reaching over all, and above all, and through all, to eternity: 'by his own blood he entered in once into the holy place, having obtained eternal redemption for us', Hebrews 9:12.

Thus in his love it appears that of him are we in Christ Jesus, just as it is of him that he is made unto us wisdom. As to that wisdom, in the length, breadth, depth, and height of it, it embraces righteousness, sanctification, and redemption: all in all, 'that, according as it is written, He that glorieth, let him glory in the Lord', I Corinthians 1:30,31.

Next the apostle shows how he had exemplified in his own person – when first he came to Corinth – the truths which now he urges upon them in their present state. That is, he illustrates by his own personal testimony the very admonition which he delivers to them in chapter one.

'And I, brethren, when I came to you, came not with excellency of speech or of wisdom, declaring unto you the testimony of God. For I determined not to know anything among you, save Jesus Christ, and him crucified.

'And I was with you in weakness, and in fear, and in much trembling. And my speech and my preaching was not with enticing words of man's wisdom, but in demonstration of the Spirit and of power:

'That your faith should not stand in the wisdom of men, but in the power of God', I Corinthians 2:1-5.

Thus the apostle records in this present epistle to them, the determination that was within himself when first he came to Corinth: this was to shut himself up to preaching Jesus Christ, and him crucified. Why? Because he knew that the preaching of the cross saved, and that they needed salvation. That was what he had made clear in chapter 1:17-25.

Paul weak? Paul in fear? Paul in much trembling? From what? Not from the fear of man, nor from the dread of persecution; but from the fear of God, and from the trembling in his presence.

But why should this be, when he came to Corinth to preach Jesus Christ and him crucified? Because he was weak, he feared, he trembled, *that all should be of God; everything should be from Christ; that each utterance should be by the Holy Ghost.*

Paul was weak, he feared, he trembled, that all should be of God, and by the power of God, and, if so, that nothing of self, nothing of the flesh, should at any time intrude. Because all these things had been judged of God in Christ, and Paul judged them in himself daily, kept under in the fear of God lest anything of man, or of Paul as a man, or of the flesh, should once appear, and so mar the testimony.

'But we have this treasure in earthen vessels, that the excellency of the power may be of God, and not of us. We are troubled on every side, yet not distressed; we are perplexed, but not in despair; persecuted, but not forsaken; cast down, but not destroyed; always bearing about in the body the dying of the Lord

Jesus, that the life also of Jesus might be made manifest in our body', II Corinthians 4:7-10.

Now, these providences brought down the flesh, and, judged within by the Spirit and mortified, kept Paul in weakness, in fear, and in much trembling: 'For we which live are alway delivered unto death for Jesus' sake, that the life also of Jesus might be made manifest in our mortal flesh', II Corinthians 4:11.

So that at a great price he obtained this freedom: 'So then death worketh in us, but life in you', II Corinthians 4:12. And thus it was that he came to Corinth preaching Jesus Christ and him crucified in weakness, in fear, and in much trembling.

In this way God's strength was made perfect in weakness, and Paul the rather gloried in his infirmities, that the power of Christ might rest upon him: 'Therefore I take pleasure in infirmities, in reproaches, in necessities, in persecutions, in distresses for Christ's sake: for when I am weak, then am I strong', II Corinthians 12:10.

Whence it is clear why Paul was weak—*made* weak, by the operation of God, both in providence and in the Spirit—and in fear, and in much trembling: this kept out the flesh, and kept the old man mortified. Wherefore Paul was of those who 'out of weakness were made strong', Hebrews 11:34.

This makes a minister, that is, a minister of the new testament, of the Spirit, and not of the letter: 'For I will show him how great things he must suffer for my name's sake', Acts 9:16.

'In all things approving ourselves as the ministers of God, in much patience, in afflictions, in necessities, in distresses, in stripes, in imprisonments, in tumults, in labours, in watchings, in fastings; by pureness, by knowledge, by longsuffering, by kindness, by the Holy Ghost, by love unfeigned.

'By the word of truth, by the power of God, by the armour of righteousness on the right hand and on the left. By honour and dishonour, by evil report and good report: as deceivers, and yet true; as unknown, and yet well known; as dying, and, behold, we live; as chastened, and not killed;

'As sorrowful, yet alway rejoicing; as poor, yet making many rich; as having nothing, and yet possessing all things', II Corinthians 6:4-10. Now these dealings of God with his servants, besides the constant inward exercises of the Spirit within in sanctification and contrariwise in mortification, these make a minister of Christ 'in weakness, and in fear, and in much trembling'.

And what motivation lies behind this constant self-judgment, suffering, and affliction on the part of the apostle, filled with the Spirit, ungrieved and unhindered: 'that *your* faith should not stand in the wisdom of men, but in the power of God', I Corinthians 2:5.

Not that Paul did not, and could not, excel in wisdom. But it was not that kind of worldly wisdom of the carnal mind in which the Corinthians were exulting, and, worst of all, exulting in contending parties about the things of Christ.

The wisdom which Paul spoke was not of man, neither by men, nor had it anything to do with this world. It was the hidden wisdom, it was spiritually received, it stood in dimensions beyond the perception of the natural mind.

This wisdom Paul could, and did, speak among them that are perfect, that is, the spiritually mature, those of full age, 'even those who by reason of use have their senses exercised to discern both good and evil', Hebrews 5:14. Whereas the Corinthians were still no better than babes: 'For ye are yet carnal', I Corinthians 3:1,3.

None of the princes of this world knew this spiritual wisdom of which Paul speaks. How could they? It was not of this world, it was of God. It was not perceptible, it was hidden. It was not in logic, it was in a mystery. It was not philosophical, it was revealed. So the worldly were blind to it, utterly in the dark about it. And hence, blind, in the dark, though very princes in this world's wisdom, yet in their benighted ignorance they crucified the Lord of glory.

For no worldly eye, no natural ear, no fleshly heart, can either see, hear, or understand that which is hidden in God, which soars to divine and heavenly realms beyond human comprehension. But *these* are the things which God hath prepared for them that love him, and, if so, to convey them spiritually by revelation in a mystery, I Corinthians 2:6-9.

Now, if this wisdom of God in a mystery was ordained before the world unto our glory, it follows, first, that it simply cannot concern this present world, nor the passage of time. Neither can it pertain to the first man Adam or his posterity.

For all these are things that pertain to what is natural, of fleshly generation, of the present world and age, and are nothing to do with eternity before the world was, or eternity when time is no more. But the hidden wisdom is *everything* to do with eternity, from everlasting to everlasting.

Likewise it follows, second, that since this wisdom of God in a mystery was ordained before the world – before time began – unto our glory – when time is no more – the world, the age, time, have nothing to do with it, neither has it anything at all to do with the world, the age, or time.

Such things – temporal things: of this age, creation and humanity – are the sole objects of worldly wisdom. But these, and wisdom concerning them, are irrelevant to the hidden wisdom of God in a mystery.

Finally, third, if ordained unto 'our' glory, *as opposed to the world and that in which men glory*, then there must be a people redeemed out of this present evil world, of another order than those who are of it, otherwise the distinction would have no validity. But it does have validity.

For God in Christ Jesus, risen from the dead, has chosen, called and created the *new* man, destined for the resurrection from death and the grave, and pertaining to the glory of the inheritance to come, world without end. Amen.

This new creation of God comes down from God out of heaven, and is of God. And so is the hidden wisdom. Hence it is incomprehensible to the natural man, who experiences none of these things. And if incomprehensible, then – to him – foolishness.

And will the Corinthians bring *this* mentality, *this* frame of mind, to bear on the evangel, or on the things of Christ? Shame on them.

'For what man knoweth the things of a man, save the spirit of man which is in him?', I Corinthians 2:11. By our own humanity we comprehend the humanity of others. From within ourselves we understand what is within others. Otherwise, such affinity would be impossible.

As well try to express one's inmost feelings, aspirations, humanity, mentality, ideals, responsibility, and immortality, holding forth in utterance to some dumb beast, or to a tree, or else a vegetable.

There is no correspondence; these lower orders of existence, though living, are so far beneath the nobility of man that communication is incapable of being realized. Nothing can be communicated man to man save by the spirit of man that is in him.

'Even so, the things of God knoweth no man, but the Spirit of God.' As a vegetable to a man; a beast to a human being; so is man to God. There is no correspondence.

No correspondence; that is, *unless* God should create anew in Christ Jesus a *new* man, gratuitously bestowing the Holy Ghost, so as to bring in life, light, and love, indwelling and filling, henceforth to communicate 'the things freely given to us of God'.

'Now we have received, not the spirit of the world, but the Spirit which is of God; that we might know the things that are freely given to us of God', I Corinthians 2:12. None of this proceeds out of the natural mind of man. All of it is communicated to our humbled, mortified, crucified minds by the Spirit of God.

'But the natural man receiveth not the things of the Spirit of God', I Corinthians 2:14. Why not? Because he has no more than the spirit of a man. He has nothing whatsoever of the Spirit of God. And should one who has the Spirit of God speak of the things revealed to him, the worldly man will think him to be a fool.

Think him to be a fool, though he utters the things of the Spirit of God. But, to the natural man, 'they are foolishness unto him: neither can he know them, because they are spiritually discerned', I Corinthians 2:14.

But he that is spiritual is full of the Spirit, is under the anointing, walks by the Spirit, is spiritually minded, and is led by the Spirit into all truth. To him, he who speaks by the Spirit, comparing spiritual things with spiritual, speaks the wisdom of God in a mystery.

As to the Corinthians, Paul, calling them his brethren, nevertheless could not speak unto them as unto spiritual, but as unto carnal, even as unto babes in Christ. He had fed them with milk, and not with meat, for hitherto they were not able to bear it, neither yet were they able.

If they were not carnal, if not still babes, Why the divisions? Why the envying, the strife, the walking as men? Why the reducing of ministry to the persons of the ministers, as if each gave his own party opinion, so that the Corinthians chose between them, creating divisions by the choice?

Paul and Apollos were nothing but labourers together with God: *the Corinthians themselves* were the building. Though let them remember who laid the foundation; who was the wise masterbuilder; and what that foundation was that the apostle had laid, I Corinthians 3:10,11.

Others had come and built upon that apostolic foundation of the Christian *ecclesia*, but let them take heed how and what they built: and that they were *sent* of God to build thereon. For it is certain that the original gold, silver, and precious stones would abide the fire of that day: but subsequent wood, hay, and stubble would not. Then, let the Corinthians grow in grace, and learn to discern between good and evil.

Having been built upon the apostolic foundation of the Christian *ecclesia*, and at that by the apostle himself, did they not know that they were the temple of God, and that the Spirit of God dwelt in them? Let no man deceive himself. If any man among them seemed to be wise in this world, let him become a fool, that he may be wise: wise, that is, in the wisdom of God in a mystery, by the Spirit of God through revelation, which is mere foolishness to the world.

Conversely 'the wisdom of this world is foolishness with God. For it is written, He taketh the wise in their own craftiness. And again, the Lord knoweth the thoughts of the wise, that they are vain.' Then let those who leaned to worldly wisdom beware.

'If any man defile the temple of God'–in context, with the introduction and propagation of worldly wisdom and carnal philosophy about spiritual things–'him shall God destroy; for the temple of God is holy.' Which temple the Corinthians were.

'Therefore let no man glory in men.' For all things were theirs. Whether Paul, or Apollos, or Cephas, or the world, or life, or death, or things present, or things to come; all was theirs; and they were Christ's; and Christ was God's, I Corinthians 3:19-23.

'Let a man so account of us', saith the apostle, 'as of the ministers of Christ, and stewards of the mysteries of God.' If of the former, then it was not them, but Christ who spoke through them, to whose indwelling they submitted in obedience. If of the latter, they would bring that forth suited to the conditions of those to whom they were sent.

The last thing that such stewards would do would be to administer above the capacity of their hearers, though it might give an impression of great eloquence and ability in the scriptures, to the admiration of the undiscerning. But as well feed babes with meat, to choke and kill them, as descend to such inhumanity.

But some judged Paul less eloquent, and therefore inferior, for this love which he bore in his stewardship, having no thought of himself, or of creating impressions. That brought him this reward from certain: 'his bodily presence is weak, and his speech contemptible', II Corinthians 10:10.

Far from reacting, or being retaliatory, the apostle in his meekness and spirituality was above such unjust criticism. Indeed, it was a very small thing that he should be judged of them. He did not even judge himself!

Why not? Because he had renounced his own knowledge, wisdom, and judgment, knowing that what things were gain to him, were now nothing but loss. Not that that justified him. No, he walked by the rule of him who said: 'I can of mine own self do nothing: as I hear, I judge: and my judgment is just; because I seek not mine own will, but the will of the Father which hath sent me', John 5:30.

Well, the Lord judged Paul, and Paul heard this just judgment inwardly by the Holy Ghost, for he both walked and spoke with a witness, under the anointing. How? In that he sought not his own will, but the will of him that sent him.

From this the Corinthians were very far, and had so much yet to which they must needs attain. Let them judge nothing before the time, when the Lord comes again to bring to light the hidden things of darkness, and to make manifest the counsels of the hearts.

And these things, for the sake of the brethren, in a figure Paul had transferred to Apollos and to himself, that they might learn not to think of men more highly than that which is written, so that none of them should be puffed up against another.

'For who maketh thee to differ from another? and what hast thou that thou didst not receive? now if thou didst receive it, why dost thou glory, as if thou hadst not received it?', I Corinthians 4:7.

Let the Corinthians observe and learn from the apostles themselves: 'For I think that God hath set forth us the apostles last, as it were appointed to death: for we are made a spectacle unto the world, and to angels, and to men.'

They were fools for Christ's sake, but doubtless the Corinthians were wise! They were weak, but who could question the strength of the Corinthians! They were despised, yet how honourable the Corinthians appeared in their own sight!

The apostles? 'Even unto this present hour we both hunger, and thirst, and are naked, and are buffeted, and have no certain dwelling place; and labour, working with our own hands: being reviled, we bless; being persecuted, we suffer it:

'Being defamed, we entreat: we are made as the filth of the world, and are the offscouring of all things unto this day.' The apostle writes not these things to shame the Corinthians, but as his beloved children to warn them.

To warn them? Yes, for though Paul had built them by Jesus Christ through the Spirit of the Lord upon the apostolic foundation of the Christian *ecclesia*, certain had come to them since, to take advantage of this apostolic labour in his absence. Hence he warns them.

'For though ye have ten thousand instructors in Christ, yet have ye not many fathers: for in Christ Jesus I'—had they forgotten?—'I have begotten you through the evangel. Wherefore'—mark that: *wherefore*—'I beseech you, be ye followers of me.

'For this cause'—observe: *this* cause—'have I sent unto you Timotheus, who is my beloved son, and faithful in the Lord, who shall bring you into remembrance of my ways'—note that: my *ways*—'which be in Christ, as I teach everywhere, in every *ecclesia*', I Corinthians 4:9-17.

He would send Timotheus, yes; but some were puffed up, as though he himself would not come unto them: but he had *begotten* them, and that through the apostolic foundation of the Christian *ecclesia*, witnessed and ratified by the Holy Ghost from heaven. Then he will know not the *speech* of them which are puffed up, but the *power*.

'For the kingdom of God is not in word, but in power.' Then what do they wish? That he should come unto them with a rod—as did those who claimed that they were Moses' disciples, yet *professed* Christ—or should he come in love, and in the spirit of meekness?

For by the rod nothing had been begotten but fear, bondage, strife, division, enmity, darkness, and confusion. But by love, and in the spirit of meekness, when the apostle came at the first, there had followed justification, remission, pardon, redemption, sonship, hope, salvation, and a certain inheritance. So what would they choose? Whom do they consider it safe to follow?

Is it their father in Christ, who begat them through the evangel by the Holy Ghost? or is it others, who came presuming to build on his work, having none of their own?

JUDGMENT CONCERNING THE WICKED; I CORINTHIANS 5:1-13

A common report of the worst kind of fornication—not so much as named among the Gentiles—on the part of one counted as a brother by the *ecclesia* at Corinth, had been bruited abroad among the Jews and unbelievers throughout the city. It was well known, and it was perfectly true.

Yet this had been ignored—indeed, treated with indifference—by the rest of the brethren.

Preoccupied and puffed up, contending for one party against another, they neither cared about, mourned over, nor brought judgment to bear among themselves concerning this wickedness in their midst, that he that had done this deed might be taken away from among them.

But to the contrary, Paul, though absent in the body, nevertheless as present in spirit, had judged already, as though he were present, concerning him that had done this deed.

In the name of our Lord Jesus Christ, when they were gathered together, and the spirit of the apostle with them, withal the power of our Lord Jesus Christ, they were to deliver such an one unto Satan—who dwelt in the world *outside* the *ecclesia*, within which the Holy Ghost dwelt—for the destruction of the flesh, that the spirit might be saved in the day of the Lord Jesus.

Their boasting was not good: they were glorying in the flesh. This was wholly reprehensible, and contrary to the doctrine and Spirit of Christ.

Let them learn from the figures under the old testament. In particular, the passover, followed by the feast of unleavened bread.

Ignoring evil in the congregation was like hiding leaven in three measures of meal. However minute the portion of leaven, did they not know that a little leaven leaveneth the whole lump? It would—and it must in its nature—spread till *everything* was leavened.

Seven days, beginning with the sacrifice of the passover lamb, and ending with an holy convocation, Israel was to eat unleavened bread.

No vestige of leaven was to be found in all their habitations throughout the feast. All that was leavened, and every particle of leaven, was to be purged out from Israel.

Well, this was the fulfilment: 'Purge out therefore the old leaven, that ye may be a new lump, as ye are unleavened. For even Christ our passover is sacrificed for us:

'Therefore let us keep the feast, not with old leaven, neither with the leaven of malice and wickedness; but with the unleavened bread of sincerity and truth', I Corinthians 5:6-8.

Ignoring evil in the congregation is as leaving leaven in meal: it will spread and increase till the whole lump is leavened.

The apostle had warned them in a previous epistle not to keep company with fornicators: but he did not so much refer to the *world*—full as it was with fornicators, the covetous, extortioners, and with idolaters: for in such a case they must needs go out of the world!—but he meant *in the ecclesia*.

Therefore to clear the matter beyond all misunderstanding he writes again now, yea, gives commandment, that they should not keep company with any man that is called a brother who is a fornicator. Is this plain enough language for them?

And not only a fornicator, but also—called a brother—not to keep company with any who are covetous, or idolaters, or railers, or drunkards, or extortioners. With such an one no not to eat. So that not only are all such to be put out, but even so much as to eat with them is execrated.

For what, declares the apostle, What have I to do to judge them that are without? Nothing at all.

As to those within, *they themselves* should have judged, long before *this* letter was written! It was their neglect of judgment *within the ecclesia* that was so grievous, for *that* was committed to them for the glory and honour of the Lord.

'But them that are *without* God judgeth. Therefore'—since all that is *within*, by the Spirit of the Lord and the apostles' doctrine, pertains to *their* jurisdiction—'put away from among yourselves that wicked person', I Corinthians 5:13.

JUDGMENT PERTAINING TO THE SAINTS: WHETHER OF THE WORLD; OF ANGELS; OF BRETHREN; OF UNRIGHTEOUSNESS; OR OF THE BODY AND THE SPIRIT; I CORINTHIANS 6:1-20

Shaming the Corinthians, the apostle asks ten questions between verse 1 and the first part of verse 9. Seven of these questions, in expressions of affront, appear in verses 1-5, and three in verses 7-9. All—whether shaming themselves to perfection, or humiliating themselves to completion—bring the apostle to a sense of outrage.

The outrage of taking matters to law before the unjust, and not before the saints! It is the saints that shall judge the world: How can the world judge the saints?

'Let the high praises of God be in their mouth, and a two-edged sword in their hand; to execute vengeance upon the heathen, and punishments upon the people; to bind their kings with chains, and their nobles with fetters of iron;

'To execute upon them the judgment written: this honour have all his saints. Praise ye the Lord', Psalm 149:6-9. And what? Take a brother to law before *these*? O, for shame!

'Know ye not that we shall judge angels?' That is at the end of this world, when the world to come shall be ushered in?

'And round about the throne were four and twenty thrones: and upon the thrones I saw four and twenty elders sitting, clothed in white raiment; and they had on their heads crowns of gold', Revelation 4:4.

From these royal thrones, set about the throne of Almighty God – depicted in a figure – shall be judged this present world at the end of the age; then, if so, likewise the *diabolos*, Satan, with all his angels; the first and second beasts; the false prophet; Babylon the whore and Babylon the city.

At the sounding of the last trump, in the day of judgment, when 'there were great voices in heaven, saying, The kingdoms of this world are become the kingdoms of our Lord, and of his Christ; and he shall reign for ever and ever', Revelation 11:15. And whose is the honour of bringing in the judgment of God upon this world, the god of it, and all his angels?

Why, it is the honour of those, in whom all the saints are summed up in a figure: 'And the four and twenty elders, which sat before God on their thrones, fell upon their faces, and worshipped God,

'Saying, We give thee thanks, O Lord God Almighty, which art, and wast, and art to come; because thou hast taken to thee thy great power, and hast reigned.

'And the nations were angry, and thy wrath is come, and the time of the dead, that they should be judged' – yes, and him that had the power of death, and all his angels with him,

Openings in First Corinthians

Revelation 20 – 'and that thou shouldest give reward unto thy servants the prophets, and to the saints, and them that fear thy name, small and great; and shouldest destroy them which destroy the earth' – namely, Satan, the destroyer, called Apollyon, with his angels, and all the fallen world.

'And the temple of God was opened in heaven' – wherein is figured the throne of God and the thrones of the twenty-four elders – 'and there was seen in his temple the ark of his testament: and there were lightnings, and voices, and thunderings, and an earthquake, and great hail', Revelation 11:16-19.

By such graphic symbolism, it appears that not only shall the saints judge the world in the last judgment at the end of time, but that they shall judge angels also. And, in time, shall such as have this honour go one against another at law before the least of those whom at the last they shall judge from the throne?

The saints shall judge angels when this life is no more: Then how much greater their competence to judge matters whilst this life yet continues? Shame on the Corinthians! Was there none wise, none able, among them, that brother went to law against brother before the very unbelievers whom at the last they are appointed to bring into the last judgment?

And if this be so – and it is so – with such a high dignity conferred upon the saints at the end of this world and beginning of that to come, then, as to the comparatively mere trifles of *this* passing age, the *least* esteemed among the brethren should more than suffice to judge the relative trivialities of this temporal and fleeting scene, I Corinthians 6:4.

But *no one* judged anything: no, they went to the jurisdiction of unbelievers instead. This was, and is, utterly a fault: better to be defrauded, than to seek amends against a brother before the courts of this world.

By so doing *all* one's brethren were defrauded of the dignity of their separation from the world, and their privileged and high standing as God's *ecclesia*. By allowing such action, they denied this heavenly and glorious inheritance.

None of the unrighteous – such as the covetous, to whom gaining money from a brother at law in this world, was more than gaining the inestimable value of the kingdom of God in the world to come – but *none* of the unrighteous shall inherit the kingdom of God.

'Neither fornicators, nor idolaters, nor adulterers, nor effeminate, nor abusers of themselves with mankind, nor thieves, nor covetous, nor drunkards, nor revilers, nor extortioners' – *now* let the covetous see in what company they are found! – 'shall inherit the kingdom of God' – and let them observe also to what destiny such characters are bound.

And such *were* some of the Corinthians: 'And such were some of you: but ye are washed, but ye are sanctified, but ye are justified in the name of the Lord Jesus, and by the Spirit of our God', I Corinthians 6:11.

On this verse I have written elsewhere, as the apostle Paul says in a certain place, 'To write the same things to you, to me indeed is not grievous, but for you it is safe', Philippians 3:1.

Or as Peter puts it in another way, 'Wherefore I will not be negligent to put you always in remembrance of these things, though ye know them, and be established in the present truth.

'Yea, I think it meet, as long as I am in this tabernacle, to stir you up by putting you in remembrance', II Peter 1:12,13.

Putting you in remembrance of what? Of the salvation of God. Of what Paul wrote also. Of the fact that 'Such were some of you: but ye are washed, but ye are sanctified, but ye are justified in the name of the Lord Jesus, and by the Spirit of our God.'

In this place there is no question of the apostle teaching the Corinthians about justification as such: that doctrine lies elsewhere. Here the doctrine is assumed.

In this context the apostle Paul shows the experience accompanying the imputing of righteousness to the ungodly: the change that this causes. I Cor. 6:11 describes the application of a previously accomplished work to the present experience of the saints.

The text shows that justification, effectually wrought at the cross, preached in the gospel, was applied with power to the Lord's people at Corinth 'in the name of the Lord Jesus, and by the Spirit of our God'.

The chosen vessels of mercy, upon whom God would make known the riches of his glory, were afore prepared unto glory when Christ died for them.

Everything was in the death of Christ. In terms of I Cor. 6:11 the death of Christ afore secured their washing, their sanctification, and their justification.

How can we tell this? First, as to washing being secured by the death of Christ, before ever it was applied by the Spirit of God, observe Rev. 1:5, 'Unto him that loved us, and washed us from our sins in his own blood.'

Here his love, which is from everlasting—'I have loved thee with an everlasting love'—preceded his dying for them, which was on the cross, when the shedding of his blood cleansed—or washed—their sins away.

It was this that the Spirit applied to them: 'but ye are washed.'

Next, as to sanctification being secured by the death of Christ, before ever it was applied by the Spirit of God, observe Heb. 13:12, 'Wherefore Jesus also, that he might sanctify the people'—

here is their sanctification – 'with his own blood, suffered without the gate.' Where sanctification doubtless is secured by the death of Christ.

'For by one offering he hath perfected for ever them that are sanctified.'

The sanctification, the securing for them of the Spirit of God, was wrought for the people of God in its entirety by the blood of Christ.

The same is true, lastly – I Corinthians 6:11 – as to justification. As has been stressed over and over again, this was secured by the death of Christ. Rom. 5:9 'being now justified by his blood.'

Justification was achieved when Christ's blood was shed. When Christ died, righteousness of God was already to the account of all those that had been, or ever should be, brought to faith.

These things, all of these things, washing, sanctification, justification, were already fully secured through the finished work of Christ at the cross for an elect and foreknown people.

In the process of time, and the experience of that people – 'I have much people in this city', see Acts 18:1,9,10 – the Spirit of God was sent to apply the work of Christ to those for whom it had been wrought.

Why? Otherwise they would never receive it, because 'it is not of him that willeth, nor of him that runneth, but of God that showeth mercy.'

So filthy, so base, so wayward, so perverse, so corrupt were these people – 'such were some of you', I Cor. 6:11 – that, were the love of God in Christ displayed before their very eyes, of themselves they would turn away.

But for such Christ died, and to such the Spirit is sent, and come they shall, for come they must, that 'no flesh should glory in his presence', I Cor. 1:29.

From their birth in the flesh they will not come, but from their birth in the Spirit they shall come, for it is written, 'which were born, not of blood, nor of the will of the flesh, nor of the will of man, but of God', John 1:13.

And so the Greek reads, I Cor. 6:11, 'But ye *were* washed, but ye *were* sanctified, but ye *were* justified', referring in the past tense to their actual present experience of what had been wrought for them before they were born.

When the mighty converting power of God turns the heart of the ungodly, there ensues a great yearning to be washed from filth, set apart from the world, and to be justified by faith.

This longing shall never be in vain. Not many days shall pass before it is said, 'But ye are washed, but ye are sanctified, but ye are justified in the name of the Lord Jesus, and by the Spirit of our God'.

This encourages the ministers of the evangel to say, 'Knowing, brethren beloved, your election of God'.

But how do they know it? Because 'our gospel came not unto you in word only, but also in power, and in the Holy Ghost, and in much assurance', I Thess. 1:4,5.

This assurance was because they knew that Christ had washed them from their sins by his own blood, when it was shed; that he had sanctified them with his own blood, when he had suffered without the camp; and that he had justified them by his blood, when he had brought in to their account righteousness of God at the cross.

All this was in the counsel and purpose of God.

What was in the life and experience of the saints was, firstly, the washing of regeneration.

By the revelation of Jesus Christ, and the quickening operation of the Holy Ghost, the interior new man was raised up in newness of life, and illuminated by the light of the glory.

It was as if cleansing streams of water washed away the old filth and corruption, purging out the guilty stains. As the word came with power, so the living streams issued forth, and thus the cleansing work was experienced.

This is called, The washing of water by the word: 'but ye are washed.'

Moreover, the saints were 'all full of the Holy Ghost'. They were strengthened with might by his Spirit in the inner man, their bodies the temple of the Holy Ghost, who took up his dwelling within their hearts.

They loved this holiness, or sanctification, caused by his inward divine presence.

This set them apart, within and without, from the world, the flesh, and the devil.

They were not conformed to this world, nor to worldly things, they walked in the Spirit, were spiritually minded, and were led by the Spirit.

The Spirit led them into all truth, glorifying Christ before their interior eyes, bringing them into an inward union and communion with the Father and the Son. 'But ye are sanctified.'

Likewise the *ecclesia* of God which was at Corinth, all of whom were the sanctified in Christ Jesus, called saints, by definition knew the blessedness of the man whose transgression was forgiven, whose sin was covered, to whom the Lord imputed not iniquity.

Openings in First Corinthians

By definition: because it was nothing other than the common experience of the work of God in justifying the ungodly that had constituted them to be the *ecclesia* which is his body.

All the saints had the same 'like precious faith', the 'faith of God's elect'.

They were justified by faith, and had come together in consequence. They were the *ecclesia* at Corinth precisely because every individual in the city without exception who had eschewed his own righteousness, fled from the wrath to come, and had experienced the blessedness of righteousness being imputed without works, was in and of that company, gathered under the preaching of the apostle, called the *ecclesia* of God at Corinth.

They had been justified in the name of the Lord Jesus, and by the Spirit of our God. This was their spiritual experience: the 'church' had not wrought it, it was not wrought by the 'church', God had wrought it, and all upon whom it was wrought were the *ecclesia*.

Every one of the saints, the sum of whom was the *ecclesia*, the body of Christ, had felt the Spirit witnessing with his spirit that he was a child of God, justified freely by grace.

From within his inmost being welled up the cry, Abba, Father.

All heaven was open to him, the old yoke clean gone, the obscuring veil taken away, the glory in the face of Jesus Christ as the body of heaven in his clearness.

The joy of the Lord was their strength; they rejoiced with joy unspeakable and full of glory, filled with all joy and peace in believing.

By grace they had been saved through faith, and that not of themselves, it was the gift of God, not of works, lest any man should boast.

But what man could boast? Where was boasting? It was excluded. By what law? of works? Nay: but by the law of faith.

Therefore they concluded that a man was justified by faith without the deeds of the law, and found this a most wholesome doctrine, and very full of comfort.

This was both the experience and the witness of the entire *ecclesia* of God which was at Corinth, every one of the sanctified, all the saints, to whom the apostle could say in spirit and in truth, 'But ye are justified'.

And yet some, perhaps most, of the saints at Corinth had been fornicators, idolaters, adulterers, effeminate, abusers of themselves with mankind, thieves, covetous, drunkards, revilers, extortioners, without God in the world, and without inheritance in the world to come.

'But ye are washed.'

That is, washed clean from every stain, all their guilt, besides every inward corruption that had ever brought forth such vile works.

Not for them the background sanctity of a 'Christian' home, or of a sheltered 'church' upbringing.

They were converted out of the world, they had been filthy, lawless, given over to greediness, fleshly lusts and worldly pleasures their selfish and ardent pursuit. But in a moment, in the twinkling of an eye, 'Ye were washed ... in the name of the Lord Jesus, and by the Spirit of our God'.

They were sanctified. Born of the Spirit in a moment, filled with the Spirit thenceforth, they were led by the Spirit away from their old companions in worldly pleasures and diversions, openly testifying of the wrath of God upon the world, and of salvation in the name of the Lord Jesus.

Separate from every form of idolatry and worldly religion, they loathed the things which before they loved.

Humbled, lowly, walking with self-distrust and self-abhorrence, shame and joy mingled as they received with meekness the engrafted word, kept in the fear of God, and rejoicing in Christ Jesus, having no confidence in the flesh.

The old things were passed away, behold, all things had become new. A new creation had come in an instant, the moment of regeneration, and they knew that they were sanctified.

Though the pleasures of sin were still in the city, though the enticements of the world were ever in their environment, though the swellings of corruption were yet felt within them, nonetheless they were indwelt by the Holy Ghost, Christ filled their hearts, the Father's good pleasure was always before them, and they could see eye to eye with the word of God, 'but ye were sanctified ... in the name of the Lord Jesus, and by the Spirit of our God'.

They were justified. God himself had imputed righteousness to them without works, freely by his grace. Instantaneously they had received the blessing.

As it was said of Peter with the Gentiles, likewise it was true of them, 'While Peter yet spake these words, the Holy Ghost fell on all them which heard the word'.

The hearing of faith was their blessing, they were of those 'who by him do believe in God', having 'obtained like precious faith with us', that is, with the apostles.

They had obtained faith, that is, it had come from God himself.

This was their joy, God had done the work, and, if so, he would complete it.

Nothing would stand that was of man, or of man's will. But, in Corinth, 'as many as were ordained to eternal life believed.'

God had imputed righteousness, and they felt that God had imputed righteousness, just as they felt that God had quickened their faith into being.

Faith was not of themselves, any more than righteousness was of themselves, all was of God, it was not of works, that is, not of the works of their will or choice, they could not boast, it was the work of God that they believed, and it was all their joy and song: God had done the work.

This would stand, and this would both bring about and secure their recovery. 'But ye were justified in the name of the Lord Jesus, and by the Spirit of our God.'

All this, every part of it, washing, sanctifying, justifying, from first to last, from heaven to earth, from God to man, from eternity to eternity, was 'in the name of the Lord Jesus, and by the Spirit of our God.'

Now, this brought justification by faith worth the name. It is justification by faith with a threefold divine witness.

Justification by faith is of the essence, it is the heart of the gospel. It is the answer to the ancient cry, 'I know it is so of a truth: but how should man be just with God?'

It is of the essence, it is the heart of the ministry of Christ from the glory, the ministration of righteousness. It is of the essence, it is the heart of the answer to the sinner's cry, the prodigal's lament, the leper's entreaty, the blind man's plea, and the yearning of the penitent.

The imputing of accomplished justifying righteousness to every heart-broken, mourning sinner is the occasion of the Spirit of the Lord GOD being upon Christ.

Openings in First Corinthians

Justification is the good tidings which the Lord hath anointed him to preach to the meek, it is that which binds up the broken-hearted, proclaims liberty to the captives, and the opening of the prison to them that are bound.

Justification is Christ's heavenly message, the divine proclamation of the acceptable year of the Lord, and the day of vengeance of our God.

Justification by faith is comfort to all that mourn, the divine appointment to all that mourn in Zion, it is the consolation in Christ, the comfort of love, the fellowship of the Spirit, and the bowels of mercies of our God.

Justification gives beauty for ashes, the oil of joy for mourning, the garment of praise for the spirit of heaviness: that they might be called trees of righteousness, the planting of the Lord, that he might be glorified.

Justification is the tree of life, the blood of atonement, the Lamb slain from the foundation of the world, the righteousness of God, the blessing of Abraham, the blessedness of David, and the bliss of all that hunger and thirst after righteousness.

Justification takes in and sounds out the death of Jesus Christ at Golgotha. Justification answers the cry, Eloi, Eloi, lama sabachthani? Justification pronounces the word, Verily, I say unto thee, Today shalt thou be with me in paradise. Justification pleads the cause, Father, forgive them, for they know not what they do.

Justification cries in triumph over sin, death, the fall, over every enemy, over the last enemy, over the judgment to come, justification cries, I say, with a loud voice, 'It is finished!'

Justification preaches redemption through the blood of Christ, the forgiveness of sins, the pardon of the sinner, the ransom of the slave, the release of the bondman, the dissolution of the old yoke, the rending of the legal veil.

Justification declares the reconciliation, proclaims substitution, shows the atonement, and affirms propitiation through faith in his blood.

Justification smiles upon the ungodly, stoops sweetly to the foul, answers mercifully to the sinful, declares God's righteousness for the remission of sins, God's justice in imputing righteousness by faith of Jesus Christ, disclosing the meeting-place of mercy and truth, the tryst of righteousness and peace.

Justification is the foundation of Zion, the door of salvation, the banner of liberty, the key of the kingdom, the hope of Israel, the establishment of the world to come, the dwelling-place of righteousness, the assurance of the inheritance, and the pledge of everlasting glory.

Justification is of the essence, the heart, of the evangel: it is the evangel, it is the evangel from which all else takes its rise, in which each doctrine is founded, upon which every truth rests, because it is that by which the death of Christ is opened, expounded, communicated, and magnified in the name of the Lord Jesus, and by the Spirit of our God.

Justification was the substance of Paul's evangelism, it was the evangelism of the apostles, by which remission of sins was preached in Christ's name to all nations, beginning at Jerusalem.

When Paul evangelized, all who believed that evangel were justified by faith. They were of the *ecclesia*: they were the *ecclesia*. This was the *ecclesia*.

There was no 'church membership', there were no other bodies, societies, or exterior organisations in the Lord's name, no rival 'churches', the very idea was antichristian; there was one *ecclesia*.

There was one body, and one Spirit, even as they were called in one hope of their calling; one Lord, one faith, one baptism; one God and Father of all, who was above all, and through all, and in them all.

This was the *ecclesia* which was in God the Father, and in our Lord Jesus Christ, I Thessalonians 1:1; II Thessalonians 1:1.

The preaching of the gospel – of justification by faith – by the apostolic ministry brought this into being, for by it the saints were gathered together in one, as members of the one body of Christ.

The preaching of justification, and the belief of it, formed and united the saints in the house of God, the *ecclesia* of the living God, the pillar and ground of the truth.

All who received the blessing were of the *ecclesia*, they were visibly united together in love, and all others outside of this body – including the vast religious edifice of formal priestly religion centred upon the outward temple – were not of the *ecclesia*, had not received the blessing, and were not of God's elect.

This was the city set on an hill, the one pool of light in a sea of darkness, the one true love in a world of enmity, the only life in a realm of death.

All the saints, in the simplicity which was in Christ, and by the power which was in the Spirit, were united with one heart and one mind under the apostolic preaching of the evangel in the beginning.

It was for this that the ministry of Christ was sent.

Anything else, or anything gathered on any other foundation, of necessity would have defied the will of God, and would have stood in the apostasy, ministering to the future disintegration of the single testimony to the unity of Father, Son, and Holy Ghost, one God, blessed for evermore. Amen.

The apostles preached doctrinally, expounding the word of God.

They brought home to the heart the condition of sinners under the law and under wrath, whilst opening the righteousness of God by faith of Jesus Christ, hour after hour, by day and by night, day after day, the gospel becoming a savour of life unto life, and death unto death to every hearer in all places.

They were hated by the world, outcast of men, persecuted by the authorities, but loved by heaven, embraced of Christ, and favoured by God and the Father.

Far from the pragmatic acceptance of the divisions, of the apostasy, of denominationalism, these uncompromising, God-taught, heaven-sent, Christ-glorifying preachers of justification by faith, the evangelists of the word of God, gathered the believers into one body, one *ecclesia*, the one unity, as it was in the beginning, is now, and ever shall be.

That is, it shall be, when justification takes its rightful place again, when men who fear God alone, and who are full of the Holy Ghost, who are not disobedient to the heavenly vision, leave all, forsake their nets, and follow him, to preach the glorious evangel of the blessed God, declaring the righteousness of God by faith of Jesus Christ through all the world abroad.

What message can compare with justification by faith?

Nothing can compare with this glorious, spiritual, heavenly, divine, and saving doctrine.

Here is a doctrine determined in the ancient settlements of eternity; ordained before all worlds in the bonds of the everlasting covenant; established in the eternal counsels of Father, Son, and Holy Ghost; sworn by the immutable oath of the Almighty; ratified by the blood of the Surety; sealed with the sevenfold seal of the Holy Ghost from heaven; and secured to the infinite reaches of everlasting glory.

Justification by faith was determined in purpose before the world was, promised in anticipation at the dawn of time, established in the blood of Christ in the midst of the ages, and shall stand to everlasting when time is no more.

When the last judgment has had the last word, when the great earthquake has shattered the earth; when the sun becomes black as sackcloth of hair, and the moon becomes as blood; when the stars of heaven fall unto the earth as a fig tree casteth her untimely figs, shaken by a mighty wind; when the heavens depart as a scroll which is rolled together, and every mountain and island are moved out of their places;

When the kings of the earth, the great men, and the rich men, and the chief captains, and the mighty men, and every bondman, and every free man, hide themselves in the dens and in the rocks of the mountains, and say to the mountains, Fall on us, and hide us from the face of him that sitteth upon the throne, and from the wrath of the Lamb, for the great day of his wrath is come; and who shall be able to stand? then shall the justified stand.

Then shall justification by faith, and the doctrine thereof, shine in her true lustre.

For the ungodly shall not stand in the judgment, nor sinners in the congregation of the righteous.

But justification shall stand; and the justified shall stand. For it is God that justifieth: Who is he that condemneth? Heaven and earth shall pass away, but these words shall not pass away.

Justification by faith shall abide the fire. When the wicked shall go away into everlasting punishment; when the 'devil'–*diabolos*–the false prophet, Babylon, and the two beasts, are cast into the lake of fire and brimstone that burneth for ever and ever; justification shall abide.

Justification shall abide the fire.

When the heavens shall pass away with a great noise, and the elements shall melt with fervent heat; when the earth shall reel to and fro like a cottage, and all faces shall be as flames; when the earth shall be burned up and the works thereof; then justification shall abide the fire.

Then shall this wonderful, this pre-eminent, this saving doctrine be marvellous in our eyes, and the Lord shall bring forth the headstone with shoutings, crying, Grace, grace unto it!

Justification shall attend the righteous into the very portals of the new heavens and the new earth wherein dwelleth righteousness.

Ever sure, ever fresh, justification shall rest in fulfilment in the place where there is no night, where the Lord God Almighty and the Lamb are the light thereof, in the place where the Lamb which is in the midst of the throne shall lead the justified, now glorified, unto living fountains of waters.

The place where God shall wipe away all tears from their eyes, where the ransomed of the Lord shall come to Zion with everlasting joy upon their heads, where they shall obtain joy and gladness, where all sorrow and sighing shall flee away.

In that place shall justification by faith, having fulfilled her office, rest content, world without end, Amen.

Then, having been washed, having been sanctified, having been justified – with *such* a justification – How is it possible, how ever could it come to pass, how dare any of *you*, having a matter against another, go to law before the unjust, and not before the saints?

Thanks be to God, it followed – it *must* follow – that such a course was abandoned; the matter was put right; all parties would rather be defrauded. So that, after *such* a word, the saints at Corinth not only submitted to the apostolic injunction, they *exemplified* it, II Corinthians 7:11.

Hence Paul continues, 'All things are lawful unto me'. They may be *lawful*—such as going to law—but they are certainly not *evangelical*! Lawful, yes, for those in this world and of it. But not for those delivered from this present evil world, and destined for glory in the world to come.

All things may be *lawful* in the world, such as meats, in any circumstances. All meats may be eaten, in the world. But if in certain situations they offend my brother, then, lawful or not, such eating is certainly not *evangelical*.

Then, a citizen's right to use the law, and utilize what is lawful, may be within his power.

But to the saints, citizens of a heavenly country, not of this world, this power is not to be used in any circumstances offensive either to one's brother, or to the *ecclesia*.

'All things are lawful unto me, but all things are not expedient: all things are lawful for me, but I will not be brought under the power of any. Meats for the belly, and the belly for meats: but God shall destroy both it and them', I Corinthians 6:12,13.

Here is sound judgment, and judgment pertaining to the saints, according to the Spirit of God in the doctrine of the apostles.

Now, passing from the truth concerning meats and the belly, the apostle considers the body—of which, naturally, the belly, the seat of the appetites, is a part. Now *this* is a matter for the saints' judgment.

The body—and the deeds of it—are for the Lord: not for fornication. Paul had occasion to speak of fornication in a particular case earlier in the epistle.

But now the natural run of the context leads him to consider the use not just of the belly but of the appetites; and not just those of the belly, but those of the whole body. And, if so, of the abuse of the body.

'Now the body is not for fornication, but for the Lord; and the Lord for the body. And God hath both raised up the Lord, and will also raise up us by his own power', I Corinthians 6:13,14. Where, as God raised up the Lord – that is, in the *body* – so shall our bodies also be raised up of God in the likeness of his glorious body. Wherefore, the body is *for the Lord*.

What? Even now? Yes, even now: 'Know ye not that your *bodies* are the *members of Christ?*', I Corinthians 6:15. If our *bodies* are the members of Christ, then what is all this nonsense about an invisible unity if our bodies are scattered throughout numerous divided denominations and meetings?

Or what the claptrap of a spiritual body of Christ, so spiritual that it is non-existent to the sight? How can *our bodies*, as his members, *be invisible*? How can *any* body, or its members, be invisible? Then, it would not be a body at all: it would be a *spirit*. But it is not: it is the *body* of Christ that is filled with his Spirit, united in the assembled members.

So to speak – as the Disraeli appointed 'Bishop' Ryle spoke to justify his politically inspired and Royalty endorsed Church of England Bishopric, and his nationally established Anglican denomination – is not only or merely in the teeth of scripture. It is not only nonsense and claptrap.

It is spiritual wickedness in denying the visibility of the body of Christ in order to excuse the sin of denominationalism in every one of its multitudinous variations.

Your bodies the members of Christ? Then, O ye Corinthians, shall you take the members of Christ and make them members of an harlot? God forbid. I Corinthians 6:15.

God forbid, for he that is joined to an harlot is one body, for two, saith he, shall be one flesh. But he that is joined to the Lord is one spirit.

Therefore flee fornication, for every other sin that a man doeth is without the body; but he that committeth fornication sinneth against his own body.

Why? Because he has made himself all of one with a whore. The harlot and he, so joined, are one flesh, not two. Then, thus he sins against his own body.

'What? Know ye not that your body is the temple of the Holy Ghost which is in you, which ye have of God, and ye are not your own?', I Corinthians 6:19.

No, not your own: 'For ye are bought with a price: therefore glorify God in your body, and in your spirit, which are God's', I Corinthians 6:20. Not our own, neither in body, soul, or spirit, all purchased, as is our person itself, purchased with the blood of Christ.

Why? For this cause: To redeem us to God, to glorify him in our body, indwelt by the Holy Ghost as his own temple, and united to Christ in our spirit, our bodies constituted withal as the members of the body of Christ.

JUDGMENT CONCERNING QUESTIONS OF MARRIAGE; I CORINTHIANS 7:1-40

Paul, obliged to descend to the Corinthians' carnal, earthly, and temporal preoccupations, answers their letter full of such questions, yet devoid of the vastly greater matters on which he had written already—and was yet to write—concerning the things of God.

It is good for a man not to touch a woman. Nevertheless to avoid fornication let every man have his own wife, every woman her own husband, with corresponding mutual obligations. But the apostle states this by permission, not of commandment, verse 6. Permission of whom? Who else but the Holy Ghost?

The apostle recommends his own estate to all, whilst acknowledging that it is the gift of God. He speaks to the unmarried and widows, that it is good for them to be even as he. But if this be beyond their attainment, rather than burn, let them marry, I Corinthians 7:7-9.

To the married who believe, the Lord commands—and the apostle reiterates—that the wife should not depart from her husband, despite what had been said in verses 1, 7, and 8. Notwithstanding, if she does depart, she must either remain unmarried, or else be reconciled to her husband, both, presumably, having remained in the congregation. Moreover, in such a case, the husband is not to put away—that is, divorce—his wife, verses 10, 11.

To the rest the apostle speaks—not the Lord—a brother having a consenting but unbelieving wife should not put her away. And a sister having a consenting but unbelieving husband should not leave him. In both cases the one believing party sets apart the other in relation to their children being holy, verses 12-14.

However—in either case—if the unbelieving depart, let them depart, since, obviously, this can no longer be prevented. Such persons depart because of unbelief; then, neither a brother nor a sister is under further obligation—that is, obliged by a broken tie—in such cases. The party wilfully deserting in unbelief beyond recovery has effectively disannulled the marriage bond, I Corinthians 7:15.

The word avoided by the Versions is *divorce*: however, this is the indisputable implication of the Greek as understood by many disparate—but equally acknowledged—authorities in the original as—for example—those who framed the Westminster Confession, and J.N. Darby of the Brethren—together with his more weighty contemporaries—not to mention many ancient fathers held in high repute.

The word 'bondage' as in 'a brother or sister is not under *bondage* in such cases', undoubtedly means bondage *to the law*. In this instance the reference is to the law concerning marriage, which had been broken by the departure of the faithless and unbelieving erstwhile wife or husband. Then 'divorce' is regarded as having taken place legally by such a departure. Witness the use of the same Greek word in Galatians 4:3, 'We *were* in bondage under the elements of the world', but now, lawfully, no longer.

Quite apart from the Westminster Confession, it may be appropriate to quote J.N. Darby, concerning the reading 'But if the unbelieving depart (divorce) let him depart (divorce). A brother or sister is not under bondage (not enslaved, that is, to the law, and may consider himself or herself unjustly divorced and therefore at liberty to remarry) in such cases', from 'The History of the Brethren', N. Noel, edited by W.F.K.

J.N. Darby comments, 'The Christian deliberately deserted by the unchristian partner was in every way free, free that is to marry: but it assumes deliberately forsaking by the one who went away. By the act of sin, sinful departure, or sinful infidelity, the tie was broken already, and judicial divorce allowed ... let them obtain a divorce, and then they are free to marry', Letters, Vol. 2, page 154.

This is of course further to the Lord's teaching in the gospels, for example Matthew 5:32;19:9, which had direct application to Israel. But now the evangel had gone out to the Gentiles, and a new thing—the *ecclesia*—had come in, creating circumstances beyond those addressed by the Son of man to the Jews that believed in Israel during the days of his flesh. This Paul implies when speaking by the Holy Ghost, I Corinthians 7:12.

Hence the further direction applicable to the Gentiles—and therefore the Corinthians—I Corinthians 7:15. Calvin has this to say: 'If the unbeliever puts away his or her partner, because of the question of religion, then the brother or sister is freed from the marriage bond by such rejection.'

Again John Calvin states concerning the meaning of I Corinthians 7:15, *'Yet if the unbeliever departs.* In this verse Paul frees a faithful husband, who is prepared to live with a wife who is an unbeliever, but is rejected by her; and similarly frees a wife, who is put away by her husband, although there is no fault on her side.

'For in those circumstances the unbeliever makes a breach with God rather than with his or her partner. Here there is a special reason, because the primary and principle bond (*vinculum*) is not merely untied, but violently torn apart', Calvin's Commentary, First Corinthians, translated by John W. Fraser, published by Oliver and Boyd, Edinburgh.

All this is both true and sound. Nevertheless if such an irrevocable situation can be avoided, it should be avoided: God hath called us to peace. Hence, prior to such irreversible departure, the possibility still existing, everything should be done to realize the hope that the unbelieving wife or husband might be saved by the believing, I Corinthians 7:15(end), 16.

In whatsoever way the providence of God distributes, so let believers walk. If the providence of God—as opposed to oneself—alters circumstances, in those altered circumstances let the believing walk accordingly. Let every man submit with contentment to that pathway which God hath ordained, since none of us is his own, but every one has been bought with a price, I Corinthians 7:17-24.

The Corinthians pursued the subject raised by *their* letter, in the longest chapter yet in the epistle, gendered by their intense interest and questioning of the matter from the apostle, who desired to speak as unto spiritual, but was forced to address the carnal. Now it is a question concerning virgins.

Paul had no commandment from the Lord, but judged that it is good for a man so to be. One bound to a wife should not seek to be loosed. One loosed from a wife should not seek a wife. But if a virgin, or one loosed, should marry, they have not sinned.

Nevertheless all such shall surely have trouble in the flesh. The apostle presses for contentment, knowing how short the time, and how near eternity, I Corinthians 7:25-31.

The apostle would have us without carefulness. He that is unmarried careth for the things of the Lord, how he may please the Lord; but he that is married careth for the things of the world, how he may please his wife.

Likewise there is a difference between a wife and a virgin: the unmarried woman careth for the things of the Lord, that she may be holy both in body and in spirit; but she that is married careth for the things of the world, how she may please her husband, I Corinthians 7:32-34.

The apostle writes such things not to cast a snare upon them, but for their own profit, that in all comeliness they may attend upon the Lord without distraction. But if a man think his behaviour uncomely, let him marry: he hath not sinned. Nevertheless he that standeth steadfast in his heart, purposing to keep his virginity, doeth well.

So then, he that giveth in marriage doeth well, but he that abstains from marriage doeth better.

For the married, death alters the case, so that a widow is at liberty to marry again, only in the Lord. But she is happier if she abide a widow, in the apostle's judgment.

And who doubts but that he writes by the Spirit of God? This concludes Paul's answer to their many questions on this subject, I Corinthians 7:35-40.

JUDGMENT CONCERNING MEATS OFFERED TO IDOLS; I CORINTHIANS 8:1-13

Touching things offered to idols, the apostle employs sarcasm against those presuming superior knowledge: 'We know that we all have knowledge.' And what use is that? 'Knowledge puffeth up.' Quite to the contrary, love edifies: it builds up.

Therefore those supposing superiority because of knowledge, looking down on others they consider ignorant, know nothing as they ought to know.

It is what – or rather whom – God knows, that is the criterion: those who love him, are known of him. None others.

Concerning eating things offered in sacrifice to idols: we know that an idol is nothing in the world: there is none other God but one. True, there be that men call gods, or lords, whether in heaven or earth. But to us there is but one God, the Father, of whom are all things, and we in him; and one Lord Jesus Christ, by whom are all things, and we by him, I Corinthians 8:1-6.

All brethren know this of the Father and the Son. More knowledgeable brethren know that idols are nothing, and mean nothing. More simple – and weak – brethren are troubled that if they should eat what was offered to idols they would be defiled.

That would be the effect on their conscience. Not that *they* – God forbid! – offer to idols, but, after the idols' priests and acolytes offered, *then* that was either sold cheaply in the shambles, or distributed freely to the poor.

Openings in First Corinthians

Now, What of such meat freely available? Or what of meat sold cheaply in the shambles, of unknown origin? Either knowing whence it came, or else not knowing, but doubting, the conscience of the poorer and more simple brethren—weak, if you will—smites them, and they are defiled, verse 7.

But—as those with knowledge realize—meat is meat is meat, neither more nor less, and neither commends us nor brings blame upon us if we eat. If we eat we are not better before God; if we eat not neither are we worse before him.

Maybe not. But if that meat is known—or even thought—at one time to have been offered to an idol, one's *brother* is stumbled, and, if he should then *follow that example of liberty*, in his case bondage is gendered, and the worst defilement of conscience ensues.

Therefore let the strong and knowledgeable take heed of liberty that stumbles the weak and ignorant, verses 8,9.

Indeed, those so bold in knowledge, so free with liberty—to get the best meat—would even sit at the table in the temple of the idol, before ever the remainder was cleared away and despatched to the shambles.

But what if one's weak brother beholds his strong brethren sitting at meat in the idol's temple? Shall he not be emboldened to do likewise? But yet in his *own* heart and conscience he cannot but condemn himself.

Then, through what one presumes to be superior knowledge, shall that weak brother perish, for whom Christ died? I Corinthians 8:10,11.

Whoso thus offends one of these little ones, to cast a stumblingblock before him, at once offends against all the brethren, wounds the conscience of the weak, and sins against Christ.

Wherefore, saith Paul, if meat make my brother to offend, I will eat no flesh while the world standeth, lest I make my brother to offend, verses 12,13.

In itself, meat, what does it matter? It was meat before being brought into the temple; it was meat when offered to a lifeless idol—which, for all its fixed graven mouth could not eat of it—within the temple; and it was meat when it was carted out to be disposed of in the shambles.

Then, what it was in the beginning, it is at the end, the interim making no difference whatsoever. That is knowledge.

But other poor and simple brethren—the weak—had not that knowledge, they could not rise to it.

Paul could: he had all knowledge; his mind was strong. Yes, but he did not despise, disparage, or dismiss the weak brother. He did not attempt with superior condescension to instruct him, either by word or example.

No, not at all. He studied his weaker brethren: he loved them: he came down to where they were. Then, he would—he could—do nothing to stumble them. Go, and do thou likewise.

[PAUL VEHEMENTLY VINDICATES HIS APOSTLESHIP - PARENTHESIS; I CORINTHIANS 9:1 TO 10:13]

[Abruptly Paul interjects four questions concerning his apostleship; his freedom; his having seen the Lord; and his fruitfulness: followed by his reproachful observation to the Corinthians that by them above all—who were the seal of his apostleship—he should be counted as an apostle.

Such a sudden interruption of his discourse, such peremptory questions, all argue that this is the beginning of a lengthy parenthesis, stung by the wounding of his heart, in which he is forced to vindicate his apostleship, verses 1,2.

Which apostleship, apparently, was disparaged by some who had come to the Corinthians in his absence—as if *their* supposed ministry were remotely comparable with *his*!—and certain among the Corinthians entertained these slurs, obliging the apostle to answer to their examination of himself and his ministry, verse 3.

For, they contended, Were not those who came to them so strong in the faith that they knew perfectly well that they could eat and drink what had once been offered to idols? Well, Paul answers, Had not *he* the same power? Then let them ask themselves from chapter 8 why he had not used it.

Were not the other apostles, they argued, distinguished in that they had the authority to go about the assemblies having their wives with them, whereas Paul did not even possess a wife? If he were an apostle, Why did he not use the same apostolic liberty? Oh? Why did not the Corinthians ask themselves from chapter 7 why he had not used that liberty?

Again, said they, Were not the other apostles—not to mention many so-called ministers—authorized—indeed, *marked out*—to forbear working in view of the importance of their ministry? Then what was Paul's ministry?

Or were Paul and Barnabas so contemptible in the eyes and mouths of others that they were disqualified from this privilege? verses 4-6.

In his reply, Paul is not afraid to quote authorities for living by the gospel one preached. Of course, this has nothing to do with the apostasy of hiring by contract on the part of sects those approved by their denominational bodies as 'reverend pastors', who contradict the presence and gifts of the Spirit in the divided congregations over which *they* are hired to preside.

As to Paul, the Corinthians were the fruit of *his* ministry: what were these others doing plucking and eating from it? And what is this, that these fruitless usurpers then denigrate the labourer who planted the vineyard? Yet the apostle, of all men entitled to use this authority, abstains from it, I Corinthians 9:7-19.

Just as Paul would abstain from meats for his weak brother's cause, and would make the gospel of Christ without charge—labouring as a brother—rather than burden the brethren, so also he condescends to the condition of those to whom he is sent.

To the Jews he became as a Jew, that he might gain the Jews. To those under law, as under law—witness his Nazarite vow; his shaving his head; his attending the Feasts in the temple—that he might gain those under law.

To those without law, as without law—though not lawless, God forbid! nor without the law of the Spirit of life in Christ Jesus—that he might gain them that are without law.

Hence, Chapter 8, to weak brethren he became as weak. And will they also blame him for that?

Blame him for coming down in love, rather than rising up in knowledge?

Whatever men were—short of lawlessness; short of denying the law of faith—he would abase himself; he would demean himself, yea, before all men, that he might save some.

And for this cause he denied himself; he buffeted his body, kept it under, humbling and mortifying himself in his apostleship. And ought the Corinthians—who would examine him—to find fault with him for this, to whom they owed their own souls besides? I Corinthians 9:20-27.

But now Paul proceeds from answering those that would examine him—though they be called brethren—to their examination of themselves. So knowledgeable?

Openings in First Corinthians

Well, Paul would not have these knowledgeable brethren to be ignorant, who gloried in having been baptized under this name or that, since all our fathers were in no less privileged a position than they.

For all the fathers were under the cloud, all passed through the Red sea, all were baptized unto Moses—note the fathers' contentment with *one* name!—in the cloud and in the sea.

They all ate the same spiritual meat—as opposed to some knowledgeable brethren who on their own ate carnal meat once offered to idols, at the expense of others, their weak abstaining brethren—and did all drink the same spiritual drink—in contrast with some among the Corinthians who drank of carnal drink in the idol's temple, to the detriment of their weaker brethren.

Moreover, that spiritual drink of which all the fathers drank sprang from the smitten Rock, which Rock, saith Paul, was Christ. So wherein were the Corinthians better than them? Rather, the fathers' unity put *them* to shame.

But for all the fathers' unity, for all their partaking of what was spiritual, for all their spiritually eating and drinking of Christ—for, observe, it is *spiritual* meat, verse 3; and *spiritual* drink, verse 4, that is, from the Rock which was *Christ*, declares Paul, verse 4—for it all, I say, with many of them God was not well pleased.

For they were overthrown in the wilderness. And this, brethren, is an example to *you*.

Although most that call themselves Brethren have a fail-safe easy-believing insurance scheme by which they defy this apostolic word, pull its teeth, cut off its hands, and flatly refuse to accept the reality of this example.

Example? They lusted after evil things, and so do some of you. But what happened to them? With examples, it follows, the same thing happens to you.

They were idolaters, sitting down to eat and drink, rising up to play. And what happened? They perished.

And, for example, they committed fornication, and fell in one day three and twenty thousand. That was more than existed in the total number of brethren at Corinth, to whom these fallen fathers are brought as an example of what happens to fornicators, whosoever they be.

These fathers tempted Christ, and because of it were destroyed of serpents. Can those to whom these are set forth an example, dare to say that they were not tempting Christ, in view of the preceding chapters of this epistle?

The fathers murmured, yes, and not least against Moses, the servant of the LORD: and what do the Corinthians that is any different?

Murmurers were, and are, destroyed of the destroyer. No ifs. No buts. It happened, and, says Paul, it happened as an example to you, I Corinthians 10:1-10.

Observe: 'Now all these things happened unto them for ensamples; and they are written for our admonition', verse 11.

Now what stiff-necked brethren, uncircumcised in heart and ears, resisting the Holy Ghost, dare gainsay this? 'Wherefore let him that thinketh he standeth take heed lest he fall', verse 12.

But, as did they, so have we a resource. It is this: 'There hath no temptation taken you but such as is common to man: but God is faithful, who will not suffer you to be tempted above that ye are able; but will with the temptation also make a way to escape, that ye may be able to bear it', I Corinthians 10:11-13.

This concludes the parenthesis, in which Paul is obliged to defend his apostleship against his examiners, upon whom he turns the tables, bidding them to examine their own conduct in the light of those examples written for our admonition, upon whom the ends of the world are come.]

Resumption of I Corinthians 8:1-13; judgment concerning meats offered to idols; I Corinthians 10:14 to 11:1

With wording appropriate to the warnings in the latter part of the parenthesis, yet entirely suited to the continuation of chapter 8:1-13, the apostle resumes his discourse: 'Wherefore, my dearly beloved, flee from idolatry.'

But if *flee* from idolatry, how then shall the dearly beloved brethren, even if knowledgeable, sit at meat, or take meat from, the very *temple* of idolatry? Let those with knowledge ponder such a contradiction.

'I speak as to wise men' – that is, *if* there *were* those who were such, Paul appeals to them directly – 'judge ye what I say', I Corinthians 10:14,15.

Because the drink suited to the brethren – whether they be strong or weak – whom Paul calls his dearly beloved, is certainly *not* to be found in the idol's temple. It is found in 'the cup of blessing which we bless'.

Neither is the meat appropriate to such brethren discovered in the temple of an idol: it is found in 'the bread which we break'.

Furthermore the company of those who bless the cup, and break the bread, is that which is called 'the communion' – but the word means 'fellowship' – of the blood of Christ, and 'the communion' of the body of Christ.

Then how can *that* company, or any *one* of that company, possibly sit in apparent communion with those gathered to eat and drink in an idol's temple, even if from no motive other than the prospect of free – or at least cheap – meat and drink?

'Be ye not unequally yoked together with unbelievers: for what fellowship hath righteousness with unrighteousness? and what communion hath light with darkness?' Moreover, 'What agreement hath the temple of God with idols? for ye are the temple of the living God'; See II Corinthians 6:14-18.

As to the unity of that body – the body of Christ – separated from the temple of idols, standing in the 'communion' – or, rather, 'fellowship' – of the blood of Christ, by which the beloved brethren were redeemed from among men, and in the communion – or, more correctly, 'fellowship' – of the body of Christ, in which they, being many, were seen as one bread, and one body, for they were all partakers of that one bread: How then can those who eat and drink in this holy communion possibly be found in an idol's temple?

The Cup and the Loaf exclude it. To this sanctified fellowship – 'I speak as to wise men; judge ye what I say' – the beloved of God were to be faithful. And why? Because 'God is faithful, by whom ye were called unto the fellowship' – or 'communion' – 'of his Son Jesus Christ our Lord', I Corinthians 1:9.

This is the communion or fellowship of the elect of God, chosen out of the world, on whom rested the blessing: 'The grace of the Lord Jesus Christ, and the love of God, and the communion' – or 'fellowship' – 'of the Holy Ghost, be with you all. Amen', II Corinthians 13:14.

Further to that which he had stated in chapter 8:1-13, observe that with the resumption of this matter, after the parenthesis, Paul brings in a new concept: that of *association*.

First, I Corinthians 10:16, that of the fellowship – or communion – of the blood of Christ, and second, that of the fellowship – or communion – of the body of Christ, also verse 16.

This is expressed by the cup of blessing which we bless on the one hand, and the bread which we break on the other: 'For we being many are one bread, and one body: for we are all partakers of that one bread', I Corinthians 10:17.

The apostle presses home this exhortation with an example: 'Behold Israel after the flesh: are not they which eat of the sacrifices partakers of the altar?'

Of course they are; the entire sacrifice was offered, and slain, at the altar, which sanctified the offering. What was not consumed on the altar was eaten by both offerer and priest; what was not eaten by both offerer and priest was consumed upon the altar.

Then *the sacrifice bound the offerer to the altar*. The association was as inevitable as it was undeniable, I Corinthians 10:18. But by an inexorable logic, *the same thing applies to what was offered to idols*.

This the apostle now enforces: 'Ye cannot drink the cup of the Lord, and the cup of devils: ye cannot be partakers of the Lord's table, and the table of devils.'

Notice that the apostle in this enforcement brings in a far stronger and more sinister element: it is no longer the cup of idols: it is the cup of *devils*; it is no more the table of idols: it is the table of *devils*.

Devils were in it: not just idols. The two were inextricable. How much stronger is *this* than his arguments in chapter 8:1-13!

Again, he speaks of jealousy. God is the *living* God: his *feeling*, his *passion* is in his love. Will they provoke his love—whose name is Jealous—by flirting at the idol's temple *with devils*?

Fear him who saith, 'Love is strong as death; jealousy is cruel as the grave: the coals thereof are coals of fire, which hath a most vehement flame.

'Many waters cannot quench love, neither can the floods drown it: if a man would give all the substance of his house for love, it would utterly be contemned', Song 8:6,7. Then, do we–dare we–provoke the Lord to jealousy? Are we stronger than he? I Corinthians 10:22.

In the remainder of the chapter, and, indeed, of this phase of the epistle, Paul repeats the conclusions reached in the beginning regarding what may or may not be lawful but which, for all that, must be subservient to expediency; to edification; and to love of the brethren.

Nevertheless, what is sold in the shambles, or else served at a table–of unknown origin–does not require or demand exhaustive and minute enquiry: accept it!

But if another knows of its provenance being derived from the idol's temple, at all costs, rise, and leave the dish uneaten and the table vacant, for the conscience sake of him that showed it.

That is what Paul would do: and with what better or more fitting words could he conclude this subject than 'Be ye followers of me, as I am of Christ'? See I Corinthians 10:23 to 11:1.

JUDGMENT CONCERNING HEADSHIP; I CORINTHIANS 11:2-16

The apostle appears to search out matters for which to praise the Corinthians, as he commends them for remembering him in everything, and that they keep the things which he delivered to them, as he delivered them–for so the Greek reads, verse 2.

What things? 'Ordinances' is not correct: it is interpolation. It is–as a verb–to give over or alongside; or–as a noun–the things given over or alongside.

Openings in First Corinthians

What things? For example, 'that form of doctrine which was delivered you', Romans 6:17; or the things—whatever this may mean—referred to in I Corinthians 11:2; and again, 'for I have received of the Lord that which also I delivered unto you', I Corinthians 11:23; once more, 'for I delivered unto you first of all that which I also received, how that Christ died for our sins according to the scriptures', see in full I Corinthians 15:3-8.

Peter refers to the way of righteousness as 'the holy commandment delivered unto them', and Jude to 'the faith which was once delivered unto the saints'. Then, 'the things delivered' may refer to doctrine, ordinances, or precepts, in the evangel given by the apostles.

Here Paul praises the saints at Corinth for remembering him in all things, and for keeping the things which he delivered, as he delivered them.

But—and there is a 'but'—there is that which he would have them know, and which now he stresses. It concerns the cause of headship, and the effect which necessarily follows from it. To convey this knowledge the apostle first lays down the doctrine, then affirms seven arguments in support of the ordinance that ensues.

The doctrine concerns authority, and the way in which this is delegated from on high in a descending order. The arguments concern the *visible signs* of the existence of that authority, and the *manifest order* by which it is made apparent.

As to the doctrine, from the Highest there are three descending realms of authority in which headship over that which is subordinate becomes abundantly clear *through this revelation*, and therefore that which follows *through its ordained visible sign*. Everything results from the truth that the head of Christ is God: then, the doctrine refers to the anointed manhood of the ascended Son of God. He is head over all; and, regarding the *ecclesia*, specifically he is the head of every man.

As to every woman, God, the head of Christ, and Christ, the head of the man, are both at remove in order of authority. The man is the head of the woman, and to him she is to submit and to maintain subordination, just as he is to Christ, and Christ to God. This is revelation: it cannot be perceived otherwise.

To fallen man and the carnal mind, to the blind and darkened—as to invisible spiritualities—sons of disobedience, all this is bewildering nonsense.

But in the last day, to all of these—evangelical, reformed, charismatic, it makes no difference—it will be a matter of terrible vengeance and fearful judgment visited upon all such disorderly rebels who make the word of God of none effect by their traditions, contending against the truth which in a vague way they profess to uphold, but actually in practice they dismiss. This shows them up to be in the fallen seed, in which Eve despised the ordinance of God conveyed to her by Adam in the day of their innocence.

Just so these excuse their women in their wilful disobedience, unable to stand before them, and thus debase their headship by such craven subservience.

Nevertheless, both the man, and the woman who enticed him, *did* surely die, and, likewise, God shall in the same manner avenge himself on all those who despise dominion, overthrow authority, deride headship, and thereby mock at the heights to which God has raised Christ, and his brethren, visibly manifest by that ordinance which was commanded to be observed in every place and in all generations throughout this earthly pilgrimage till the resurrection and glory at the coming again of Christ.

Then where shall these be, and what shall they find? They will be shown up to be disobedient and continually rebellious, and God shall mock at their calamities, who mocked at his ordinances, when all is vindicated in its due and proper place.

Headship is one thing, and it is a revealed truth to which Christendom is virtually oblivious. Why is this? Because, lacking revelation, Christendom can no more perceive such invisible spiritualities than can a blind man see visible objects. It is one thing, I say, that God is the head of Christ; that Christ is the head of every man–begotten of God–and that the man is the head of the woman–that is, of all women who name the name of the Lord. That is the truth, and it is a *revealed* truth in the apostolic doctrine. It comes down from God out of heaven, through Christ, to the brethren, and thus the sisters are under this threefold ascending authority.

Observe: since this came down from God out of heaven, and is the abiding order of authority from the Highest, it follows that I Corinthians 11:2-16 can have nothing to do with earthly geographical locations, neither with national or local customs. It is *heavenly revelation* concerning *divine authority* and it is *over all* and *throughout time*. Nothing can change that.

However, headship is one thing, the *sign* of it is another. The first is revealed apostolic doctrine concerning invisible spiritual realms and realities, the second is the corresponding revealed apostolic ordinance outwardly signifying those invisible spiritual realities.

This signification is seen–and, mark, this is a *revelation*–in the uncovering and covering of the head in all forms of prayer and every kind of prophecy on the part of the man and the woman respectively. The apostle enforces this with seven unanswerable arguments.

But why, someone will ask, the uncovering and the veiling–for that is the meaning of the Greek: *thorough veiling*–respectively? But I have already shown the meaning of the apostle: it springs from *headship*. So what else are you going to cover?

The fact is that men and women are visible, but God and Christ are not. Therefore what is *visible* is to represent the invisible, so as to manifest the order of God in Christ. That is, the man sets forth the place of Christ over him, and, because Christ is his immediate—but *invisible*—head, shows by *the absence of covering*, that, when he prays or prophesies, *there is nothing and no one between him and Christ*.

Not so the woman. When the woman prays or prophesies, she is commanded to make manifest that there *is* a stratum of authority between her and Christ, namely, the man. To make this visibly clear, the opposite is required of her to that which is required of the man: she *thoroughly covers*—cover or veil is brought down upon—*her head*. This sets forth the place of the man, her visible head, and his authority in Christ over her, and shows her submission and subjection both to the doctrine and ordinance of God by the Spirit.

Seven times over the apostle presses home the truth with invincible logic to those who know and love the truth. He argues in turn from consistency; from authority; from creation; from origination; from economy; from nature; and from usage.

Yet the perversity of those who lie by styling themselves as 'evangelical' remains contentious, not obeying the truth. They regurgitate matter impossible of digestion such as Corinthian custom, prostitution, temporary and local institutions, and I know not what other deceivableness of unrighteousness, to overturn truth as plain as daylight and as enduring as the sun.

Oh, then they will have it that a woman's hair is her covering! What? Hair a veil?

And what? If her hair is her covering veil, then for her to pray uncovered means that she prays hairless, or shorn.

And what? If it be a shame for her to be shorn or shaven, 'let her be covered', verse 6. But if her hair were her veil or cover, and if it be shorn, then how can she be covered? She cannot put back her shaven locks!

'But if it be a shame for a woman to be shorn or shaven'—which, according to the intent of these twisters of the truth must mean 'uncovered'!—then, commands the apostle, 'let her be covered.' But in such a case as they propose, she *cannot* be covered; for *they* say her *hair* is her cover, and, lo, it is all *gone*! Behold, they have made it impossible for her to be covered.

Thus observe the ludicrous dilemma of those who twist the plain meaning—and irony—of the apostle, that, if the woman wishes to usurp the man's place, then let her be shorn like a man! However, since that would be too shameful, then let her veil—*katakaluptō, thoroughly veil down upon*—her head, hair and all. This cuts off such contemptuous and unrighteous cavilling.

But now they object, Oh, but verse 15 says expressly that 'her hair is given her for a covering'. It is. And if these perverse meddlers were not so covered with darkness and ignorance, they would have seen that the Greek here is *not* that for *thorough veiling, katakaluptō,* but that for *something cast around, peribolaion.*

And what is 'cast around' her head? Why, her 'long hair', verse 15, by which nature itself—if not prevented by the scissors of worldly fashion—teaches the comeliness of veiling the *entire head, hair and all,* when in spiritual exercise towards God, namely, praying or prophesying. This is clearly indicated by the distinct word previously used in the Greek, *katakaluptō,* which, of course, in itself incorporates the actual word 'veil', so that it cannot possibly be confused with 'hair'.

And so the custom or ordinance was understood and practised in all the churches of God, I Corinthians 11:2-16. It still is; but never in the conspicuous depositories of congregational disobedience.

PART TWO

JUDGMENT CONCERNING ASSEMBLING TOGETHER

CHAPTERS 11:17-15:58

PART TWO

JUDGMENT CONCERNING ASSEMBLING TOGETHER
CHAPTERS 11:17-15:58

(1) THE LORD'S SUPPER, CHAPTER 11:18-34

At I Corinthians 11:17 the epistle enters into a new phase. Before it had been a question of individual matters, and of how individuals should walk: now it is a question of the *ecclesia* as such, of corporate matters, of how the saints assemble together, and walk together.

This change in aspect is obvious from the words 'For *first of all*, when ye come together in the church', verse 18. If *first of all*, then none of what follows had been introduced previously. Why not? Previously, the apostle addressed the saints as such; but now, he addresses the whole in their coming together, in assembly, in their congregating.

This is not to say that up to now the right – or wrong – conduct of the saints did not affect the whole: it did. Then, for good or ill, righteousness and righteous judgment should be exercised individually for the benefit of all. Now, it is no more a question of the walk of one affecting all: it becomes a question of the walk of all the assembly as one affecting the whole assembly.

This change of vision does not mean that what had been addressed to the individual was not to be practised in the assembly. For example, when the whole *ecclesia* prayed, the uncovered heads of the brethren would be those who rose and gave utterance on behalf of all.

In fact, in the assembly, women were forbidden to speak at all, whereas, in suited circumstances, they might pray and prophesy individually – if gifted of the Spirit – outside of the gathering.

Nevertheless, silently praying with and under the man, the veil would without doubt remain upon their heads, for, whether within or without, the man was their head, and, whether vocal without or silent within, they would be in prayer – and thus thoroughly veiled – in both instances.

Neither godliness, righteousness, order, nor comeliness could possibly be less emphatic because of changed circumstances that can never dismiss – though they might increase – the obligations of obedience.

Far from the Lord's supper indicating divisions, it manifests unity. Then, since Paul had heard that there were divisions among them, it was not the Lord's supper which they ate when they came together. If not, in that, they came together not for the better but for the worse.

Yet for it all, those who kept in the unity were by these divisions – or schisms – the more made manifest by the unruly spirit and party contention of the – several – others, and thus, owning the head and abiding in the Holy Ghost, could not but be the subject of the approval of all, as they kept in stillness and submission despite the contending strife and mounting din all around them.

It is essential to grasp the situation at Corinth exactly as the report of it was conveyed at the time to the absent apostle, causing him to write as he did in I Corinthians 11:17-34. Particularly note the words: 'When ye come together therefore into one place, this is not to eat the Lord's supper. For in eating every one taketh before other his own supper: and one is hungry, and another is drunken. What? have ye not houses to eat and drink in? or despise ye the church of God, and shame them that have not? What shall I say to you? shall I praise you in this? I praise you not', I Corinthians 11:20-22.

Paul adds the significant correction 'Wherefore, my brethren, when ye come together to eat, tarry one for another. And if any man hunger, let him eat at home; that ye come not together unto condemnation', I Corinthians 11:33,34.

Observe from these words the degeneration into which the Lord's supper had fallen, so much so that Paul declares it not to be the Lord's supper at all—'this is not to eat the Lord's supper'—such was the division and disorder at Corinth.

How could this have occurred? No forms of the 'Lord's supper' in existence today, no matter how they had degenerated, could possibly result in a chaos parallel with that described at Corinth: the *elements* for such a kind of degeneration as Paul describes simply do not exist today. But why not? What were those elements?

For whatever collapsed *then*, did so from the original institution of the ordinance delivered by the apostle in the beginning, where, evidently, he accepted *every element and circumstance as a background to the Lord's supper, which, later corrupted, led to the abuse which this epistle sets out to correct. Yes, and without changing the original elements, circumstances, and background of the institution itself.*

The question is this: What had been ordained originally, and against what background wholly acceptable to the apostle, that, subsequently, had fallen into such dire abuse?

Notice carefully that the apostle reproves them in certain cases for bringing a large meal to assuage hunger: not for bringing a meal in itself. If it were a question of hunger, Well: eat and drink at home, *then* come with a smaller supper. But to gorge in front of those who could afford next to nothing, then to become drunk – adding insult to injury – as if one's poorer brethren were beneath notice, was wholly unacceptable conduct.

Paul likewise reproves them for not – each with his supper – waiting for one another, so as to eat together; not to say that those who brought more ought to have shared with those who had little. All this, however, was apart from – and evidently before, since some did not wait – I say, this meal was apart from and evidently before the Lord's supper. As such, when they came together to eat, they were to wait for one another, verse 33.

This meal was not to satisfy the cravings of hunger, but the bonds of unity, in which fellowship, surely, 'he that gathered much had nothing over: and he that gathered little had no lack.' This is what should have been so conspicuous in their care the one for the other. Then, doubtless, the Lord's supper followed naturally.

But unlike the meal together, the Lord's supper entailed their partaking of but one loaf – 'for we being many are one bread, and one body: for we are all partakers of that *one* bread', I Corinthians 10:17 – for 'the bread which we break, is it not the *fellowship* of the *body of Christ*?'. Likewise the cup. One cup – '*the* cup of blessing which we bless, is it not the *fellowship* of the *blood of Christ*?', I Corinthians 10:16. Where the one signifies Jesus' *own* body, and the other his *own* blood.

If so, then, of necessity, but *one* loaf, and but *one* cup. It was *this* that was made manifest in the supper by the *entire body of*

Christ, already redeemed by his blood, united as one in fellowship, 'till he come'.

The practice of the saints taking a meal together in fellowship was no novelty, in which case that it should be followed by the ordinance—as it appears at Corinth, in the *only* epistle in which the supper is mentioned—seems as harmonious as it is suitable.

Indeed *the* Last Supper itself had been preceded by a meal from which it naturally followed. Though this were the passover, still, it provided a precedent, withal in a substantial meal of no small consequence. Paul must have had such a precedent in mind when he wrote, 'Christ our passover is sacrificed for us: therefore let us keep the feast, not with old leaven, neither with the leaven of malice and wickedness; but with the unleavened bread of sincerity and truth', I Corinthians 5:7,8.

The only other assumption, that the one loaf—'This is my body'—and cup—'This is the new testament in my blood'—had degenerated into a situation where *everyone* took at least their own loaf, many with meats and other foods, plus their own flagon of wine, is simply untenable. Of necessity, logic inexorably points to the degeneration of *a common meal*, and, with it, either the abuse or neglect of that which should have followed concerning the Lord's supper.

In the context of correcting such a situation, Paul does not censure them for taking their common meal in fellowship—only the abuse of it—but he does reiterate that which he had instituted at the first when he had delivered to them the ordinance which should have followed of course and in due order.

There is no question of either meal being other than that called 'supper'—the evening meal—equally the apostle has nothing to say concerning any particular day on which this is taken: indeed, one might infer that it was every day of the week. Whatever was lacking in the Corinthians it was certainly not enthusiasm. Nor did the apostle see the need to impose upon them some hireling or voted 'elders', in order to cure an ill by a worse disease.

Much less is revealed about the Lord's supper than is commonly supposed. As to its origin, the Last Supper, apart from the actual historical record of that event, only Luke records the utterance of the word—and therefore the implication of memorial ordinance—'remembrance'. Furthermore, strictly this is with reference to the bread alone; albeit 'likewise', in relation to the cup, *may* imply the same kind of repetitive memorial, but it does not say so explicitly.

The second—and only other—reference to the Lord's supper, this time uniquely and unequivocally designating the bread and the cup in terms of a repetitive memorial of the body and blood of the Lord—to be kept by the *ecclesia*—occurs in the first epistle of Paul the apostle to the church at Corinth. Nowhere else.

Whilst the term 'breaking bread' occurs in the Acts of the Apostles—for example, 'breaking bread from house to house'; and, 'the disciples came together to break bread'—to suppose from such an expression that this is anything other than taking a meal in common is nothing more than wishful thinking.

The fact that bread was broken in the Lord's supper does not imply that it was never broken at any other time: on the contrary, without the specific mention of the Lord's supper—not to say the addition of the cup—the words 'breaking bread' ought to be read as they were intended: to take a meal in which the staple loaf or loaves were divided among the participants.

This rather points to the common meal—the 'feast of charity'—indicated in I Corinthians 11, and—again absurd—in II Peter 2:13 and Jude 12. As to the Lord being known in the breaking of bread to the two disciples at Emmaus—supposed by those who would impose their prejudices upon the scriptures to have reminded the twain of nothing other than the Last Supper—they were not at the Last Supper!

Besides, of vastly greater significance, and certainly of stupendous effect upon the memory, was the Lord's taking, blessing, and breaking first five loaves to feed five thousand, then seven loaves to feed four thousand, events vastly more momentous, and impressive upon the memory. *That* was miraculous; the Last Supper was not.

And, incidentally, the two disciples may well have been *there* when those heavenly wonders were wrought by the Lord, whereas they were certainly *not* there at the Last Supper.

It was therefore far more likely that it was the *miracles* that sprang to their mind – revealing the Lord – when 'he was known of them in the breaking of bread'. But when – like the Roman Catholic Mass – a sect is formed over the single incidence – and only clear reference – to but one ordinance so as to eclipse all others – however numerous may be the references to *them* – then what distortions; what wishful thinking; what reading into scripture may one *not* expect?

However, sufficient unto the day the righteous judgment that pertained from the epistle – and pertains to us – concerning the Lord's supper.

(2) THE UNITY OF THE SPIRIT IN THE BODY OF CHRIST, CHAPTERS 12:1-13:13

The Gifts and Baptism of the Spirit

Before proceeding with this new – and corrective – passage in the first epistle to the Corinthians – that is, Chapter 12:1-13 – it seems appropriate to remark on the consistent evangelical principles by which the apostle rectifies any and all deviations and errors on the part of the Corinthians; and, moreover, to notice with care that by which he does *not* correct them.

What do I mean by this, especially at such an advanced point in the epistle? I mean that for all the error, all the misconduct—one might even add despite certain riotous and lawless elements not only among them but tolerated by all of them—a most conspicuous feature appears in the apostle's response which it is of the utmost importance to note.

What is this? It is Paul's consistent appeal to the evangel of Christ.

Never once is the law brought in to correct the error. Not at all does the apostle appeal to the ten commandments to counter the deviation. No, not for any one thing. But this would most surely have been the case had those who framed the so-called Westminster Confession been at this business, or had those who insist on the law as 'a rule of life' addressed the conditions at Corinth.

Then how much more would the pallid and vitiated mimics of those Puritans—now calling themselves 'reformed': the impudence!—have set about wagging their pygmy legal fingers upon every occasion!

But what have any of these sterile deviates from the evangel, or the least part of their impotent legal court of appeal, to do with the matter? What? appeal to *the letter that killeth*, in order to restore to life? Paul *always* appeals to *the evangel of Christ*.

From which it is evident—and ought well to be noted—that such confounded legalists preach *another* gospel, and, I affirm, *another* Jesus, with *another* spirit, and have *another* ministry than that of the apostles of Christ, who handle everything upon an entirely different basis, namely, that of the evangel alone, by which deliverance from the law and the legal rule is for ever assured through the death of Christ.

(i) *The Spirit of God*

In I Corinthians 12:1 the apostle first comes to things spiritual. Not that such things had been neglected hitherto: indeed, in either verb or noun form, out of some twenty-six new testament references, fifteen of these occur in this epistle, of which I Corinthians 12:1 is the ninth.

This epistle contains far and away the greatest number of references to *pneumatikos*, whatever the precise grammatical form. And yet the Corinthians were not those whom one would have thought to be the most spiritual in practice!

The word *gifts*, as in spiritual *gifts*, I Corinthians 12:1, is nothing but interpolation. There is no precise English equivalent to the Greek. One might say literally 'spiritualities', but this does not at all cover the whole range of the Greek word. Other alternatives include 'things spiritual'; 'that which is spiritual'; and 'spiritual matters', but none of these quite does justice to the original.

However, the alternative renderings do make the idea perfectly clear.

Paul is to speak to the Corinthians, and correct them, over things that were spiritual. Regarding such things, he would not have them to be ignorant.

Nevertheless, from the past—in a more sinister context—there was that in this realm of which they certainly were *not* ignorant: 'Ye *know* that ye were Gentiles, *carried away* unto these dumb idols, even as *ye were led*', I Corinthians 12:2.

The idols were dumb, but that invisible spiritual power which carried them away to them was not dumb. The idols were dumb, they knew that, but willingly enough they followed those spirits that led them to them, and that knowingly: 'Ye know that.'

They knew that they were 'carried away', as men say, 'beside themselves', because of the licentious abandonment associated with idolatry, so that far from resisting they welcomed the heightened excitement which these animated spirits induced in their already eager lusts.

But they knew precisely what was happening when they were 'carried away'. Likewise when they 'were led'. They knew it was wrong. But they followed the inward urging within their passions, animated by the spirit that now worketh in the children of disobedience.

Why? Because by following these interior influences in their senses, they knew that the pitch of their excitement when taking part in the vile practices of idolatry would be far greater than if merely left to themselves. Hence they followed the spirit by which they 'were led', and they did so knowingly.

Today, the people are just as carried away in their pleasures, just as led in their excitements, but, unlike the Gentiles of old, they are utterly blind to the supernatural and demonic influences to which they give themselves up in order to fulfil their lusts.

But where did all this lead the Corinthians? Into idolatry, riotousness, fornication, and drunkenness. But had not such wickedness been rebuked *among them still* in the earlier part of the epistle? Then to what spirit were such persons giving themselves over in the church – or *ecclesia* – of God?

Wherefore Paul gives them to understand what it is to be moved within, and led in the interior, by the Spirit of God. For they must never forget in their emotional excitement – or in that abandonment – to which they gave themselves so easily: *there were more spirits abroad to take advantage of such states than the Spirit of God.* Wherefore, 'believe not every spirit, but try the spirits whether they are of God', I John 4:1.

Negatively: 'No man speaking by the Spirit of God calleth Jesus *anathema*', I Corinthians 12:3. But whoever would do that? The legalists would, and did, and so did those who sought to bring back the law under the guise of a 'rule of life'.

Openings in First Corinthians

They protest? It is the protest of liars: the Jesus they profess is another Jesus. But the Jesus they deny is the true Jesus. Then, by their Antinomian and unevangelical heresy–whosoever they are, it maketh no difference to me: God accepteth no man's person–*denying that Christ by his death lawfully delivered us not only from the penalty of the law, but also from the law itself, therefore they abhor, reject, and cry 'anathema' against such a Jesus as this, and such a lawful deliverance as the apostle enjoined.* Nevertheless *this* is the true Jesus.

Here is the very doctrine of Galatians; just as these same legal heretics are those exposed by II Corinthians 11:3,4 and 13-15. Denying Jesus *as he is in truth, outraged at the violation of their so-called 'systematic theology' by the reality of that redemption through which we have been set free from the law, being delivered by his death from the entire legal system for ever,* they subtly reintroduce *another Jesus, which fictional character they pretend kept the law for us in his lifetime, yet brings us back into bondage under its–supposedly sanctionless!–legal rule for the rest of our lifetime.* Outraged at the very idea of any other *Jesus, namely, Jesus as he is in truth, with venomous fury they hiss at such a Redeemer so offensive to their legal system: 'anathema'.*

Then–I Corinthians 12:3–*they have not, and cannot have, the Spirit of God.* They have another, an opposing, a wholly different spirit. Read 'Justification by Faith'; and read 'Deliverance from the Law: the Westminster Confession Exploded'. That is, if you would save yourselves from this untoward generation, and find the truth, as the truth is in Jesus.

Positively, no man can say that Jesus is the Lord–that is, say 'Lord Jesus'–but by the Holy Ghost. Men do not glorify him: the Spirit glorifies him. Men do not speak of him: they use his name to speak of themselves. Men do not submit to Jesus as Lord: they claim his name and power to lord it over others. O, it is not by might, nor by power, but by my Spirit, saith the Lord: *nothing* can be done aright but by him, and in him, and through him.

The Spirit of God has come to magnify the Lord Jesus: not to assist men in using his name to magnify themselves: 'He shall glorify me; he shall not speak of himself.' Then, how much less shall those whom he leads to say 'Lord Jesus', speak of *themselves?* The Spirit of truth always speaks of *him*, never of *himself*; always glorifies *him*, never *himself*; always leads to *him*, never to *himself*.

By this we know that Christ is always magnified and exalted by the Holy Ghost, who on the one hand safeguards from error, and whatever derogates from the Lord's glory, and on the other *always speaks of Christ, and upholds the doctrine of Christ, exulting and triumphing in those whom he indwells with the victorious exclamation from the heart:* 'Jesus is LORD!'

By this we know the Spirit of God.

(ii) The Gifts of the Spirit

Since this entire phase of the epistle is concerned with unity, the apostle now shows the unity of divine persons revealed in the new testament, yet, in this unity, divine activity, demonstrating the diversity of gifts, administrations, and operations respectively.

This diversity proceeds from each divine person revealed in the new testament, demonstrably manifesting the oneness of God in three persons through the revelation of Christ. Then how can the Corinthians possibly detach, say, gifts from the Giver; ministries from the Administrator; or operations from the Operator, setting these things at variance the one against the other, as if everything did not proceed from each divine person respectively, and as if divine persons were not one in the Godhead?

Yet this divine unity and united activity was what the Corinthians were denying in effect, particularly as they vied, envied, and competed one against another in respect of their distinctive and differing gifts. Now this concerns spiritual things, brethren.

But all their spiritual gifts, however differing, *manifested the one person of the Holy Ghost*: 'But the manifestation of the Spirit is given to every man to *profit* withal': not to *contend* withal.

Gifts are to profit: not to divide; not to dissent; not to envy; not to argue; not to create schism. But *to manifest the Spirit*. That is, the making visible, with supernatural implications, *of what is otherwise unseen, namely, the unity of the Spirit*.

To make visible – manifest – what is invisible, namely, the presence of the divine Giver of the gifts, one in the Godhead with the Father and the Son. 'But all these worketh that one and the selfsame Spirit, dividing to every man severally as he will', I Corinthians 12:11.

Then what was this, that there were divisions among them, and contentions, to further which each separate party *used the gifts he had received to uphold his own particular sectarian position?*

What is it? It is schism, and of the worst sort, against the unity of the Spirit, and of the one body, contrary to him, and against themselves.

From the context, and the following passage on the body of Christ in the same chapter, it is evident that the gifts of which the apostle speaks are, first, from the Holy Ghost, and, second, within the body. The name that is given to such gifts is, singular, *charisma*, and, plural, *charismata*.

The *charismata* listed in I Corinthians 12:8-10 by no means indicates a fixed and inevitable series of gifts. The gifts may vary greatly from one *ecclesia* to another, and, judging by the apostle's injunction to 'covet earnestly the *best* gifts', I Corinthians 12:31, may even change from one gift to another within the same congregation.

Then, to presuppose either *fixed lists* or *inevitable gifts* is to superimpose the will of man and contradict the will of the Spirit who 'divideth to every man severally as *he* will', I Corinthians 12:11.

In the case of the *charismata* selected as an example by Paul in I Corinthians 12, it is well to note both the order and number of those given. Besides this, since he speaks of the 'best' gifts, it follows that these must be less than the total number listed; otherwise, were none better than another, there could be no 'best'.

Besides this, there appears an evident flexibility in the prospect of improving one's profitability to the whole body, by ascending from an inferior to a superior gift to profit, thus showing the Spirit's willingness to answer to a man's spiritual aspirations to the benefit of his brethren by the very best *charisma*.

Then, it would be crass ignorance to be bound by the letter—the *dead* letter—as opposed to the living Spirit indicated in I Corinthians 12:8-10.

What *is* certain, in the unity of the body of Christ, indwelt by the Holy Ghost, is that 'the manifestation of the Spirit is given to *every* man to profit withal', I Corinthians 12:7; that such a manifestation is at once spiritual, supernatural, and divine; and that the manifestation takes the form of various gifts bestowed by the one Spirit of God, as it is written, 'But all these worketh that one and the selfsame Spirit, dividing to every man severally as he will', I Corinthians 12:11.

If so, there is none without a gift, but all the gifts together in harmony make clear that there is one Spirit; one Lord; and one God and Father, who is above all, and through all, and in all. *That* is what the gifts—whatever they may be—are *for*, and it is *that* which the effectual working of every part makes manifest.

Then, this applies *only* in the body of Christ, *never* in a schism, or on a lesser, divided ground such as denominationalism.

Openings in First Corinthians

Equally, it is impossible for it to apply where a hired so-called minister or priest takes the pre-eminence and does everything himself, the congregation remaining mute under his presumed ministrations.

Now consider the gifts mentioned by Paul in this place: First, the word of wisdom; second, the word of knowledge; third, faith; fourth, the gifts of healing; fifth, the working of miracles – literally, the inworkings of acts of power – sixth, prophecy; seventh, discerning of spirits; eighth, kinds of tongues; ninth, interpretation of tongues.

Oh? Where is the tenth? Mark my words, there is far, far more behind the choice of the apostle as to these *charismata* than appears on the surface, or on face-value to the superficial. Let would-be 'copiers' beware, and more than beware.

Now therefore carefully examine this ninefold list against the background already made manifest in this highly corrective epistle. Corrective, yes, but it is wonderful to behold the love of the apostle for his own children in the faith, and the care he lavishes upon them lest they should be overwhelmed by the rebukes which they richly deserved in so many areas.

Yet Paul finds occasion to praise them again and again, nor once does he lose heart despite the chaotic and erroneous depth of their fall. He never once forgets, or lets slip out of his mind, the calling and power of God put forth in their beginnings.

Such a remembrance enables him to say in the present tense what none but the eyes of one in the very spirit of I Corinthians 13 could possibly consider to be a realistic description of the state he sets out to correct.

But he remembers – and reminds them – full of the encouragement of love: 'I thank my God always on your behalf, for the grace of God which is given you by Jesus Christ; that in every thing ye are enriched by him, in all utterance, and in all knowledge; even as the testimony of Christ was confirmed in you: so that ye come behind in no gift; waiting for the coming of our Lord Jesus Christ: who shall also confirm you unto the end, that ye may be blameless in the day of our Lord Jesus Christ. God is faithful, by whom ye were called unto the fellowship of his Son Jesus Christ our Lord', I Corinthians 1:4-9.

Still, despite the love that beareth all things, believeth all things, hopeth all things, endureth all things, that never faileth, nevertheless all things must be corrected by the word of the truth of the evangel, and this the apostle fails not to bring home in due order to the *ecclesia* at Corinth.

First, to one is given by the Spirit the word of wisdom. That may have been so prior to their being led astray, and it may be so in theory, but in practice the apostle enquires, 'Is it so, that there is not a wise man among you?', I Corinthians 6:5.

There is about the nine *charismata* a kind of gentle – and unspoken – irony, which he who had eyes to see would have discerned.

For not only is the list of *charismata* in I Corinthians 12:7-11 an objective statement of general principles – as opposed to its being an account of what existed at that time in Corinth as a matter of fact – that is, it is general teaching, not historical record; but the apostle so selects and arranges the nine examples of *charisma* that the Corinthians – did they reflect upon it – might well perceive a hidden rebuke in the issue.

Is it the word of wisdom? Yet they had become enamoured with the wisdom of this world. But Christ, the wisdom of God in a mystery, had never been made known by the wisdom of the wise, which God had made foolish by the Cross. Christ was made known by the spiritual wisdom, even the hidden wisdom of God in a mystery, which stands in the gift of the Spirit.

Which *spiritual* wisdom was precisely what they lacked, not what they possessed. Read Chapters 1 to 12.

Or is it the word of knowledge? Well, both wisdom and knowledge were said to be in a word – the *word* of wisdom; the *word* of knowledge – and that word was the word of the truth of the evangel, the doctrine of Christ, whom the Spirit, the same Spirit, would glorify in the midst of the assembly by his own divine gifts.

This both magnified Christ, honoured the Father, and united the brethren. Now, brethren, where was that divinely given, spiritually conveyed word of wisdom, and word of knowledge, from that one and the selfsame Spirit, who should work such divine wonders among you, so unmistakably from God, indwelling the *ecclesia*, in Father, Son, and Holy Ghost?

Again, the Spirit gave faith, not man. It was not man's conjuring tricks in the letter and form, it was the power of God in the Holy Ghost. And whence came, and what was so evident from this divine manifestation of the Spirit? Why, that faith came by hearing, and hearing by the word of God. But what prevailed at Corinth? The apostolic word of God, or the contending voices of man?

Fourthly, gifts of healing. Note that this is in the plural. Well, so were their schisms, divisions, parties, contentions, and verbal conflicts that set one against another. These – being in the plural – needed *gifts* of healing, and many healings at that, before the body was made sound from its bruises and self-inflicted wounds.

Oh, *they* needed the gifts of healing most assuredly, who, failing to profit from the infallible word of wisdom by the Spirit, the incontestable word of knowledge – that is, of Christ by the same Spirit – were yet rent with *their* divisions and lacerating encounters. Was it not evident that they stood in such dire need of the healing of the Spirit, to bring them into the wholeness of unity by the gentleness and meekness of Christ, through the mystery of the gospel?

Fifth, 'working of miracles', declares the Authorized Version; but, more literally, this is 'the gift of inworking of acts of power'. How they needed *that*, in due sequence of wisdom, knowledge, faith, and healing, to prevent anew their abuse of external words and formal truths, that these might not again be carnally corrupted in and by their diverse mouths of contention, but inwrought by the power of God in the unity of the faith, and of the one and the selfsame Spirit.

O that thus their faith should not stand in the wisdom of men, but in the power of God; not in the dead letter which killeth, but in the quickening Spirit who giveth life.

But this cannot be without the *inworking* of acts of *power*, by which their *hearts* should be comforted, being knit together in love, and unto all riches of the full assurance of understanding, to the acknowledgement of the mystery of God, and of the Father, and of Christ. Thus all should be united *within* by the indwelling of God in Father, Son, and Holy Ghost. What a gift of grace *this* would be!

Next, prophecy. But had this *really* been among them, then surely the Spirit would have declared his being grieved; and, the inevitable future consequences of their unruly conversation and conduct having been foretold by the mouth of the prophet, they should surely have been shocked into repentance, and brought under the fear of God in mortification.

To another is given the *charisma* of discerning of spirits. But if *this* were so evident, and being exercised to the profit of all, how was it that the 'knowledgeable' took meat at the idols' temples, or else knowingly bought it in the shambles, since those with whom they went to such feasts 'were Gentiles, *carried away* unto these dumb idols, even *as they were led*', I Corinthians 12:2?

Did such a *charisma* as discerning of spirits exist at Corinth, then would no warning sound, no plea of love for the weak brother, have arisen in their midst? Were this gift in evidence, how then should it have fallen to the absent apostle to expostulate, 'Concerning *spirituality*, brethren, I would *not* have you to be ignorant', I Corinthians 12:1?

Had this gift been in evidence, and exercised, they would *not* have been ignorant. And yet still the resource was in that one and the selfsame Spirit, brethren: then whence and why the lack?

Next–and eighth–Paul mentions the Spirit giving to another divers kinds of tongues. Well, the Spirit *may* bestow such a gift, to speak in terms of general principle; or in terms of objective teaching it may be said that he is able to do so; but be that as it may: at Corinth the reality stood elsewhere!

For what diverse kinds of tongues had the Corinthians? Was it those freely given for edification by the one Spirit, or was it the clamour of contending parties, all speaking at once, and each determined to drown out the other?

Thus with the Corinthians it was indeed *divers kinds*–yes, and all at once–of *tongues*, note the plural. And though at the day of Pentecost by such wondrous heavenly gift the descended Holy Spirit marvellously glorified the ascended Christ, the promise of the Father filling as one the entire body, whilst they spake in the tongues of the nations of those about them, this was a far cry from–indeed, by Paul's gentle irony, it was *the very opposite to*–the clamour that existed at Corinth.

Hence, above even the best gifts, Paul yearned earnestly for his beloved children to discover the transcendent inner motive of 'a more excellent way': 'that ye all speak the same thing, and that there be no divisions among you; but that ye be perfectly joined together in the same mind and in the same judgment', I Corinthians 1:10.

Thus, by the nature of the true Gift; by the unity of the divine Giver; and by the appeal to the apostolic precedent, Paul almost imperceptibly guides them to the peerless divinity of the thirteenth chapter.

Ninth, and lastly, the apostle adds 'to another the interpretation of tongues'. Would God one among them, filled with the Spirit, and gifted by the grace of God, had interpreted for them *their* tongues, as they used them in practice, even as the gift of the Spirit, in peace and unity, interpreted the gift of another in the tongues sent down from heaven.

But now *their* tongues rose up on earth, and clashed in the flesh, and who shall interpret this?

Why, Paul shall, and that with a yearning love, a kindly wisdom, and the gentlest of implied rebukes, so that by the word of truth, by the power of God, and by the armour of righteousness, they might as one man be brought down in humility, conviction, self-condemnation, and heart-felt repentance.

And that is precisely what came to pass: 'For godly sorrow worketh repentance to salvation not to be repented of: but the sorrow of the world worketh death. For behold this selfsame thing, that ye sorrowed after a godly sort, what carefulness it wrought in you, yea, what clearing of yourselves, yea, what indignation, yea, what fear, yea, what vehement desire, yea, what zeal, yea, what revenge! In all things ye have approved yourselves to be clear in this matter', II Corinthians 7:10,11.

Then why did Paul stop at nine *charismata*, seeing that *ten* would have indicated completeness, in this case, of the *charismata*? Why? To draw attention to the fact that any number of gifts were as nothing without the Giver, that is, without God's unspeakable gift in the Son of his love, and, in truth, *that* was missing.

But as Paul continues from the twelfth chapter of the First Epistle to the Corinthians, he progresses from indicating their lack, to supplying their need by Christ Jesus in his doctrine unto them. Where? In the thirteenth chapter. Here he enlarges upon the missing, the tenth, the unspeakable gift of God.

Withal, thereby he sets forth unto them a more excellent way than all the gifts besides. How can this be? Because the chapter describes the indwelling of the Giver, one in deity with the Father and with the Son. 'Because the love of God is shed abroad in our hearts by the Holy Ghost which is given unto us', Romans 5:5.

Or as John put it, '*Herein* is our love made perfect' – or complete – I John 4:17.

However the *charismata* – the gifts of the Spirit in the body – objectively selected by way of admonitory instruction in I Corinthians 12:7-11, by no means embrace the entire compass of the various *charismata*, nor does that place represent the sole record of *charismata* in the new testament.

In Romans 12:6-8 Paul lists gifts – save for the one common instance of prophecy – whose range reaches to quite a different character, a range quite missing from I Corinthians 12:7-11, for all that the latter passage includes certain gifts omitted from the Romans text. Still the *range of character* is greater in Romans. Yet both – being gifts of the Spirit in the body – are called *charismata*.

Whereas Romans begins with prophecy, adding ministry, then teaching, and next exhortation – compatible in a sense with at least four, if not five, of the Corinthian *charismata*, since all are *vocal* – the last three *charisma* in Romans are distinct in essence from all those given in the Corinthian epistle. So much so, that one might be surprised that the three *were* gifts of the Spirit.

Observe: 'Giving'. Giving? What, at Corinth, where 'one is hungry, and another is drunken'; and, 'each one *taketh* before other *his own* supper'? See I Corinthians 11:21. Evidently, this singular gift in the body at Rome achieved in that assembly a far more gracious and benign effect from its presence and exercise.

Again, 'Ruling'. But who or what ruled at Corinth? Where, 'I speak to your shame. Is it so, that there is not a wise man among you? no, not one that shall be able to judge between his brethren?', I Corinthians 6:5. Rule? At Corinth? What rule, in that calamitous scene of chaos and disorder?

Then how beneficent and peaceable the gift of one for the blessing of all in rule by the Holy Ghost at Rome?

Lastly, 'Showing mercy'. But what mercy was shown to the brother in debt when taken to court by his creditor, I Corinthians 6:6,7? What mercy to the thirsty by the drunken, I Corinthians 11:21? What mercy to the hungry by the full, I Corinthians 11:21,22?

How Corinth would have benefited by the presence of this grace, this *charisma*, conspicuous at Rome, had it been present and in exercise among those who gloried in their contentious abuse of the nine gifts which, had even *they* been employed, might have spared the apostle the many tears and much anguish that forced him thus to write to his beloved children.

Whereas nine at Corinth indicates coming short of completeness, the seven at Rome points to the attainment of perfection. Then why are whole contemporary sects, and entire modern delusions, so enamoured of Corinth at its worst state – copying for all that they are worth, since the divine original and reality clean escape them – when the apostle labours with tears and anguish in his doctrine gently to deliver them?

I say, why so exalt the Corinthian *nine*, as if nothing perfect existed? Why? Because such ignorant persons are of the same carnal nature as that into which the Corinthians had fallen, but without their divine beginnings, and without the holy apostle to correct the lamentable issue.

Hence their inept misconstructions feed their lust for religious excitement, display, and even abandonment, the flesh – and the spirits – taking occasion through their blind perversion of the truth of the evangel of Christ, namely, of the apostles' doctrine, discipline, fellowship, and ordinances.

The apostle Peter likewise speaks of *charisma* – that is, gifts of the Spirit in the body of Christ – declaring 'As every man hath received the gift' – *charisma* – 'even so minister the same one toward another, as good stewards of the manifold grace of God.' This might well include Giving; Ruling; and Showing mercy, besides other gifts of like character.

However Peter goes on to emphasize that which is most to edification in their assembling together: 'If any man speak, let him speak as the oracles of God; if any man minister, let him do it as of the ability which God giveth: that God in all things may be glorified through Jesus Christ, to whom be praise and dominion for ever and ever. Amen', I Peter 4:10,11.

Where, note, as to being assembled together, the *charisma* to which Peter draws attention above all other relate, first, to 'speaking'. This must be 'as the oracles of God'. And this is only right, as befits the exercise of the gift of the Holy Ghost. Last, 'ministering', which as filled with the Spirit, and thus careful in the fear of God, must be of necessity 'as of the sufficiency which God giveth'.

Here we may well see the seven; yes, but where are the nine? Still going to the priest? Better the tenth, worshipping and pouring out thanksgiving at the feet of Jesus.

The tenth never got to the priest. Here is the *charisma* of mercy! Rather, the tenth saw where the healing truly lay, not only in this life, but in that which is to come. And he was a Samaritan; see Luke 17:11-19.

Openings in First Corinthians

Before leaving this passage, I Corinthians 12:7-11, it is well to take notice of what are called 'miraculous' signs and gifts of the Spirit in the body of Christ: as though others, less conspicuous, were not. As has been said, *all* such gifts pertain *to the body of Christ*.

The *charismata* have nothing to do with the schisms, divisions, and denominations – not to mention independencies – into which Christendom has fallen. Nor have they to do with sects or movements *based on so-called manifestations*, which, in practice ignoring – as if it were of no consequence – I say, *ignoring* the unity of the body from which such schismatics are divided, namely *the body of Christ*, pretend to and mimic such things *as the end of their existence*.

What, schismatics mimic the manifestations which really did attend and glorified *the body of Christ* at the beginning? As if their invented human means at the last were more than the authenticated divine reality at the first? Or as if the apostles, the witness of Father, Son, and Holy Ghost, and the testimony of Holy Scripture might as well be ignored? Not to mention their blasphemous conjuring in order to beguile the foolish and the simple, as they ape that to which they have neither right, authority, justification, or calling.

However, it is remarkable that neither the apostle Peter, nor yet the apostle John, have *one word* to say of outwardly 'miraculous' *charisma*, much less of so-called 'tongues', witness I Peter 4:10,11, where the entire emphasis is on gifts of the Spirit in speaking and ministering. As to John, he does not so much as mention *charismata*, or, indeed, *any* miraculous signs in the *ecclesia*, though he has three epistles, one revelation, and seven churches in which to do so.

Besides this, Paul says *nothing* of *that kind of sign or manifestation* in Romans 12:6-8, a passage just as much devoted to *charismata* as is I Corinthians 12:7-11.

Regarding the later epistles, or the ministers of God under and following the apostles, besides the all-important pastoral epistles – *indicating what should follow after the apostles' departure* – the silence is deafening. Not because the Holy Ghost did not indwell the *ecclesia* just as much as at the beginning, or that the gifts of the Spirit were given to *any less a number than every man in the assembly*, but because the emphasis – as indicated by Romans, Peter, and the Johannine epistles – *lay upon those vocal gifts by which the apostles' doctrine should be reiterated spiritually to the end of the age.*

Not that these vocal gifts were *less* miraculous, or *less* of the Spirit: but, so much the more as the end approached, *they were the more necessary.*

Besides, the miraculous signs and wonders wrought by the apostles, and through the laying on of their hands, and in the manifestation of the gifts of that one and the selfsame Spirit in the one body, *had more than sufficiently given testimony by miracles, signs, and wonders* to the witness of God that this was *his ecclesia.* Just as had the wonders wrought in the land of Ham, and the signs shown in the field of Zoan, when Israel came out of Egypt.

And what shall I more say of the parting of the Red Sea, the bringing of water out of the rock, the descent of the heavenly manna, or the terrible judgments by which Jehovah bore record to his authority resting upon Moses and Aaron?

These are to be remembered continually, as the psalmist often exhorts us. But, given, did these things cross over Jordan with them? Did the Rock follow them after they came into the land? Did the manna still fall when they ate the finest of the wheat in their inheritance? Did the Red Sea continue parting at the words of 'faith' by zealots long afterwards? Certainly not.

The previous signs, miracles, wonders, and manifestations were more than sufficient to give divine attestation to Israel's beginnings, but they merely *attended* the giving of the law, and of the testimony, and of the prophetic word. Having been given, repetition – divorced from their original significance – would have *distracted* from what was *actually* central and *really* abiding.

Had these signs continued – human nature being what it is – such passing wonders would have appeared to man as vastly more significant and important than the vital, permanent, and everlasting *truth*. That is, *unalterable* and *absolute* truth, in the giving of which miracles were no more than transient and suitably placed signposts for future generations to mark and read in the unfolding passage of time.

Witness the worship of the brazen serpent, which had long since ceased to have any significance. Yet, because *once* it was vested with miraculous powers, thereafter the superstitious and credulous bowed down and craved present signs and wonders on the basis of its past history. However, the righteous ground it to powder.

Therefore miracles, once having been given, passed away. But, 'To the law and to the testimony, if they speak not *according to this word*, it is because there is no light in them.'

Then, let the people rejoice in the remembrances of their beginnings; but *now*, let them attend upon the testimony of Israel, the law of Moses, the judgments given to Jacob, the prophetic word, and, indeed, to that which was committed to them, namely, the oracles of God.

Just so in the *ecclesia*. We need every part as much of the divine indwelling as they had in the beginning; we need every whit as much of the appropriate gifts of the Spirit in the assembly as were theirs at the first; but, whilst remembering with joy the original apostolic witness, we know that our need is for that which is appropriate for us *today*, that we may *keep alive in the new testament, that is, in the testimony of Jesus, which is the Spirit of prophecy*.

Openings in First Corinthians

I say, we need these divine and inward things to remember and declare the words of our Lord Jesus Christ and his holy apostles; to keep the faith; to obey from the heart the form of doctrine delivered unto us; to hear continually the apostles' doctrine reiterated by the Holy Ghost; to have the doctrine of Christ sound in our ears constantly.

We need these things to hear the Lord's voice in the assembly; yes, and to witness the distribution of the suited gifts—even according to the closing record of the new testament scriptures—by that one and the selfsame Spirit, that, holding fast the form of sound words, we might abide in that which was—and is—central from the beginning.

And what was—and is—central from the beginning? The apostles' doctrine and fellowship, the breaking of bread and prayers, for in the hearing and continuance of this lies our salvation and safety, even as it is said, 'truly our fellowship is with the Father, and with his Son Jesus Christ'.

In a word, we need to continue—to abide—in one Spirit, abundantly able to give gifts to every man in the unity of this one body, suited to the times and conditions of the recovery of these selfsame things in our own age.

(iii) The Spirit and the Body

'For as the body is one, and hath many members, and all the members of that one body, being many, are one body: so also is the Christ', I Corinthians 12:12.

Observe the words 'For as', indicating that what follows is either an explanation, illustration, or analogy of what had been said before.

What had been said before? 'All these'—manifestations of the Spirit between one and another among many brethren—'all these worketh that one and the selfsame Spirit'—that is, they are a variety of supernatural yet audible and visible manifestations *which show that one divine person spiritually and invisibly indwells the entire number of the assembled saints in unity.*

However, that one divine, invisible and spiritual person manifests his presence in unity 'dividing to every man severally as he will', I Corinthians 12:11.

Now Paul is to illustrate and open this spiritual mystery—albeit this divine reality—by an analogy: it is the analogy of the body. To introduce this, he uses the words 'For as'.

'For as the body is one, and hath many members, and all the members of that one body, being many, are one body.' Here he shows the relation of the members to the body.

Not only has the body many members, but each one of that number is essential to make up the whole. The whole is called the body, and this whole is much, much more than the sum of the parts.

Nevertheless *each single part*—or every member—is necessary if one is to speak of the body as a whole. The absence of but one—though it be the very least—member precludes having a sound body. All together *are* the body. Their union *constitutes* the body.

Considered in themselves, each is a member. Together, they are many members. In union they are the body.

The explanation, the visible illustration, the analogy is clearly apparent. Let this, however, be pressed home: the body as a whole is comprised of many members in particular, yet so united as to present a visible, tangible organic entity.

Physically the members grow into and are connected together as one. The bones support all; the sinews connect all; the joints give movement to all; the flesh covers all; the breathing aerates all; the blood replenishes all; the nerves sensitize all; the circulation renews all; the skin encloses all: yes, but above all, *the life quickens all*. Now, here is much more than the sum of many members. *The body is more than all.*

Now, declares Paul, 'So also is the Christ', I Corinthians 12:12. Properly translated – as opposed to transliterated and truncated – this should read 'So also is *the Anointed'*. Incidentally, note the definite article.

But the anointing is not that of oil poured out by Moses upon the head of Aaron the high priest, flowing down to the skirts of his garments, and therefore covering all members – which was a tangible figure – it is of the *Holy Ghost*, which is an intangible reality.

Then, it is not outward, but inward. It is not visible, but invisible. It is not human, but divine. It is not earthly, it is heavenly. It is not natural, it is supernatural.

Maybe: *but it still flows down from the Head and it still covers – or, rather, fills – all the members in one body, one with and united to the Head.*

Then the members, which, with the Head, constitute that one body, are seen as one with him, and hence it is said in consequence of the anointing, 'So also is the Anointed', or, 'So also is the Christ'.

That is, so also is *his* body. It is one, tempered together in union; it has many members, united together in one, each member having his own place in the body. There are many members, yes, but all are necessary to make up the whole.

The united whole constitutes his body; less does not: the whole is in obvious and undeniable union, each essential member in his place, and all united together as an entity. This is true of the entire *ecclesia*, and it is represented in the manifold wisdom of God in *each ecclesia*.

Manifested: though spiritual and invisible in the *anointing*, it is visible and manifest in the unity.

For Paul is speaking of *the assembly*. This is evident through the unity of the brethren. Are *they* invisible? As it pertains to their union with Christ, and with the Holy Ghost, and in their interior *spiritual* union with each other, yes.

But since *that interior union* separates them from the world to be together as one, and since that separation is *to the assembly, visible in their assembling*, then, *visible indeed*.

For, whatever is inward, it is *within their bodies*. And *in the body* they are assembled. Then, their unity is abundantly—*and bodily*—made manifest. 'So also is the Christ.'

It is true, in the anointing, of each member it is said, 'he that is joined to the Lord is one spirit'. Yes, but the *'he'* that is so joined in one spirit, is, in and of himself, in the body. As it is written, 'Know ye not that *your bodies* are the members of Christ?'—or, of the Anointed?—I Corinthians 6:15,17.

Then—*bodily*—it must follow, however divine, however supernatural, however mystical, however spiritual, however invisible *this inward union*, it is of *absolute necessity that it becomes corporeally visible in the* gathering of the *assembly*: 'So also is the Christ.'

It is worthy of note that 'there are diversities of gifts, but the same Spirit', I Corinthians 12:4, corresponds with verses 7-11, namely, *what the Spirit is to the body, and the body to the Spirit*. Just as 'There are differences of ministries, but the same Lord', I Corinthians 12:5, answers to verses 12-27, that is, *what the Lord is to the body, and the body to the Lord.*

Openings in First Corinthians

One thing is certain: there is nothing individual in itself, much less independent, in either case: *everything* is corporate, whether in the whole *ecclesia*, or in any given manifestation of that whole, for example, at Corinth.

This observation utterly cuts out all denominationalism, every form of independency, and each affectation of individualism, including sects based on the *notion* of one body, whilst in doctrine and practice denying it, such as the various schisms of Brethrenism, besides those founded on an entirely false interpretation of the baptism of the Spirit, such as Pentecostalism in its many divisions, including the craze of the 'Charismatic' delusion.

On the contrary, as to both the gifts of the Spirit and the administrations from the Lord, *there is one body, to which corresponds one Spirit*: 'One body, and one Spirit, even as ye are called in one hope of your calling; one Lord, one faith, one baptism, one God and Father of all, who is above all, and through all, and in you all', Ephesians 4:4-6. 'So also is the Christ', I Corinthians 12:12.

The members of his body are so inwardly joined, ingrafted, grown together, and interconnected as one in the Spirit—'their hearts being *knit together* in love'—that the outward manifestation of this interior unity is clear and plain to all.

They themselves visibly present—in each place, and all in every place—I say, they themselves present a real, visible and manifest unity, a united company, a separated assembly, a mystery of union and communion in one and the selfsame Spirit, that nothing else will suffice as an analogy but to say, They are 'one body'. That is, So also is the Christ.

But not as it were the literal body of a person, who in and of himself fills that body with his own life. For the apostle speaks in a mystery of *the body of Christ*.

It is *his* life that fills the one body, both as a whole, and as manifest in each place. It is *God's* power that sustains that one body, *his* energy, in every place, and in all places joined as one. It is the *Spirit's* anointing that bestows the interior fulness, in each several manifestation of the one body, and in that one body in itself as a whole. 'So also is the Christ.'

So that it is not simply a question of persons in spiritual agreement, or sharing a common spiritual experience. It is *the indwelling of divine persons*.

In particular, I Corinthians 12, the indwelling of the person of the Holy Ghost; for this is in the context of 'spiritualities'. In this passage the body is not mentioned in connection with the Head in heaven, much less is it, itself, seen as in the heavenlies.

In First Corinthians *the body is seen on earth, as constituted by the divine person of the Holy Ghost, descended so as to indwell the whole in his own person*. This is that one and the selfsame Spirit the manifestation of whose gifts, both supernatural and diverse, declare in their unity the invisible but unmistakable presence of the divine Giver, the one indwelling person of the Holy Spirit of God: 'So also is the Christ.'

The Authorized Version renders the first part of the next verse, 'For by one Spirit are we all baptized into one body', I Corinthians 12:13, but this translation is not correct. It could not be correct, not only because it misrepresents the Greek, but also because it contradicts what is asserted elsewhere.

What is asserted elsewhere? Why, that *Christ* baptizes with the Holy Ghost. Matthew 3:11, '*he* shall baptize you with the Holy Ghost'; Mark 1:8, '*he* shall baptize you with the Holy Ghost'; Luke 3:16, '*he* shall baptize you with the Holy Ghost'.

Is not this testimony enough to establish the truth that the one who baptizes with the Holy Ghost is Jesus Christ, the Son of God?

If not, hear once more from the record of John the Baptist: 'And John bare record, saying, I saw the Spirit descending from heaven like a dove, and it abode upon him. And I knew him not: but he that sent me to baptize with water, the same said unto me, Upon whom thou shalt see the Spirit descending, and remaining on him, *the same is he which baptizeth with the Holy Ghost*. And I saw, and bare record *that this is the Son of God*', John 1:32-34.

Whence it is evident – from all four gospels – beyond all controversy that it is the Lord Jesus Christ, the Son of God, and he alone, who baptizes with the Holy Ghost.

Then why have the Authorized Version translators contradicted this – and thus confounded the English reader – by declaring: 'For *by one Spirit* are we all baptized into one body', I Corinthians 12:13, where, they say, *the Spirit himself* baptizes, namely, baptizes all into one body?

Then, according to them, since it is clear that the baptism referred to is that of the Holy Ghost, the Spirit himself both does the baptizing and is the baptism.

For if by the Spirit we are baptized, then, *the Spirit baptizes of his own Spirit*. If so, not content with contradicting the clear fourfold testimony of the gospels, the translators go on to make the verse a confusion – if not a nonsense – within itself.

Then what ought it to read, and where lies the error? This place *ought* to read, 'For *in* one Spirit are we all baptized into one body'; that is, the *Son of God* baptizes all into one body *in one Spirit*.

The error lies in mistranslating the Greek preposition ἐν, *en*. The translators at once contradicted all four gospels, confounded divine persons, obscured the work of God, and made a nonsense of the verse, by imposing the English word 'by', as if it translated the Greek '*en*'.

It does not. It confuses it. The Greek is translated properly by the preposition 'in', giving the correct sense, 'For in one Spirit are we all baptized into one body', I Corinthians 12:13.

The translators have no excuse whatsoever. They had good precedents in any case, but *would* follow the wrong ones. Rightly, Tyndale, 1535, rendered '*en*' as 'in'. And so did Coverdale, 1535.

Thereafter – with almost unbroken monotony – the succession of translators – all we like sheep have gone astray: that is, one after the other, seeing nothing but the backside of the sheep in front – mangle the Greek, make this place to confound itself, contradict the gospels, and, in truth, make a mock of divinity.

The Great Bible, 1540, begins this confusion, despite the correct translations of its predecessors. No, they must change 'in' for 'by', as if the Greek were irrelevant beside their confounded prevarications.

This error was followed by the Geneva Bible, 1562, and the Bishops Bible, 1602. The Roman Catholic Rheims Version, 1582, shames these Protestants, upholding against them the correct translation 'in'.

Not so the next Protestant Bible, namely the King James – or Authorized Version – of 1611, which follows the corruption 'by'.

To the contrary, notwithstanding the committee having been duped by Westcott and Hort, the Revised Version, 1881, with its sly substitution of a Greek edition based on sheer fallacy, yet gives the correct 'in'. Alas! must we be shamed by these also?

The Revised Standard Version, 'updating' the Revision of 1881 in 1946, boldly peels off the sheep's clothing of superficial corrections and reverts to type, much more comfortable in the wolf-skin of 'by'.

So there you have your clerical and 'scholarly' record.

Openings in First Corinthians

Young – of Concordance fame – emphatically insists upon 'in': 'For also in one Spirit we all to one body were baptized.'

I suppose I should quote J.N. Darby, who renders this part of the verse with characteristic and imperious assumption: 'For also in [the power of] one Spirit we have all been baptized into one body', where the words in brackets actually are pure invention, like so many of those Brethren traditions and conceits that still manage to persuade the ignorant that their outward forms, unwarranted assumptions, and impertinent conclusions are 'scriptural', or, as they now like to put it – irrespective of version – 'bible based'. But enough of this miserable dust.

The text reads in fact 'For also in one Spirit are we all baptized into one body.'

Also? 'For also'? As well as what? To get the sense, read the context: 'So also is the Christ.' Or, rather, 'the Anointed'. Hence in continuity the passage is as follows: 'So also is the Anointed. For also in one Spirit are we all baptized into one body.'

Where the anointing, under the Anointed, inwardly flowing down upon and into every member, is likened – also – to the baptism of the Spirit, just as the baptism of the Spirit – 'for also' – is much like to the anointing.

Where is the difference?

The anointing pertains to that divine, interior, mysterious, and spiritual unction in which God marks us out by the Holy Ghost as being united to Christ: it is the infallible mark that we are his, and one with him under the anointing.

The baptism of the Spirit is in a sense more intimate. It brings in *one body*. It is not only that the members are anointed, marked out as Christ's by the Spirit, but by the baptism of the Spirit, the Spirit himself *indwells all the members in his own person*, *so as to constitute the whole one body in Christ*: 'So also is the Anointed. For also in one Spirit are we all baptized into one body', I Corinthians 12:12,13.

The expression 'Baptism of the Holy Ghost' occurs some seven times in the new testament.

The words were first spoken by John the Baptist before the baptism of Jesus, and are recorded respectively in Matthew, Mark, and Luke, each referring to the same occasion.

The fourth reference is in John, who records the Baptist's testimony to the Son of God—that it is he who shall baptize with the Holy Ghost—shortly after the baptism of Jesus.

Observe that in the first three gospels the Baptist prophesies, 'He shall baptize *you* with the Holy Ghost', where *you* refers to those penitent Jews who had received and obeyed the prophetic ministry of John, having confessed their sins and been baptized of him in Jordan.

Without doubt some, and in all probability all, of the number of the apostles had received the baptism of John. Exceptions are possible, but unlikely.

In the unlikely event, then they would have been baptized by the first disciples, 'Jesus made and baptized more disciples than John, though Jesus himself baptized not, but his disciples', John 4:1,2.

As to all the apostles being baptized—probably by John, but otherwise by the first disciples—observe, 'Except a man be born of *water* and of the Spirit, he cannot enter into the kingdom of God', John 3:5.

And how could the apostles, who were sent of Christ to preach the kingdom of God, not first themselves have entered into it? And, if so, initially by water.

In the evangel according to John, the prophecy that the Son would baptize with the Holy Ghost is not confined to the 'you', namely, to the repentant and obedient remnant out of all Israel.

John broadens the scope, declaring of the Son of God, 'The same is he which baptizeth with the Holy Ghost', John 1:33, where the whole emphasis is upon the one who baptizes, not those who are baptized.

Thus John hints of a people far beyond the remnant according to the election of grace called out from among the Jews. 'Is he the God of the Jews only? is he not also of the Gentiles? Yes, of the Gentiles also', Romans 3:29.

After the first four references to the baptism of the Holy Ghost – Matthew, Mark, Luke, and John respectively – two further instances appear in the Acts of the Apostles.

Jesus, risen from the dead and appearing to the apostles whom he had chosen, virtually repeats the words which the Baptist spoke in Matthew, Mark, and Luke: 'For John truly baptized with water; but ye shall be baptized with the Holy Ghost not many days hence', Acts 1:5.

Likewise in Acts 11:16, Peter, giving an account of the way in which the Holy Ghost fell upon the devout Gentiles, reiterates words previously spoken: 'And as I began to speak, the Holy Ghost fell on them, as on us at the beginning. Then remembered I the word of the Lord, how that he said, John indeed baptized with water; but ye shall be baptized with the Holy Ghost. Forasmuch then as God gave them the like gift as he did unto us, who believed on the Lord Jesus Christ; what was I, that I could withstand God?', Acts 11:15-17.

This quotation – Acts 11:15-17 – is the sixth occasion on which the expression Baptism of – or in this case, be baptized with – the Holy Ghost appears in the new testament, and the second in

Acts. The seventh and last incidence is in I Corinthians 12:13, the text in question.

However the exposition of this place is not just a matter of the seven occasions on which the actual expression 'Baptism of the Holy Ghost' occurs: indeed, the *words* are not used in Acts 2, the very chapter describing the descent and shedding forth of the person of the Holy Ghost to fill the one hundred and twenty disciples in the upper room, when they were all together with one accord in one place on the day of Pentecost.

Moreover there are two further instances in which what occurred answers so nearly to Acts chapter 2 that – though, like Acts 2, not actually called the baptism of the Spirit in the text – these occasions undoubtedly refer to a repetition of the same thing.

The first concerns the Samaritans, Acts 8:16,17, the second the – presumably – Gentile disciples at Ephesus, Acts 19:2-6.

In both cases note the laying on of the hands of those called to the apostolate: 'Then they' – namely Peter and John – 'laid their hands on them' – that is, the Samaritans who had believed Philip's preaching and had been baptized in the name of the Lord Jesus, yet upon whom the Holy Ghost had 'not yet fallen'; but when the apostles laid their hands on them – *then* 'they received the Holy Ghost'.

In the other case the disciples at Ephesus, who knew no more than and had received nothing save John's baptism, thereafter, when Christ Jesus was preached unto them, were – again – baptized, this time in the name of the Lord Jesus. 'And when Paul had laid his hands upon them, the Holy Ghost came on them; and they spake with tongues, and prophesied. And all the men were about twelve', Acts 19:2-7.

Furthermore, there are passages in at least two of the epistles which indicate that those concerned had been baptized with the Holy Ghost on a previous occasion, namely, when first they had received the grace of God.

'Truly the signs of an apostle were wrought among you in all patience, in signs, and wonders, and mighty deeds', II Corinthians 12:12, although nothing of this is mentioned in the narrative of the beginning of the work of the Lord at Corinth, Acts chapter 18.

Again, 'He therefore that ministereth to you the Spirit, and worketh miracles among you, doeth he it by the works of the law, or by the hearing of faith?', Galatians 3:5. But there is no record of this in Acts or anywhere else.

Quite apart from these specific instances, there are suggestions from the early ministry of the apostles—particularly in the case of Paul—that not only the baptism of the Holy Ghost, but miracles, signs, and wonders followed of necessity, given to those called into the *ecclesia* by the evangel of Christ.

I say, 'into the *ecclesia*', for, observe, it is 'He shall baptize *you*'—not *thee*—'with the Holy Ghost', Matthew 3:11; Mark 1:8; and Luke 3:16. Likewise, 'For also in one Spirit *are all we* baptized into *one body*', I Corinthians 12:13.

Then, the baptism brings in *that which is corporate*. It is not at all individual, save that the individual is incorporated into the one body of Christ.

Whence it follows that the end in view with the baptism of the Spirit is not so much what *he* is for *me*. It is altogether what *we* are for *him*, united together as one body in Christ.

(iv) The Baptism of the Spirit

Of tongues I shall have occasion to speak later, but it is *essential* to note that tongues *no more than accompanied* the baptism of the Holy Ghost on certain notable occasions. If so, they were, as such, distinct from that baptism, in and of itself.

Then, the baptism of the Holy Ghost could and did—according to the narrative—occur without the speaking in tongues, for example, as in the case of the Samaritans, Acts 8:15-18.

No mention of tongues appears in Romans, Thessalonians, Philippians or Galatians, for example: but it is unquestionable that all these were baptized with the Holy Ghost.

On the other hand, silence does not necessarily imply absence: note that the first Ephesian disciples—when Paul the apostle laid hands on them—received the Holy Ghost 'and'—immediately—'spake with tongues, and prophesied', Acts 19:6. Yet in the great epistle to the saints at Ephesus, Paul, writing much later, makes no mention of tongues.

So that even from the earliest days of the apostles it is necessary to observe that the incomparable gift of the baptism of the Holy Ghost, so as to form one body in Christ, vastly transcended—and transcends—the sign of tongues which by no means necessarily accompanied that baptism.

Moreover, whilst the laying on of the apostles' hands—subsequent to Acts 2—appeared in a number of cases as that which conveyed the baptism of the Holy Ghost, this was not invariably the case. Note the instance of Cornelius: 'While Peter was yet *speaking*'—not while Peter was yet *laying on hands*, of which nothing whatsoever is said—'the Holy Ghost fell on all them which heard the word', Acts 10:44.

So that hasty and rash conclusions should be avoided. At this point what one may safely deduce is that the baptism of the Holy Ghost is a thing in and of itself; it is not at all a thing which must necessarily be followed by the sign of tongues; again, that the baptism of the Holy Ghost invariably followed and was never disassociated from the effectual preaching of the apostles' doctrine, and at that, in the new testament, by the very apostles themselves.

Moreover the laying on of the apostles' hands was not necessarily a criterion. The preaching was a criterion, under which the hearing of faith became manifest by the baptism of the Holy Ghost.

Finally, one should mention that the significant manifestations in Acts answer to the words of the Lord Jesus immediately preceding the ascension: 'Ye'–that is, *the apostles whom he had chosen*, Acts 1:2–'Ye shall be witnesses unto me both in Jerusalem, and in all Judea, and in Samaria, and unto the uttermost part of the earth', Acts 1:8.

Jerusalem, Judea, and Samaria are obvious, from Acts chapter 2 to Acts chapter 8.

'The uttermost part of the earth'–within the limits of Acts–has a twofold testimony in the significant baptism of the Gentiles, first of Cornelius' gathering, Acts 10, then that of those at Ephesus, Acts 19.

What remains is that one should remember that–taking for granted the addition of I Corinthians 12:13–*these references include, and, with objective fairness, expand, the–only–seven occurrences of the expression, the baptism of the Holy Ghost*. Then, a sense of proportion must be maintained, especially in relation to the many–and *later*–works and books recorded in the remainder of the new testament.

For example, whilst unquestionably the baptism of the Holy Ghost–*let it always be remembered, given so as to constitute the body of Christ, exclusively and invariably*–must have occurred in the later epistles; yet neither that, nor any miraculous signs–unless it were the deceitful duplications of the Adversary–appear in the closing records.

Nothing could be more conspicuous by dint of absence than either the words 'baptism of the Spirit', or any *charismata* whatsoever, in the Pastoral Epistles. Yet these were written to ensure the continuation of the apostolic ministry and fellowship in the apostle's absence. Hence these scriptures were of paramount importance for those approaching the end of the apostolic presence and close of the new testament. And if so, how much more for us from that time to this? So why the silence concerning the baptism and the miraculous gifts?

Take the other later epistles. Peter was a chosen eyewitness. He was at Pentecost. No one had more experience. He gave forth the first words after the baptism and shedding forth of the Holy Ghost at the very first. Likewise he explained the reason for and nature of the tongues with which they then spake: then *why no mention of any of these things in the very much later First and Second Epistles of Peter?*

The baptism, evidently, was taken for granted as having taken place. As to miracles, these, apparently, as with Israel of old, had fulfilled their office: *the thing signified, the reality itself, remained.* And this Peter addressed.

Nothing in Jude, I, II, and III John? But John, like Peter, had been at the heart of the matter in Acts 2. But no word of this in the three later – if not last – epistles.

Why not? Only one explanation adequately answers this question. Miracles had fulfilled their office. That to which they *had* borne testimony under the apostles and apostolic churches remained on record in Acts and the earlier Epistles – or, indeed, the Gospels – just as the testimony of the Pentateuch – particularly Exodus and Numbers – remain on record for Israel in the succeeding millennia till the coming of Christ.

Then what corresponding apostolic testimony? This. *This* is the *heart* of that testimony: 'the word of the Lord endureth for ever. And *this* is the *word* which by the *gospel* is *preached* unto you', I Peter 1:25. The eternal Spirit bore – and bears – equal witness to that word of the truth of the gospel, and will bear it, in all those sent of Jesus Christ to the end of the age, for the Spirit is truth.

The Book of Revelation? Seven churches, yes, but neither a single mention nor one hint of the baptism of the Spirit, or of miraculous gifts. But signs, wonders, miracles, and delusions – for the last times – in abundance from Satan and the second beast. 'To the law and to the testimony: if they speak not according to this word, it is because they have no light in them', Isaiah 8:20.

In conclusion, consider the last word on this very matter, recorded in yet another of the later epistles, one written under no less an authority than the Apostle of our profession.

'How shall we escape, if we neglect so great salvation' – not, neglect so great a *baptism*; nor so great *signs*: but, not neglect the *reality*; not neglect *the thing signified*, namely, *so great salvation* – 'which at the first began to be spoken' – mark that, *what matters is conveyed by speech* – 'spoken by the Lord, and was confirmed unto us' – where *us* is a further generation, like ourselves – 'unto us by them that heard him' – that is, confirmed unto us by the apostles that heard him, in the first generation – 'God *also* bearing *them* witness' – that is *also* meaning *as well as* bearing witness to the Lord when *he* spoke: *also* bearing witness to the chosen apostles and eyewitnesses, when, in turn, *they* spoke – 'God also bearing *them* witness' – not *us* witness: *them* witness – 'both with signs and wonders, and with divers miracles, and gifts of the Holy Ghost, according to his own will?', Hebrews 2:4.

Just as the manna ceased, the pillar of cloud and fire departed, the water from the Rock which followed them withdrew, having fulfilled their office when Israel entered into the land, so it is with us, in terms of the apostolic signs, since we have entered by so great salvation into the rest that remains for the people of God, being baptized into one body in one Spirit, our signs—the signs of the *new* covenant—likewise having reached the satisfactory conclusion of their abundant witness.

What remains? These things remain: 'There is one body, and one Spirit, even as ye are called in one hope of your calling; one Lord, one faith, one baptism, one God and Father of all, who is above all, and through all, and in you all', Ephesians 4:4-6.

The gospel—the evangel—abides; the baptism of the Spirit remains. The fellowship of the apostles, which is with the Father, and with his Son Jesus Christ, that continues.

But I repeat, the *signs* of an apostle, the generation of the apostles, these have ceased, having fulfilled their purpose. But the word of the Lord endureth for ever. The Son is upon his Father's throne, the Spirit abides below: *these bear witness to the evangel, the doctrine of Christ*. The vain pursuit of signs and wonders—once having been given under the safe hands of the apostles—but diverts attention from the one thing needful in the things that abide.

The facts speak for themselves. Nothing less than what has been said *explains the facts*, both then at the first, thereafter till the close of Revelation, and since, even until this present time.

I am obliged to add that not only—over a lifetime—am I aware of 'Pentecostal' and 'Charismatic' claims concerning miracles, signs, wonders, healings, and of course 'tongues', in modern times, but that I have without prejudice in my early days—before being established more perfectly by the Spirit of truth in vital experience by Holy Scripture—having first been converted at twenty years old, entered enthusiastically into their extravagances. But out of them all the Lord delivered me.

Moreover, since then, far from sitting in an armchair or at some comfortable meeting and gullibly swallowing up everything dished out by 'Pentecostal' and like-minded 'missionaries'

Openings in First Corinthians

in the 'Foreign field' to the 'Home base'—namely, from primitive countries to America and Britain—I have gone to see for myself.

In every case of close enquiry and examination of those whom the scriptures call the heathen, I found exaggeration, more than equalled by the superstitious witchcraft to which such excitable, ignorant, and credulous poor people were already prone. Some instances could not be explained naturally, but that was very rare, and in any event matched by spiritual evil and followed by blasphemy.

Likewise I found neither the reality of the doctrine of Christ, nor the *true* inward work of the Holy Ghost—read 'Saving Faith'—nor yet the love of *the truth*. There was no question of the superabounding enthusiasm, sacrifice, or sincerity of the peoples so easily swayed.

But let armchair and excitable—nevertheless sedentary—meeting enthusiasts remember that the financial support of these 'missionaries'—together with those of the Society backing them—increases in proportion to the tales of miraculous wonders reported from 'the field' to the 'home base'.

Let them also remember that a fool and his money are soon parted. I may add, so also are self-styled 'Pentecostals' and 'Charismatics' parted, not merely from sound common sense, but—not at all infrequently—quite literally from all reason.

And let not these—or anyone else—accuse me of limiting the power of God. They invent it; we proclaim it: but as it is in truth, that is, in the full inworking of so great salvation, together with the revelation both of the person and work of the Holy Ghost in glorifying Christ by the evangel.

I say, We proclaim it: and we do so as called of God, declaring nothing but that which agrees and harmonizes with that tenor of doctrine, narrative, and fellowship commanded by the Lord to be followed faithfully after the decease of the apostles.

More: unlike these erroneous persons, I teach according to the doctrine of Christ and his holy apostles the *truth* of the baptism of the Holy Ghost, namely, that it is always to bring in and to incorporate into *one body*, about which I have found these fanatics totally ignorant, though it pertains to the most precious things of the inner sanctuary. But then, What do they care about *the love of the truth, that they might be saved?*

Rather, their trust is in so-called manifestations, supposed signs, and in what they presume to be the Spirit, yet a spirit who speaks of himself, glorifies them, and has little or no interest in *the truth*.

Is that plain enough English for you?

Of course there is a baptism of the Holy Ghost: I have expounded it to you as it is in holy writ. But *one body in Christ always follows from it*. Of course the Spirit gives gifts – '*charismata*' – but neither in the perfect list of these in Romans, nor in Peter – and who knows best, he or them? – do they appear as *outwardly* miraculous.

And of course the baptism even today is given to those who seek one body in Christ. But not to those who ignore it, who glorify themselves by pretending to it, who rend the body of Christ by forming a sect over it, and who say and do not.

That is, they say over and over 'baptism of the Spirit', yet in works do not have it, but rather deny it in its very essence and divine purpose by their unruly pretence.

However, as to those who know and love the truth, though they have erred and gone out of the way, nevertheless by grace it abides true of them, 'For also in one Spirit are we all baptized into one body', I Corinthians 12:13.

The origin of the words 'baptize with the Holy Ghost' is to be found in the ministry of John the Baptist, in a prophecy concerning Christ which contrasts *Christ's coming ministry with John's present one*. 'I indeed baptize you with water, but he shall baptize you with the Holy Ghost', Matthew 3:11, Mark 1:8, and Luke 3:16.

Nevertheless, contrast or not, John's baptism not only prefigured that of Christ, it was a visible earthly manifestation of that invisible heavenly effusion which was to come.

Therefore the baptism of John was a *figure* of the baptism of the Holy Ghost, and, in fact, the latter expression is derived from the former, so that John prophesied of Christ baptizing from the ascended glory–having received the promise of the Holy Ghost from the Father in view of the completion and perfection of his substitutionary work on earth–I say, John prophesied of this in terms of his own faithful work in baptizing the penitent Jews in the river Jordan.

John baptized in the wilderness, and preached the baptism of repentance for the remission of sins to the Jews–and to all that remained of the remnant of Israel–saying, 'Repent ye: for the kingdom of heaven is at hand', adding, 'I indeed baptize you with water unto repentance: but he that cometh after me is mightier than I, whose shoes I am not worthy to bear: he shall baptize you with the Holy Ghost, and with fire.'

This mighty word was with power, for the Holy Ghost was upon John, and from the beginning of his preaching in the wilderness 'there went out to him Jerusalem, and all Judea, and all the region round about Jordan, and were baptized of him in Jordan, confessing their sins.'

Here was the repentant remnant of the election according to grace. These repented with a repentance not to be repented of, filled with contrition and godly sorrow, openly confessing their sins, and publicly being baptized of John.

What was the vision before them? The One that should come after John, who was mightier than he, who should baptize them with the Holy Ghost, bringing in the Kingdom of God, which was at hand.

For they knew, they sensed, it was witnessed in their hearts, 'Except a man be born of water and of the Spirit, he cannot enter into the kingdom of God', John 3:5.

Hence they were baptized unto John's baptism, thus to be born of water, looking and searching earnestly for the One of whom John spake, because he would baptize them with the Holy Ghost, that they might be born of the Spirit, and enter into the Kingdom of God.

Neither shall this fail of application, nor shall the spiritual voice of John crying in the inward wilderness of the soul cease, preparing the way of the Lord, till the Lord comes again.

These things are spiritual, but of them Paul would not have you to be ignorant, but discerning, for it remains a truth that whoso climbs up some other way is a thief and a robber.

Now consider the significance of John's baptism as – in a figure – it opens the mystery of the Son of God baptizing with one Spirit into one body, where those thus baptized are viewed as the members of his body.

This cannot be envisaged naturally, for the simple reason that the members of one's body are not only a corporeal whole, they are energized by the same vitality; quickened by the same life; they are sensitized by the same nervous system; renewed by the same life-giving blood; replenished by the same breathing; upheld by the same skeletal system; are of one physical appearance; have the same joints and bands; are clothed with the same supple skin; are of distinct physical integration; are of singular visible composition; and, above all, are the possession of that unique living soul whose outward structure is thus constituted as a physical entity – in itself unique – in the oneness of its many members.

Openings in First Corinthians

Together these many members make up the material composition of the unity of one person's body: But how can *many* such persons—each with his own separate bodily frame—no matter how united in mind and heart, be regarded as the *members* of the *one* body of Christ? How can this be explained?

Mysteries cannot be explained. But by spiritual experience they can be both opened and unveiled. And they can be signified in a figure.

Therefore, again, consider John's baptism. Here were the bodies of many persons, who, having received in their hearts and minds the searching words of John the Baptist, confessed their sins, and alike waded into the river Jordan to be baptized of John.

One river; but many immersions. One river; but poured out over many. Many immersions, but into one Jordan; many on whom the waters were poured out, but waters from one and the same river.

Thus, when John baptized, all the many penitents stood in the water, and out of the water.

More or less of every one of their bodies was submerged, so that what appeared seemed—as it were beneath the surface—to be invisibly united the one to the other by the same river in which all stood and out of which that which was visible of each one emerged. So it was when John baptized. His disciples stood in and were united by that depth of the one flowing river.

Moreover, that of their bodies which did appear above the surface of the water shone all wet and glistening with the waters of baptism poured out over them. But the waters were one, and were from one and the same river.

Then said John, 'I indeed baptize you with water'—*thus* he baptized them with water—'but he shall baptize you with the Holy Ghost.'

Now, the Spirit is likened to the river of the water of life or to the water from the smitten Rock which followed Israel in the wilderness. Which Rock, saith Paul, was Christ. But the water from that Rock signified the Holy Ghost, which Christ—once smitten—having been exalted, received of the Father, and shed forth upon his disciples.

Here is no outward river: 'He that believeth on me, as the scripture hath said, out of his belly shall flow rivers of living water. But this spake he of the Spirit, which they that believe on him should receive: for the Holy Ghost was not yet given; because that Jesus was not yet glorified', John 7:38,39.

Here are waters not only to the spiritual ankles, but also the knees, rising to the thighs, deepening to waters to swim in: a river of the water of life in which all those who are baptized are spiritually immersed and united.

That is, inwardly. For Jordan was outward, and in those natural waters some half or more of their bodies themselves were immersed, and this could be seen. But the waters of the Holy Ghost cannot be seen, and, invisibly, these fill the spirit and soul of the many baptized therein.

And these things being spiritual—and not natural or visible—neither this spiritual river, nor that baptism of the Spirit, can be seen outwardly or by the carnal sight. Nevertheless, like a mighty flowing river, the one person of the Holy Ghost, issuing forth as the water of life, immerses the members of Christ in the inward man, and fills the hidden man of the heart.

These spiritual waters flow continually into those upon whom they have been shed forth, uniting them in one Spirit, so as to constitute one body, every part as much as—indeed much more than—the figure of Jordan of old flowed about and appeared to unite in one those under John's baptism.

Nevertheless, for all that the baptism of the Spirit from the glorified and heavenly Son is *inward*, so that all are *inwardly* united in one divine person, *this oneness still takes place within their bodies. So that though their spirit and soul is made one, yet their bodies of necessity remain distinct.*

However, within themselves, Christ himself, by the Spirit, fills the one body. Then, *their* bodies signify *his* members. They stand out in that way, as hitherto John's disciples at one and the same time stood in and out of Jordan.

Hence, those baptized in the Holy Ghost are *visibly* one, and *must* be visibly one. 'Know ye not that your *bodies* are the members of Christ?', I Corinthians 6:15.

Christ fills us by the Spirit, who, in turn, himself constituted us inwardly as one body for the indwelling of the Son. Then we *in the wholeness of our being* are his members, and, together, constitute the body of Christ. Just as our own bodies, each one, constitute the outward expression of our own indwelling person and life, so also is the Christ: 'for also in one Spirit are we all baptized into one body.'

And if the baptism with the Holy Ghost is to bring in one body, What is it now? Now it is that *the truth of the one body, of the baptism of the Holy Ghost, has been quite lost, and is, alas, equally unsought, for all the delusions of man and duplications of the Adversary.*

For beyond all shadow of doubt it is evident, *the baptism of the Holy Ghost is corporate, it is to bring into one body. And if this is not the consequence, then what is claimed to be the baptism is not only wholly invalid, it is downright iniquitous, and, at that, in the holy things of the inmost shrine.*

But–as opposed to the imitations of man; the delusions of self-persuasion; the conjuring tricks of hirelings; or, more sinister, the supernatural workings of the Deceiver—the Corinthians, together with all those at the beginning, *really were baptized in one Spirit into one body.*

This was under the ministry of the holy apostle; it was with the power of God; it was of the heavenly glory; it was from the exalted Son of God; it was through the promise of the Father; and it was in the mighty presence and power of the Holy Ghost in the inner man of the assembled believers, that is, *when* they believed.

This made them one, not in themselves alone, but one in the indwelling person of the Holy Ghost. And not one in the indwelling person of the Holy Ghost only, but one in the fulness of him that filleth all in all, so as together to constitute, with all saints—here manifested at Corinth—one body in Christ.

At Corinth? But of old there had been enmity in the city of Corinth; there had been a middle wall of partition at Corinth; there had been distance betwixt Jew and Gentile at Corinth; the Jews at Corinth would not so much as set foot, let alone sit at meat, with the unclean Gentiles at Corinth.

Then what was this? Out from among the Jews, it was the calling according to the election of grace. Upon the Gentiles great light had arisen in thick heathen darkness, and God had separated the light from the darkness: 'a light to lighten the Gentiles, and the glory of thy people Israel.'

To both Jew and Gentile, God from heaven, the Son from glory, the Spirit on earth, had sent an elect vessel, a chosen apostle, 'to open their eyes, to turn them from darkness to light, and from the power of Satan unto God, that they may receive forgiveness of sins, and inheritance among them which are sanctified by faith that is in me', Acts 26:18.

And now together as one were all baptized in one Spirit into one body.

'Whether we be Jews', to whom first Paul testified that Jesus was Christ, and, when they opposed themselves, called down their blood on their own heads. But Crispus, the chief ruler of the synagogue, and all his house, believed, separating with all other believing Jews from the synagogue.

'Or Gentiles', of whom the Lord said, 'I have much people in this city', and, 'many of the Corinthians believed, and were baptized.'

'Whether we be bond or free'; God is no respecter of persons–though *we*, ourselves, as men, ought to give honour to whom honour is due, which is according to sound doctrine–with God there is no difference, no, neither between bond or free, nor Jew or Gentile, in the like bestowal of this baptism of the Spirit. And so Peter himself testified to the Jews at Jerusalem, 'Forasmuch then as God gave them the like gift as he did unto us, who was I, that I could withstand God?', Acts 11:17.

Yet such a gift to slaves under bondage? But the world's distinctions, whether social or religious, have no place with God. 'Hath not God chosen the poor of this world'–to be–'rich in faith?'

God has chosen us despite our low estate; and the Son knows the elect, and baptizes every one of those whom the Father gave to him; withal, the Spirit is poured out in baptism alike upon all, joining every member together as one–whether Jew or Gentile, bond or free–in the unity of the one body of Christ.

'And have been all made to drink into one Spirit', I Corinthians 12:13. In closing the verse, the apostle employs another illustration. The allegory which he uses now also shows the manner of the union, and, likewise, it is taken from water.

The figure envisaged is that of many who are drinking from one river. They are all drinking into that one river. The river is one, and the water is one. But these men come–not in self-will: they have been *made* to drink!–and all kneel at the river, and all drink.

Now every one has the water of the river within themselves, but, drinking their fill, as they take in the water continually, carrying it dripping from hand to mouth, what is within them is joined in one stream with what they are presently imbibing, which in turn is united with the waters from which they drink.

Thus, in a certain manner, each is joined to the other by what all receive whilst drinking together from the same river.

So it is with spiritualities: with what is of the Spirit. Inwardly our parched souls, made thirsty by the voice of one crying in the wilderness, by the preparatory work of God, cried out for the water that Christ could give, which would satisfy the thirsty soul, giving also to us that fulness—waters to swim in—which we clearly perceived others before us had experienced.

Weeping and crying, in our gasping—'I opened my mouth, and panted', Psalm 119:131—we were like the hart that panteth after the waterbrooks: 'so panteth my soul after thee', Psalm 42:1.

Then, at length, within ourselves sounded the words, 'I will pour water upon him that is thirsty, and floods upon the dry ground', Isaiah 44:3; and thereupon, 'He brought streams also out of the rock, and caused waters to run down like rivers', Psalm 78:16.

The waters came down, they ran down, they descended from 'the river of God, which is full of water', Psalm 65:9, so that he turned our wilderness into a standing water, Psalm 107:35, yea, the rock of our stony hearts into a standing water, the flint of our souls into a fountain of waters, Psalm 114:8.

Hence each one of us could say, and that by experience, 'When the poor and needy seek water, and there is none, and their tongue faileth for thirst, I the LORD will hear them, I the God of Israel will not forsake them. I will open rivers in high places, and fountains in the midst of the valleys: I will make the wilderness a pool of water, and the dry land springs of water', Isaiah 41:17,18.

Therefore have all we been made to drink into one Spirit, I Corinthians 12:13. For Christ having been smitten for us on earth, having justified and redeemed us by his blood, the third day was raised from the dead. Being seen of those witnesses chosen of God, called by the Son as his apostles, after forty days he ascended up into heaven.

Some ten days thereafter, when the day of Pentecost was fully come, there came a sound from heaven as of a rushing mighty wind, and it filled all the house where they were sitting. And there appeared unto them cloven tongues like as of fire, and it sat upon each of them. And they were all filled with the Holy Ghost, and began to speak with other tongues, as the Spirit gave them utterance. And there were dwelling at Jerusalem Jews, devout men, out of every nation under heaven.

Now when this was noised abroad the multitude came together, and were confounded, because every man heard them speak in his own language. Peter declares this to be the fulfilment of Joel's prophecy, the baptism of the Holy Ghost, saying of the Son, 'Therefore being by the right hand of God exalted, and having received of the Father the promise of the Holy Ghost, he hath shed forth this, which ye now see and hear', Acts 2:33.

This is to be baptized with the Holy Ghost. This was the beginning, but there is no ending: the Son baptizes still. This also is to be made to drink into one Spirit which also has no end. For all were, and are, made to drink into that one and the selfsame Spirit, in fulfilment of the figure.

For the measure imbibed by each one, as one shed forth upon the whole, fills the one body in union with that divine person who, invisibly and spiritually, unites all in and with himself. And, if so, it follows of course, each is united the one with the other in him, 'for we have *all* been made to drink into one Spirit.' Then, if thus one with him, also united to each other.

Furthermore, we are full, yea, overflowing, because above even such overwhelming blessing as this, the Spirit, flowing from the Father through the Son, joins us in one with the Son.

And not the Son only, for, in the acknowledgement of the fellowship of the mystery, we *experience* that he and his Father are one; then, in the same Spirit, we are united in spirit with the Father through the Son of his love: 'and truly our fellowship is with the Father, and with his Son Jesus Christ', I John 1:3.

This is to 'have all been made to drink'–*drink*–'into'–*into*–'one Spirit', I Corinthians 12:13.

Hence we can echo in our own inward experience the words of Jesus, 'If thou knewest the gift of God, and who it is that saith to thee, Give me to drink; thou wouldest have asked of him, and he would have given thee living water', John 4:10.

For he who slakes his thirst of the water that is in this world must at last cease from drinking. And then he shall thirst again.

'But'–saith Christ–'whosoever drinketh of the water that I shall give him shall never thirst; but the water that I shall give him shall be in him a well of water springing up into everlasting life', John 4:14.

With outward, visible, natural water–that of the world–of necessity one thirsts again in proportion to the length of the period extending from the last time that one drank. Not so with the heavenly, invisible, spiritual water, namely, that of the Son from the glory, in the person of the Holy Ghost.

For this divine, mysterious, heavenly, glorious, spiritual, invisible, and living water, *in its very nature, never has cessation from its outpouring and upspringing, nor do those who receive the gift ever cease to drink therefrom.*

Therefore, they 'never thirst again'. Nor could such spiritual thirst ever be possible, because they have 'all been made to drink into *one Spirit*', I Corinthians 12:13.

Again, such as these cannot but reiterate the words of Jesus, 'If any man thirst, let him come unto me, and drink. He that believeth on me, as the scripture hath said, out of his belly shall flow rivers of living water. But this spake he of the Spirit, which they that believe on him should receive: for the Holy Ghost was not yet given; because that Jesus was not yet glorified', John 7:37-39.

But now he *is* glorified, and, being glorified, it follows, the Spirit has been given. And, if given, then they that believe on the Son must have received him.

This being the case – and from the words of Jesus it must be the case – again it follows of necessity, first, that they have come to him and drank; and, second, that out of their bellies flow rivers of living water.

But then, given the reality of which both drinking and rivers were the figure, this is neither more nor less than that which is written in the event, namely, that they that believe on him 'have all been made to drink into one Spirit', I Corinthians 12:13.

And what is this?

This is *none other – given the unity of the deity in Father, Son, and Holy Ghost – none other than 'As thou, Father, art in me, and I in thee, that they also may be one in us'*, John 17:21.

The Body of Christ and the Gifts

Already having opened the truth concerning the gifts and baptism of the Spirit, I Corinthians 12:1-13 – briefly touching upon the subject of the body of Christ – next the apostle Paul applies the figure of the body, I Corinthians 12:14-26.

Here he is not at all referring *directly* to the body of Christ. He points to the physical frame, by way of allegory drawing inferences from the relation of one's body to its members, and one's members to that body.

However—despite the vast differences—with propriety certain parallels may be drawn between one's own body and its members, and the body of Christ and its members. That is, the inferences drawn in I Corinthians 12:14-26 may in a figure be transferred to the members of the body of Christ, and to that body itself.

Hence, whilst this passage refers to the human frame, because it does so with but one object in mind, at the last the apostle concludes, 'Now ye are the body of Christ, and members in particular', I Corinthians 12:27.

In principle verses 14-26 present two propositions in relation to the body and its members. The first appears in verse 14: 'For the body is not one member, but many.' This proposes *one body but many members*, and is expounded by way of allegory in I Corinthians 12:15-19.

The second proposition is in verse 20: 'But now are they many members, yet but one body.' This shifts the emphasis, declaring *many members yet but one body*. This is opened by similar allegory between verses 21-26.

In the first, Paul argues from the body to the members; in the second, from the members to the body. Although seemingly simple—the members addressing one another—the force of the apostle's propositions, and their respective conclusions, seen aright, comes with powerful impact to the Corinthians. To the contemporary situation in modern-day 'Christianity', the application is absolutely devastating.

(i) One Body but Many Members

Consider the first proposition, 'For the body is not one member, but many', I Corinthians 12:14. This postulates *one body but many members*, upon which the apostle enlarges in verses 15-19. This proposition *seems* to state the obvious, but by it the apostle presses home the truth. For by making much more obvious what is natural, he directs them the more diligently to consider the spiritual implications of these things in the body of Christ.

To this end Paul supposes two members of one's body able to deny the purpose of their existence. Showing the folly of this, the apostle questions the denial imagined regarding each member respectively. His questions make the two members' statements appear ludicrous. He concludes this immediate context with the truth of verse 18, and the question of verse 19.

To return to the two questions. These are imagined as being asked by the foot and the ear respectively. Suppose the foot – had it power to speak – should say, 'Because I am not the hand, I am not of the body.' Again, imagine the ear – assuming it could speak – saying, 'Because I am not the eye, I am not of the body.'

But, allowing the licence of the figure, such speech is preposterous. To show *how* preposterous, the apostle dismisses the vanity of such foolish statements by the repeated question, '*Is it therefore not of the body?*'. That is, assuming the foot and the ear, because they are not the hand and the eye, *should* be capable of saying, 'Therefore I am not of the body', I Corinthians 12:15,16.

Just *suppose* – imagines the apostle – these members should so speak: Well, *what difference would it make?* None at all. Speak away with such vain froth: '*Is it therefore not of the body?*' The empty words, light as air, *change nothing in reality*. What these members say, or do not say, does not decide things, or alter anything.

The truth is that both members are what they are because God has created them so. Moreover they are not created to be what they are in order to be independent of the body itself. The member is what it is, not for itself, or for its own sake, but it is what it is for the body, and for the body's sake.

Whence it follows that no member exists for itself: it exists for him whose body it is, into which that member is incorporated. It is *what* it is, and *where* it is, because God has so created the body that each member is exactly what is necessary in the place in which it is set. *That* member would be useless were it set elsewhere. It is created naturally to function—according to its fashion and form—expressly where it has been placed, and placed perfectly in order to realize its full usefulness to the body as a whole.

How suited therefore the figure employed by Paul, imagining two such members to be in the position of speaking, and doing so as severing themselves from the body—if they could—because such members, rejecting their own nature, deny the very purpose of their existence. And for what cause? For this cause: they are neither of the nature nor in the place which they fancy for themselves: then, vexed, they refuse to accept that they are members of the body at all. Are they therefore not of the body?

Then what clamouring members are these? Such presumption arises from considering nothing other than themselves. From questioning, Why am I not this? Or, Why can I not be that? And whining, Well, if I am not *this*; or if I cannot be *that*; then I am not of the body, and disassociate myself from the body. But is it therefore not of the body?

Such a member—supposing it could do so—should rather give thanks. And if it were possible that it should ask questions, ask these questions: How can I respond more fully, more efficiently, to him to whose body I belong, so as to please *him*, being what I am? How can I function in harmony and co-ordination with each other member, every one in its proper place and due order, so as to serve him whose members we are?

Thus the purpose for the existence of the members of the body, every one, would be fulfilled. And the reason for the being of each member, unique in its place in the body—in concert with all—would be realized.

Openings in First Corinthians

But are these inferences, drawn from the members of one's body—and their imaginary speech—suited to the state of the body of Christ at Corinth? They were suited to *correct* that state. For, whatever their condition, still, all had been baptized in one Spirit into one body, and all repented with a repentance not to be repented of—II Corinthians 7:8-11—besides which, all were of the same mind and the same judgment, all spake the same thing, and all were gathered into the unity of the one *ecclesia of God* at Corinth.

But is the state that was at Corinth, which this epistle generally—and that figure of the body particularly—was sent to correct, in any way comparable to the state of the contemporary professing church? No, it is not. There is not the remotest resemblance between the two. They are as far apart as the east is from the west.

Whatever the faults of the Corinthians, they existed within the unity of the only assembly or *ecclesia* in that entire city, and also in all the earth. However the Corinthians might have erred, nevertheless, they *had* all been baptized in one Spirit into one body. No matter how the Corinthians had strayed, they had strayed one from the other, or from the apostle, *within the integrity of the only visible gathering that existed.* That integrity—called into the fellowship of God's Son, into the unity of Father, Son, and Holy Ghost, *manifestly set forth in the ecclesia*—that integrity, I say, remained unbroken.

Contemporary Christianity—in all its forms—is the direct opposite of that original unity, the unity of the one body of Christ. Brethrenism claims—or used to claim—that it is the exception; but this is palpable nonsense: there are more divisions and sects at war with each other in Brethrenism, than there are in those from whom they had separated in order to disintegrate into this splintered and fragmented contradiction of even the semblance of unity. And where is the unity of *one body*—visibly manifested—in that?

Openings in First Corinthians

As to the rest of Christendom, consisting as it does of numerous denominations, independencies, parties, groups, and sects, each in fact divided from the other; all having their own peculiarities, dogma, and systems; every one with a mixed congregation comprised of believer and unbeliever, the world and the church, light and darkness; the preponderance being for the worst: What of this? This mixed multitude of divisions is as irreconcilable as it is incurable. As prophesied in holy writ, it is irremediable: from it, all that is of God should repent, depart, and cry for the unity of *one* body.

Then can they agree in nothing? Yes, they can agree in two things. First, they can agree to tolerate this evil which, together, they embody, saying nothing whatsoever about it, either in their own party, or in that of others. Second, they can agree in their divided entities stoutly to defend the *status quo*, and this alike by utterly shutting their eyes and ears to the least sight or the faintest sound of the truth of God's *ecclesia* as it was in the beginning, is now, and ever shall be: O, tacitly they can agree together wholly to ignore the truth of the one body *of Christ*!

Yet even this, so-called 'evangelicals' will justify in their iniquity, claiming that the body is invisible; that its members are scattered like so many indiscernible ghosts; that they merge imperceptibly each one among and with the worldly, divided, invented, disobedient divisions of Christendom; that they abide wraith-like – unknown, unseen, unaware, uncomprehending – invisible amidst the membership of unbelieving congregations. And this is the unity of one body? Oh, yes, they say, and 'Bishop' Ryle saith it: and who is this Disraeli-appointed Ryle to overturn the everlasting gospel?

Ah, but, says the evangelical, the body is hidden in the professing church. But it is not a church: it is a series of disparate denominations, sects, independencies, and divisions. And it is not a profession: for if there is one thing that they do *not* hold, nor will they ever profess, it is the faith once delivered to the saints.

And of all the contradictions in terms, none is so farcically blatant as the absurdity of the words 'an invisible body'. An invisible body is no body at all: it is a spirit. 'Know ye not that your *bodies* are the members of Christ?', I Corinthians 6:15. *Inwardly* those baptized in one Spirit are united in one; yes: but also *outwardly* those spiritually in union are likewise united *in one body*. Its unity is *visible*. You can see it. If not, it is no body.

But the truth is, 'evangelicals' dare not admit what stares them in the face: the body of Christ is a reality in the word of God, and in the Spirit of truth, from which they have utterly fallen, so that *it no longer appears*. What appears is that like the Pharisees of old 'these are they that justify themselves'. Yes, and in so doing, condemn the preciousness of the body of Christ to the Head. If not, let them admit of it, and confess and forsake their sin.

Let them be like the Jewish remnant according to the election of grace, which, as one man, repented at the preaching of John, and, openly confessing their sins, were baptized of him in Jordan. Let them heed the cry, 'Come out of her, my people'. Let them cleanse themselves from all filthiness of the flesh and spirit. Let them 'come out from among them, and be separate'. Let them go forth unto Christ *without the camp*. They will not find themselves alone.

So has the Spirit been grieved in the past, and in this present generation, in which we and our fathers have sinned, that his divine influences have been well-nigh withdrawn, and in their place a lying spirit with his fleshly incitements has deluded multitudes. And since they would not receive the love of the truth, God has given them over to their delusions. Nevertheless, to the remnant that is left, a voice cries in the wilderness.

We who are of this remnant are to repent, and return, and be united in one Spirit—for 'there is one body, and one Spirit, even as ye are called in one hope of your calling'—that it may appear again that the body of Christ is a reality, so that the world may know that the Father sent the Son; and know it, precisely because of this reality of fellowship – the apostles' fellowship – in Father, Son, and Holy Ghost.

And should it be that there are those who have repented in a place, and received the truth: let them not suppose that we fulfil all the mind of the Lord, till we in every place are so united. Thus not only do we manifest the unity of the Spirit among the members of the one body of Christ in the *ecclesia* in which we are called; but also in all the earth – in demonstration of the Spirit and of power – we show forth as one this unity, under the Head, of the whole body, the one *ecclesia*.

This is that, in the light and to the realization of which by the Spirit, we are called, and to which we should come with heart-broken penitence, with mourning and humility, for the failure and sin of which we and our fathers have been the cause.

Till we are fully returned to this – not only in a given locality; but in the unity of *one* body throughout the whole earth, of all who are so met in every place – we declare, in practice, however we delude ourselves in theory, 'Because I am not the hand, I am not of the body'. And again – for in the mouth of two or three witnesses every matter is established – 'Because I am not the eye, I am not of the body'. But if God hath wrought at all in thee, Art thou not of the body?

To assert independence from the one body of Christ – so as to join ourselves in the sin of schism with what *must* be infinitely less – is, in effect, by one's life, volition, and direction, to deny both the body of Christ, and that one is a member of that body. Independence of the body therefore is as impossible to true members, as it is to the real members of one's own body. If not, what does the figure, and what does the passage, mean?

How this shows up the Charismatic delusion – among others – in which, claiming the baptism of the Spirit, supposing to seal that claim by the twofold extravagance of the loss of self-control on the one hand, and the pretence to 'signs'—such as gibberish—on the other, these impostors *eschew the body of Christ, properly so-called*. Do they not? Are they not found, gleefully expressing themselves, united with their congregations, whether in Roman Catholic, Anglican, Nonconformist, Brethren, Independent, Group, or House-meeting?

I Corinthians 12:17 demonstrates by two simple questions the indispensability of many members in one body. This appears in the necessity of many needed—but quite different—functions. To these functions, respectively, the members correspond; for them, as a whole, they were created, and do exist. Hence the irony of Paul's two rhetorical questions.

'If the whole body were an eye, where were'—*the function of—* 'hearing?' *That* function, necessitates an *ear*. And only the corresponding member can perform the required function. How essential then, the variety, co-ordination, and unity of the members to the body. How can—with the wildest imagination—the whole body be an eye? How can it be a body unto itself?

And whilst asserting its independency, will it yet have the temerity to profess that it—so mean, so small, not to say disobedient, a member—is sufficient for the Head of the body to indwell, that *thus* he might fully express *himself*? What presumptuous folly! *A man cannot express himself through an eye only.* A man is so constituted that he needs every member of his body for full self-expression.

One can *see* through an eye: it *is* an essential *part* of self-expression: but *only* a part. It requires *all* the parts, every member, the whole of the functions, working together as one under the direction of the head, in order that a person should achieve self-expression.

Any one member, any single function, is *not* an expression, but only a part, a contributory function, of the full expression.

He whose body it is requires the co-ordinated unity of the whole range of functions from every member, enlivened together in harmony, to express the fulness of his personality who indwells the whole.

Hence the irony of Paul's question: as if one member were – or possibly could be – the whole body. The very idea is at once grotesque, fantastic, and repellent. One member can never be the body, much less a body unto itself. Yet 'evangelicals' have for generations acted *in practice* upon the presumption that it is so.

Is it any wonder that ICHABOD is written over our portals, and that, in wrath, the *presence of God* has departed from us, after *so long* a time of patient longsuffering, of enduring our inventions, to see if at last our fathers or we might come to repentance and reformation?

In the same verse – I Corinthians 12:17 – the apostle, as if to call another witness against such a gross impossibility, repeats the question in terms of the faculty of hearing: 'If the whole body were' – no more than the faculty of – 'hearing, where were the' – faculty of – 'smelling?' The absurd folly of such a proposition in nature, though ludicrous, serves a vital purpose: by giving voice to the inanity of the very idea in natural things, Paul presses home the truth that such an aberration were even more shocking in spiritual things.

As if any one member could so bloat itself as to eclipse all the others, making out that nothing signifies save *this* member!

Would not he whose body it is – allowing of the figure used by Paul – say to it, What doest thou? But if it replied, I am here to express your lordship over me! What would be the rejoinder but this: Thou fool! Am I so small in thy sight? I need you; but I need *every other member with you*. I need your function; but I need *every other member to function in harmony also*: only *thus* am I expressed.

Openings in First Corinthians

'So also is the Christ', I Corinthians 12:12.

That is, just as 'God hath set the members *every one of them in the body, as it hath pleased him*', I Corinthians 12:18, 'so also is the Christ'. However, strictly – except by allusion – verse 18 does not refer to the body of Christ, but to the body of man in the creation.

Then how could such a creation, both in its parts, and in the sum of those parts, be other than 'very good', so that 'God *rested* on the seventh day from all his work which he had made'?

Then, consistent with God's nature, his rest, and his own image, man reflected, down to the very least member, the divine perfection of the work of him who set every member in the body, as it pleased him.

Wherefore observe that, *firstly*, it hath pleased God perfectly to form each member so that it is ideally adapted to perform its function; *secondly*, that all the members – whether paired or single – are set in that place in the body admirably suited – in concert with every other member – to its use; *thirdly*, that – save for pairs: as hands, eyes, or ears, for example – each member is essential for that distinctive use for which it, alone, was created and set in the body; and *fourthly*, that God hath set all together, each in its respective place, so that the whole body, perfectly synchronized and harmoniously responsive, answers to the head, according to the volition and will of him whose body it is, to the glory of God.

This end and result of the creation of the body of man, and this setting of the members of that body so agreeably in concert with perfect efficiency of movement and energy, is what is called 'as it hath pleased him'. For what pleases God is order, perfection, harmony, subjection, and beauty. Thus the members set in the body were 'as it hath pleased him', and, viewing his work in creation, it gave to God such pleasure that it is written, 'behold, it was very good'.

And if this be so with the creation and setting of the members of the body of man, shall it be *less so* with the members of the body of Christ? My brethren, these things ought not to be. Then why is it that the holy apostle is obliged thus to write?

'And if they were all one member, where were the body?', I Corinthians 12:19. This verse concludes the first proposition of the apostle, namely, *one body but many members*. What a conclusion! What? Must the apostle needs conclude such a proposition with the words, 'And if they were all one member, where were the body?'. Yes, for shame, he must.

Irrespective of what member and function was bestowed upon those at Corinth, what was it that each actually usurped to himself—or, for shame, herself—in their assembling together? What was it that made them appear 'all one member', so that the mentally sound unbeliever should declare them to be mad? What was it? It was that they were all tongues. They '*all* spoke with tongues', and, it appears, all at once, I Corinthians 14:23. Then, 'Where were the body?'

And this, remark, during the lifetime of the apostles, in an apostolic age when it was granted to them, and to the *ecclesia* raised up under their authority, to show forth such signs and wonders, as in parallel at the commencement with Israel.

Yet, even in such auspicious apostolic beginnings of the *ecclesia*, these very same early miraculous signs evidently were what the Corinthians abused, both in the apparently mad bedlam of their assembling, and in their usurping what was in fact 'a sign, not to them that believe, but to them that believe not', I Corinthians 14:22.

And this, I say, in a day when such signs *were* given, under the safe hands of the apostles, to indicate to the whole world, and the entire age, *God's* inauguration of the new testament, and his bringing in of the body of Christ at the beginning.

(ii) Many Members yet but One Body

Verse 19 concludes the apostle's first proposition, *one body, but many members*, I Corinthians 12:14, which he expounds between verses 15-19. It also leads naturally to his second proposition, which follows immediately, namely, *many members, yet but one body*, I Corinthians 12:20, the opening of which appears in verses 21-26.

In the first case Paul had argued from the body to the members. The body embraced all the members. They were all members, which, together, constituted that body. The number of the members, the variety of their functions, the diversity of their appearance, made no difference to – in fact, it conspired to enhance – the truth of the one body.

That is the emphasis of the divergence of so numerous yet distinct a conjunction of members: *together*–and they *are* together–*they constitute one body*. 'One body but many members.' Thus the difference and variety of the many members *stress*, not *contradict*, the unity of the body, I Corinthians 12:14-19.

Although the alteration of the emphasis in the second proposition may appear so slight that it seems a distinction without a difference, obviously this cannot be so: rather, it should be clear immediately that such a weighty matter must be considered from every aspect, and in each nuance of meaning.

Then, it is emphatically and distinctly true that it behoves the apostle now to stress that *there are many members, yet but one body*, I Corinthians 12:20, where Paul argues not from the body to the many members, *but from the many members to the one body*. Consider this.

The members have 'need' one of the other in the one body. This word 'need' appears twice, verse 21. Likewise the members have a 'necessity' each one of the other, in the nature of the one body, verse 22. *That* is the issue in these verses: the *need*; the *necessity*; namely, *the need, the necessity of every member to the whole body*. That is what Paul feels compelled to impress upon the Corinthians.

The fact of varied members, of their differing characteristics, of their distinct nature, of their diverse function, of their unique appearance, *cannot disassociate those members from the one body*. Whatever their differences, each and all belong to the body, and *to nothing else but the body*.

The very idea of severance from the body as if to operate in connection with some alternative organism – much less organisation – is an impossibility in nature, a transgression against creation, and a grotesque parody of all that is lawful, proper, and orderly.

Yet has not this concept become the norm in the organisations, systems, denominations, societies, schools, 'charities', and other superfluous growths and cancers of modern Christendom? As if the members *could* be considered in connection with anything other than the one body? For there is but *one* body.

But Christendom, in its nature, stands in a multitude of independent structures, not one of which existed in the new testament. None of this can possibly be justified by holy scripture, which declares with categorical emphasis – however many or diverse the true and living members – 'yet but *one body*', I Corinthians 12:20.

Whence it follows that no function can be exercised by any member independent of the one body. Nothing else exists to those members *but* one body. All members, however varied; all functions, notwithstanding their diversity; *pertain exclusively to the one body*.

No other organism – much less organisation – exists to the members save that one corporate entity of him whose body it is.

All the members are of that one body, whether great or small, weak or strong; often or little used: *'yet but one body.'*

As in the first proposition the apostle again supposes, for the sake of argument, that one member might ask hypothetical questions or make theoretical statements to another. Specifically, the eye to the hand, or the head to the feet.

But, there being *'yet but one body'*, these members *cannot* make such impossible hypothetical statements as this: 'I have no need of you.' They have *every* need of each other, and, vastly more important, the body itself has the utmost necessity of all the members, none excluded.

The eye say to the hand, I have no need of thee? But the hand is of the utmost necessity to the eye, otherwise, what is *seen* cannot be put to *use*. Why not? Because the eye is not a hand. The eye which sees, requires the hand which works.

Besides, transcending the hypothesis, What is this, that the members speak of themselves with such presumptuous impudence? It is for *him whose body it is, whose members these are*, to speak, or not to speak; to direct, or not to direct, every single one according to his own will.

The whole is one co-ordinated organism for the self-expression of him whose body it is: then what is this height of arrogance–given the figure–that the members dare to speak–much less to act–as if they were each detached bodies in and of themselves?

The head say to the feet, I have no need of you? But the head can neither stand nor can it proceed in motion without the feet. The feet cannot function as the head, nor can the head fulfil its purpose without the feet.

Both head and feet act in concord, not to do the work of the whole body, but to function as unique and diverse members of that body, so that the entire body, with *every* member, may give due expression to the personality of him to whom all belongs as one. Without this, there *is* no body: only dismemberment.

Next, making a further comparison between the members of one's body, Paul speaks of differences of another sort: some are 'feeble'; others 'uncomely'. That is, relative to those which appear 'honourable', or 'more comely'.

What of this? Does this make them less members than the others, or of meaner value? Can this be a cause of one despising another, or of some rejecting those held by them to be inferior? God forbid: else where were the body's unity? or of what use are such disjointed and contradictory members to the person whose body it is?

'Nay, much more those members of the body, which seem to be more feeble, are necessary: and those members of the body, which we think to be less honourable, upon these we bestow more abundant honour; and our uncomely parts have more abundant comeliness.

'For our comely parts have no need: but God hath tempered the body together, having given more abundant honour to that part which lacked: that there should be no schism in the body; but that the members should have the same care one for another.

'And whether one member suffer, all the members suffer with it; or one member be honoured, all the members rejoice with it. Now ye are the body of Christ, and members in particular', I Corinthians 12:22-27.

By 'feeble' the apostle refers to those members which are especially vulnerable, lacking natural protection. For example, the eye: how sensitive, how susceptible to injury – in a word, feeble – this member appears. Then, every member instinctively moves to guard and protect such a member in case of danger.

The same applies to the ear, should some foreign matter threaten this orifice: the head flinches, the hand flies to defend the vulnerable and exposed member, and the feet run from the area of danger.

Thus nature itself teaches—and instinctive reaction instructs—that all the members of the body as one fly to the protection of those members weaker than themselves. Every member by a kind of natural reflex hastens to defend and strengthen that which is more feeble, thus bestowing 'more abundant honour', because 'all the members' have 'the same care one for another'.

Now Paul draws attention to another relative difference between the members of the body: some are 'uncomely', whereas certain others are 'comely'. But should this be the cause of 'schism in the body' according to nature? Certainly not. Once more, nature itself teaches quite the opposite.

An 'uncomely' member is one not prepossessing in sight. Yet upon these also we bestow 'more abundant honour'. For example, the feet. Hardly the most attractive members, these might well be considered 'uncomely'. Yet, especially in Paul's day, and in other parts of the world to this day, though less honourable, upon these it is at once natural, necessary, and courteous to bestow special attention.

John the Baptist considered himself unworthy so much as to unloose the latchet of the Lord's shoes, let alone wash his feet. Simon the Pharisee, however, disdained even—at the least—to provide the expected water for the Lord to wash his own feet when entering the house. For, said Jesus, 'thou gavest me no water for my feet', Luke 7:44.

The Lord himself washed the disciples' feet, much to the consternation of Peter, who considered it utterly beneath the Lord to wash the feet of one as unfit as himself. Indeed—much like to John the Baptist—far from having *his* feet washed, he thought it unworthy in himself so much as to attempt to wash the *Lord's* feet: 'And shalt *thou* wash *my* feet?'

Where, in those days of open shoes or sandals, before entering the house it was considered both proper and decent to wash the feet: to bestow honour, that is, on one's own or others' uncomely members. Whence it appears that thus to bestow honour upon the uncomely members was universal in practice.

Hence the suitability of the apostle's application, I Corinthians 12:23, for the hands serve, the eyes guide, and the joints supply, as one bends to wash and cleanse these lowliest and least comely of members. That is, *every other member* combines in recognition of the significance of *these*, in and to the *whole* body, notwithstanding their uncomeliness!

From this point Paul begins to apply lessons from the figure of the body to the members of the body of Christ with much more direct and pointed attention. For example, the use of the word 'schism', I Corinthians 12:25, a word impossible to apply accurately to one's own body, but tragically applicable to the members of the body of Christ.

But God has tempered–bound, given cohesion, compounded, blended–the body together, 'that there should be no schism in the body'. The Greek *schisma*, or *schizō*, has been rendered 'division; rent; schism'; or 'break; divide; rend; open'.

This indicates a rent, cleft, or division. Now, this cannot refer to the body naturally, for in such a case it would imply amputation; dismemberment; severance; or mutilation.

Then Paul is applying the word *schisma* to the members of the body of Christ spiritually. It is a direct application. The apostle means that in the body of Christ, wherever found, such is the work of God in 'tempering' the members of the body together, *that in consequence there should be*–or, one might say, *there could be*–no *schism.*

On the contrary, because of the Father, the Son, and the Holy Ghost, all 'the members should have the same care one for another', I Corinthians 12:25, 'that there should be no schism in the body'.

'And whether one member suffer, all the members suffer with it.' In effect, as it is true of one's own body, this is fulfilled in the body of Christ. If the eye or ear be afflicted, or should some laceration or severe bruising affect a part, such is the pain of that single member that one's whole body seems to be nothing but that member! Namely 'all the members suffer with it', until the suffering be eased, and healing finally takes place.

'Or one member be honoured, all the members rejoice with it.' Here the apostle barely waits to give the figure, but with it proceeds immediately to the application. For hardly will a member of one's own body be 'honoured'; yet, certainly, this may be true of a member of the body of Christ.

Nevertheless when excellence is performed by the hand at work, or by the feet in running, or else the eye in sharpness of vision, then it is true that a sense of well-being and of satisfaction floods the whole body.

So when a member of the body of Christ excels in the things of the Lord, and in the work of God, or in spiritual matters, far from envy, disparagement, or sour jealousy being the result, *in the body of Christ*, every single member as it were glows with pleasure and satisfaction at the grace manifested in that member.

How is this love so wonderfully fulfilled? Because 'now are they many members, *yet but one body*.' Whereas in the organisations of religion after the flesh, at the excellence or being honoured of one, the rest of the dead congregation rather give place to 'hatred, variance, emulations, wrath, strife, seditions, heresies, envyings', Galatians 5:20,21.

And why is this? Because it is as Christ said, 'He that gathereth not with me scattereth'. And, because the invention of these divisions is after the flesh, the works of the flesh they will do. Hence such reactions are inevitable in those carnal assemblies which—for all their loud claims and professions from the bible—stand in nothing but the works of man under the dead letter.

Whereas the love of God is shed abroad in the hearts of those who are of him made members of the one body of Christ. Christ fills the body, and his light, life, and love are made manifest in each member, and all the members together as one, having been baptized in one Spirit into one body.

And seeing that this body is of Christ, what life other than his should appear in the members of that body? Then, when one member is honoured, grace reigns, humility rules, love triumphs, and all the members rejoice with it together as one. For 'ye *are* the body of Christ, and members in particular', I Corinthians 12:27.

This verse concludes the entire passage—I Corinthians 12:14-27—in which, under two propositions, the apostle demonstrates the analogy between one's own body, and that of the body of Christ. He had argued first from the relation of the members to the body, and last, from that of the body to the members, concluding the whole with the plain statement 'Now *ye* are the body of Christ, and members in particular'.

However from this point onward to the end of the chapter, Paul begins to open a mystery not previously mentioned, and to reveal the existence of gifts other than those of the Spirit bestowed upon the members of the body of Christ, about which he had spoken hitherto.

Furthermore, to clarify the difference, he also shows the relationship between that which he *had* expounded in I Corinthians 12:7-27, and that which he is *about* to reveal between verses 28-31, the closing verses of this chapter.

(iii) Gifts of Christ; Gifts of the Spirit

The apostle commences, 'And God hath set some in the church' – or, rather, 'God hath set certain in the *ecclesia*'– I Corinthians 12:28. Carefully note the change in Paul's description.

Observe that the words 'hath God set' had been used of the members in the body: 'But now *hath God set* the members every one of them in the body, as it hath pleased him', I Corinthians 12:18. Next mark that in verse 28 the apostle repeats the words 'God hath set', not now concerning all the members of the body, but rather 'some'– or 'certain'–whom 'God hath set' *in the ecclesia*: 'And *God hath set* some in *the church*', I Corinthians 12:28.

Yes, but why *repeat* the expression, 'God hath set'? Why change the former reference to 'the members', to the latter expression, namely, to 'some', or rather 'certain', pointing elsewhere? And why is Paul firstly *inclusive* of the members, embracing *all* the members, verse 18, then secondly *exclusive* in relation to 'certain', that is, to 'some' only, verse 28?

And why does the first reference state 'in the body', verse 18; whereas the second–to the contrary–affirms specifically 'in the church', verse 28?

First, Why are certain said to be set in the *ecclesia*, verse 28? Elementary: because they are not said to be set in the body.

Why are the members said to be set in the *body*, verse 18? Elementary: because they are not said to be set in the *ecclesia*.

It is simply a question of discerning the mind of the Spirit, and of observing the distinctions in the counsels of God.

Then, whilst *God's setting them*, respectively, is descriptive of the same operation of God, *the wording of the Spirit is such that the same operation is applied twice.*

It is a twofold operation, and the reason is *that it pertains to two different spheres, and concerns two distinct kinds of gifts.* Without discerning this, without observing the distinction, all is confusion. With the discernment, given the observation, everything becomes clear.

Hence observe that every member is said to be set in the body. Likewise mark that only 'some'—*certain*—*persons* are said to be set in the *ecclesia*. These persons are, respectively, 'first apostles, secondarily prophets, thirdly teachers', verse 28.

'After that'—mark well: *after* that—a different matter entirely is mentioned, and mentioned in order to show *the contrast*. That is why it is brought in: 'After that miracles'—this should be, *powers*—'then gifts'—plural: *charismata*—'of healings, helps, governments, diversities of tongues.'

Now these are not *persons*, as was the former case: these are objective gifts. No person is said to possess them: it is simply a formal list of *charismata*, not said to have been personified at all: it is merely objective. Why? *To show the contrast 'After that'*.

After what? After the *persons* whom God hath set in the *ecclesia*, verse 28.

Whereas the apostle *had* been speaking of the body—whether the figure of the body, or the body of Christ itself—this referred to the body and its members *as manifested at Corinth*. There is one body, and *that* is what is brought to light wherever the saints are gathered in the baptism of the Spirit. Then, *there* the one body is distinctively apparent, according to the manifold wisdom of God. In *this* case, at Corinth.

But now in verse 28 *the apostle is no longer speaking of the body of Christ at Corinth, nor of its members, neither yet of the charismata bestowed upon them in the gift of that Spirit who, himself, in person, fills the body*. Now the apostle is speaking of another realm, far wider than that of the body at Corinth, and of other gifts, of far more profound import than the *charismata*.

That is, he is speaking of the *entire ecclesia*, and of those persons whom God hath set in such a realm as this. Thereupon Paul introduces another class of gifts altogether, not previously mentioned.

That is why the apostle repeats the words 'God hath set', verses 18 and 28.

Note the words. First, they are uttered to emphasize that this is the work of God: 'God hath set ... as it hath pleased *him*', verse 18. *Him*, notice. Then this is nothing to do with *man*: this is altogether to do with *the operation of God*.

All the attempts of man—and these are many and various—to copy the work of God and the operation of his hands begin and end in shame, disgrace, and departure, a hollow charade which mocks man's inability to his face. The work of God is inimitable, transcendent, divine: 'God hath set.' It is all of God's initiative, and wholly of the power of God. It is *in this* that his presence is known.

But I return to the question: Why repeat the clause of verse 18 in verse 28? Because the apostle in his doctrine wishes to make clear that *what* God hath set in the first instance is entirely distinct from *what* he hath set in the second.

He sets entirely different things; but the sovereign operation, the divine initiative, the power of God in his work of 'setting'— as such—is the same: that is, the same work of God, twice put forth, inaugurates two different effects.

However the repetition of verse 18 in verse 28 is worded in such a way that we cannot fail to grasp this vital distinction:

Openings in First Corinthians

The same kind of operation of God actually respects two entirely different things. That is why in the first case 'God hath set' the members in the body; and in the second, that 'God hath set' certain chosen persons in the *ecclesia*.

So that what God hath set in the body at Corinth *is another thing altogether* than that which God hath set in the *ecclesia* at large.

From which it follows that there are two quite distinct realms of divine operation, and that there are two entirely different classes of gifts.

'God hath set some in the church'—or, rather, I repeat, 'hath set certain in the *ecclesia*'—'first apostles, secondarily prophets, thirdly teachers.' 'After that' it is another question altogether, the exposition of which must be deferred until it is clearly understood what is meant by 'certain in the *ecclesia*'.

First apostles. In fact, these gifts—for the eleven, together with Paul, the twelfth, are *themselves* the gifts—*preceded* the church, or the *ecclesia*. They were chosen, called, prepared, and sent *in order to bring in the church or ecclesia*.

That choice, calling, preparation, and sending were all things completed *before* they began preaching, in consequence of which those saved were thus constituted God's assembly on earth.

So it was when the apostles continued to preach and teach the word of life: 'the Lord added to the church daily such as should be saved.' But, like Paul with the Gentiles, *their apostleship preceded the raising up of the ecclesia*.

Then what comparison can *these*—whose persons *are* the gift—I say, what comparison can these have with the *charismata*? Obviously, they are *another kind of gift altogether*.

They are not members of the body to whom a gift—*charisma*—has been given. They are *themselves* the gift sent before either *ecclesia* or body were called into existence under their ministry.

Then what of 'secondarily prophets, thirdly teachers'? These are gifts in themselves sent to labour under the apostles, either to accompany them, or to establish and extend their work together with them. No wonder a different word is used for such gifts as these, whether apostles, prophets, or teachers.

Paul here refers to the *domata*, first of all the twelve apostolic eyewitnesses, then, in due order, certain others, all alike being regarded as having been sent from the Lord in glory, to call out, increase, and establish the *ecclesia* of God, the body of Christ. Only *after* that, come gifts in the body, namely, the *charismata*.

The 'some' or 'certain', verse 28—individually *doma*, collectively *domata*—are gifts personified: they have an office in virtue of their persons. Their persons *are* the gifts, and that described in terms of their office: first apostles, secondarily prophets, thirdly teachers.

But the members of the body have not an office: *they* are given a gift. Such gifts, *charismata*, are given to their persons, as members of the body. *They* are not the gifts; these gifts of the Spirit are given to *them*. These gifts are things given to persons, namely, to the members of the body of Christ.

Hence, of God, by the Spirit, *charismata* are things persons are enabled to do; what they are gifted to do, as members of the one body of Christ.

The *domata*, however, are *the persons* sent by Christ to raise up the church, or *ecclesia*, before as yet it had existence; or else to establish and extend it, once called into being by the apostolic ministry.

Hence, considering the *ecclesia* either in a view of its being called into existence, or as having been gathered by the saving truth of the evangel, *the actual persons* used of God, sent of Christ, and anointed by the Spirit to do this work, are themselves the gifts, that is, the *domata*. They are the gift of Christ to the *ecclesia* as a whole, hence it is said, 'God hath set certain in the *ecclesia*, first apostles, secondarily prophets, thirdly teachers.'

The apostle continues, 'After that'. After what? After *those* unique, distinct gifts *of chosen persons*, there are other gifts–not sent to the *ecclesia* at large, but still *in* it: for, to the Corinthians, the body and the *ecclesia*, and the *ecclesia* and the body, were both identified at Corinth–other gifts that is, given to every one of the members of the body of Christ, here considered as the assembled Corinthian saints.

These gifts were the *charismata*, of which Paul–having indicated three distinct *doma*–now–'*after this*'–lists five *charisma*, namely powers; gifts of healing; helps; governments; and diversities of tongues.

Note that of these *charismata*, verse 28, the apostle adds two which were omitted in the previous list of nine mentioned in I Corinthians 12:8-10.

What is the difference between *charismata* and *domata*?

Charismata are gifts given *in* the body; *domata* are gifts given *to* the body. *Charismata* are raised up by the Spirit below; *domata* are sent down from Christ above. *Charismata* are gifts given to every member of the body; *domata* are persons given to edify the whole body.

Charismata function in the manifestation of the body in a given place. *Domata* minister to each manifestation of the body in every place. *Charismata* are gifts of the Spirit raised up *in* the body on earth; *domata* are ministers of Christ sent down from heaven *to* the body on earth.

But quite rightly the question will be pressed, since *charisma* and *doma* have alike been translated 'gift' in English, What is the difference in the Greek? Where is the distinction between the two Greek words?

There is a distinction, and I will indicate it; but, first, it must be said that the distinction is a subtle one. So much so that what matters most is not the difference in meaning between the two Greek words, *but that to which the apostle reserves the use of each one respectively, either to the gifts of the Spirit on earth on the one hand, or those of the Son of God from heaven on the other.*

The first of these two Greek words is set apart to indicate the gifts of the Spirit raised up on earth and bestowed upon all the members of the body of Christ in any given place. The second Greek word is retained in order to describe the gifts sent down from heaven by Christ ascended into the glory: gifts, that is, limited to those ministers whom he himself chooses, calls, prepares, and sends.

Sends? Yes, sends from the glory of heaven, for the perfecting of the saints, for the work of the ministry, and for the edifying of the body of Christ in every place, and throughout the age, commencing with the unique foundation of the twelve apostles.

Both *domata* and *charismata* belong – respectively – to large families of words having several branches, each family possessing its own distinct root.

This becomes apparently complicated not only by a similarity of use between the two families, but in some branches by a cross usage resulting in duplication when describing one and the same thing.

Then, in certain cases, whilst there may be a distinction in wording, the fact that certain of these words are used alternately for the same purpose gives the appearance of a distinction without a difference.

Not so, however, with the use of that particular branch—springing from the root—indicated by the word *domata*; nor yet with the analogous *charismata*, developed in turn from its own distinctive origins.

Here, clearly and precisely, there is a consistent difference between that which is reserved for the gifts of Christ *to* the body, and that set apart to describe the gifts of the Spirit *in* the body.

Entire sects have been formed over—what was in fact—the misapplication of the one to the exclusion of the other.

For example, inciting every person, irrespective of the Spirit, to attempt that for which not one was gifted—*the meanwhile quite dismissing the office of minister, as indicated by the word domata*—the Brethren suppose themselves to be 'scriptural', on the basis of their ignorant assumptions from I Corinthians 12:7-27 and 14:26-35; likewise Romans 12:4-8.

Here is nothing other than sheer—indeed, breath-taking—presumption concerning *charismata*, whilst remaining contemptuously dismissive of *domata*. If *this* is not ignorance concerning spiritual—not to say doctrinal and experimental—things, What is?

On the other hand there exist the various priestly, clerical, and pastoral systems, in which one salaried person, 'ordained' by a particular party to take pre-eminence over everyone else—however gifted—on no basis other than honour received from the respective ministerial education scheme peculiar to his—or her!—given sect or denomination.

Yet these diverse parties vehemently agree as one man to presume to justify this gross aberration on the ground of their misapplication—or *is* it *merely* misapplication?—of the word *domata*, quite blotting out the very memory of the existence of the truth of the *charismata*.

However, to return to the question of the precise meaning of the two words, it is certainly true that this calls for a fine distinction. It is equally true, however, that the greater significance lies in the restraint of the Spirit in each particular context, as a result of which the words *charismata* and *domata* are reserved to indicate the gifts of the Spirit in the body on earth, or the gifts of Christ from the glory, respectively.

As to the actual distinction between the two Greek words in and of themselves, *Charisma* is a gift which points to the disposition of the giver. It *is* a gift, but one which *as such* reflects the benevolent character and bounteous nature of the *giver*.

On the other hand *Doma* emphasizes the gift *itself*. *What* it is that is given. The gift is free, unmerited, and unsought. It is at once generous and magnanimous. The Greek word indicates a gratuitous present.

Although neither the singular *doma* nor the plural *domata* appear in the text of I Corinthians 12, nevertheless what the word describes – and for which it is duly reserved – *does* appear, and it is this that should be observed as of the greater significance.

Then where does that which *domata* describes appear? In the verse in question: 'God hath set certain in the *ecclesia*, first apostles, secondarily prophets, thirdly teachers', I Corinthians 12:28.

Nevertheless, the *burden* of the apostle in First Corinthians lies in his describing the *charismata*, not in indicating the *domata*. That is why – of all the epistles – this truth occupies so large a part, unmatched elsewhere in the new testament, although it is true that Romans 12:4-8 contributes considerably to the revelation of the mind of the Spirit concerning such charismatic gifts.

Just so, the revelation of the *domata* appears to be concentrated in one book in particular, namely, the Epistle to the

Ephesians. Nevertheless, as with *charismata* and the Romans, likewise the four evangelists—Matthew, Mark, Luke, and John—together with the Pastoral Epistles, contribute greatly to what is revealed concerning the *domata*.

And this is not to mention the Acts of the Apostles—of the *apostles*, note—and other places in which what is sent down and given from the Son of God in heaven—despite that the Greek word itself may not actually appear in the text—*show* the wonderful kindness and work of the Lord from the glory in sending those rare and choice gifts, his own sent ministers.

(iv) Christ's descent; ascent; and the Gifts

The apostle points clearly and definitively to the δόματα, *domata*, in Ephesians 4:8; 'Wherefore he saith, When he ascended up on high, he led captivity captive, and gave gifts unto men.' These gifts are the *domata*: 'first apostles, secondarily prophets, thirdly teachers', I Corinthians 12:28, compare Ephesians 4:11.

The immediate context of Ephesians 4:8 may seem to present difficulties to the reader, but in fact it greatly supports the truth which the apostle is about to open. 'But unto every one of us is given grace according to the measure of the gift of Christ', Ephesians 4:7. As in the case of Ephesians 3:7, this verse utilises the related Greek word δωρεά, *dōrea*.

Complexities arise from the assumption that 'every one of us', Ephesians 4:7, refers to all saints. It does not. It refers to the *domata*, those chosen out from all saints to be the ministers of Christ to them. Were the pronouns in this context to be observed, all difficulties would be resolved. Then the verse would appear to substantiate, not vitiate, Ephesians 4:8.

The apostle spoke of 'I' as opposed to 'you', verse 1. He had spoken of 'the body'; of 'ye'; of 'your'; verse 4. Again, he referred to 'all', namely, 'in *you* all', verse 6. *Then* he said 'But'. That is, *in contrast*, verse 7, '*But* unto every one of *us*.' Us? Us in contrast with whom? With you. 'But every one of *us*', verse 7, in contrast with '*you* all', verse 6.

If not, why change the pronouns? If not, why contrast the verses? If not, why does the apostle limit the measure of 'the gift of Christ' to the *domata*, verse 7, as opposed to his having expanded 'the gifts of the Spirit' to the whole body, verse 4?

If not, why does the apostle proceed immediately to extend verse 7 with the 'Wherefore' of verse 8, which, without question, speaks of the *domata* sent in the gift of Christ *to* all saints, that is, *to* the body?

It follows, it must follow, verse 7 is *inclusive* of every one of the *domata*, whatever the respective measure of the gift of Christ–ascended–in each. Whence it is evident that verse 7 must be *exclusive* of the body and its members, to whom and for whom each *doma* is sent 'for the perfecting of the saints, for the work of the ministry, for the edifying of the body of Christ', verse 12, so long as Christ reigns on high, and the saints exist below.

'Wherefore he saith', verse 8. Wherefore? But this word means 'On account of which, or, on which account.' That is, *on account of the preceding verse*, 'he saith'. Namely, *because of what had just been stated in verse 7, it follows*, 'When he ascended up on high, he led captivity captive, and gave gifts'–δόματα, *domata*–'unto men', Ephesians 4:8.

'Wherefore' following on *so as to elucidate verse 7, in which the gift of Christ was given to every one of 'us'*, the apostle explains the nature of the gift of Christ given unto every one of us, and none other, namely, the gift–or rather, the gifts–of the ascended Son of God from the excellent glory of heaven. Then, indubitably, the *domata*.

So the text reads; so the word *domata* demonstrates; so the context demands; and so both grammar and logic require in the conjunction of verses 7 and 8 beyond a peradventure. *Ergo*, verse 7 *must* refer to the *domata* and to the *domata* alone. *Quod erat demonstrandum.*

'Wherefore he saith, When he ascended up on high, he led captivity captive, and gave gifts unto men', Ephesians 4:8. This verse is a remarkable quotation from Psalm 68, which in itself speaks of entirely different events and occurrences in Israel, and, at that, in strange, mysterious, and apparently disconnected utterances, which, put together, make the psalm hard of interpretation.

From one such apparently random and arbitrary statement, abruptly the following words are uttered: 'Thou hast ascended on high, thou hast led captivity captive: thou hast received gifts for men; yea, for the rebellious also, that the Lord God might dwell among them', Psalm 68:18.

This is the verse quoted by Paul in Ephesians 4:8. It is the more remarkable that the psalmist does not appear to address – or even to be speaking of – Christ, and that even the events poetically portrayed concerning the history of Israel are at once disjointed and highly mystical in utterance throughout the context. Nevertheless, the apostle plucks out this verse and applies it to the ascension, further to his expounding the nature of the *domata*.

Without such an application by the apostle, it is impossible that anyone should have brought so obscure a verse to bear on the *domata*. However, by the inspiration of the Spirit, Paul not only does so, but moreover brings Ephesians 4:7 right into his exposition of the gifts of Christ *by this very quotation*, witness the introductory words, '*Wherefore he saith*, When he ascended up on high'; *then* follows the reference to Psalm 68:18.

Indeed, the psalms *do* speak of the ascension, albeit in a mystery. For example, 'The Lord said unto my Lord, Sit thou at my right hand, until I make thine enemies thy footstool', Psalm 110:1. This is quoted by Peter on the day of Pentecost, not now of the resurrection, of which David prophesied, and the apostles were witnesses, but of the ascension itself, in which the Son was exalted to the right hand of the Father, there to reign till his foes should be made his footstool, Acts 2:33-35.

Likewise the following Psalm: 'God is gone up with a shout, the LORD with the sound of a trumpet. Sing praises to God, sing praises: sing praises unto our King, sing praises. For God is the King of all the earth: sing ye praises with understanding. God reigneth over the heathen: God sitteth upon the throne of his holiness', Psalm 47:5-8.

Again, prophetically viewing Christ in the ascension the psalmist declares, 'For thou, LORD, art high above all the earth: thou art exalted far above all gods', Psalm 97:9. And this David echoes in Psalm 68:18, 'Thou hast ascended on high, thou hast led captivity captive.'

I do not intend to enlarge upon the mysteries of Psalm 68 as a whole, nor is this necessary. Suffice it to say with Peter that 'the prophets enquired and searched diligently, who prophesied of the grace that should come unto you: searching what, or what manner of time the Spirit of Christ which was in them did signify, when it testified beforehand the sufferings of Christ, and the glory that should follow.

'Unto whom it was revealed, that not unto themselves, but unto us they did minister the things, which are now reported unto you by them that have preached the gospel unto you with the Holy Ghost sent down from heaven; which things the angels desire to look into', I Peter 1:10-12. Of these things, Psalm 68:18, provides a choice example.

Because of the obvious difficulties in understanding the sequence of utterance in Psalm 68, whilst I have no intention of opening the psalm in its entirety, I will drop a few hints for the benefit of the reader concerning the context of verse 18.

The context is that of God arising and triumphing over his enemies on behalf of his people. He takes up the poor and despised, the captive outcasts of Israel in the distant lands of their bondage. He takes captivity captive. He calls his inheritance together. He leads them through the wilderness. He magnifies his glory at Sinai in the presence of all the people.

God arose, and his enemies were scattered. Pharaoh and his host perished in the Red sea. This victory, God's deliverances, made the earth to tremble, as he marched through the wilderness. The report thereof declared his goodness for the poor. This word was published by a great company. It was *God's* salvation.

From the land of their captivity, through the wilderness, God marched with his people, the land of their inheritance before their faces. The kings of Canaan fled apace. Zion was his choice. The mountains of Canaan trembled. The inhabitants of the land melted before the mighty power of God, his chariots, and his angels.

For his people got not the land in possession by their own sword, neither did their own arm save them: but thy right hand, and thine arm, and the light of thy countenance, because thou hadst a favour unto them. From the land of Egypt, Canaan was his objective, Zion his choice. This was the mountain of his inheritance.

As to the Canaanites, those who held the land in captivity, together with those whose stronghold was mount Zion, who held mount Zion captive, God scattered them all. The LORD arose to possess his holy mountain, he took mount Zion, that is, he ascended up on high, he led captivity captive. Here he chose to dwell. He would dwell among men, moreover giving gifts to the rebellious.

This made the earth to shake, the hills to leap. For the hill of God is as the hill of Bashan: an high hill as the hill of Bashan. Why leap ye, ye high hills? Zion is the hill which God desireth to dwell in; yea, the LORD will dwell in it for ever.

Thou hast ascended on high, thou hast led captivity captive: thou hast received gifts for men; yea, for the rebellious also, that the LORD God might dwell among them, Psalm 68:18.

But this ascent—as appears in Ephesians 4:8—has a double meaning. That which was true in Israel was but a figure, a type, a shadow of good things to come, the substance of which should appear in the gospel of Christ. For, speaking through the first, initial, and outward circumstances, the Spirit declares of Christ in prophecy through the psalmist, speaking across the ages to the Son of God, '*Thou* hast ascended on high', Psalm 68:18.

'Wherefore he saith, When he ascended up on high, he led captivity captive, and gave gifts unto men', Ephesians 4:8. But this is not carnal: it is spiritual. It is not the earthly shadow: it is the heavenly reality.

Here is no mere ascent of a literal earthly mount in the land: here is the ascension into the heights of heaven by the victorious Son of God, in which he brings many sons to glory, whilst all his foes are made his footstool. This is called, 'leading captivity captive', and, in consequence, from the glory, 'giving gifts'— *domata*—'unto men.'

However, the heights of the ascension can only be measured correctly from the point at which all commenced. This was not the grave. Much less was it from the earth after the resurrection. The point from which the Spirit measures the ascent of Christ is lower by far than both the earth and the grave.

This the apostle reveals in the following verses: 'Now that he ascended, what is it but that he also descended first into the lower parts of the earth? He that descended is the same also that ascended up far above all heavens, that he might fill all things', Ephesians 4:9,10.

Where the emphasis *first* is upon the *descent* of the Son of God. Because *that first* is the measure of the ascension. The height of his ascent is measured from the depth of his descent. And that descent is said to be 'into the lower parts of the earth', Ephesians 4:9.

In one sense the descent began from the deity and above all heavens. 'In the beginning was the Word, and the Word was with God, and the Word was God', John 1:1. 'And the Word was made flesh', John 1:14. Likewise, he 'being in the form of God, thought it not robbery to be equal with God: but made himself of no reputation, and took upon him the form of a servant, and was made in the likeness of men', Philippians 2:6,7.

These passages speak of the descent of the deity, in the person of the Son, at the incarnation. So that 'God was manifest in the flesh', I Timothy 3:16. This declares the deity incarnate, and, if so, predicates a descent that staggers the imagination. Nevertheless, it is not the descent emphasized in Ephesians 4:9.

Ephesians 4:9 *presumes* both incarnation and crucifixion. But in fact the verse *commences* by stressing the depth of his descent *after burial. Then* he descended 'into the lower parts of the earth.' This brings one to the threshold of a vital part of the evangel that is virtually universally ignored, if not downright contradicted. But it is the evangel. It is the doctrine of Christ. It *cannot* be ignored, much less contradicted, if one holds to the faith.

It is vital to perceive that Ephesians 4:9–and many other verses elsewhere–speak of what Christ did in the Spirit *whilst* his body lay dead in the tomb.

When the verse says 'he also descended first into the lower parts of the earth' it is impossible to suppose that this refers to his *body* being put in the sepulchre, which, in fact, was hewn out of rock *above the surface* of the earth, witness the stone rolled away from the mouth of the empty grave into which the first witnesses *walked*.

Besides, 'the lower parts of the earth' is synonymous with Revelation 5:3,13, where a distinction is made between 'in earth' or 'on earth' and 'under the earth', a metaphor for the underworld, just as is the expression 'the lower parts of the earth', Ephesians 4:9.

Moreover the depth of his descent 'into the lower parts of the earth', verse 9, is set in contrast with the height of his ascent 'far above all heavens', verse 10.

Where, if he has ascended up far above all that is visible or even imaginable over and above the heavens themselves, then it follows—since the descent and ascent are put in juxtaposition—that he first descended far below all that is visible or even imaginable beneath the depths of the earth or the burial places of the dead, namely, 'into the lower parts of the earth', or, the underworld.

David also speaks of a distinction *after* the death and burial of Christ, but *before* his resurrection, saying, 'Thou wilt not *leave* my *soul* in hell'—Hebrew, *sheol*, the underworld—'neither wilt thou suffer thine Holy One to *see* corruption'—that is, of the *body*, Psalm 16:10.

The apostle Peter, speaking by the Holy Ghost, interprets this prophecy on the day of Pentecost quoting David exactly, saying 'Thou wilt not leave my soul in hell, neither wilt thou suffer thine Holy One to see corruption', Acts 2:27.

Peter discerns this quotation from David, declaring that 'he seeing this before spake of the resurrection of Christ'—and, if so, of the period *after* his death but *before* his resurrection—'that his *soul* was not *left* in hell'—Greek, *hadēs*, the equivalent of *sheol*, the underworld—'neither his *flesh* did see corruption', Acts 2:30,31. This makes a clear distinction between the *soul* of Christ, after death, in respect of the underworld, and the *flesh* of Christ, after death, lying in the grave.

Paul confirms this truth in another way, asking a hypothetical question, as if in the place of those in doubt, 'Who shall descend into the deep? (that is, to bring up Christ again from the dead)', Romans 10:7. But Faith cries in triumph, There is no need; God hath raised him from the dead.

Nevertheless, to be valid, the rhetorical question *must assume the truth that after death Christ was in the deep*. If so, his *soul* descended into the deep. Now 'deep' here translates the Greek *abussos*, which answers to 'the abyss', another expression indicating the underworld. Then, into that, namely, 'the lower parts of the earth', or *sheol*, or else *hadēs*, his soul descended.

As to *what occurred* during the period between this descent of his soul, whilst his body lay dead in the sepulchre, and the time when he—that is, in his body—was raised from the dead by the glory of the Father, this is taught with perfect clarity in a passage so central to the evangel and to the mystery of the faith, that Paul states concerning this vital revelation: 'And without controversy great is the mystery of godliness', I Timothy 3:16.

The apostle continues, 'God was manifest in the flesh, justified in the Spirit, seen of angels, preached unto the Gentiles'—the Greek is *ethnos*, properly, Nations; that is, ethnic diversities— 'believed on in the world, received up into glory.' This completes the verse, I Timothy 3:16.

This verse utterly confounds both clergy and commentators, and, above all, wholly puzzles the theologians, not to mention equally self-conceited and know-all Brethren: but why? Elementary, my dear reader. Why? *because they know nothing about the great* mystery of godliness, being at once proud, dead, unspiritual, unexperimental, and lost in the dark mists of their disobedient inventions in place of the divine and heavenly mystery of the faith once delivered to the saints.

Hence, whilst to the simplest child it is obvious that I Timothy 3:16 consists of a series of six *consecutive* statements, because these supposedly mature know-alls cannot explain them in sequence, yet being too proud to confess their ignorance, they pretend – against even their own better judgment–that the statements are *random*, having no sequence at all! But if this is not God blinding their eyes, What is?

The verse commences, '*God was manifest in the flesh*'. This was the very first beginning of the descent, as has been demonstrated. The verse concludes, '*received up into glory*'. That was the uttermost end of the ascent, as has been clearly shown from the like contrast between descent and ascent in Ephesians 4:9,10.

Then how in heaven, on earth, or under the earth, can the four statements bracketed between his *descent* and his *ascent*, not on the one hand be *consequential*, and on the other, not refer to what happened in sequence between his descent and his ascent?

And, since these people think to evade the exposure of their incompetence by railing at me that I ought not to judge them– but it is Christ in me who judges them – in passing let me ask these haughty pretenders who *say* that they know what the verse means, Why no crucifixion? Why no death? Why no mention of the resurrection?

Come now: you know everything; I am nothing but a judge: then I invite you to show your knowledge, and confound my judgment. You say that you are of God, and that I cannot be, because I judge. Come now; if you are of God. Then tell us the meaning. But all we get from you is deafening silence: 'And the people answered him not a word', I Kings 18:21.

Of course they answered him not a word, any more than these answer me not a word, because God never put a word in their mouths, who go about as if they know everything; whereas he fills my mouth with his words, though of myself I know nothing.

This is the great mystery of *godliness*. Because God was manifested in the flesh. Every statement concerns the descent of the deity, and finally, the ascent into glory. If of the deity, even in such a context of being manifest in the flesh, one can never speak of death: only of what God did. He was manifested in the flesh, and, as to *that*, he was justified in the Spirit.

That is, *everything he came to achieve as becoming manifest in the flesh, had been achieved, and achieved with triumph*. He was wholly vindicated and justified in his having been made manifest in the flesh. But, first—mark that, *first*—that justification was *in the Spirit*. Not in the flesh in which he had been manifest from the first.

Nevertheless, because he *was* justified, this means that he had *finished the work which he came to do*. The Spirit justified this, and verified it by a sevenfold witness, *immediately victory had been won*. Now, as to the flesh, that means *after the cross, and following the burial*.

But these statements concern God; they concern *the deity*. Then, not the flesh in which he was manifested, but he who was manifested in that flesh, is now traced from descent to ascent, in all that is most critical of his divine pathway. At this point, *everything accomplished for ever*, immediately, but *immediately*, he was justified in the Spirit.

Then—and not till then—*then* he was 'seen of angels'. So that this could not refer to those angels who had seen him at and following the incarnation, or during the period of his being manifest in 'the days of his flesh'. This must refer to those angels *who had not seen him thus*, who, following the justification of all his work on earth, *in the Spirit saw him now*.

Why? I will tell you why. Because having wrought everlasting victory to perfection, justified in the Spirit, in that same Spirit *he went down and proclaimed the same to these spirits here called angels*. Proclaimed, yes; and no more. *They* were left in everlasting chains, under darkness, unto the judgment of the great day. These were the angels that sinned, II Peter 2:4.

Next, *after* this – for the angels, being greater in power and might, were to see – and hear the proclamation – first. These were the angels that sinned, and caused to sin, in the days of Noah. But the sinning nations, carried away in the flood with the destruction of the old world, came next in order.

To these the tremendous voice of Almighty God echoed and re-echoed in the depths of the underworld as it proclaimed – the Greek is *kērussō*, to proclaim; to announce; or to herald – the vindication of Noah, and of the election of God, *seen* in his having been justified in the Spirit. And, by the Spirit, he made the proclamation.

What a justification this was! How great, you shall know when you behold with your eyes the whole of time from the beginning unfold – and, as it were, unreel – before your astounded vision in the last, the great day of judgment.

As to the souls of those wicked nations which perished in the flood, called the old world, following this proclamation, their doom sealed, these await with anguish and trembling the resurrection of the unjust, and the sentence of everlasting punishment in the great day of God. *They* know it: do *you* know it?

Immediately following, the ascent begins. First, from angels and men in the underworld, to whom had been thundered out the tremendous vindication of God from the beginning of time up to the overwhelming victory of the cross. A victory achieved, that is, *before* the descent. And now, from the deep ascending up to the face of the earth, he is *'believed on in the world'*.

God, who was manifested in the flesh, justified in the Spirit, seen of angels, proclaimed unto the nations, is now 'believed on in the world'. That is, he is risen. Then what can they say who are his, but, falling on their face, cry out 'My Lord *and my God*', John 20:28. Now, *these* believed on him in the world.

So the eyewitnesses affirmed, saying, 'That which was from the beginning, which we have heard, which we have seen with our eyes, which we have looked upon, and our hands have handled, of the Word of life; for the *life was manifested*, and we have seen it, and bear witness, and show unto you *that eternal life*', I John 1:1,2.

What is this but that *God* was manifested in the flesh, justified in the Spirit, seen of angels, proclaimed unto the nations, and now–*as God*–believed on in the world. But God in three persons:

'We have *seen*, and show unto you *that eternal life*, which *was* with the Father'–before being manifest in the flesh–'and was manifested unto *us*.' Supremely manifested, that is, as victorious over all, when, on earth, risen from the dead, one with the Father and with the Spirit, he was seen for forty days. If so, 'believed on in the world'.

First by the eyewitnesses: 'Him God raised up the third day, and showed him openly; not to all the people, but unto witnesses chosen before of God, even to us, who did eat and drink with him after he rose from the dead', Acts 10:40,41. This is to be 'believed on in the world', that is, following his prior descent into the lower parts of the earth, yet before his being received up into glory.

'He rose again the third day according to the scriptures: and that he was seen of Cephas, then of the twelve: after that, he was seen of above five hundred brethren at once; of whom the greater part remain unto this present, but some are fallen asleep. After that, he was seen of James; then of all the apostles. And last of all he was seen of me also', I Corinthians 15:4-8. This is to be 'believed on in the world'.

'Until the day in which he was taken up, after that he through the Holy Ghost had given commandments unto the apostles whom he had chosen: to whom also he showed himself alive after his passion by many infallible proofs, being seen of them forty days', Acts 1:2,3. This is to be 'believed on in the world'.

Finally–yet not finally to perfection: finally in the great mystery of godliness revealed in six consequential statements in I Timothy 3:16–'received up into glory.' This is the height of the ascension, of which we cannot now speak particularly, since we have yet somewhat to add to the opening of the words, 'he also descended first into the lower parts of the earth', Ephesians 4:9.

The apostle Peter enlarges upon this essential evangelical truth of the great mystery of godliness, when, consonant with 'seen of angels' in I Timothy 3:16, he declares, 'God spared not the angels that sinned, but cast them down to'–it is not 'hell' at all; neither is it *hadēs*, nor yet the abyss: it is *tartarus*, the deepest depths–'delivered into chains of darkness, to be reserved unto judgment', II Peter 2:4.

Of these Peter wrote earlier, saying that Christ was 'put to death in the flesh, but quickened by the Spirit: by which also he went and'–it is not 'preached': it is *kērussō*, as in I Timothy 3:16– 'proclaimed unto the spirits'–not *souls* notice: *spirits*; that is, the angels that sinned.

For 'he maketh his angels spirits', Hebrews 1:7. Then, though fallen angels, still *spirits* – 'in prison; which sometime were disobedient, when once the longsuffering of God waited in the days of Noah', I Peter 3:19,20. This verifies the truth opened in I Timothy 3:16.

The book of Jude also confirms the truth of the fallen angels being confined in the deepest depths: 'And the angels which kept not their first estate, but left their own habitation, he hath reserved in everlasting chains under darkness unto the judgment of the great day', Jude 6.

To these, even though they were in the deepest depths, the proclamation reached, heralding the glorious triumph of God over all the age, every enemy, and, here in particular, over all the consequences of the disobedience of the angels whose sin brought about the judgment of the old world.

To such depths – the deepest depths – the proclamation of the victory – reaching throughout all ages and over all time – was sounded forth by him who descended into the lower parts of the earth.

The apostle Peter goes even further than the scope of I Timothy 3:16 in the following scripture: 'For this cause *was the gospel preached*' – this is *not* '*kērussō*', to make proclamation; it is *euaggelizomai, to preach the evangel* – 'also to them that are dead, that they might be judged according to men in the flesh, but live according to God in the spirit', I Peter 4:6.

Who were those dead whose life when in the flesh was judged? Who preached the gospel unto them? When did this take place? And what was the effect?

Those dead whose life in the flesh was judged were the old testament saints. The end of these, after death, was utterly different from that of sinners. Nevertheless, the souls of both went to the underworld, but their existence *there* was entirely separate. The saints were those 'carried by angels' into 'Abraham's bosom'. Sinners were those separated into a place of torment.

'And it came to pass, that the beggar died, and was carried by the angels into Abraham's bosom: the rich man also died, and was buried; and in *hadēs*'—it should not be 'hell': it is *hadēs*—'he lift up his eyes, being in torments, and seeth Abraham afar off, and Lazarus in his bosom', Luke 16:22,23. Then, they were not *so* far apart as not to be visible to each other.

Nor were they so distant that they could not communicate: 'But Abraham said, Son, remember that thou in thy lifetime receivedst thy good things, and likewise Lazarus evil things: but now he is comforted, and thou art tormented.

'And beside all this, between us and you there is a great gulf fixed: so that they which would pass from hence to you cannot; neither can they pass to us, that would come from thence', Luke 16:26. No doubt in this parable Jesus used metaphor. But what of that? It is metaphor used by the Lord to convey *the truth*.

That truth denoted the souls of men whose bodies had died being strictly divided into that seed reckoned as children of Abraham by faith, and those faithless sinners who were not counted for the seed. These were separated by 'a great gulf' but, in the parable, it was possible to communicate, at least by vision and speech, from one side to the other.

Hence the one *sheol*, or underworld, was divided on the one hand to the blessing of Abraham's bosom, and, across the impassable gulf, on the other hand to the torment of the curse. After death the souls of all the dead were irrevocably committed to the one or other.

That is, until God was manifested in the flesh, and justified in the Spirit. Namely, until Christ through death destroyed him that had the power of death, that is, the devil, and delivered them who through fear of death were all their lifetime subject to bondage, Hebrews 2:14,15.

That is, until Messiah finished the transgression, made an end of sins, made reconciliation for iniquity, and brought in everlasting righteousness, Daniel 9:24. Namely, until in death Christ accomplished redemption for all that by faith had looked for salvation from the coming Messiah since the beginning of the world until the cross, and for all that should ever believe on him after the cross till the end of the world.

That is, until in the fulness of his glorious accomplished victory, Christ descended in the Spirit to proclaim to the angelic spirits in prison and to the tormented souls of the nations in *hadēs* the triumph in which they had neither believed from prophecy, nor obeyed with foresight. For he 'was seen of angels, proclaimed unto the nations', when he 'descended into the lower parts of the earth.'

That is, until in his descent by the Spirit he 'preached the gospel to them that are dead' from righteous Abel to believing Noah, thence to every one who had died in the faith which Abraham had yet being uncircumcised, all resting in Abraham's bosom, till the mighty conqueror who had accomplished their redemption at last, preached the same in his descent thereafter.

This which he had just accomplished was that which they had believed would be fulfilled when he came. Thus he was the Lamb slain from the foundation of the world, believed upon by all who died in faith, looking to him and for him who should justify them by his blood at his coming. This he had done. And that he preaches to their believing souls.

This is called his 'preaching the gospel to them that are dead.' Though in Abraham's bosom, yet still both Abraham and all the great multitude of believing souls yearned for the fulfilment of all that in which they had trusted, for which they died in faith.

In their lifetime it had been evident that they were the righteous, or the just, for, 'the just shall live by faith'.

And now their faith was justified, for when Christ preached the gospel to these that were dead, behold, their lifetime—being judged according to the life of faith which they had lived in the days of their flesh—itself declared their belief and trust in the coming Messiah.

Thus they were judged according to men in the flesh, for that which they had believed afar off when they were alive in the world, was what they heard in the Spirit by the gospel now being preached unto them. That very gospel, yea, that same Jesus, albeit seen and heard dimly in their lifetime, was what they saw and heard so clearly in the gospel presently being preached unto them by their descended Redeemer.

That was what, and *he* was whom, they had believed in the days of their pilgrimage, and now, their redemption having been fully accomplished, their justification already having been wrought, they were in spirit to ascend with him to heavenly glory, 'the spirits of just men made perfect', Hebrews 12:23.

'The spirits of just men made perfect'? To whom else *can* this refer but to the old testament saints, and *all* the old testament saints, namely *every one* of those just men? 'Made perfect'? Yes, since the time that Christ preached the gospel to their awaiting souls in Abraham's bosom, carrying their—relative—captivity captive as he led them up to the perfection of heavenly glory.

That 'we are come' unto these, Hebrews 12:22, who are ourselves justified under the new testament, shows that—there being none other just men than these—these are the just who had died in faith under the old testament. They await us; we are come unto them; or, we are yet coming unto them.

Where are they now? Not in Abraham's bosom in the underworld as was once the case before Christ descended, but now in glory, for they first, then we, are 'come unto mount Sion, and unto the city of the living God, the *heavenly* Jerusalem, and to an innumerable company of'—holy—'*angels*'.

We are come 'to the general assembly and church of the firstborn, which are written *in heaven*, and *to God the Judge of all*, and *to the spirits of just men made perfect*, and *to Jesus* the mediator of *the new covenant*'—that stands in everlasting heavenly glory— 'and to the blood of sprinkling'—namely, *on the propitiatory before the Majesty on high*, Hebrews 12:22-24.

Of this victory of the cross, a certain witness—among others— was borne immediately: 'Jesus, when he had cried again with a loud voice, yielded up the ghost. And, behold, the veil of the temple was rent in twain from the top to the bottom; and the earth did quake, and the rocks rent;

'*And the graves were opened; and many bodies of the saints which slept arose*, and came out of the graves *after* his resurrection, and went into the holy city, and appeared unto many', Matthew 27:50-53. Here is a witness indeed. The souls of *all* were delivered. But the bodies of *some* were a sign.

The Lord's ascent in victory, triumphing over all by the cross, bringing to glory every single saint who had ever believed upon him, all the just who had lived by faith, and who had died in faith, whose souls had patiently waited in Abraham's bosom: What is this? It is called 'leading captivity captive', Ephesians 4:8.

As to the glorious heavenly height to which the whole of this erstwhile captivity was led, this is the inheritance, Colossians 1:12, of those who now 'live according to God in the spirit', I Peter 4:6.

This Christ achieved by his death for all the old testament saints *after* he descended, and *when* he had ascended: 'Wherefore he saith, When he ascended up on high, he led captivity captive, and gave gifts unto men.'

'Now that he *ascended*'—leading so great a multitude of once captive souls, who had awaited his redemption by faith—'what is it but that *he also descended first'*–descended first? But descended where?–'into the lower parts of the earth', Ephesians 4:8,9.

Hence it is that when *we* die after the flesh, our souls immediately ascend to be with the Lord. Thus John in vision sees all the elect–signified by the twelve patriarchs and the twelve apostles–in the twenty-four elders on thrones about the throne of God and of the Lamb.

Whence it follows that–unlike the old testament saints who waited–we who are in and of the new testament, falling asleep, are carried in our souls immediately into the heavenly glory, thence to 'be ever with the Lord'.

'He that descended is the same also that ascended up far above all heavens, that he might fill all things', Ephesians 4:10. Here two things immediately impress the reader. First, *this was a verified, witnessed, attested historical event.* It happened, and it was seen to have happened.

Second, over and above the basic *fact* of the historical event, what was *not* seen by the eyewitnesses was *the height to which the ascension reached.* It passed from view when the eye could see no more. Then, it entered into dimensions beyond human capacity to comprehend. It passed all understanding, because it lay beyond man's faculties to grasp.

But faith believes and grasps the doctrine that sets forth the ascension, fully acknowledging that the bodily ascent of Christ 'above all heavens' lies utterly beyond man's natural ability even to imagine. Then don't imagine it.

Simply receive the truth and believe it. And know this: you will surely find it so in the end, at the coming again–and descent–of Christ. Blessed are they that have not seen, and yet have believed, John 20:29. This refers to the resurrection of his body. Then how much more of his ascension?

And so Peter tells you: 'Whom having not seen, ye love; in whom, though now ye see him not, yet believing, ye rejoice with joy unspeakable and full of glory: receiving the end of your faith, even the salvation of your souls', I Peter 1:8,9.

Thus Paul cautions us against the carnal mind and natural intellect, assuring us that his apostolic warfare was against such things, 'Casting down imaginations, and every high thing that exalteth itself against the knowledge of God, and bringing into captivity every thought to the obedience of Christ', II Corinthians 10:5.

Wherefore? Because nothing is more destructive of faith than human reasoning. Which is not surprising, since 'To be carnally minded is death.' Worse: it is death unnaturally animated by implacable hostility: 'because the carnal mind is enmity against God', Romans 8:7. Why? Because it is fallen. It is earthly, sensual, and devilish, James 3:15. It cannot believe, it will not believe, and it is enmity against belief: 'For whatsoever is not of faith is sin', Romans 14:23.

Then it is by faith that, believing ourselves risen again with Christ, we 'seek those things which are above, where Christ sitteth on the right hand of God.' Indeed, dead to reasonings, imaginings, worldly and unbelieving thoughts, the just live by faith: 'for ye are dead, and your life is hid with Christ in God', Colossians 3:1-3. This is to answer by faith to the revelation of the height of the ascension.

Mark tells of the eyewitnesses of the ascension: 'So then after the Lord had spoken unto them, he was received up into heaven, and sat on the right hand of God. And they'–the eleven–'went forth, and preached everywhere, the Lord working with them, and confirming the word with signs following. Amen', Mark 16:19,20.

John however records the words of Jesus himself to Mary Magdalene, after he was risen from the dead: the Lord declares the triumph of his death for his own – calling them 'my brethren' – even though he had not yet ascended to his Father. But he sends her with this message: 'Go to my brethren, and say unto them, I ascend unto my Father, and your Father; and to my God, and your God', John 20:17. This testifies to the height and to the glory of the ascension.

Luke bears record precisely of that which was seen by the eleven: 'And he led them out as far as to Bethany, and he lifted up his hands, and blessed them. And it came to pass, while he blessed them, he was parted from them, and carried up into heaven', Luke 24:50,51. So that their last view of him, as he ascended, was that of his nail-pierced hands lifted up together with his voice, blessing them indeed. And so it is to this day.

For their word was blessed to multitudes and generations, whether spoken or written, as he saith, 'But ye shall receive power, after that the Holy Ghost is come upon you: and ye' – the eleven – 'shall be witnesses unto me both in Jerusalem, and in all Judea, and in Samaria, and unto the uttermost part of the earth.

'And when he had spoken these things, *while they beheld*, he was taken up; and a cloud received him out of their sight. And while they looked steadfastly toward heaven as he went up, behold, two men stood by them in white apparel;

'Which also said, Ye men of Galilee, why stand ye gazing up into heaven? this same Jesus, which is taken up from you into heaven, shall so come in like manner as ye have seen him go into heaven', Acts 1:8-11.

When the Holy Ghost had been shed forth on the day of Pentecost, Peter, standing up with the eleven, bore witness first to the resurrection of Christ, then to his ascension, calling David to record: 'For David speaketh concerning him, I foresaw the Lord always before my face, for he is on my right hand, that I should not be moved:

'Therefore did my heart rejoice, and my tongue was glad; moreover also my flesh shall rest in hope: Because thou wilt not leave my soul in *hadēs*, neither wilt thou suffer thine Holy One to see corruption. Thou hast made known to me the ways of life; thou shalt make me full of joy with thy countenance.

'Men and brethren, let me freely speak unto you of the patriarch David, that he is both dead and buried, and his sepulchre is with us unto this day. Therefore being a prophet, and knowing that God had sworn with an oath to him, that of the fruit of his loins, according to the flesh, he would raise up Christ to sit on his throne;

'He seeing this before spake of the resurrection of Christ, that *his* soul was not left in *hadēs*, neither *his* flesh did see corruption. This Jesus hath God raised up, whereof we all are witnesses', Acts 2:25-32. This is both the prophecy and the *eyewitness account* of the resurrection of Jesus, 'Whom God hath raised up, having loosed the pains of death: because it was not possible that he should be holden of it', Acts 2:24.

The testimony to Christ's ascension—forty days after his resurrection—now follows: 'Therefore *being by the right hand of God exalted*, and having received of the Father the promise of the Holy Ghost, *he* hath shed forth this, which *ye* now see and hear.

'For *David* is not ascended into the heavens: but he saith himself, The LORD said unto *my* Lord, Sit *thou* on my right hand, until I make thy foes thy footstool. Therefore'—continues Peter—'let all the house of Israel know assuredly, that God hath made *that same Jesus*, whom ye have crucified, both Lord and Christ', Acts 2:33-36.

This concludes the *eyewitness*—as well as the *prophetic*—testimony to the *ascension* of the *risen* Lord.

David had uttered and written the prophecy which Peter quotes on the day of Pentecost *some one thousand years before*.

Openings in First Corinthians

Now, How can anyone reasonably doubt the resurrection and ascension, seeing such things were both spoken and recorded in close detail *even before the millennium preceding that in which these things took place?* And this is not to mention the *eyewitness* in the event.

How could this be, had not God revealed the future so long before on the one hand, and set aside all natural laws, bringing to light dimensions undreamed of and staggering all reason on the other hand? Yet, doing both so as *indisputable facts* irrefutably supported the supernatural mysteries *in both cases.*

If any desire a proof of the infallible inspiration of holy scripture, this provides it: just as much because of what was *foreseen in detail* a thousand years before it happened, as in the case that the same thing was *witnessed by impeccable eyewitnesses*—plural—a thousand years later. Then, beyond any shadow of doubt, let all men be advertised *that the ascension really took place, and that Christ really is on the right hand of God at this moment.*

Let no one overlook the truth that it is the factual evidence to the ascension of Christ that is presented in holy writ. Nothing less than *facts*, concerning first David, then the eleven, appear before the reader, in the light of time and eternity, of things first foreseen, then visibly outworked, next witnessed and verified, and finally passed into the heavens.

Thereafter, all being invisible, outside of human comprehension, and pertaining to dimensions beyond all faculties and senses to realize, it is a matter of what was revealed by inspiration of the Holy Ghost to the chosen apostles in the doctrine of Christ, and recorded in the epistles of the new testament.

What is revealed concerning the work of Christ in the ascension may differ from one epistle to another. For example, in Ephesians it is a question of Headship. In Hebrews, however, it is a matter of Priesthood. But since the present state of the enquiry concerns the ascension as such, whilst Headship is the ultimate question, the revelation from Hebrews regarding Priesthood is of no mean weight to establish the doctrine.

Consider: Concerning the Son it is revealed – revealed, mind: all this doctrine is spiritually *revealed* by the Holy Ghost *after* the Son had passed from the sight of the apostles into the heavens – 'When he had by himself purged our sins, *sat down on the right hand of the Majesty on high*', Hebrews 1:3.

Again: 'To which of the angels said he at any time, *Sit on my right hand, until I make thine enemies thy footstool?*', Hebrews 1:13. Or consider this: 'Thou crownedst him with glory and honour, and didst set him *over* the works of thy hands: Thou hast put all things *under his feet*', Hebrews 2:7,8.

Once more: 'Seeing then that we have a great high priest, *that is passed into the heavens*, Jesus the Son of God', Hebrews 4:14.

Likewise, 'Christ glorified not himself to be made an high priest; but he that said unto him, Thou art my Son, today have I begotten thee'–that is in the resurrection from the dead, Acts 13:33–'As he saith also in another place'– concerning the ascension, and following the resurrection, Acts 2:34, Psalm 110:1,2, and 4–'Thou art a priest for ever after the order of Melchisedec', Hebrews 5:5,6.

See now what *revelation* flows down from the glory: 'For such an high priest became us, who is holy, harmless, undefiled, separate from sinners, *and made higher than the heavens*', Hebrews 7:26. 'We have such an high priest, *who is set on the right hand of the throne of the Majesty in the heavens*', Hebrews 8:1.

'For if he were on earth'–even though risen from the dead, as he was those forty days – 'he should not be a priest, seeing that there are priests that offer gifts according to the law', Hebrews 8:4; 'But now hath he obtained *a more excellent ministry*'–that is, above all heavens, according to the evangel – Hebrews 8:6.

'But Christ being come an high priest of good things to come, by a greater and more perfect tabernacle, not made with hands, that is to say, not of this building; neither by the blood of goats and calves, *but by his own blood he entered in once into the holy place, having obtained eternal redemption for us*', Hebrews 9:11,12.

'For Christ is not entered into the holy places made with hands, which are the figures of the true; *but into heaven itself*, now to appear *in the presence of God* for us', Hebrews 9:24.

And let the weight of the following passage, delivered by inspiration of the Holy Ghost, concerning things unseen, sink down into the ears of him that hath ears to hear: 'But this man, after he had offered one sacrifice for sins for ever, *sat down on the right hand of God; from henceforth expecting till his enemies be made his footstool*', Hebrews 10:12,13.

Or this: 'Having therefore, brethren, boldness to enter into *the holiest* by the blood of Jesus, by a new and living way, which he hath consecrated for us, *through the veil, that is to say, his flesh*; and having *an high priest over the house of God*; let us *draw near* with a true *heart* in full assurance of faith', Hebrews 10:19-22.

How greatly, therefore, does the ascension inspire us to keep 'Looking unto Jesus the author and finisher of our faith; who for the joy that was set before him endured the cross, despising the shame, *and is set down at the right hand of the throne of God*', Hebrews 12:2.

Nevertheless it is not his ascension in order to occupy the office of Priesthood, as in Hebrews, but rather his ascending to fulfil the position of *Headship* that concerns the epistle to the Ephesians. And if of *Headship*, then to make manifest the mystery of the *Body*. And if of the *Body*, then of the heavenly gifts essential to bring in this same fellowship of the mystery.

Hence Paul stresses the exaltation of Christ even from so great a glory as that of his resurrection from the dead: 'and set him at his own right hand in the heavenly places, far above all principality, and power, and might, and dominion, and every name that is named, not only in this world, but also in that which is to come.'

Indeed, from such an ultimate descent, to such an absolute ascent, how can this his sovereign majesty over all be surprising? 'And hath put all things under his feet, and gave him to be the head over all things to the *ecclesia*, which is *his body*, the *fulness of him* that filleth all in all', Ephesians 1:20-23.

'Whereof', declares Paul, 'I was made a minister.' How was this? 'How that by revelation he made known unto me the mystery.' The mystery? Yes, of the unsearchable riches of Christ, 'to make all'– saints–'see what is the fellowship of the mystery', Ephesians 3:3,7-9.

Whereof he was made a minister? Oh? Who made him a minister? Evidently, Christ, from the excellent glory. For from thence came the voice from heaven, 'For I have appeared unto thee for this purpose, to make thee a minister', Acts 26:16.

How should Christ from above the heaven of heavens do this? He should do it by his divine and heavenly initiative in calling Paul to the office of minister, a unique *doma*, the gift of Christ from heaven.

'Whereof I was made a minister, according to the gift'–that is *dōrea*, a word closely related to *doma*–'the gift of the grace of God given unto me by the effectual working of his power', Ephesians 3:7. That was how it was done. That was how he was made a minister. *And I tell you of a truth, for all man's invented substitutes, there is no other way into the ministry, just as there can be no other 'ministers' entitled to the name*.

How *could* there be any other ministers, or any other way, when *the Son of God from heaven* sends the ministers he calls *domata*, and when the *effectual working of God's power* gives them–*dōrea*–the ability? Where is man in that? Where is the 'church' in that? Where are 'divinity schools' in that? There is *nothing* of any such things in that. The real thing is *all of God*.

By this means, Christ having ascended, the Holy Ghost having descended, the saints are brought into the fulness, and into the knowledge of the fulness. 'And hath put all things under his feet, and gave him to be the head over all things to the *ecclesia*, which is his body, the fulness of him that filleth all in all', Ephesians 1:22,23.

But first, he descended. 'He that descended is the same also that ascended up far above all heavens, *that he might fill all things*', Ephesians 4:10. Nothing in the deepest abyss below, nothing in the glory far above all heavens, but that he took it all in, and *that* in person, putting all things in their place relative to his victory, his authority, and his proclamation, 'that he might fill all things'.

Further to which–to affirm which–by the Holy Ghost from heaven, by the effectual working of God's power, by his sole sovereign initiative and authority, from far above all heavens *he ordained and does ordain every single one of the ministers whom he sends*.

'And he gave'–Ephesians 3:8; 4:7,8,11; *here is the root of the word domata*–'he gave some, apostles; and some, prophets; and some, evangelists; and some, pastors and teachers', Ephesians 4:11.

In a word *he gave* his own chosen, called, prepared, ordained, and sent *ministers; he gave their persons*; some to be this, some to be that, some to be the other, but all *given alike*–in a mystery–*from the ascension, far above all heavens*, and all as one called by the common name given to the ministers of Christ from the glory, namely, the *domata*, Ephesians 4:8,11.

It is of this that the apostle Paul speaks precisely when he declares, 'And God hath set some in the *ecclesia*, first apostles, secondarily prophets, thirdly teachers', I Corinthians 12:28.

In order to show the distinction between these heavenly gifts of Christ from his ascended glory, as opposed to the gifts of the Spirit descended to glorify Christ in the body on earth, the preceding doctrine has been opened.

So that the first, second, and third gifts mentioned in I Corinthians 12:28, respectively, indicate the *doma*, each in his proper rank, yet, as a whole, all having those distinctive features unique to the *domata*.

Whereas First Corinthians does not reveal the position of the *ecclesia* in relation to Christ in the ascension – but rather in terms of the Spirit during the time of pilgrimage on earth – Ephesians does: and hence it is from this epistle that the brief mention of the *domata* in I Corinthians 12:28 has been elucidated.

'After that' – continues the apostle – 'after that miracles' – that is, works of power – 'then gifts' – *charismata* – 'of healings, helps, governments, diversities of tongues', I Corinthians 12:28.

The most obvious distinction between 'apostles, prophets, teachers', and *after that* 'miracles, gifts of healings, helps, governments, diversities of tongues', I Corinthians 12:28, lies in the fact that the former – the *domata* – are *persons*, whereas the latter – the *charismata* – are not: they are *gifts given to persons*.

And yet in one sense – despite the disparity – there is a relation between the two. Indeed, the very words 'after that' seem to imply a certain potential inter-relationship between the *domata* and the *charismata*. And this is reinforced by the apostle with the words concerning the *charismata*, 'covet earnestly the *best* gifts', I Corinthians 12:31, in which brethren are encouraged to reach out to the highest in order that they might edify the most.

Coveting earnestly the best gifts may well lead to the Lord taking up in a far wider, heavenly, and divine way those whose excellence appeared in their charismatic ministry in the body of Christ where it had pleased God at the first to set them.

Timothy provides the perfect example of this. During Paul's first great apostolic circuit, he preached and taught the evangel for some time at Iconium, then Lystra, and also Derbe. On his return he confirmed the disciples in each city, exhorting them to continue in the faith, ordaining elders in each *ecclesia* with prayer and fasting.

Then, the brethren would have been graven upon his heart, and he would have observed the operation of God, the work of the Lord, and the ministration of the Spirit in each of the three congregations. If so, he would have rejoiced in the faith and background of Timothy, his mother Eunice, and his grandmother Lois. This young man was already marked out.

After a very considerable passage of time Paul returned, and, not to his surprise, found that in the interval Timothy 'was well reported of by the brethren', not only in the *ecclesia* in which he met, but likewise in the two congregations gathered in the adjoining cities. Here the brethren gave evidence of Timothy's 'making full proof of thy ministry'.

From that time forth Paul took him to be with him in his apostolic labours. This had been confirmed by prophecy—whether in the *ecclesia* at Iconium, Lystra, or Derbe—and by the laying on of Paul's hands, with the laying on of the hands of the presbytery. From then on a new field opened up to the young man whom Paul calls 'my dearly beloved son'.

But what was Timothy's ministry in terms of gift? First, in his own city, then, increasing, in the two adjoining assemblies, it was that of the exercise of his gift from the Spirit, nor was this ever to depart from him: it was but to increase in him.

Wherefore Paul exhorts, 'Neglect not the gift'–*charismatos*–'that is in thee', I Timothy 4:14. And again, 'Stir up the gift'–*charisma*–'of God, which is in thee', II Timothy 1:6. If so, Timothy began with the gift of the Spirit bestowed upon him in the body. In this he abounded and increased in his love for the brethren. And for this cause Paul took him to be with him.

How could one deny that as Paul's 'own son in the faith', with whom Paul associated himself in addressing the epistles to the *ecclesia*, Timothy, who was 'my workfellow', and 'fellowlabourer in the evangel of Christ', commanded to ordain overseers, servants, and elders, receiving the charge in the absence of the apostle, I say, Who could deny that after such faithful diligence, the gift–*doma*–of Christ did not rest upon 'brother Timothy'?

This progression, this elevation, this taking up the choice gifts, coupled with earnest zeal, of the Spirit and by the Lord, appears to the encouragement of all whose motive is nothing other than love. For this cause alone such 'covet earnestly the best gifts'. Thus, for example, prophecy, first a gift of the Spirit, transcends to become 'prophet', distinctly a gift from Christ.

Wherefore all are drawn in their measure to increase by the magnanimity of the Spirit, and by the gift of the grace of Christ, that love should find its fullest expression, unhindered and unlimited, from charity out of a pure heart, and a good conscience, and of faith unfeigned.

No wonder then, that Timothy is to 'do the work of an evangelist', II Timothy 4:5, a gift proper to the *domata*, Ephesians 4:11. Nothing but encouragement for faith; nothing but enlargement for love; and nothing but fulfilment in the 'perfecting of the saints, the work of the ministry, the edifying of the body of Christ', Ephesians 4:12.

Then, 'according as God hath dealt to every man the measure of faith', the saints are exhorted to increase in all humility and lowliness, each preferring the other in love, but every one encouraging the other to go on to perfection in fulness, for, 'Whosoever will, let him take the water of life freely'.

With the ascension of the Son above all heavens to the right hand of the Majesty on high, presenting the full accomplishment of his redemptive work, effectual from the beginning of the world till the last day of its dissolution, he received of the Father the promise of the Holy Ghost, which he shed forth abundantly on the day of Pentecost.

This brought in the body of Christ. In the light of the First Epistle to the Corinthians, the body is viewed as constituted by the Holy Ghost dwelling within the saints united in the faith in their pilgrimage here below. This position, however, is not that envisaged in Ephesians, where the body of Christ is seen as one with the Head in the heavenlies, and dead with Christ to all below. First Corinthians hardly views the saints in connection with the ascension as such: all the focus is upon the body on earth.

The analogy of this appeared in the tabernacle in the wilderness, in which the presence of God abode in the midst of Israel from just after their deliverance from Egypt until their entrance into the promised land. This was the testimony throughout their pilgrimage. In a figure, it was let down from heaven.

The tent of witness had no fixed abode on earth: it was moveable: it had no floor. The presence of God was passing through the wilderness with the pilgrim people of God, till they ascended into the promised land. Just so 'the testimony of Christ was confirmed in you', I Corinthians 1:6.

Had they fallen? Yes, but, 'God is faithful', I Corinthians 1:9, and the apostle labours for them in prayer and by letter. All things having been set in order on earth, therefore, according to the word of God and the nature of the testimony, finally the pilgrim *ecclesia* is caught up to the glory of heaven in I Corinthians 15.

Openings in First Corinthians

This is the glory that shines before the face—yea, and in the heart—of all those travelling in unity through the wilderness of this present world as pilgrims and strangers with their pathway set onwards toward Zion. It is this inshining glory that illuminates the body of Christ on earth.

Nevertheless God makes full provision for this pilgrimage of the *ecclesia*, the body of Christ, filled with the Holy Ghost on earth. For 'God hath set some in the *ecclesia*, first apostles, secondarily prophets, thirdly teachers, *after that* works of power, *charismata* of healings, helps, governments, diversities of tongues', I Corinthians 12:28.

Following on from the three classes of *persons* whom God hath set in the *ecclesia*, first apostles, secondarily prophets, thirdly teachers—though not here expressly so-called, yet still *domata*—the apostle proceeds to denominate certain *charismata*. These, of course, are not persons, but *gifts*, given to members of the body of Christ.

Five such *charismata* are mentioned, three of which had been named before in the hypothetical list in I Corinthians 12:8-10. But two had not. Nor were these two—quite apart from the *domata*—immaterial to the Corinthians. They were *essential*. Yet they were conspicuous by their absence.

When one considers the division, the fornication, one brother taking another to law, the incest, the riotous assembly, the abuse of the supper, the neglect of warnings, the eating and drinking not only what had been offered to idols, but consumed at table within the temples of those idols, the abuse of the sign of tongues, the disorderly behaviour of women, the allowance of division and disorder, disbelief in the resurrection, and I know not what else; I ask, Who was 'helpful'?

Those of the house of Chloe were 'helpful', I Corinthians 1:11. They which were approved by standing fast in the one unity despite the divisions all around them were 'helpful', I Corinthians 11:19. Above all, Paul was 'helpful', and, standing with him, brother Sosthenes, I Corinthians 1:1. All these were helpful.

Yes, but where was the *gift of the Spirit*, most surely needed in plurality in the unhelpful chaos at Corinth, namely, the gift of 'helps', I Corinthians 12:28?

Who desired *that* gift? It was non-existent. Indeed, it was despised. But the Corinthians *needed* help–in the spiritual gift of it; *and* as multiplied–more than they dreamed of: yet help was the last thing the various opinions and divisions thought that they required. To them, *others* needed it: and *they* shouted it. But the truth was, they *all* needed 'helps' from the Spirit.

Equally–if not more–was it so with 'governments'. The riotous meetings, the carnal divisions, the absence of control, the breakdown of authority, the erroneous factions, the appalling misbehaviour, all this gave rise to the conclusion that they were ungovernable. And so did the total absence of any with the spiritual gift of 'government'. Save, such was the extent of the damage, a plurality was called for: 'governments', I Corinthians 12:28.

Lastly, Paul names 'diversities of tongues'. That, they had in abundance, one party babbling, even shouting as if in Babel– none hearing or understanding the other–one party ranting unintelligibly in contention against another. And *this* they seemed to consider the best gift, and the one most desired by all? Yet what they put first, the apostle puts last, *after* helps and governments.

Besides, Paul calls tongues a *sign*, and a sign for those *outside the ecclesia*; not *a gift for those inside it*. See I Corinthians 14:21-25. Paul does not forbid to speak in tongues, no. But he makes an absolute condition of doing so *that another must thereafter give the interpretation*, I Corinthians 14:27,28. But how can one supposedly speaking in tongues *know beforehand* whether another will interpret or not? He *cannot* know. *Then* what?

Besides this, no more than two or at most three should speak in or by *any* identical gift, I Corinthians 14:27-29. Moreover, not only must no woman speak in tongues in the *ecclesia*, no woman must speak *at all* in the *ecclesia*, I Corinthians 14:33-40. But which sect, denomination, apostasy, independency, or division has not broken bounds and forsaken the foundation over this?

And yet for all that, how gentle; how kind; how encouraged to *expect* their acceptance of correction—despite everything—how much in remembrance of their wonderful beginnings, the apostle shows himself to be—full of the love of Christ, withal in righteousness—abiding steadfastly in faith, hope and love. Neither was he to be disappointed, II Corinthians 7:9-11.

Such is the fruitfulness and blessing of the *domata*, the gifts of Christ to the body, especially in that of the apostle: that perfect unity, in heart and speech, in judgment and deference, I say, perfect unity, the unity of one body, was restored. The gifts of the Spirit harmonized in one, and grace reigned through righteousness unto eternal life, whilst truth and peace pervaded throughout the entire *ecclesia*.

(v) Seven Questions on the Gifts

In closing this part of the epistle, Paul asks—to set them pondering—seven questions. In a way these questions bring together the gifts of Christ *to* the body, and the gifts of the Spirit *in* the body, I Corinthians 12:29,30.

In what way? In that, if pondered, the questions yield a priceless truth. All that is given from heaven; all that is bestowed on earth; all is to purpose. Divine purpose. And that purpose is *one*. Let the Corinthians consider it.

'Are all apostles?' No. There are twelve apostles. There were eleven. During the time after the ascension, whilst they were to wait for the coming of the Spirit, before he came—neither the Lord nor the Spirit being present; nor any such notion commanded—the eleven cast lots—*cast lots?*—for a twelfth apostle, as it were at the fall of a dice! But *afterwards* the Lord chose—who alone *could* choose—the twelfth from heaven.

Twelve apostles and no more. Their names are in the foundations of the walls of the city, Revelation 21:14.

The apostolic witnesses were entrusted with the revelation. They set forth the same in writing. That is the new testament. There is no appeal from this, no exceptions to it, and nothing can be added thereto. It is absolute: by it from Christ in heaven the apostles were sent to preach and teach the evangel and *thus* to establish the *ecclesia*. That is no *ecclesia* which is not so established. However large or venerable, it is a sham: a fraud.

The word committed unto the apostles is the foundation, of which Christ himself is the chief corner stone. There is no other, and there can be no other.

'Are all prophets?' No they certainly are not, Paul, neither would the vast majority have the faintest inkling of the *cost*, experimentally, doctrinally, and devotionally, neither of the years and decades of the suffering affliction and spiritual discipline which preceded the appearing of such *domata*.

Take John the Baptist for an example, to whose prophetic witness the Lord bore such a great testimony, John 5:35; John 3:5; I John 5:6. 'He was in the deserts till the day of his showing unto Israel', Luke 1:80. Oh? And how long was he *there*? And what did he *do* over those decades?

Let those who talk so glibly about 'prophets' answer *these* questions, and they may *just* begin to understand why, in his decade and a half of preparation, the Lord said of Paul, for example, 'I will show him how great things he must suffer for my name's sake'. As to John, no wonder that 'all men counted John, that he was a prophet indeed', Mark 11:32.

Nor would so many discount the prophets sent of the Lord under the old testament, as it is this day. But these prophesied of Christ. Of David, being a prophet, Peter testified, declaring that he foresaw Christ being raised from the dead: 'He seeing this before spake of the resurrection of Christ', Acts 2:31.

And of Christ, his sufferings and glory, spake all the prophets, Isaiah, Jeremiah, Ezekiel, Daniel, Hosea, Joel, Amos, Obadiah, Jonah, Micah, Nahum, Habakkuk, Zephaniah, Haggai, Zechariah, Malachi, and many others withal, not to mention that Moses also wrote of Christ, John 5:46,47.

Hence Christ preaches *from these* of the new testament, the evangel, saying, 'O fools, and slow of heart to believe all that the prophets have spoken: ought not Christ to have suffered these things, and to enter into his glory? And beginning at Moses and *all the prophets*, he expounded unto them in all the scriptures the things concerning himself', Luke 24:25-27.

The unique gift of the prophets continued after the sending of the apostles: 'And in these days came prophets from Jerusalem unto Antioch', Acts 11:27. 'And Judas and Silas, being prophets also themselves, exhorted the brethren', Acts 15:32. 'There came down from Judea a certain prophet, named Agabus', Acts 21:10. And what of the two mystical prophets in Revelation 11:3,4?

With so great a cloud of witnesses, is it any wonder that Paul declares of the *ecclesia* of God, concerning the mystery of Christ, 'Which in other ages was not made known unto the sons of men, as it is now revealed unto his holy apostles and prophets by the Spirit', Ephesians 3:4,5?

Moreover as to the old testament prophets Peter testifies, 'Unto whom it was revealed, that not unto themselves, but *unto us* they did minister the things, which are now reported unto you by them that have preached the evangel unto you with the Holy Ghost sent down from heaven', I Peter 1:12.

Hence the apostle Paul concludes, 'Now therefore ye are no more strangers and foreigners, but fellowcitizens with the saints, and of the household of God: *and are built upon the foundation of the apostles and prophets*, Jesus Christ himself being the chief corner stone', Ephesians 2:19,20.

Whereas it is unquestionable that—particularly following the ascension—the apostles and prophets mentioned above constitute those of the *domata* sent from heaven by the Lord of glory, nevertheless *the gift* of prophecy was and is also raised up by the Holy Ghost on earth under the same new testament, being bestowed upon chosen members of the body according to his own will. For example, from such charismatic members 'the prophecies'– note the plurality–'went before' upon Timothy, I Timothy 1:18.

Furthermore Philip the evangelist, whose house was at Caesarea, was one of the seven upon whom the apostles' hands had been laid. 'And the same man had four daughters, virgins, which did prophesy', Acts 21:9, where without doubt this refers to the *charisma* bestowed upon them.

Likewise the word to the assembled *ecclesia*, 'Let the prophets speak'– here, those members of the body on whom the Spirit had bestowed the gift–'two or three, *and let the other judge*. If anything be revealed to another that sitteth by, let the first *hold his peace*. For ye may all prophesy'–who *can* prophesy– '*one by one*, that all may learn, and all may be comforted', I Corinthians 14:29-31.

The prophet, and the gift of prophecy, opens what was hidden. Prophets have openings into the revelation, and can uncover from the sum delivered by the apostles. So that although the word was there, the meaning was hidden, but by prophecy it was uncovered.

That is, what had been once delivered to the saints was uncovered, not to say applied by the Holy Ghost and with power to effect conviction. Moreover the prophets—more or less—made known the mind and will of God, each in their own generation.

'Are all teachers?' As with the previous question concerning the prophets, just as the prophet may be either a gift of Christ from heaven or else prophecy may be a gift of the Spirit on earth, so it is with teachers and teaching. It is not that Paul is blurring the distinction: quite deliberately he is drawing out an important matter of fact.

In Ephesians 4:11 prophets are the second *doma*; but in Romans 12:6 prophecy is the first *charisma*. The first is from Christ ascended to the body, and stands in the heavenly gift of the person of the prophet; the second is from the Spirit descended in the body, and resides in the spiritual gift bestowed upon persons on earth.

Likewise Ephesians 4:11 reveals that the teachers—together with pastors—themselves are the fourth of the *doma* given from Christ in glory, whereas in Romans 12:7 'he that teacheth', as a member of the body, is given this supernatural gift of the Spirit abiding in the body upon earth—namely, the *charisma*—as 'having then gifts'—*charismata*—'differing according to the grace that is given to us', Romans 12:5,6.

From which it is to be observed that the apostle—in challenging whether *all* had the selfsame ministry—names gifts: whether persons, or that which is bestowed upon persons, either of *domata* and *charismata*—for all their differences in origin, ability, and character—*had every single one of the brethren but one and the same gift?*

'Are all teachers?' No, but there *are* teachers in each assembly, and there *are* teachers of the assembly. So with prophets and prophecy. In either case the gift may be of the character of *doma* or that of *charisma*. Yet this dichotomy introduces a lesson to which the apostle is leading: the *divine objective* in giving *any* gifts – of whatever character – answers to a *common end, whatever* the nature of the gifts. It is to fulfil an *eternal purpose*.

Teachers? They recall the apostolic doctrine. They bring to remembrance the prophecy. They do not originate, but by the Lord from heaven, or from the Spirit on earth, they reiterate. Their gift is to repeat what had been opened. They 'bring to remembrance.' By the word of the Lord and by the power of the Spirit the teachers expound, enlarge, and declare what had been opened by the apostles and prophets.

Of the seven gifts about which the apostle questions the Corinthians in this place – as if to challenge them – the remaining four are without doubt *charismata*. Challenge them? Indeed, for the Corinthians conducted themselves as if what they considered to be the more spectacular and stridently vocal gifts were on the one hand common to all, and on the other as if they excluded any other gifts whatsoever.

'Are all workers of miracles?' – it should be, works of power; that is, are *all* gifts works of power? – 'Have *all* the gifts' – *charismata* – 'of healing? do *all* speak with tongues? do all interpret?', I Corinthians 12:29,30.

Do *all* speak with tongues, question six? No, of course not; any more than *all* are apostles, question one. Then why did the Corinthians behave to the contrary? They had not so learned Christ, no, nor the body of Christ. Nor would the Spirit support what was to the contrary of the apostles' doctrine. How could he? for he is the Spirit of *truth*. Indeed 'the Spirit *is* truth', I John 5:6.

As to 'interpretation', who cared about *that* among them? Every man, each party, spoke as if neither word nor reason existed above their babbling.

'But covet earnestly the best gifts', says the Authorized Version, I Corinthians 12:31, although the reader may prefer the more literal 'But be zealous of the better *charismata*'. Why? Were there worse? Necessarily, there were *less* than the *best*. And would they covet the worst?

Then these less than best must have been at least relative to the most profitable, yet the Corinthians' fleshly zeal coveted the least – or worst – above all, and at that, for the wrong reasons.

What? as if there were no other, let alone better, *charismata*? What? all covet the same one thing, and that for carnal show, babbling away in tongues which none understood but themselves, if even *they* knew what they were ranting about? For this was exactly the case with them; just as it is the case with their far more erroneous imitators to this very day.

(vi) The More Excellent Way

'And yet show I unto you a more excellent way.' And, thanks be to God, by the Spirit and through the truth, in much soul-travail with earnest prayer and fasting, through many tears, and out of a heart torn with love, *the apostle prevailed in leading them therein*.

Prevailed, yes, and more than prevailed, this great gift of Christ from heaven to the body of Christ at Corinth. So that at the last he could say with tears of joy, 'The grace of the Lord Jesus Christ, and the love of God, and the communion of the Holy Ghost, be with you *all*. Amen', II Corinthians 13:14.

Then what had happened to them? *God* had happened to them, to deliver them out of their carnal backsliding, to save them from their fleshly energy, to subdue fallen nature, to exalt Christ, to grant them submission to the truth declared so earnestly and graciously by the apostle. All that had happened.

And this had followed: 'Ye were made sorry after a godly manner, that ye might receive damage by us in nothing. For godly sorrow worketh repentance to salvation not to be repented of: but the sorrow of the world worketh death.

'For behold this selfsame thing, that ye sorrowed after a godly sort, what carefulness it wrought in you, yea, what clearing of yourselves, yea, what indignation, yea, what fear, yea, what vehement desire, yea, what zeal, yea, what revenge! In all things ye have approved yourselves to be clear in this matter', II Corinthians 7:9-11.

For they came to see not only their abuse of the gifts, yea, but their forcing in the flesh of one or two gifts in particular which *all* had emulated at the expense of what was *actually* proper to *each* one; and, at that, with fiery zeal and in carnal contention, abusing divine things to exalt the flesh.

Yea, more, they came to see that *all* gifts were means to an end, not an end in themselves. Whether it were the *domata*, or whether it were the *charismata*, or whether it were a relative form of the same gift in both kinds, it made no difference to the *reason* for which God had set all, be it in the body, or in the *ecclesia*.

For all in all, God had a purpose, an eternal purpose. When the gifts answered to *that*, they justified their existence, and profited by their use. And what was that eternal purpose? It was 'a more excellent way'.

It was to be made perfect in love, I John 4:17. It was that 'the love wherewith thou hast loved me may be in them'–all of them; and all of them together in unity–'and I in them', John 17:26.

It was that the body should be filled with the light, life, and love of the Head, dwelling in one in Father, Son, and Holy Ghost: 'As thou, Father, art in me, and I in thee, that they also may be one in us: that the world may believe that thou hast sent me', John 17:21.

Then of a truth every member of the body would echo from the heart and in the Spirit the words of that apostolic *doma* set apart and sent to them with the words of life and of the Spirit of God, 'that they all may be one', John 17:21.

What words of life are these? Why, those of that more excellent way: 'Though I speak with the tongues of men and of angels, and have not love, I am become as sounding brass, or a tinkling cymbal.

'And though I have the gift of prophecy, and understand all mysteries, and all knowledge; and though I have all faith, so that I could remove mountains, and have not love, I am nothing.

'And though I bestow all my goods to feed the poor, and though I give my body to be burned, and have not love, it profiteth me nothing.

'Love suffereth long, and is kind; love envieth not; love vaunteth not itself, is not puffed up, doth not behave itself unseemly, seeketh not her own, is not easily provoked, thinketh no evil; rejoiceth not in iniquity, but rejoiceth in the truth;

'Beareth all things, believeth all things, hopeth all things, endureth all things. Love never faileth: but whether there be prophecies, they shall fail; whether there be tongues, they shall cease; whether there be knowledge, it shall vanish away.

'For we know in part, and we prophesy in part. But when that which is perfect is come, then that which is in part shall be done away. When I was a child, I spake as a child, I understood as a child, I thought as a child: but when I became a man, I put away childish things.

'For now we see through a glass, darkly; but then face to face: now I know in part; but then shall I know even as also I am known.

'And now abideth faith, hope, love, these three; but the greatest of these is love.'

(3) THE MANIFESTATION OF THE GIFTS IN THE ASSEMBLY, CHAPTER 14:1-40

Since this is a corrective passage, the apostle handles the matter under four distinct heads:

FIRST: PAUL COMPARES THE USEFULNESS OF PROPHECY WITH THE LIMITATION OF TONGUES, I CORINTHIANS 14:1-25.

SECOND: HE DIRECTS THE ORDERLY MANIFESTATION OF GIFTS WHEN COMING TOGETHER IN THE *ECCLESIA*, I CORINTHIANS 14:26-33.

THIRD: THE APOSTLE FORBIDS WOMEN TO SPEAK OR ASK QUESTIONS, BUT TO BE UNDER OBEDIENCE IN THE *ECCLESIA*, I CORINTHIANS 14:34,35.

FOURTH: PAUL STRESSES THAT THE WORD OF GOD CAME *UNTO* THEM, NOT AROSE *FROM* THEM. THEN, LET EVERY ONE OF THEM ACKNOWLEDGE WITHOUT GAINSAYING THAT THE DOCTRINE AND DISCIPLINE OF I CORINTHIANS 14:1-40 *ARE THE COMMANDMENTS OF THE LORD*, VERSES 36-40.

To proceed:

FIRST: PAUL COMPARES THE USEFULNESS OF PROPHECY WITH THE LIMITATION OF TONGUES, I CORINTHIANS 14:1-25.

'Follow after love, and desire spiritual gifts, but rather that ye may prophesy', verse 1. The word 'gifts' – in italics in the Authorized Version – is an interpolation.

The Greek is very difficult to render precisely in English: spirituality; what pertains to the spirit; spirituals. Perhaps. But like 'what is spiritual', all these are clumsy in translation.

If I were to give the literal impression, I should read: 'Pursue love, and be zealous of spirituality, but rather that ye may prophesy.' But by 'spirituality' in this place Paul refers to their giving themselves over to spiritual impressions, resulting in unintelligible sounds.

Hence he says immediately: 'For he that speaketh with a tongue, speaketh not unto men, but unto God: for no man understandeth him; howbeit in the spirit he speaketh mysteries.'

Mysteries indeed, not only to others but apparently to himself also, since 'my'–own; let alone others–'understanding is unfruitful', verse 14.

Nevertheless, carried away in emotional response to spiritual impulse, the tongue is loosed beyond control of either understanding or judgment, either to him who speaks, or to those that hear.

In no case does Paul suggest foreign languages in Chapter 14: it is clear that what is heard is out of control–quite deliberately, however spiritual the cause–and unintelligible to *anyone* save an hypothetical interpreter.

The most charitable view one can take of verse 2 is that the one speaking in tongues is overwhelmed beyond control by divine and spiritual mysteries.

Paul is saying, If so, evidently it is still possible to control the tongue, whilst retaining the divine impression, and by so doing edify the whole *ecclesia*: that is, *'rather* that ye may prophesy.' Because he that prophesieth speaketh unto men–so that thus they can understand and follow what has been received–'to edification, and exhortation, and comfort.'

Whereas, verse 4, for all the noise made to no purpose for the hearers, he that speaks in a tongue edifies no one but himself. But he that controls his spirit, and declares the mystery intelligibly—which Paul calls 'prophesying'—edifieth *the whole ecclesia*.

Which is preferable? The apostle makes abundantly clear which is preferable, verse 4.

As to being wholly given to what is spiritual, so as to be zealous of receiving what is from the Spirit, such was the value that the apostle clearly placed on their earnest zeal that he desires no check to be put upon *this*, even though it meant for the time present that they all *should* continue speaking with tongues: without any loss to their enthusiasm he seeks to turn the same zeal in them towards prophecy. For surely he detested the least appearance of that dead and inert apathy which the Lord describes as 'lukewarmness'.

Yet for all that, whilst encouraging their fervour, still, *for their own mutual profit*, he would direct that same zealous spirituality into the intelligible utterance of what each one received from the Spirit.

'I would that ye all spake with tongues, but rather that ye prophesied: for greater is he that prophesieth than he that speaketh with tongues, except he interpret, that the *ecclesia* may receive edifying', verse 5. But if he interpret, Why the tongue first? for, to all intents and purposes, the interpretation then becomes prophecy!

Suppose *Paul* did what *they* were doing. If he came to them, would they wish *his* speech to be gibberish like theirs, of which they could understand not a word? They would not. No, because that would lose all the value of the life-giving apostolic ministry of the new testament by which they had been begotten of God.

Then—though on a lesser plane—Why do among themselves, what they could not bear from him, if he came to them? 'Now, brethren, if *I* come unto you speaking with tongues, what shall *I* profit you?', verse 6. Profit them? In such a case, no more than the same thing was of profit among themselves. Can they not see this obvious lesson?

But if Paul came speaking to them either by revelation, or by knowledge, or by prophesying, or by doctrine, clearly and intelligibly, so that all understood, how profitable *this* would prove to be.

Will they then cast aside such inestimable blessing for meaningless and incoherent babbling? No they will not. Then why do to themselves in Paul's absence what they would not wish him to do to them were he present?

Using the illustration of a pipe – or flute – then of an harp, and finally a trumpet, Paul signifies the absolute necessity of intelligible sounds in order to communicate to others.

Such instruments are useless of themselves, being without life. That is, unless one either blow air, pluck with the fingers, or sound through the mouthpiece.

However, this alone produces nothing save a tedious monotone, a jangling discord, or a raucous blast: meaningless sounds from living men through dead instruments.

But once the flautist, blowing through the pipe, uses his expertise appropriately to stop the holes with his fingers, then what ordered tones in sequence delight the ear.

Or else the harpist plucking the strings with cunning, selecting and moderating each in turn, or running a part or the whole in a kind of liquid flow: then how lovely the harmony to the hearers.

But in each of these cases the arrangement of the music must be known beforehand, so that the piper pipes the appointed score with skill, the flautist plays the predetermined notes with accomplished control, and the harpist harps upon his stringed instrument to give a distinctive cadence.

Thus in each case the notes harmonize, and the rhythm blends so as to give forth a sweet melody, a thing impossible save by the foreknowledge of the composition, and hence the control of the sound.

As to the trumpet, everyone knows that the force of air must be directed by the different positioning of the lips in order that clear and distinct notes–both in tone and length–may be trumpeted: 'For if the trumpet give an uncertain sound, who shall prepare himself to the battle?', I Corinthians 14:8.

Now all these things are true of lifeless instruments, namely, that musicians must not just blow aimlessly, or strike chords at random, but must know the score beforehand, taking up the instrument to play skilfully, giving a distinction in the notes played.

If so, how much more should the necessity of regulation in sound apply to those voices which give forth a cacophonous babel of unintelligible discord? Clearly, as with music, all should be *regulated* in order to render an *intelligible* sound, so that every one of the hearers might understand and be edified.

Otherwise, despite that men take up the instrument of the tongue, and for all that they speak through their mouth with the voice, the sound is meaningless to anyone unless it be regulated according to intelligible utterance: 'How shall it be known what is spoken? for ye shall speak into the air', I Corinthians 14:9.

Indeed, since the noises have no signification and the resultant sounds are meaningless gibberish to everyone–including the speaker–the hearers may well say of such a tongue, since they themselves give forth the like incoherent babble–and all at one and the same time–'I shall be unto him that speaketh a barbarian, and he that speaketh shall be a barbarian unto me', I Corinthians 14:7-11.

'Even so ye' continues the apostle; that is, 'even' as with the figure of the tuneless and discordant pipe, harp, or trumpet, 'so ye' bawling at each other like barbarians, oblivious of one another's language, raising your voices one at the other—as if you can make up for incomprehension by increasing the volume to a crescendo—thus create a situation little short of ludicrous: nevertheless, 'Even so ye'.

'Even so ye, forasmuch as ye are zealous of spiritualities, seek that ye may excel to the edifying of the *ecclesia*', just as musicians who know their parts and play their instruments accordingly, and as those who speak the same language.

If so, on the one hand as opposed to a discordant cacophony, and on the other, as distinct from two alien barbarians who rant at each other meaninglessly, none knowing the tongue of the other.

'Wherefore let him that speaketh in a tongue pray that he may interpret', verse 13. But in such a case what of the following verse: 'If I pray in a tongue, my spirit prayeth, *but my understanding is unfruitful*'? But if my understanding is unfruitful, How can I possibly interpret? Yet if I *could* interpret, and my understanding *were* fruitful, then *that* would eliminate the use of the tongue in the *first* place.

And if, after all, I *were* able to interpret *afterwards*, then—given the hypothesis—such an interpretation would be tantamount to prophecy. And, saith Paul—as opposed to tongues—prophecy would be for the edification of all. In that case, Why the tongues?

Clearly, though addressed never so gently, the implication of the apostle is inescapable.

And likewise, What of this: 'If any man speak in a tongue ... let one'—that is, *another* one—'interpret'? see verse 27. By all that has been said already, even to the most prejudiced, three things intrude themselves.

First, if the understanding of the one who speaks in a tongue be unfruitful, it follows of necessity that this means that *he* knows not *what* he says. It is highly doubtful—his understanding being unfruitful—that he even knows what he *means*. Then, How can he possibly interpret to others? verses 13,14.

Second, if a man may only speak in a tongue—in the *ecclesia*—provided *another* interprets—the idea of his own unfruitful understanding enabling him to be his own interpreter being merely hypothetical—then he is *not* to interpret what he himself spoke in a tongue. See verse 13 *cf* verses 27,28.

Third, even in the case of a man wishing to speak in a tongue in the *ecclesia*, since he may only do so under the condition that another interprets thereafter, *de facto* he is prevented in his wish *because of the impossibility of his knowing in advance whether the interpretation will be given to another or not.*

So that whilst carefully nurturing the spiritual zeal of the Corinthians, and doing nothing to dampen their ardour, nevertheless the apostle, both by his advocacy for the superiority of prophecy, and by the discipline he administers on the exercise of tongues in the *ecclesia*, whilst under no sense forbidding it as such—indeed laying down ordinances which, given an interpreter, allows for it—yet still, their obedience to these ordinances being granted, it is difficult to see how the use of tongues in the *ecclesia* would be possible thereafter.

Hence in the next verses Paul unites the spiritual enthusiasm—one might almost say abandon—in which the Corinthians' emotions, if not passions, were carried away by the intensity of their feelings, with the sobriety and solid control of their *nous*—for so the Greek reads—a word better translated 'mentality' than 'understanding':

'For if I pray in a tongue, my spirit prayeth'—through the excitement of the emotions and passions from spiritual impressions—'but my *nous*'—my mentality—'is unfruitful', verse 14.

Why, Paul? Because it is *all* spiritual excitement without *any* comprehending mentality.

That is, I do not know *what* I am saying. I know only what I am feeling. Then, bring both feeling and mentality together under control: 'What is it then? I will pray with the spirit, and I will pray with the *nous*'–mentality–'also: I will sing with the spirit, and I will sing with the *nous* also.'

But if not,What? 'Else when thou shalt bless with the spirit'– carried away in song or blessing beyond comprehensible words –'how shall he that occupieth the place of the uninstructed'– uninstructed, that is, in just *what* is going on in such meetings –'say Amen at thy giving of thanks, seeing he knoweth not'– Greek, *has no idea of*–'what thou sayest?'

How could he know? It is all unintelligible babel to him.

'For verily'–Paul does not doubt it–'*thou* givest thanks well, but *the other* is not edified.' Yet the edification of others–in the *ecclesia*–is the object of *all* vocal activity, I Corinthians 14:14-17.

For their encouragement, both in private and the assembly– lest they feel rebuked, or disconsolate, over this apostolic–but most considerate–discipline in the Spirit, Paul adds, 'I thank my God, I speak with tongues more than ye all', verse 18.

But what did the apostle actually *mean* by this? The same kind of tongues as they meant? Perhaps; yet certainly not in the *ecclesia*.

Because immediately he states, 'tongues are for *a sign*'–which was hardly the case with the Corinthians–besides, 'a sign, *not to them that believe*', verse 22. Wherefore it is hardly likely that Paul gave forth in tongues *as they did*.

To be consistent with verse 22, verse 18 must suppose that Paul spake in tongues more than they all *to them that believe not*.

Openings in First Corinthians

Then, in what tongues? For example, the Hebrew tongue, incomprehensible to most of the Corinthians, but not to those unbelievers at Jerusalem: 'And when there was made a great silence, he'–Paul–'spake unto them in *the Hebrew tongue*.'

Besides this, he spoke Greek–preaching the evangel to unbelievers in that tongue–and used the same language to write his epistles; besides this, there is a strong probability from the range of his journeys that he spoke in the varied Greek dialects.

Again, being a citizen of Cilicia, dwelling in the city of Tarsus, there can be no doubt but that he had the tongue of that people also by it preaching to them that believed not.

Once more there can be little question but that Paul spoke Latin, not only from his being a free-born Roman, but also from his years spent in the city of Rome. Hence his ability to converse freely with Romans, whether the centurion and chief captain at Jerusalem, the Romans at Caesarea, or to Julius, a centurion of Augustus' band, to whom Paul was committed on his journey in custody to Rome.

Indeed, the Romans themselves testified at Jerusalem, 'this man is a Roman', Acts 22:26, and a free-born Roman at that, verse 28. Then can anyone doubt that he would have had the Latin tongue?

And–quite apart from other tongues peculiar to the different peoples to whom he was sent–such as the Syrians of Damascus–is not this 'speaking in tongues more than ye all'? And was not this 'a sign to them that believe not', carrying the evangel intelligibly to them?

Or, if it be a matter of revelations and of spirituality, Paul excelled all, being caught up to the third heaven, hearing unspeakable words, which it was not lawful for a man to utter, II Corinthians 12:2-4.

But if not lawful, Paul would not utter them, no not in any tongue. And if unspeakable, Paul *could* not utter them, since no tongue sufficed to utter what could not be spoken. And what can be more spiritual than that?

Not as if Paul mentioned the incident till writing the second epistle to the Corinthians, from which it is evident that he restrained himself in all things that he might benefit the brethren: 'Yet in the *ecclesia* I had rather speak five words with my *nous*, that by my voice I might teach others also, than ten thousand words in an unknown tongue.'

Whereupon he exhorts the brethren not to be children – or childish – in *intelligence*, but to grasp the reason for what he was saying as *intelligent* men – that is, in mature manhood. See I Corinthians 14:18-20.

At this point therefore he appeals to the scriptures of the prophets: 'In the law it is written, With men of other tongues and other lips will I speak unto this people; and yet for all that will they not hear me, saith the Lord.

'Wherefore tongues are for a sign, not to them that believe, but to them that believe not: but prophesying serveth not for them that believe not, but for them which believe', verses 21,22.

Concerning tongues as a sign to them that believe not, there was nothing incoherent about it: 'And they were all filled with the Holy Ghost, and began to speak *with other tongues*, as the Spirit gave them utterance' – that is *other* than their *own* tongue, or language – 'And there were dwelling at Jerusalem Jews, devout men, out of every nation under heaven.

'Now when this was noised abroad, the multitude came together, and were confounded, because that every man heard *them* speak *in his own language*.'

And they, though devout Jews, yet unbelievers, 'marvelled, saying one to another, Behold, are not all these which speak Galileans? and how hear we every man in our own tongue, wherein we were born?

'Parthians, and Medes, and Elamites, and the dwellers in Mesopotamia, and in Judea, and Cappadocia, in Pontus, and Asia, Phrygia, and Pamphylia, in Egypt, and in the parts of Libya about Cyrene, and strangers of Rome, Jews and proselytes, Cretes, and Arabians, we do hear *them* speak *in our tongues* the wonderful works of God', Acts 2:4-11.

Now, *this* was tongues with a witness. And this was tongues with a witness to *unbelievers*. Where *the saints* knew not the tongue in which they spoke, but the interpretation, respectively, was given by the hearing of fifteen different nations, in the tongues wherein they were born.

Other cases of tongues, as with Cornelius' company, and those at Ephesus, were likewise a sign, not least to the apostles themselves, that God would justify the Gentiles also—a thing at first unbelievable to them.

Of this Peter, called to account at Jerusalem, could not but testify, saying, 'Forasmuch then as God gave them'—who, from being Gentile unbelievers, were brought to faith—'*the like gift as he did unto us*, who believed on the Lord Jesus Christ; what was I, that I could withstand God?

'When they heard these things'—that what happened to *them*, at Pentecost, had happened *to the Gentiles also*—'they held their peace.'

Wherefore tongues are for a sign, not to them that believe, but to them that believe not. In which sign, note, the speakers had no knowledge of the tongue which they uttered, and the interpretation came from the unbelieving foreigners who heard.

As to Corinth, this was another thing altogether: it was to *them that believe*, which is all wrong, and turns the scripture upside-down. Besides this, *there was no question of foreign languages.*

It was not a matter of 'Are not all these which speak Corinthians?' It was more a matter of 'Are not all these which babble Barbarians?'

Interpret? They were all too preoccupied with 'speaking in tongues' every man for himself, till there was not one who was left to interpret.

And not to interpret by translating some foreign language *outside*, but to puzzle over 'mysteries' indeed within. Within? But yet, out of all the *ecclesiai* in the new testament, within that peculiar to Corinth alone.

Still, how patient and longsuffering the apostle appears in his ministry, anxious to encourage their zeal, whilst guiding them into a more excellent way, to more edifying prophecy, withal for the time being forbidding nothing at all.

Nevertheless, the truth which he states, without applying it, save leaving it to their *nous*, stands from the day of Pentecost till the end of time: 'Wherefore tongues are for a sign, not to them that believe, but to them that *believe not.*' That is to those without.

As to those *within*, that is, '*them which believe*', in the same verse the apostle sets everything in stark contrast: 'but'—mark that: *but*—'prophesying serveth *not for them that believe not*, but for *them which believe*', I Corinthians 14:21,22.

But for all the great weight of that which the apostle had pleaded up to this point, he makes yet one further appeal to the Corinthians, that they themselves might see good reason for favouring utterance by prophecy, in their own minds being persuaded of the unsuitability of tongues in the meetings of the *ecclesia*.

'If therefore the whole *ecclesia* be come together into one place, and all speak with tongues, and there come in those that are unlearned, or unbelievers, *will they not say that ye are mad?*'

That was their present witness. Mad.

'But if all prophesy, and there come in one that believeth not, or one unlearned, he is convinced of all, he is judged of all: and thus are the secrets of his heart made manifest; and so falling down on his face will worship God, *and report that God is in you of a truth.*'

That was the witness Paul desired for them in the future.

Well, What would they? Madness, and the common reputation for it? Or God's indwelling, and the general report that they had become his habitation?

The apostle presents a choice amounting to this: Will they have tongues and madness? or will they have prophecy and sanity? See I Corinthians 14:23-25.

This leads the apostle to the next head in the passage from I Corinthians 14:1-40:

SECOND: HE DIRECTS THE ORDERLY MANIFESTATION OF GIFTS WHEN COMING TOGETHER IN THE *ECCLESIA*, I CORINTHIANS 14:26-33.

From the preceding passages and especially the context it is abundantly evident that 'tongues' were coveted above all by the Corinthians, who had been beguiled into supposing that the use of this gift was the height of spirituality in the *ecclesia*. But it was not.

Nor was this sign – or gift – for them that believe at all, but for them that believe not, Chapter 14:22.

Prophecy, however, was another matter altogether, verses 23-25. Paul had made this crystal clear.

However, he does not forbid tongues: he puts the gift – or sign – in perspective, relegating it to its comparative status and due order according to the ways of God in those apostolic times at the beginning in which he writes.

I say 'apostolic times' for it must be borne in mind constantly that such a period was as unique to the inauguration of the new testament as was the receiving of the law and the signs following the deliverance of Israel from Egypt until the crossing of Jordan into the promised land under the old testament.

The *origination* of both testaments, ordained under each respective Apostle, was marked by a period of miracles, signs, and wonders never intended to be repeated in subsequent generations, nor – as the history of Israel demonstrates – *were* they repeated, though they *were* constantly to be had in remembrance.

The cessation of the falling of the manna from heaven; of the water from the Rock which followed them; or of the pillar of cloud and of fire which guided them, did not make the subsequent generations *less* of Israel after they crossed the river of Jordan.

What it did was to make the *continuation of Israel in the doctrine delivered by Moses* to be marked out as divinely given by the unique and distinguishing features manifest at their beginnings. Just so in the new testament.

Now, however, the apostle continues, 'How is it then, brethren? when ye come together, every one of you hath a psalm, hath a doctrine, hath a tongue, hath a revelation, hath an interpretation. Let all things be done unto edifying', Chapter 14:26.

It is essential to grasp the background of this passage, over against the accretions of the ages, layer upon layer, and the accumulation of both traditions and prejudices, under which it has been continually and increasingly buried during the intervening centuries, not least by those who suppose themselves to be so scriptural that they judge everyone *other* than themselves to be guilty of this grotesque form of tumidity.

'How is it then, brethren? when ye come together', verse 26, answers to 'If therefore the whole *ecclesia* be come together into one place', verse 23.

First enquire, If all the brethren, that is, the whole *ecclesia*, be come together in one place, then how on earth can that *place* be called the *ecclesia* or 'church'? It cannot.

The *ecclesia* or 'church' is said to come together *into that place*, not that *the place* into which the *ecclesia* or 'church' came was called by the name of those who came into it! Then, in those apostolic times, all the brethren, the entire *ecclesia*, came together into one place.

But now it is different.

A motley congregation, the majority of which – even by their own standards – are not converted, and the conversion even of the core minority would certainly be questionable by apostolic standards, I say, if these come together on a sectarian basis – that is, on the basis of a 'membership' divided from the unity of one body – into a building more or less conformed to a certain architectural pattern, which they have the temerity to call 'the church' or 'their church', and, at that, with a denominational name appended, What follows?

It *must* follow that *they cannot be* the *ecclesia* or 'church', they themselves bearing a twofold witness against themselves. First, by the misapplication of the term. Second, by the added qualification of their denominational title.

Thus, those of that denomination 'go' to 'their' church. How can this be? Because *the place* into which they come is named deceitfully. Not to say, denominationally.

And, for all their pretensions, I do not see that the substitution of 'meeting' or 'hall' for 'church' *makes the slightest difference unless those who come together do so in the unity of the one body, that is, in the one fellowship which is in the Father, and in his Son Jesus Christ, abiding in the communion of the Holy Ghost.*

For *that* was what Paul meant when he said, 'How is it then, brethren? when ye come together', and, 'If therefore the whole *ecclesia* be come together into one place'.

But what *men* mean by 'going to church' is as far removed from the context of the apostle – and the remotest possibility of any application of his words – as the north pole is distant from the south.

Self-styled 'biblical' congregations may hide this truth – for example by housing-estate style 'modern' halls, or whatever.

But everybody knows what these adapted buildings represent – with their modest hints of some updated 'ecclesiastical' feature or another – just as much as if these were the modern spawn of ancient cathedrals, with which, in practice, the superstition of multitudes associates as being worthy of a like – if lesser – veneration.

And why not? For, within, if not a font, there is a baptistery. If not a sacristy, there is a vestry. If not an altar, there is a table. If not a reading desk, there is a pulpit. If not a priest, there is a pastor. If not a pastor, there are 'speakers'.

And in the minds of worldly, unconverted people – not dispossessed of common sense by the prejudice of religious bias – what is the difference? A difference in kind, but not a difference in substance.

Openings in First Corinthians

How unlike the times when 'brethren, *ye* come together'! 'How is it then, brethren? when *ye* come together'? For a start, no one brought, or could bring, a bible. The old testament rolls were far and away too inaccessible, and the hand written and copied books of the new testament—such as they were at that time and place—were as yet neither collated nor assembled.

At most—and that but rarely—there would be an apostolic epistle written to them or to others nearby to be read by an able brother to the entire assembly. But no one individual possessed his own copy, much less his own bible, and certainly not his own new testament.

Neither had they any written psalms, songs, or hymns. In fact, they came empty handed, having no books of *any* kind to bring, or to find laid out for them on arrival.

Whatever was written was written by the Holy Ghost on fleshy tables of the heart.

As to writings on tables of stone, or rolls of parchment, apart from unavailability, the balance of probabilities weighs heavily against the majority of the Corinthians—not to say, the saints of the new testament, many of whom were slaves—being able to read or write at all.

Then, all depended upon the anointing by which they needed not that any man teach them, namely, the inward spiritual writing on the heart by the Holy Ghost from heaven, *and the inspired memory of what they had received from the preaching and teaching of the apostolic ministers of the new testament.*

Hence, in coming together in one place, the apostle's insistence upon the participation, verification, and witness of at least *two*, or, appropriately, *three*, when ministering any gift among themselves. This was nothing less than imperative.

It is an absolutely vital fact to be fixed in the mind that they depended upon the Holy Ghost to bring to their remembrance what had been taught to them, just as much as the accurate memory of those psalms, hymns, and spiritual songs agreeable to the doctrine of Christ.

Hence the necessity of verification by another in the exercise of any one gift: 'If any man speak in an unknown tongue, *let it be by two, or at the most three*'–far from the entire number!–'*and that by course*'–not all at once!–'and let *another* interpret', I Corinthians 14:27.

Again, 'Let the prophets speak *two or three*, and *let the other judge*. If any thing be revealed to another that sitteth by, *let the first hold his peace*', verses 29,30.

Thus, since *memory* was the crucial issue, the apostle enjoins an order in which *corroboration was assured* by at least one, if not two, others.

Observe likewise his patience and gentleness with the Corinthians in the allowance of tongues *within* the assembly, and *to* believers, despite what he had declared in verse 22, not to say verses 23-25.

However, since his allowance of tongues was conditional upon an interpreter, it is difficult to see how tongues could be exercised in the assembly, since it would have been impossible for one so speaking to know beforehand whether an interpretation would follow or not.

In any event *the principle* of two or at the most three in the exercise of any one gift held good, and *that* was the main issue.

Nor does *our* possession of a complete bible–old and new testament–together with the–now at last available–invaluable psalms, hymns, and spiritual songs, *alter the principle of dependence upon the interior witness and inwriting of the Holy Ghost leading us also, where reference to what is written takes the place of remembrance of what had been spoken.*

The same injunctions still apply, because they are principles in their nature, and, if so, enduring in their application.

Once again notice the wording: 'How is it then, brethren? when ye come together, every one of you hath a psalm, hath a doctrine, hath a tongue, hath a revelation, hath an interpretation', verse 26.

And again, 'If therefore the whole *ecclesia* be come together into one place', verse 23. Note carefully that this was *the* meeting of the saints, of all the brethren, of the whole *ecclesia*.

No suggestion exists that the taking of the Lord's supper in fellowship after their meal together was at a *different* time or place. The inference is that it was at *this* time and place.

But *the functioning of the gifts in conveying the word of God by the Holy Ghost through the appropriate members of the body transcended all.* Whatever else may have taken place when 'the whole *ecclesia* be come together into one place', or when brethren 'come together', the declaration of the word of the truth of the evangel was paramount.

The Supper–or 'Breaking of Bread on Lord's Day Morning' as some so unscripturally, unsoundly, and inaccurately denominate it–or the so-called 'Gospel Meeting'; the Prayer Meeting; or the Meeting for Fellowship, and suchlike: all these things might and perhaps in some cases did accompany that paramountcy: *but nothing equalled it.*

Whatever *was* ordained, accompanied it. *This* was *the* meeting of the saints; of all the brethren; of the whole *ecclesia*, and, it appears this involved *everything*.

Indeed, the *conception* of this passage leads to the supposition of *one* meeting–*this* meeting–for everything, and, in all likelihood, *every night of the week*, cessation from work permitting. Mark that well, in this apostate day of apathy and lukewarm half-heartedness.

In contrast, then, in those early times everything that they did was all done *in one and the same meeting*, and at that 'daily', when 'the whole *ecclesia* be come together into one place', and, 'brethren, when ye come together.'

I repeat: *then* not only was all in one, but in all probability it was *every day*. Why repeat this? Because it *should* be repeated, and that in our own times.

Carefully notice the nature of the coming together of the *ecclesia* in the exercise and manifestation of the gifts of the Spirit in the body of Christ. What appears so clearly is that it *was* the *body of Christ* that came together 'into one place' and as 'brethren'. Hence there followed the *manifestation of the gifts of the Spirit in the body, as assembled in one for edification*.

What followed? 'Every one of you hath a psalm, hath a doctrine, hath a tongue, hath a revelation, hath an interpretation.' And, since it *was* 'every one of you' the apostle admonishes the brethren to wait in due order, that all might be edified: 'Let all things be done unto edifying', verse 26.

Here there is not the slightest resemblance to divided memberships coming together each in its own separate quarter to hear a hired priest, 'ordained' minister, 'trained' pastor, or presumptuous 'brother'. No priest, minister, pastor, or usurper appears in any place whatsoever in this passage dealing exhaustively and apostolically with the coming together of the body of Christ into one.

No such grotesque impositions as have mushroomed since, existed in the one *ecclesia* of God. The gifts of the Spirit in and from the members of the body in and of themselves provided the whole of the ministry and the entirety of the edification. This is not to say that the apostles were then present, or that their giving the apostolic ministry is the subject of this passage.

It is to say that *this* is the apostles' doctrine for the gathering together into one place of the *ecclesia*, where *this* answers to the manifestation of the gifts of the Spirit on the part of those to whom such gifts were given, for the edification of the whole.

That is, 'Every one hath' by the same Spirit, that which harmonized with all other manifest gifts for the edification of the entire body, and in the agreement and unity of the conscience and judgment of every one of the brethren.

'Every one hath.' Not 'the pastor hath'; not 'the priest hath'; not 'the minister hath'; not 'every presumptuous usurper hath': quite apart from *such fictional impositions and impostors as these, plying their trade in the divisions outside of the body, nevertheless within the body*, 'every one hath'.

As to 'the pastor': there was no pastor. As to the 'priests': they had passed away with the old covenant. As to Brethren imitations: there were no Brethren imitations.

As to the booked and arranged Speakers, such things were unheard of in that 'whole church come together into one place', when 'brethren, ye come together' and 'every one'—gifted by the Holy Ghost in one body—'hath a psalm, hath a doctrine, hath a tongue, hath a revelation, hath an interpretation', I Corinthians 14:26. .

Nothing else existed in the *ecclesia*, the body of Christ. No, nor in this entire epistle, namely, that epistle singled out and devoted to expounding once and for all the manifestation of the gifts of the indwelling Spirit in the coming together of the *ecclesia*, the body of Christ, into one place.

Then, when the brethren were thus come together, one rule prevailed: 'Let all things be done unto edifying.' That is, not all at once, but one after the other. And not one gift alone but each differing *charisma* in due order unto edification.

Now for the time being allowing for tongues in the assembling of the *ecclesia*, despite that the drift of the context had been to the contrary, the exceeding gentleness of the apostle, his moderation towards their excess falling short of outright prohibition or sudden closure; the apostle continues.

'If any man speak in an unknown tongue, let it be by two, or at the most three, and that by course'—as opposed to everyone presuming the same gift, and that all at once—'and let one interpret.'

But, as has been said, How shall the two, or at most three, speaking in tongues by course, *know* that they will be followed by that interpretation without which they are to keep silence? 'But if there be no interpreter, let him keep silence in the *ecclesia*; and let him speak to himself, and to God', verse 28.

Next, Paul comes to prophecy. The same principle applies, though the gift differs: 'Let the prophets speak two or three, and let the other judge. If any thing be revealed to another that sitteth by'—who has judged by the Spirit what had been prophesied—'let the first hold his peace.'

For such a revelation, enlarging or contracting the previous prophecy, would be all one as if he that received the revelation were a prophet also: 'For ye may all prophesy one by one'—one *after* the other—'that all may learn, and all may be comforted.'

'And the spirits of the prophets are subject to the prophets.' If so, then each must receive from and submit to the furtherance and enlargement of others in sequence, not claiming that the spirit in him gave him the right to interrupt whomsoever followed.

On the contrary, the spirit of the prophets being subject to the prophets, the previous speaker must meekly receive the further revelation of the other prophets, added to his own contribution, each in his own order, so that the judgment of all being edified and comforted by this witness of diversities of gifts—but the same Spirit—the entire *ecclesia* is comforted.

Openings in First Corinthians

See I Corinthians 12:4 and likewise I Corinthians 14:29-33. 'For God is not the author of confusion, but of peace, as in all the *ecclesiai* of the saints.'

Such a verse, embracing that commensurate discipline following from the apostolic authority through which the Lord himself directed the doctrine and fellowship received by all the *ecclesiai* of the saints, brings Paul to the next revelation of the new testament commanding the coming together of the *ecclesia*, that is, the gathering together into one place of the body of Christ.

THIRD: THE APOSTLE FORBIDS WOMEN TO SPEAK OR ASK QUESTIONS, BUT TO BE UNDER OBEDIENCE IN THE ECCLESIA, I CORINTHIANS 14:34,35.

Further to the truth that 'God is not the author of confusion, but of peace, as in all the *ecclesiai* of the saints' the apostle immediately follows with the commandment of the Lord, and word of God, necessary for the achievement and continuance of such a divinely given peace, namely, 'Let your women keep silence in the *ecclesiai*'–not just the *ecclesia* at Corinth, note: it is not in the singular, *ecclesia*; it is plural, '*ecclesiai*'.

Then, this commandment of the Lord necessarily extends *everywhere* and to *all generations*–'for it is not permitted unto them to speak; but they are commanded to be under obedience, as also saith the law', verse 34.

The law? Where in the law? The *Torah* for instance. Genesis for example. Of this, recorded in the first book of Moses, 'nature itself teacheth you', as saith the apostle, I Corinthians 11:2,11-16.

Teacheth you what? The difference between the creation of the man; the forming of the woman from the man; the woman being deceived; the bringing in of the Fall–because she *would* answer the serpent, and *would not* ask her husband–and the difference between the man and the woman before God, and especially *since the judgment of the Fall*, Genesis chapters 2 and 3, concerning which the apostle teaches the truth, I Timothy 2:11-15.

The law also confirms this truth and commandment elsewhere in the *Torah*, not least with the offerings and the feasts—which the *men* of Israel were to offer—and for the same reason. 'Thrice in the year shall all your *menchildren* appear before the Lord God, the God of Israel', Exodus 34:23.

It is true that in special circumstances there were offerings for women—as in childbirth or an issue—but although these were given by the woman *they must be offered by the priest*.

Indeed, as to all the chief and continual offerings it is 'If any *man* of you bring an offering', Leviticus 1:2. And, at that, though the man did much, the priest did more, actually bringing the offering both to the altar and before the LORD.

As to women, they did nothing; and as for priestesses, they belonged to the detestable abominations of the heathen, from which Israel was utterly to separate himself, and which he was perpetually to abhor and abominate.

As also saith the law. Not to mention the gospel. Then, 'Let your women *keep silence* in the *ecclesiai*: for it is not permitted unto them to speak; but they are *commanded* to be *under obedience*, as also'—that is, *besides* the evangel; *as well as* the gospel; so *also*— 'saith the law', I Corinthians 14:34.

'And if they'—the women—'will learn any thing, let them ask their husbands at home'—which is what Eve did not do; but Sarah did, who embodied this meek submission and subjection to God, to Christ, and to her husband, as the apostle Peter carefully instructs you, I Peter 3:5,6.

As to the rest, the apostle Paul adds *'for it is a shame for women to speak in the ecclesia'*, I Corinthians 14:35.

Openings in First Corinthians

FOURTH: PAUL STRESSES THAT THE WORD OF GOD CAME *UNTO* THEM, NOT AROSE *FROM* THEM. THEN, LET EVERY ONE OF THEM ACKNOWLEDGE WITHOUT GAINSAYING THAT THE DOCTRINE AND DISCIPLINE OF I CORINTHIANS 14:1-40 *ARE THE COMMANDMENTS OF THE LORD*, VERSES 36-40.

With a mixture of asperity and indignation the apostle allows some of the outrage that he feels to appear in the closing verses. 'What?' How this bursts out!

And so it would again today against every know-all so-called 'brother' with a head full of dead scriptures—of whatever version—and a heart full of presumption—over whatever notions—who thinks that such impudence can supersede the four vital questions, 'How then shall they call on him in whom they have not believed? and how shall they believe in him of whom they have not heard?

'And how shall they hear without a preacher?'—mark that: *hear*, not *read*; and a *preacher*, not the *dead letter*: the Ethiopian eunuch had that; Cornelius had that—'And how shall they preach, *except they be sent?*'

And if *sent*, then such divine, heavenly apostolic ministers as these who bring the word of faith which we preach, and who bring it unto us with the Holy Ghost sent down from heaven, ought to be received with all heartfelt humility and submission.

And if these are sent to bring to us the word of faith, How come you deny them, pick up a bible—of whatever version, about which background you know nothing—and without fail confound it, add to it, subtract from it, multiply it, divide it, and yet profess it, *when you were never sent, no, nor ever received any one thing from God out of heaven to bring to the people?*

What? Came the word of God out from you? No, it did not. It came unto you only; or else, properly received and rightly so-called, *it never came unto you at all.* For you can be sure of this: *the dead letter in your hands will never be a substitute for this mighty work of the living God in those who are sent by the Holy Ghost.*

However, that word *was* sent, and it *did* come to the Corinthians, and hence, their conversion was a living testimony to the power of God. And, notwithstanding that later they erred, yet despite all, he who was sent to them in the power of God still had such a divinely given hope of their recovery, for all their need of so much and varied correction, that he was not to be disappointed.

'Or came it'–the word of God–'unto you only?' What can they do, who must own the sending of Paul to Corinth, the Lord saying to him in a vision in the night, 'Be not afraid, but speak, and hold not thy peace: for I am with thee, and no man shall set on thee to hurt thee: for I have much people in this city', Acts 18:9,10?

They can but bow in shame and contrition of heart. And what can *they* do, who, unconverted, nowadays lift themselves up, every man unsent, who must book speakers, filling up the vacant dates themselves by both necessity and presumption, thrusting themselves into that to which God never called them.

And what? Being unconverted, they gain no converts. Being uncalled, they cannot call others. Being unsent, they can never arrive. Being dead, they can give no life.

But putting on a show, they act out and do all that they can, with as bright a pretence as possible, attracting those as light and chaffy, as vain and carnal as themselves, worldlings all, till the whole is got together in the flesh over a dead bible–of whatever version–and a frothy form of religion.

But it was never so at Corinth. What? Paul declares that the word of God, in life and power, *came unto them only*. It never came out from them. Which is what they could not deny, and did not deny, but humbly confessed, as witnessed by the second epistle to the Corinthians from Paul, an apostle of Jesus Christ by the will of God, and Timothy, brother, unto the *ecclesia* of God which is at Corinth, with all the saints which are in all Achaia.

Here it is evident that even the most disputatious and contentious had been brought to a broken spirit and contrite heart, being subdued of God, and made submissive in the Holy Ghost.

But first Paul says, 'If any man think himself to be a prophet, or spiritual, let him acknowledge that the things'—all the things, every one of the things, in the whole epistle without exception, and especially in chapter 14—'that I write unto you *are the commandments of the Lord.*'

But should anyone question anything whatsoever, then 'Ignorance' was writ large across his forehead: and who will hear anything from such a man as that? Since he is obdurate, let him be dismissed. 'If any man be ignorant, let him be ignorant.'

In conclusion the apostle conveys his solicitude concerning them, studying the welfare of his own dear children in the faith, full of helpfulness and encouragement.

'Wherefore, brethren, covet to prophesy, and forbid not to speak with tongues. Let all things be done decently and in order', I Corinthians 14:39,40.

This ends the chapter, and the entire eleventh division of the epistle.

(4) THE EVANGELICAL TRUTH OF THE RESURRECTION OF THE DEAD, CHAPTER 15:1-58.

In this closing passage under the heading of 'Judgment Concerning Assembling Together' the apostle declares to the *ecclesia* at Corinth the evangel which he preached unto them, which they received, and in which they stood.

But why declare this? Because of the error of some among them, who, not only forgetting what they had received, substituted that which struck at the heart of the evangel.

What struck at the heart of the evangel? The denial of the resurrection of Christ from the dead.

The apostle shows that without belief in the resurrection, they had neither the evangel, nor the faith, nor yet any hope whatever either in this life or the next. Hence his insistence upon the truth that the resurrection of Christ lay at the very heart of the apostles' witness and doctrine in the belief of which alone salvation was assured.

'Moreover, brethren, I declare unto you the gospel which I preached unto you, which also ye have received, and wherein ye stand; by which ye are saved, if ye keep in memory what I preached unto you, unless ye have believed in vain', I Corinthians 15:1,2.

As was the case with each successive instance following on from the *first* occasion on which the apostle specifically addressed the *ecclesia* at Corinth *as assembled together*–'For *first* of *all*, when ye come together in the *ecclesia*', I Corinthians 11:18 – so in this the *last* instance: *the passage is corrective.*

Throughout this long chapter – I Corinthians 15:1-58 – the apostle is occupied with the correction of their error regarding the resurrection of the dead.

This is revealed in the following crucial statement, put in the form of a question, concerning the departure from the truth of certain at Corinth: 'Now if Christ be preached' – by all the apostolic eyewitnesses testifying together with one voice –'that he rose from the dead, *how say some among you that there is no resurrection of the dead?*', I Corinthians 15:12.

The challenge sounded out by Paul's question in this place provides the reason for the answering corrective doctrine which he declares everywhere else, from the first verse to the last.

The fact that the apostle reiterates the truth of the evangel 'by which ye are saved'; that this must be 'kept in memory';

and that faith must be kept alive – 'unless ye have believed in vain' – go together to demonstrate that vague statements, recited creeds, sentimental feelings, simple professions of an otherwise undefined 'Jesus', much less a mere 'acceptance' or 'committal', *are not enough* – according to I Corinthians chapter 15 – to warrant either the apostolic meaning of believing, or that of the faith of the evangel, or, of course, of salvation itself.

How does I Corinthians 15 demonstrate this?

Because it *insists* on the truth of the resurrection being integral to the evangel; that it is the evangel *itself* that saves; and that faith cannot respect Christ, nor can Christ be believed upon, *save through that evangel given by the Father, spoken by the Son, witnessed by the Holy Ghost, and declared by the apostles.*

And *that* evangel incorporates the resurrection.

So, 'how say some among you that there is no resurrection of the dead?', I Corinthians 15:12.

The faith that saves, the evangel that is to be believed, the apostles' doctrine that declares the word of life, the doctrine of Christ that brings into union with the Father and the Son, in a word, *this* evangel declared by Paul, I Corinthians 15:1, finds its strength in the sum of its parts. '*It* is the power of God unto salvation', Romans 1:16.

All, but *all*, the parts are essential rightly and in balance to declare him who *is* the truth.

To believe in Christ is to believe *the evangel* of Christ. To profess a 'Jesus' or a 'Christ' *without* that evangel is to be *anti* Christ. To profess only a part of the evangel, discarding another part – such as the resurrection – evinces a false profession: no true faith at all.

Christ is expressed, and expresses himself, through the evangel, the whole of the evangel, and nothing other than the evangel. This was declared once for all by the eyewitnesses, the chosen apostles. It was 'declared' unto us.

The word of God came not out from us, it came unto us only. Then, we cannot discard what we will, retain what we wish, or invent what we want.

The sole expression of Christ is in the truths of the evangel, completely in order, perfectly in proportion, and wholly in balance: then and there the glorious evangel shines, and shines in the face of Jesus Christ.

It is *this* that is to be both preached and believed: *all of it; not just some of it; much less a 'Jesus' without it; or, worse, some alternative to it.*

Christ, who is the truth, is expressed in the truths of the evangel, *all of which together as a whole constitute the truth, from which any missing part*–such as the resurrection of Christ from the dead–*nullifies the whole.*

Observe that it is this verity by which the Spirit inspires the apostle in his corrective doctrine concerning the truth of the resurrection in I Corinthians chapter 15.

FIRST; THE APOSTOLIC DECLARATION AFFIRMS THE INDISPENSABILITY OF THE TRUTH OF THE RESURRECTION TO THE INTEGRITY OF THE EVANGEL OF CHRIST, I CORINTHIANS 15:1-11.

If so, it behoved the apostle to clarify that evangel as a whole, as he declared it when first he preached to the Corinthians: 'Moreover, brethren, I declare unto you the gospel which I preached unto you,

'which also ye have received, and wherein ye stand; by which also ye are saved, 'if ye keep in memory what I preached unto you'–or, more literally *'by which also ye are being saved, if ye hold fast what word I evangelized to you'*–'unless ye have believed in vain.

'For I delivered unto you first of all that which I also received.'

At this point the apostle forthwith but briefly summarizes for their benefit and memory that very evangel which he had evangelized to them 'first of all', or, *in the first place*, I Corinthians 15:1-3.

So that before commencing his brief summary–or definition–of the evangel in its essence, the apostle recalls to their remembrance the circumstances and manner of their having received it at the time, and, indeed, of their then holding it fast as a whole.

To this end the apostle states the things in which he himself was–or else had been–active. Firstly, why he was writing this at that present time: 'I declare unto you', present tense, verse 1. Thus he is about to recall to them in writing that which he had done for them in the past.

It was to be a written declaration stating the apostle's current recollection of his past activity–and their beginnings–at Corinth.

His past activity? That which he had done for them in the beginning? He had preached the gospel unto them. Here the apostle recalls the very first thing which he had done at Corinth: 'I declare'–now–'unto you the gospel which I *preached*'–then–'unto you', I Corinthians 15:1.

The first verb is in the present, the second in the past tense.

This is the apostle's recollection of what he had done for them at the very beginning when he came to Corinth.

'I declare unto you *the evangel which I evangelized to you*', verse 1. He repeats this in verse 2: 'I preached unto you', or, literally, *'what word I evangelized unto you.'*

He is going to bring home to them at present that which he had preached unto them – the evangel which he had evangelized – in the past.

Why? Because some among them said *now* what they had neither heard, nor would have dared to say *then*. What was this? That there is no resurrection of the dead, verse 12.

But *this*, declares Paul, *utterly contradicts the evangel by which they had been evangelized: it attempts to overturn that word which he had evangelized unto them when first he came among them.*

Then, he is going to jolt their memories by reiterating the evangel by which they should be saved: 'unless ye have believed in vain', verse 2.

In declaring again the evangel which he had evangelized long before, the apostle is emphasizing the fact – the *obvious* fact – that when first he came to Corinth, he had preached *the evangel*, and that in its very essence, verse 1.

If so, what they heard, received, and believed *then*, was 'the word of truth, the evangel of your salvation', Ephesians 1:13. Observe, it is *the* evangel.

There is none other: 'But though we, or an angel from heaven, preach any other evangel unto you than that which we have preached unto you, let him be accursed. As we said before, so say I now again, If any man preach any other evangel unto you than that ye have received, let him be accursed', Galatians 1:8,9.

Observe that the apostle is speaking of a *body of truth*, namely, the *body of truth which declares the person and work of Christ*. That body of truth was the sum of every single one of its essential parts, of which none was more significant than that which declared *the resurrection of Christ from the dead*.

Hence Paul's emphasis on the evangel strikes at the enormity of the presumption adopted by 'some among you' that either the evangel, or any part of the evangel, could ever be considered as optional, subject to mutation, or else alterable: 'How say some among you that there is no resurrection of the dead?', verse 12.

This evangel is described under various terms in the new testament: for example it *is* the new testament. It is called 'the doctrine of Christ.'

This doctrine declares the things – *things*, mark it – that constitute those essential, related, and balanced truths by which the Holy Ghost through the apostles enshrined the truth, the whole truth, and nothing but the truth concerning Jesus Christ, namely, the 'things most surely believed among us', Luke 1:1.

'But continue thou' – though all about seemed to be falling away – 'continue *thou* in the *things* which thou hast learned and hast been assured of, knowing of whom thou hast learned them', II Timothy 3:14.

What things? 'The form of sound words, which thou hast heard of me, in faith and love which is in Christ Jesus', II Timothy 1:13. This 'form' – delineation; pattern – answers to those truths which as a whole constitute the evangel of Christ.

This is the apostles' doctrine, in which the early *ecclesia* continued steadfastly, Acts 2:42. It is the word, in the truth of which, if they continued, then were they Christ's disciples indeed; 'and ye shall know the truth, and the truth shall make you free', John 8:31,32.

Again, the evangel is called 'the faith once delivered unto the saints', Jude 3. Delivered to the saints, note, not the academics.

Man's creation of a separate priestly caste – of 'clergy' ordained to administer 'sacraments' to the 'laity' – largely secured the apostasy, in which education took the place of revelation;

clerisy took the place of Spirit-filled saints; divinity faculties took the place of the calling, discipline, and teaching of Jesus Christ through the Holy Ghost from heaven; and 'theology'– whatever *that* means – took the place of 'the faith once delivered unto the saints'.

Now, *that* faith is what the apostle calls *the evangel*, I Corinthians 15:1,2.

Whence take notice that the apostles were sent to evangelize, and what they evangelized was *the evangel*. The way in which this was received was by *believing*.

The ministers of Jesus Christ received grace and apostleship 'for obedience to the faith among all nations, for his name', Romans 1:5.

Those who heard and received such apostolic ministers sent 'into all the world to preach the gospel', Mark 16:15, 'obeyed from the heart that form of doctrine which was delivered to them', Romans 6:17, and, 'He that believeth and is baptized shall be saved; but he that believeth not shall be damned', Mark 16:16.

Where 'believing' means wholly submitting to and receiving from the heart *all the evangel*, in *all its parts*, and *in the whole*, that is, sincerely yielding the whole-hearted obedience of faith to the entirety of the apostles' doctrine, the doctrine of Christ, the form of sound words, the faith once delivered, the new testament, the word of truth, namely, *the evangel*.

If so, this is to come to *the knowledge* of the truth. For it is *knowledge* – in the inward and spiritual reception of it – to which one responds in the evangel. Hence those who believed were 'transformed by the renewing of their *mind*.' It is *the truth* that is believed.

Then, it is not just the *experience* of Christ: above all, it is the *knowledge* of Christ. The first is *felt*: the last is *believed*. Experience – true or false – only concerns that which one feels about him personally; but believing concerns *what he is in himself*.

One *feels* subjective experience, and this is within *oneself*; but one *believes* objective doctrine, and *that* is what *he* is, *in and of himself*.

In the one case everything is confined within *you*; but in the other instance everything is expanded to *him*. That is what is meant by believing.

One believes *the evangel*, and Paul declares that this is exactly the truth which he preached when he evangelized the evangel at the beginning in Corinth. If so, now, 'How say some among you that there is no resurrection of the dead?', verse 12.

Those 'some among you' would never have said that at the beginning. Then, what Paul preached unto them, they, together with all, heartily received. Had they forgotten? They must needs keep in memory the evangel which the apostle evangelized unto them, because *nothing else, and nothing less* would save them.

Do they contend? Then must the apostle conclude that they had believed in vain?

'I declare unto you the evangel which I evangelized unto you, which also ye have received, and wherein ye stand; by which also ye are saved, if ye keep in memory what I evangelized unto you, unless ye have believed in vain.

'For I delivered unto you first of all that which I also received', I Corinthians 15:1-3. In that Paul says that he *delivered* the evangel, it follows that nothing that he preached was initiated, contrived, or invented by him. It was not his opinion in religion: it was his part faithfully to deliver the message on behalf of the sender.

What he delivered was wholly the message of the one from whom he had received it: the apostle neither added to it, subtracted from it, multiplied it, divided it, or substituted anything of his own – or anyone else's – in place of it: what was given to him – no more, no less – that he delivered unto them.

It was not even that he delivered his own experience of Christ, that is to say, his *own* testimony. He received what he was to deliver, and that was what he passed on faithfully.

It was not what Christ had done to or in him: that would be *his* testimony: it was what God had done in Christ; that was *God's* testimony. The message was the evangel of God concerning his Son, a message complete within itself.

It was *God's* testimony concerning his own Son, which Paul had received of him by the Holy Ghost under the anointing. It was the *testimony of Christ* which he had received from God out of heaven in its entirety, and passed on to them, delivering that message to them faithfully, exactly as he had received it.

His place had been to act as a messenger on behalf of the one who had sent him, an ambassador, a post, who, having this charge, did no more than deliver the message that was his responsibility to pass on to the recipients.

This message – the evangel – Paul describes as 'that which I also *received*'. How did he receive it? He received it in a unique, apostolic manner. He received it from the Father, by the Son, through the Holy Ghost: 'I certify you, brethren, that the evangel which was preached of me is not after man. For I neither received it of man, neither was I taught it, but by the revelation of Jesus Christ', Galatians 1:11,12.

As to that, the Son himself – uniquely and apostolically – appeared to Paul, saying, 'I have appeared unto thee for this purpose, to make thee a minister and a witness both of these things which thou hast seen, and of those things in the which I will appear unto thee', Acts 26:16.

Hence Paul speaks of 'the dispensation of the grace of God which is given me to you-ward: how that by revelation he made known unto me the mystery', Ephesians 3:2,3.

And again, referring to the evangel, Paul says, 'Whereof I was made a minister, according to the gift of the grace of God given unto me by the effectual working of his power. Unto me, who am less than the least of all saints, is this grace given, that I should preach among the Gentiles the unsearchable riches of Christ', Ephesians 3:7,8.

Once more: 'I am made a minister, according to the dispensation of God which is given to me for you, to fulfil the word of God', Colossians 1:25.

Then, this evangel which the apostle delivered unto the *ecclesia* at Corinth was that which he had received by revelation from God, concerning the person and work of Christ, a dispensation having been given to him to deliver as he had received it, which was what he had done faithfully throughout his ministry, and not least at Corinth.

What he received was all of God, and what he delivered was all of God, and, moreover, he had done so as sent, delivering the evangel not in word only, but also in power, and in the Holy Ghost, and in much assurance, I Thessalonians 1:5.

Thus he declares unto them in this present epistle the things that he had done when first he came to them in times past: he had evangelized the evangel. He had delivered unto them the evangel. And, before ever he came to them, having been called to the apostolate, he had received that evangel by revelation from the Father, by the Son, and through the Holy Ghost.

Moreover, this same evangel was a profound mystery, it brought into the fellowship of the mystery: nevertheless, not all its profundity, but the clarity of its first principles, the evangel of Christ in its essence, 'first of all' Paul had delivered to the *ecclesia* at Corinth.

At this point in I Corinthians 15:3 Paul enunciates the essence of the evangel even as 'first of all' he had delivered unto them that which he had received of God.

He declares the things – mark that: the *things* – most surely believed among us, Luke 1:1, in which, beginning with the person of Christ, he proceeds to affirm his death, burial, and resurrection.

Next he enumerates in order the chosen eyewitnesses of these attested and verified *historical facts*, evidently seen by those who ate and drank with him after he rose from the dead, Acts 10:39-42.

'For I delivered unto you first of all that which I also received, how that Christ died for our sins according to the scriptures.' How much is revealed by this opening declaration of the evangel! That the Messiah, the Christ, promised ever since the foundation of the world, *had actually come*. Moreover, he had come *to die*. Further, he *had* actually died.

But his was no ordinary death. How could it be? What? Of the Messiah, who should come into the world, known – however dimly – of all nations even to the ends of the earth, as saith the wise men from the east, 'Where is he that is born king of the Jews?'.

Likewise the Samaritan woman: 'I know that Messias cometh, which is called Christ: when he is come, he will tell us all things', John 4:25.

And this dim flicker persevered in the consciousness of all nations – as 'To the unknown God', Acts 17:23 – however enlightened or debased; but now, saith Paul, *He has come*. And *come to die.*

Why? Because 'Christ Jesus came into the world to save sinners', I Timothy 1:15, and, if so, by dying in their place.

Openings in First Corinthians

Whose place? Directly in this epistle 'our' refers to Paul together with the Corinthian *ecclesia*. Then, not all the city of Corinth, but those called out of it, even as saith the Lord at the beginning, 'I have much people in this city', Acts 18:10.

Not, I have the whole population of this city; but, 'I have much people'–out of the population–'in this city'. For the sins of these, Christ had died, as it is written by Paul the apostle to the *ecclesia* at Corinth, 'Christ died for *our* sins according to the scriptures', I Corinthians 15:3.

But what is a death 'according to the scriptures'? It is a sacrificial death; a substitutionary death; an atoning death; and it is an effectual death, all to put away sin by the sacrifice of himself.

It is a death depicted in the burnt offering, the meat offering, the peace offering, and the sin offering; in Abel's lamb and Abraham's ram; in the continual burnt offering; in the passover lamb; in the sacrifice of *Yom Kippur*, the day of atonement: *that* kind of death.

It is a death 'according to the scriptures' as saith the holy prophets which have been since the world began.

For example, the prophet Isaiah: he prophesied of a death 'according to the scriptures' saying, 'Surely he hath borne our griefs, and carried our sorrows: yet we did esteem him stricken, smitten of God, and afflicted. But he was wounded for our transgressions, he was bruised for our iniquities: the chastisement of our peace was upon him; and with his stripes we are healed.

'All we like sheep have gone astray; we have turned every one to his own way; and the LORD hath laid on him the iniquity of us all.'

And again, 'for the transgression of my people was he stricken.' Once more, 'by his knowledge shall my righteous servant justify many; for he shall bear their iniquities', Isaiah 53:4-6,8,11.

Now, this is a death, a substitutionary, sacrificial death, a death 'according to the scriptures'.

In that 'Christ died for our sins according to the scriptures', this does not mean some general, universal atonement effectual only when the will of man makes it applicable. On the contrary, it means a precise, particular atonement, in which he *actually took away the sins of those for whom he died at the moment at which he died*.

His shed blood was witness that *those sins were actually taken away for ever*: 'covered' by the blood, never again to appear before the righteous judgment and all-searching eye of Almighty God. They were gone for ever, *then*.

Hence the apostle stresses positively, 'Christ died for *our* sins according to the scriptures' for it is certain that all those for whom he died—including Paul and the *ecclesia* at Corinth—had their sins blotted out by the blood of Christ, when that blood was shed in death.

Hence Jesus saith 'This is my blood of the new testament, which is shed for many for the remission of sins', Matthew 26:28. Where notice, first, that it is the blood that was shed that remits the sins, not the believing upon it. What is believed upon is that *the blood, once shed, actually remitted, dismissed, those sins at that time*.

And, secondly, Jesus himself limits the application of the shed blood to the sins of 'many', a word which could only have been used because he deemed it necessary to qualify the number, lest any should suppose 'all'. Now, they cannot. Not for sins. Sin is another question.

As to sins, all those whose sins are forgiven them *had those sins blotted out when Jesus' blood was shed*. It was shed 'for the remission of sins', namely, of the 'many' in and under the new testament.

This is confirmed in the epistle to the Hebrews, where the writer affirms 'Christ was once offered to bear the sins of *many*', Hebrews 9:28. Here the sins, laid upon Christ, were *borne*, and, if so, borne *away*.

When? When 'Christ was once offered', namely, at the cross.

Whose sins? 'the sins of *many*', that is, of all those redeemed to God by the blood of the Lamb *out of* every kindred, and tongue, and people, and nation, Revelation 5:9.

From which reference, notice, *blood* redeemed them, the blood of the Lamb, *when he was slain*, Revelation 5:9.

It is *this* that is meant, and to which the Holy Ghost bears witness, when it is said, 'Christ died for *our* sins according to the scriptures'.

By 'scriptures' in this place the apostle refers to the thirty-nine books of the old testament. But since the reference is apostolic, and in writing, it is proper to include the twenty-seven books of the new testament, given by the pen of the holy apostles after the ascension of the Lord Jesus, and following the descent of the Holy Ghost, who 'led them into all truth' besides 'bringing all things to their remembrance'.

Thus he embraces the entire inspired record of the books of the new testament, to be included—as implied—under the term 'scriptures', even as Peter testified of Paul's writings, counting them all of one with the 'other' scriptures, namely, the entire old testament, II Peter 3:16.

'And that he was buried', I Corinthians 15:4. 'And when they had fulfilled all that was written of him, they took him down, and laid him in a sepulchre', Acts 13:29.

This confirms his death with a witness: 'But when they came to Jesus, and saw that he was dead already, they brake not his legs:

but one of the soldiers with a spear pierced his side, and forthwith came there out blood and water.' 'Then took they the body of Jesus, and wound it in linen clothes with the spices, as the manner of the Jews is to bury', John 19:33,34,40.

From thence, they 'beheld the sepulchre, and how his body was laid', Luke 23:55.

'For', saith Jesus, 'as Jonas was three days and three nights in the belly of the great fish; so shall the Son of man be three days and three nights in the heart of the earth', Matthew 12:40.

Yet though his corpse was removed from the face of the earth, his dead body wrapped in grave clothes in the depths of the sepulchre, mute witness by its absence to all that had been taken away in death, yet he saw no corruption. 'Because thou wilt not leave my soul in *hadēs*, neither wilt thou suffer thine Holy One to see corruption.'

Where David, being a prophet, spake not of himself, but of Christ, 'that *his* soul was not left in *hadēs*, neither *his* flesh did see corruption', Acts 2:27,31. This word of Peter, quoting David, was given on the day of Pentecost.

Paul later confirms the same, saying, 'Thou shalt not suffer thine Holy One to see corruption', Acts 13:35 – no, not *see* corruption – even though his dead body lay in the grave those three days and three nights 'according to the scriptures'. This was attested by many witnesses, not only of his own disciples; but of the Roman authorities; their soldiers; the centurion; and the rulers and people of the Jewish nation.

'And that he rose again the third day according to the scriptures', I Corinthians 15:4. Of the resurrection from the dead, Peter testified on behalf of all the apostles: 'And we are witnesses of all things which he did both in the land of the Jews, and in Jerusalem; *whom they slew and hanged on a tree.*' That was what *they* did.

'Him God raised up the third day, and showed him openly; not to all the people, but unto witnesses chosen before of God, even to us, who did eat and drink with him *after he rose from the dead.*' And that was what God did. Acts 10:39-41.

Paul shows how the resurrection on the third day was 'according to the scriptures', declaring 'But God raised him from the dead', adding, 'And we declare unto you glad tidings, how that the promise which was made unto the fathers'–according to the scriptures–'God hath fulfilled the same unto us their children, *in that he hath raised up Jesus again*;

'As it is also written'–apart from the promise in the scriptures, 'also' the following prophecies appear in the psalms–'in the second psalm, Thou art my Son, this day have I begotten thee'–that is, from the *dead*. This day? Which day? The third day, 'according to the scriptures'.

'And as concerning that he raised him up from the dead'– according to the scriptures–'now no more to return to corruption, he saith on this wise, I will give you the sure mercies of David. Wherefore he saith also in another psalm, Thou shalt not suffer thine Holy One to see corruption.

'For David, after he had served his own generation by the will of God, fell on sleep, and was laid unto his fathers, and saw corruption: but he, *whom God raised again*, saw no corruption', Acts 13:30,32-37.

If this be not 'according to the scriptures' what is according to the scriptures? Here is a promise to the fathers, repeated again and again over the entire old testament. Further to which Paul quotes two psalms of David, and yet another insight into the future, to behold the resurrection from the dead, foretold by the prophet Isaiah.

And, remark, it is Jesus' *body* that was raised: he was raised *bodily*. His *body*–which in the case of all humanity save his, upon burial, saw corruption – 'as in Adam *all* die'; 'he was laid unto his fathers, and saw corruption' – the *same* body, this *same* Jesus, was physically raised from the dead, never having seen corruption, for ever to reign in life far beyond the reach of the grave, the other side of death.

That was the reality which gripped the apostles.

'Behold my hands and my feet, that *it is I myself*' – it is *the same body: the marks show it* – 'handle me, and see; for a spirit hath not flesh and bones, as ye see me have', Luke 24:39.

Likewise Jesus, risen *in the body*, the *same* body, the marks of the crucifixion upon him, saith to Thomas, 'Reach hither thy finger, and behold my hands; and reach hither thy hand, and thrust it into my side: and be not faithless, but believing', John 20:27.

That is, believing *in the resurrection of the same body, as such, from the grave in which he had been laid in death three days and three nights before.*

This was the truth, the astounding truth, the truth that vindicated Christ's coming, his life, his words, his death, his burial, all that had been achieved in death, every ancient prophecy that had passed upon him, his future glory, and his coming judgment.

'Because he' – God – 'hath appointed a day, in the which he will judge the world in righteousness by that man whom he hath ordained; whereof he hath given assurance unto all men, *in that he hath raised him from the dead*', Acts 17:31.

This, I say, *this* was the reality that gripped the apostles: *they were witnesses of his resurrection from the dead.*

'And as they spake unto the people, the priests, and the captain of the temple, and the Sadducees, came upon them, being grieved that they taught the people, and preached through Jesus the resurrection from the dead', Acts 4:1,2. 'And with great power gave the apostles witness of the resurrection of the Lord Jesus: and great grace was upon them all', Acts 4:33.

From the beginning this astounding verity, witnessed by their own eyes, ears, and hands, *gripped the apostles*. There *was* a resurrection of the dead, *witness the bodily resurrection of the Lord Jesus*.

'Whom God hath raised up, having loosed the pains of death: because it was not possible that he should be holden of it.

'For David speaketh concerning him'–his resurrection being according to the scriptures–'I foresaw the Lord always before my face, for he is on my right hand, that I should not be moved: therefore did my heart rejoice, and my tongue was glad; moreover also my flesh shall rest in hope:

'Because thou wilt not leave my soul in *hadēs*, neither wilt thou suffer thine Holy One to see corruption. Thou hast made known to me the ways of life; thou shalt make me full of joy with thy countenance.

'Men and brethren, let me freely speak unto you of the patriarch David, that he is both dead and buried, and his sepulchre is with us unto this day.

'Therefore being a prophet, and knowing that God had sworn with an oath unto him, that of the fruit of his loins, according to the flesh, he would raise up Christ to sit on his throne; he seeing this before spake'–and wrote in the scriptures some one thousand years before the event–'*of the resurrection of Christ,*

'That *his* soul'–not David's soul, who spoke and wrote of Christ a millennium before; but Christ's, of whom David prophesied– '*his* soul was not left in *hadēs*, neither *his* flesh did see corruption.

This Jesus hath God raised up, whereof we all are witnesses'; so testified Peter on the day of Pentecost, Acts 2:24-32.

'And that he was *seen* of Cephas, then of the twelve: after that, he was *seen* of above five hundred brethren at once; of whom the greater part remain unto this present, but some are fallen asleep.

'After that, he was *seen* of James; then of all the apostles. And last of all he was *seen* of me also, as of one born out of due time', I Corinthians 15:5-8.

Now here are the holy apostles, chosen of God as eyewitnesses, impeccable in their truthfulness; here are above five hundred just, holy, and true brethren at once, most living when Paul wrote; here is James, a very pillar of rectitude; and here Paul himself, whose witness is true, and ye know that he speaks truth.

These all testify with one voice – the voice of unimpeachable honesty, and that by the Holy Ghost – not to add the voices of David and Isaiah, some one thousand years before, verified in the event – *one voice, I say, that, bodily, in the body in which he was crucified, witness the marks in his hands, feet, and side, bodily Jesus rose from the dead.*

And these all, seeing both it and him with their own eyes, speak to the ends of the world of what they witnessed infallibly, declaring the truth by the Holy Ghost from heaven.

Then, 'How say some among you that there is no resurrection of the dead?', I Corinthians 15:12.

How? For by so doing you make a lie of that evangel of which the apostle had shown – and *is* showing – *that the resurrection is an integral part*; you make a lie of the testimony of the Holy Ghost, who records that he rose from the dead, and bears record to this day; you make God a liar, who declares that he raised Christ

Openings in First Corinthians

from the dead; you make the Son of God a liar, who showed himself alive after his passion by many infallible proofs.

Moreover, you set aside as worth nothing more than a pack of lies the eyewitness of all the holy apostles, of Cephas, James, Paul himself, and above five hundred brethren at once.

And, despising so great a testimony as this, of God and man; heaven and earth; time and eternity; life and death; this world and the next; of all the apostles and five hundred brethren: I say to you, Tell us: Who are you?

Who do you think you are, and what have you seen, or what do you know? or how will the balance go, you laid on the one side, and this infallible, irrefutable, incontrovertible testimony, with all those who bore witness, on the other side?

'How say some among you that there is no resurrection of the dead?'

Next the apostle writes about himself, 'as one born out of due time'. The meaning is that as an *apostle* he did not come forth when he should have done. Thus he employs a kind of irony against himself, depreciating his apostleship in relation to the twelve.

'For I am the least of the apostles, that am not meet to be called an apostle, because' – before he was so called – 'I persecuted the church of God', I Corinthians 15:9.

The twelve were called by the Son of man on earth in Israel, during the days of his flesh; Paul was called afterwards outside Damascus by the Son of God from heaven when he had entered into his glory.

But if this was the will of him who called every one of the apostles, who is he that shall require him to give an account of his matters?

For, saith Paul, '*By the grace of God* I am what I am: and his grace which was bestowed upon me was not in vain; but I laboured more abundantly than they all: yet not I, but the grace of God which was with me.

'Therefore, whether it were I or they, *so we preach, and so ye believed*', I Corinthians 15:10,11.

SECOND; THE INDISPENSABILITY OF THE TRUTH OF THE RESURRECTION TO THE INTEGRITY OF THE EVANGEL ENFORCED AGAINST THOSE WHO ERRED AT CORINTH, I CORINTHIANS 15:12.

Now here is the explanation for the apostle's emphasis on the evangel which he preached at the beginning in Corinth; of his recalling their reception of it; of the necessity of their continuing in it; of salvation being exclusive to it; and of his defining so clearly the very essence of the evangel itself; and, finally, besides all this, leading up to the explanation for the first four verses, the names and number of the witnesses of the resurrection of Christ from the dead, verses 4-11.

But what is the explanation? why all this? Because 'some among you' denied the resurrection of the dead, verse 12.

That is the reason for the earlier passage: *no one can deny the resurrection without denying the evangel in its essence*. It was *that* which the apostle had established in the opening verses.

As to them, where were the 'some' among them at the beginning? Then, all as one man had received the evangel, the whole evangel, and nothing but the evangel, preached by the apostle sent to them, verse 1.

And where were the 'some among you' in the interval? Not apparent until now? Indeed, there were not 'some' apart from 'all', at the beginning; nor, presumably, until comparatively recently.

For 'all' received the *whole* evangel at the first.

It was that 'wherein ye stand', and had stood up until now, namely, until 'some among you' fell away from the truth and in effect denied their standing: and openly, too, having no shame about 'saying' what denied both resurrection and evangel.

But let them be under no delusion: they were denying their own salvation: 'by which also ye are saved.'

But 'some among you' had forsaken that evangel, the rather inviting perdition than embracing salvation.

One must constantly recall the evangel, if one is to be saved at last: 'by which also ye are saved *if* ye keep in memory what I preached unto you', verse 1.

But they, the 'some', had expunged from their memories the integrity of the evangel, and, if so, these preferred erroneous heresies, apparently having believed in vain.

Was it so? Was it true that some had come to this: 'unless ye have believed in vain'? If not, 'How say some among you that there is no resurrection of the dead?', verse 12.

Note therefore the strength behind the opening words of the twelfth verse: 'Now if Christ be preached that he rose from the dead.'

If he be preached? But he was so preached! Such preaching was integral to the essence, the most basic truth of the evangel, as had been shown.

'For I delivered unto you first of all that which I also received, how that Christ died for our sins according to the scriptures; and that he was buried, and that he rose again the third day according to the scriptures', verses 3,4.

This *was* the preaching of the evangel. It was *the evangel itself*. Then why '*If* Christ be preached that he rose from the dead', verse 12?

For there *are* no 'ifs' or 'buts'. Christ *was* so preached. Yes, and at that preached by whom? By the holy apostles. Namely, by the eyewitnesses chosen of God.

By Cephas; by the twelve; by James. After that, by all the apostles, confirmed by above five hundred brethren at once.

And, finally, preached by Paul also, even as he clearly testified: 'Moreover, brethren, I declare unto you the evangel which I evangelized unto you.'

Then, these things being so, and they were so, 'how say some among you'—how *can* you say it? how *dare* you say it?—'that there is no resurrection of the dead?', I Corinthians 15:12. What is this but 'they that observe lying vanities forsake their own mercy', Jonah 2:8?

Third; the disastrous effect upon the integrity of the evangel resulting from the denial of the resurrection, I Corinthians 15:13-19.

In this passage the apostle reproves and convicts those who denied the resurrection of the dead despite their erstwhile confession of that evangel which they had heard and received in the beginning. Then, at the present, 'How say some among you that there is no resurrection of the dead?'.

This denied their first faith.

Moreover, such an appalling error—once granted—would result in disastrous consequences. Five disastrous consequences. Very well then, let them consider what they are saying:

First; if they were right 'that there is not a resurrection of the dead'—for so the Greek reads: it was not simply Christ's resurrection that they denied; they were saying *that there is not a resurrection of the dead at all*—then, if so, it must follow of necessity *that neither had Christ risen from the dead!*

'If there be no resurrection of the dead, then is Christ not risen', I Corinthians 15:13. Or, to render the Greek grammatical form, 'But if a resurrection of [the] dead there is not, *neither has Christ been raised.*'

In a word, Paul is saying, Unless *all* the dead rise, then *none* rise. Conversely, if *one* rose from the dead, then *all* must rise from the dead.

As sure as if *one* be born of woman, *all* are born of woman, and as certain as if *one* die, so *all* die – these things being immutable certainties – *so also is the resurrection*: if *one* rose, *all* will rise.

And who is he that can contend against the universal and immutable verities of the birth and death of all mankind? Then let none contend against the concomitant truth of the resurrection, attested by many infallible proofs witnessed of the one man, Christ Jesus. For if *all* rise not, 'then is *Christ* not risen', verse 13. But verses 4-8 show that Christ *is* risen. Then *all* shall rise, and there *is* – and must be – a universal resurrection of the dead.

Second; if they were right – God forbid – 'that there is not a resurrection of the dead', then Christ could not have risen: for, as Paul had shown, either the dead rise, or the dead rise not. And if *all* the dead rise not, then *none* of the dead rise.

As certainly as the birth of *one* man attests the birth of *all* men; and as surely as the death of *one* man presages the death of *all* men, so infallibly does the resurrection of *one* ensure the resurrection of *all*. For it is no more ludicrous in the face of *one* resurrection to deny the resurrection of *all*, than it is in the birth and death of *one* man to conclude that these events are not common to the whole of mankind.

Now let those who say that there is no resurrection consider what they do. One, they make the apostles' preaching vain, verse 14, or, as the Greek has it, 'then void is our proclamation'.

Obviously: for the apostles proclaimed the opposite to that which these affirmed. The apostles preached the truth of the resurrection and the judgment to come, namely, that God 'hath given assurance unto all men, in that he hath raised him'–the man Christ Jesus –'from the dead', Acts 17:31.

But these said, 'there is no resurrection of the dead'. And, if not, 'then is our preaching vain'. Two, 'and your faith is also vain', I Corinthians 15:14.

That is, such 'faith' as remained to them, after they had lacerated the truth, and left the evangel in tatters. What 'faith' was that? Well, that *somehow* Jesus still loved them, and *one way or another* they would be forgiven. The apostle calls this 'vain'. Vain faith. Or, as the Greek has it, 'and void also is your faith'. It will not, and it cannot, save.

Three, 'Yea, and we are found false witnesses of God; because we have testified of God that he raised up Christ: *whom he raised not up, if so be that the dead rise not.*'

Then, are we liars, or are they liars? Do we make God a liar, or do they make God a liar? One or the other is true.

And this also is true: if *one* man rises, all men rise. If all men rise not, no man rises. But we testify of God that he *did* raise one man, Christ Jesus. This, they contradict by denying the resurrection of all men: 'whom he raised not up, if the dead rise not', I Corinthians 15:15.

Third; if they were right–God forbid–'that there is not a resurrection of the dead' then it must be true after all that Christ rose not: for it is certain that he died, yea, was both dead and buried. 'For if the dead rise not, then is not Christ raised', I Corinthians 15:16.

Where either *man as such rises*, or, *man as such does not rise*. And, if but *one* man rose, then *all* must rise. But these said 'the dead rise not', and, if not, 'then is not Christ risen'.

If not, then *who* was it that so many and such impeccable eyewitnesses both handled and saw? 'That which we have *seen* and *heard* declare we unto you, that ye also may have fellowship with us: and truly our fellowship is with the Father, and with his Son Jesus Christ', I John 1:3.

Fourth; if they were right 'that there is not a resurrection of the dead', three things must follow: one, their faith is vain. There is nothing to believe, because nothing is corroborated.

Indeed, since Christ plainly taught that he would rise again on the third day, then *nothing* that he said, and *nothing* that he did, can be believed, *if that failed to happen*. Then, their faith is vain.

Two, they are yet in their sins. Even *if* they believed that he took their sins upon himself *in* death, and yet *after* death rose not, evidently he took them not *away*.

Resurrection was the witness, the only possible witness, that his death was effectual before God to take away sins; which he took not away, if he rose not: 'ye are yet in your sins.'

Three, all those who died in faith, with all those who have since fallen asleep in Christ, died and fell asleep under a delusion: if *he* rose not, it is certain that *they* will not rise.

Hence, observe the consequences 'if Christ be not raised'. One: 'your faith is vain.' Two: 'ye are yet in your sins.' And three: 'then they which are fallen asleep in Christ are perished', I Corinthians 15:17,18.

Fifth; if–God forbid–they were right 'that there is not a resurrection of the dead', then yet three further things follow of necessity.

One, we have no hope in this life. Fearful, black, unknown terrors face us the moment we die: in view of *that*, this present life is filled with hopelessness.

Two, neither have we any hope in the life to come. Since there was nothing to give us hope under the sun in the land of the living, what hope can there be under the blackness of darkness in the unending world of lost souls into which we must pass immediately upon death?

Three, knowing this, unable – unlike the vain fools – to forget such things for one single moment, then, through fear of death, we are all our lifetime subject to bondage.

This brings down the old yoke; it lays us under an intolerable burden; it binds us hand and foot with the chains of horror; and it shuts fast the two leaved gate beyond recovery.

In a word, 'If in this life only we have hope' – and even had we *this* fleeting relief, knowing what we do of the fearful terrors that await us beyond the grave, then – 'we are of all men most miserable', I Corinthians 15:19.

FOURTH; THE INDISPENSABILITY OF THE TRUTH OF THE RESURRECTION TO THE REALIZATION OF THE COUNSEL AND PURPOSE OF GOD, I CORINTHIANS 15:20-28.

'But now is Christ risen from the dead, and become the firstfruits of them that slept', I Corinthians 15:20. 'But' – as opposed to all the cavilling of every disputer in the whole world: in contrast, *but* – 'now *is* Christ risen from the dead.'

Now? When? 'the third day according to the scriptures', verse 4. Consider that day; consider the signs on that day:

'There was a great earthquake: for the angel of the Lord descended from heaven, and came and rolled back the stone from the door, and sat upon it. His countenance was like lightning, and his raiment white as snow: and for fear of him the keepers did shake, and became as dead men.

'And the angel answered and said unto the women, Fear not ye: for I know that ye seek Jesus, which was crucified. He is not here: for he is risen, as he said. Come, see the place where the Lord lay. And go quickly, and tell his disciples that he is risen from the dead; and, behold, he goeth before you into Galilee; there shall ye see him: lo, I have told you.

'And they departed quickly from the sepulchre with fear and great joy; and did run to bring his disciples word. And as they went to tell his disciples, behold, Jesus met them, saying, All hail.

'And they came and held him by the feet, and worshipped him. Then said Jesus unto them, Be not afraid: go tell my brethren that they go into Galilee, and there shall they see me', Matthew 28:2-10.

'Then the eleven disciples went away into Galilee, into a mountain where Jesus had appointed them. And when they saw him, they worshipped him: but some doubted.

'And Jesus came and spake unto them, saying, All power is given unto me in heaven and in earth. Go ye therefore, and teach all nations, baptizing them in the name of the Father, and of the Son, and of the Holy Ghost: teaching them to observe all things whatsoever I have commanded you:

'And, lo, I am with you alway, even unto the end of the world', Matthew 28:16-20.

Once more: 'And when the sabbath was past, Mary Magdalene, and Mary the mother of James, and Salome, had brought sweet spices, that they might come and anoint him. And very early in the morning the first day of the week, they came unto the sepulchre at the rising of the sun.

'And they said among themselves, Who shall roll us away the stone from the door of the sepulchre? And when they looked, they saw that the stone was rolled away: for it was very great.

'And entering into the sepulchre, they saw a young man sitting on the right side, clothed in a long white garment; and they were affrighted.

'And he saith unto them, Be not affrighted: Ye seek Jesus of Nazareth, which was crucified: he is risen; he is not here: behold the place where they laid him. But go your way, tell his disciples and Peter that he goeth before you into Galilee: there shall ye see him, as he said unto you', Mark 16:1-7.

'Now when Jesus was risen early the first day of the week, he appeared first to Mary Magdalene, out of whom he had cast seven devils', Mark 16:9.

'After that he appeared in another form unto two of them, as they walked, and went into the country', Mark 16:12.

'Afterwards he appeared unto the eleven as they sat at meat', Mark 16:14.

'And he said unto them, Go ye into all the world, and preach the gospel to every creature. He that believeth and is baptized shall be saved; but he that believeth not shall be damned', Mark 16:15,16.

'So then after the Lord had spoken unto them, he was received up into heaven, and sat on the right hand of God. And they went forth, and preached everywhere, the Lord working with them, and confirming the word with signs following. Amen', Mark 16:19,20.

And again: 'Now upon the first day of the week, very early in the morning, they came unto the sepulchre, bringing the spices which they had prepared, and certain others with them. And they found the stone rolled away from the sepulchre. And they entered in, and found not the body of the Lord Jesus.

'And it came to pass, as they were much perplexed thereabout, behold, two men stood by them in shining garments:

and as they were afraid, and bowed down their faces to the earth, they said unto them, Why seek ye the living among the dead?

'He is not here, but is risen: remember how he spake unto you when he was yet in Galilee, saying, The Son of man must be delivered into the hands of sinful men, and be crucified, and the third day rise again', Luke 24:1-7.

'And, behold, two of them went that same day to a village called Emmaus, which was from Jerusalem about threescore furlongs. And they talked together of all these things which had happened. And it came to pass, that, while they communed together and reasoned, Jesus himself drew near, and went with them.

'But their eyes were holden that they should not know him', Luke 24:13-16.

'Then he said unto them, O fools, and slow of heart to believe all that the prophets have spoken: Ought not Christ to have suffered these things, and to enter into his glory?

'And beginning at Moses and all the prophets, he expounded unto them in all the scriptures the things concerning himself. And they drew nigh unto the village, whither they went: and he made as though he would have gone further.

'But they constrained him, saying, Abide with us: for it is toward evening, and the day is far spent. And he went in to tarry with them. And it came to pass, as he sat at meat with them, he took bread, and blessed it, and brake, and gave to them. And their eyes were opened, and they knew him; and he vanished out of their sight.

'And they said one to another, Did not our heart burn within us, while he talked with us by the way, and while he opened to us the scriptures?

'And they rose up the same hour, and returned to Jerusalem, and found the eleven gathered together, and them that were with them, saying, The Lord is risen indeed, and hath appeared to Simon.

'And they told what things were done in the way, and how he was known of them in breaking of bread. And as they thus spake, Jesus himself stood in the midst of them, and saith unto them, Peace be unto you.

'But they were terrified and affrighted, and supposed that they had seen a spirit.

'And he said unto them, Why are ye troubled? and why do thoughts arise in your hearts? Behold my hands and my feet, that it is I myself: handle me, and see; for a spirit hath not flesh and bones, as ye see me have.

'And when he had thus spoken, he showed them his hands and his feet.

'And while they yet believed not for joy, and wondered, he said unto them, Have ye here any meat? And they gave him a piece of a broiled fish, and of an honeycomb. And he took it, and did eat before them.

'And he said unto them, These are the words which I spake unto you, while I was yet with you, that all things must be fulfilled, which were written in the law of Moses, and in the prophets, and in the psalms, concerning me.

'Then opened he their understanding, that they might understand the scriptures, and said unto them, Thus it is written, and thus it behoved Christ to suffer, and to rise from the dead the third day: and that repentance and remission of sins should be preached in his name among all nations, beginning at Jerusalem.

'And ye are witnesses of these things', Luke 24:25-48.

'And he led them out as far as to Bethany, and he lifted up his hands, and blessed them. And it came to pass, while he blessed them, he was parted from them, and carried up into heaven', Luke 24:50,51.

Yet again: 'Mary stood without at the sepulchre weeping: and as she wept, she stooped down, and looked into the sepulchre, and seeth two angels in white sitting, the one at the head, and the other at the feet, where the body of Jesus had lain.

'And they say unto her, Woman, why weepest thou? She saith unto them, Because they have taken away my Lord, and I know not where they have laid him.

'And when she had thus said, she turned herself back, and saw Jesus standing, and knew not that it was Jesus.

'Jesus saith unto her, Woman, why weepest thou? whom seekest thou? She, supposing him to be the gardener, saith unto him, Sir, if thou have borne him hence, tell me where thou hast laid him, and I will take him away.

'Jesus saith unto her, Mary. She turned herself, and saith unto him, Rabboni; which is to say, Master.

'Jesus saith unto her, Touch me not; for I am not yet ascended to my Father: but go to my brethren, and say unto them, I ascend unto my Father, and your Father; and to my God, and your God', John 20:11-17.

'Then the same day at evening, being the first day of the week, when the doors were shut where the disciples were assembled for fear of the Jews, came Jesus and stood in the midst, and saith unto them, Peace be unto you. And when he had so said, he showed unto them his hands and his side.

'Then were the disciples glad, when they saw the Lord. Then said Jesus to them again, Peace be unto you: as my Father hath sent me, even so send I you.

'And when he had said this, he breathed on them, and saith unto them, Receive ye the Holy Ghost: whose soever sins ye remit, they are remitted unto them; and whose soever sins ye retain, they are retained.

'But Thomas, one of the twelve, called Didymus, was not with them when Jesus came. The other disciples therefore said unto him, We have seen the Lord. But he said unto them, Except I shall see in his hands the print of the nails, and put my finger into the print of the nails, and thrust my hand into his side, I will not believe.

'And after eight days again his disciples were within, and Thomas with them: then came Jesus, the doors being shut, and stood in the midst, and said, Peace be unto you.

'Then saith he to Thomas, Reach hither thy finger, and behold my hands; and reach hither thy hand, and thrust it into my side: and be not faithless, but believing. And Thomas answered and said unto him, My Lord and my God.

'Jesus saith unto him, Thomas, because thou hast seen me, thou hast believed: blessed are they that have not seen, and yet have believed', John 20:11-29.

Moreover the Acts of the Apostles records the great power with which the eleven gave testimony to the resurrection of the Lord Jesus. For example, in the opening words the writer looks back on the ministry of the Lord, declaring 'all that Jesus began both to do and teach'.

Then, again, he looks forward to his risen administration from the glory, the other side of death, affirming that 'he was taken up, after that he through the Holy Ghost had given commandments unto the apostles whom he had chosen:

'To whom also he showed himself alive after his passion by many infallible proofs, being seen of them forty days, and speaking of the things pertaining to the kingdom of God', Acts 1:1-3.

'And when he had spoken these things, while they beheld, he was taken up; and a cloud received him out of their sight', Acts 1:9.

'This Jesus hath God raised up, whereof we all are witnesses', Acts 2:32.

'Unto you first God, having raised up his Son Jesus, sent him to bless you, in turning away every one of you from his iniquities', Acts 3:26.

But 'as they spake unto the people, the priests, and the captain of the temple, and the Sadducees, came upon them, being grieved that they taught the people, and preached through Jesus the resurrection from the dead', Acts 4:1,2.

Boldly the apostles testified that which they had seen, in the power which they had received, namely, 'Jesus Christ of Nazareth, whom ye crucified, whom God raised from the dead', Acts 4:10.

So that 'with great power gave the apostles witness of the resurrection of the Lord Jesus: and great grace was upon them all', Acts 4:33.

Hence Peter declared on behalf of all the apostles, 'And we are witnesses of all things which he did both in the land of the Jews, and in Jerusalem; whom they slew and hanged on a tree: him God raised up the third day, and showed him openly; not to all the people, but unto witnesses chosen before of God, even to us, who did eat and drink with him after he rose from the dead.

'And he commanded us to preach unto the people, and to testify that it is he which was ordained of God to be the Judge of quick and dead', Acts 10:39-42.

But there was one born out of due time, the last of the apostles, who saw him not as did Peter and the others, on earth, but uniquely, in heaven, whence the apostle Paul was called to the apostolate from the heights of glory:

'And it came to pass, that, as I made my journey, and was come nigh unto Damascus about noon, suddenly there shone from heaven a great light round about me. And I fell unto the ground, and heard a voice saying unto me, Saul, Saul, why persecutest thou me?

'And I answered, Who art thou, Lord?

'And he said unto me, I am Jesus of Nazareth, whom thou persecutest', Acts 22:6-8.

No wonder therefore that central to the evangel sounded forth the testimony of Paul the apostle before all the Jewish religious authorities: 'But this I confess', declared he, 'that after the way which they call heresy, so worship I the God of my fathers, believing all things which are written in the law and in the prophets:

'And have hope toward God, which they themselves also allow, that there shall be a resurrection of the dead, both of the just and unjust', Acts 24:14,15.

Now Paul was not an eyewitness during the forty days in which Christ, risen from the dead, appeared to the eleven. Then how did he know of and bear witness to the resurrection?

Because *his first acquaintance with him with whom the other apostles ate and drank after he rose from the dead, was after he had ascended into heaven.*

Their last view of him was in the cloud that received him out of their sight when he was caught up to heaven as he ascended. *Paul's* first view of him was without a cloud after he had ascended into his glory, being sat down at the right hand of the Father.

But whether the eleven, or Paul, all the apostles as one man had this testimony: *he whom they saw was risen from the grave, the other side of death, alive for evermore in that very body in which he had been crucified, death defeated, the grave vanquished*, even as saith the Lord from the glory of heaven to the last of the apostles: '*I am Jesus*.'

If so, not only risen, not in the act of ascending, but seated in glorious exaltation at the right hand of the Father. *In the body*. Then, it follows – it *must* follow – there *is* a resurrection of the dead.

'But *now* is Christ risen from the dead.' If *now* – a recurring present – how shall we know of the resurrection? In the same way as the Corinthians.

Yet, as they experienced, so do we: for all the *infallible* proofs; for all the *impeccable* eyewitnesses; for all the *immutability* of the scriptures: until our blinded hearts are enlightened; until our darkened minds are illuminated, until God, who commanded the light to shine out of darkness, shines in our hearts to give the light of the knowledge of the glory of God in the face of Jesus Christ, *we cannot believe*.

Now, however, God has opened the eyes of our understanding, and, behold, we *see*. Not as the chosen eyewitnesses saw, who saw literally, but, enlightened by the Father from heaven, receiving in *that* light the testimony of the holy apostles, *now we see spiritually*.

No less than they, we too are blessed, as saith Jesus, 'Blessed are they that have *not* seen, yet have *believed*', John 20:29.

Wherefore a vast multitude, whom no man can number, preceded us, but included us, *who also have seen spiritually, and believed*, as it is written, 'Whom having not seen, ye love; in whom, though now ye see him not, yet believing, ye rejoice with joy unspeakable and full of glory: receiving the end of your faith, even the salvation of your souls', I Peter 1:8,9.

This is that of which Jesus spake, saying, 'This is the will of him that sent me, *that every one which seeth the Son*, and' – in consequence of this *seeing* – 'believeth on him, may have everlasting life: and I will raise him up at the last day', John 6:40.

Of this inward, spiritual *seeing*, in consequence of which the light shines on and through the apostolic eyewitness, one can say, 'But *now* is Christ risen from the dead', because every one of those in the secret declares from the heart, 'One thing I know, that, whereas I was blind, now I see', John 9:25.

This *seeing* the world receiveth not, though outwardly and formally it may profess the record of the eyewitnesses.

It may: but it is sightless, and in the dark, and, whatever the profession, it is not that of saving faith, as saith Jesus, 'The world seeth me no more'.

No, the world seeth him no more, but to those illuminated by the Father, he saith, *'but ye see me*: because I live, ye shall live also', John 14:19.

'But *now* is Christ risen from the dead', I Corinthians 15:20.

'And become the firstfruits of them that slept.' The term 'firstfruits' refers to an old testament figure typical of Christ in relation to his people.

The expression 'them that slept' indicates all those who ever have, or ever will, 'fall asleep', that is, die in the faith of Christ, having been laid to rest in union with him.

Openings in First Corinthians

As to their bodies, even to this very generation, having 'fallen asleep', these sleep on.

But the 'firstfruits' does not sleep on. He is risen: 'But now is Christ risen from the dead.'

In relation to the *bodies* of the sleepers in Christ, though sleeping still, the promise of the harvest is certain in the firstfruits: 'But now is Christ risen from the dead, *and become the firstfruits of them that slept*', I Corinthians 15:20.

'Seven weeks shalt thou number unto thee: begin to number the seven weeks from such time as thou beginnest to put the sickle to the corn', Deuteronomy 16:9.

'And thou shalt observe the feast of weeks, of the firstfruits of wheat harvest.' 'The first of the firstfruits of thy land thou shalt bring unto the house of the LORD thy God', Exodus 34:22,26.

'When ye be come into the land which I give unto you, and shall reap the harvest thereof, then shall ye bring a sheaf'—observe: *one* sheaf—'of the firstfruits of your harvest unto the priest: and he shall wave the sheaf before the LORD, to be accepted for you: on the morrow after the sabbath'—mark that: *on the morrow after the sabbath*—'the priest shall wave it', Leviticus 23:10,11.

So that at the time the green ears of the wheat harvest just begin to ripen, then, here and there, in the most advantageous, sheltered, and sunny situations, an ear or two would appear golden ripe, in advance of and anticipating the whole harvest.

These relatively few advanced ears were cut off at the stalk from the ground and gathered together, a kind of witness of the whole harvest yet to come.

This sheaf, called the firstripe sheaf, was offered on 'the morrow after the sabbath'.

The cutting off of the firstripe sheaf from the earth answered to the day of the passover in the type, when Christ hung on the cross and was put to death: 'he was cut off out of the land of the living', Isaiah 53:8.

The morrow after the sabbath, namely, the first day of the week, this firstripe sheaf was waved by the priest before the Lord. In the figure, all the harvest was seen in him in his death and burial: 'he was cut off out of the land of the living: for the transgression of my people was he stricken', Isaiah 53:8.

Now, risen, severed from the earth, on the day of the resurrection, he appears as set forth wholly free of all root or connection with or in this present world, held up in priestly hands, waved in joy and triumph, an exultant demonstration *that nothing of the earth, or of the world, or of time, was in this victorious liberty before all the heavens.*

However, when the priest waved the firstripe sheaf, not only that sheaf in itself, but in those full and abundant ears *all the harvest was signified.*

'He shall wave *the*'–singular–'sheaf before the Lord, to be accepted for *you*'–plural; Leviticus 23:11.

From the day that the firstripe sheaf was waved the counting began. This counting ended forty-nine days later.

Of that last day it is written, 'When the day of Pentecost was fully come, they were all with one accord in one place. And suddenly there came a sound from heaven as of a rushing mighty wind, and it filled all the house where they were sitting.

'And there appeared unto them cloven tongues like as of fire, and it sat upon each of them. And they were all filled with the Holy Ghost', Acts 2:1-4.

This, the beginning of the *ecclesia*, and of the constitution of the body of Christ, was in itself significant of all who should be conformed to the image of God's Son, Romans 8:29.

If so, of the final harvest. A week of weeks, seven days seven times over – seven being the number symbolizing perfection – indicates perfection perfected.

Typified on the day of Pentecost, such perfect consummation has its true fulfilment in the reaping of the harvest at the last day.

Whatever was true of that firstripe sheaf, must be true of the whole harvest.

Hence, as the firstripe sheaf was carefully gathered by being put to the sickle, the harvest of that from which the firstripe sheaf was taken must likewise be reaped: 'And he that sat on the cloud thrust in his sickle on the earth; and the earth was reaped', Revelation 14:16.

'And he shall gather his wheat into the garner', Matthew 3:12. 'Gather the wheat into my barn', Matthew 13:30.

'The harvest is the end of the world', Matthew 13:39.

'But now is Christ risen from the dead, and become the firstfruits of them that slept', I Corinthians 15:20.

It is of the essence in I Corinthians 15:20-28 that one neither loses sight of the context, nor errs from the discipline of its constraints. The context is exclusive to the second man not the first; to the evangel not the law; to Zion not Sinai; to the resurrection of the just not of the wicked; to what is in Christ not what is in Adam; to the heavenly inheritance not the earthly; to the counsel of God and his purpose, not that of man or of this present world.

In context the apostle goes on to speak of the harvest of which Christ had been the firstfruits.

He does not speak of any other harvest; there is another, but he does not speak of it: that is not his subject. Here, he is concerned only with what pertains to Christ, namely that resurrection of which his own resurrection had been the harbinger.

It is the truth of the resurrection in Christ which constrains the apostle to reach upwards to the stupendous heights which culminate in the climax of verse 28: it is the indispensable truth of the resurrection in connection with the evangel: it is the resurrection *of the ecclesia*.

It is not a question of how that resurrection is a blessing to *us*. It is a question of what that resurrection brings in for *God*.

First and foremost, the evangel of Christ is not centred upon man: above all, what is in view is the glory of God. It is not *our* salvation; *our* service; *our* sanctification; *our* resurrection; *our* inheritance that is pre-eminent: all these things are subservient to the counsel, purpose, and glory of God, and find their significance in relation to *that*.

It is a question of 'what is the hope of *his* calling', and, 'what the riches of the glory of *his* inheritance in the saints', Ephesians 1:18.

The evangel is firstly *for God*: *his* will; *his* counsel; *his* purpose; *his* inheritance; *his* glory: *that* was foremost in the faith of Jesus Christ, and therefore in the evangel, and hence in the resurrection of the dead.

Therefore the reality of the resurrection of the just, of the *ecclesia*, of the harvest of which Christ was the firstfruits, brings to pass God's counsel and purpose. That is why Paul now sets forth for the instruction of the Corinthians the tremendous truths of verses 20-28.

'For since by man came death, by man came also the resurrection of the dead. For as in Adam all die, even so in Christ shall all be made alive', I Corinthians 15:21,22.

Whereas the first part of each of the two verses appears to be negative, this is not so in fact. Actually the apostle employs the truth of the judgment of God upon Adam and the dire consequences to the whole of his posterity as a contrasting figure of the very opposite that is true in Christ.

Whatever is negatively true of man in Adam, much more is the opposite positively true of man in Christ.

There are *two* men, and their respective seeds. It is imperative to grasp and hold this distinction. Likewise that what is true of each of the two, respectively – in consequence of their having acted on behalf of all those whom they begat – by a law of necessity becomes true of all those begotten by them.

Then, since 'by man' – the first man – 'came death', the parallel holds good: 'by man' – the second man – 'came also the resurrection of the dead.'

The resurrection of the dead? Yes, *to all those seen in himself and of himself, on whose behalf the second man acted, to whose account God reckons his action, and who are in consequence begotten in him.* And none other.

Then, since 'in Adam all die', a negative fact that cannot be controverted, equally – yea, how much more! – in the *last* Adam a positive consequence must follow to his posterity as surely as he himself rose from the dead.

That is, by a law of necessity, all *his* seed, on whose behalf he acted, who are begotten in him, *must become partakers of his actions*: in a word, 'even so in Christ shall all be made alive.'

It cannot be overstressed that in the will, counsel, purpose, and creation of God there are *two* men, not one. The failure to perceive this makes confusion worse confounded and brings down darkness and obscurity upon the minds of men.

Hence the god of this world, who blinds the minds of them that believe not, exploits men's incredulity at such a distinction to the utmost. Then they will never see light.

The revelation that there is not only a first Adam, but also a last; that there is not only a first man, but likewise a second; *and that these are entirely distinct, as are those begotten from them; besides the consequences of their actions upon their respective seeds*: these are paramount truths that form the basis of Paul's argument in I Corinthians 15:20-28, and to a very much greater extent in Romans 5:12-21.

So that 'since by man came death', and, 'as in Adam all die', are not expressions employed by the apostle as negative discouragements to the Corinthians. On the contrary, what is true of Adam, the first man, is used to show that *exactly the opposite must be, and is, much more true of Christ, the second man, and, if of him, then of all his seed.*

Hence far from having a negative effect verses 20 and 21 redound to the glory of God in Christ, revealing a hidden mystery, a purpose from before the foundation of the world, utterly transcending the man of this world, the world itself, and all that happens in the world from its creation to its dissolution.

The glorious triumph of Christ for all those chosen in him from before the foundation of the world – and therefore before the creation of Adam – rings with the shout of victory and resounds again and again from one end of the vault of heaven to the other; from eternity across time to eternity; to echo for ever through everlasting ages in the fulfilment of the purpose of God in the glorious inheritance of the kingdom of our God, and of his Christ, world without end. Amen.

Openings in First Corinthians

This is the prospect that Paul the apostle sets before the *ecclesia* at Corinth in the resurrection from the dead.

'But every man in his own order: Christ the firstfruits; afterward they that are Christ's at his coming', I Corinthians 15:23, where 'afterward' refers to the resurrection of 'they that are Christ's'—and, if so, of the *ecclesia* at Corinth—a resurrection precisely commensurate with the figure of the reaping of the whole harvest, seen in figure fifty days before, when the firstripe sheaf had been put to the sickle, reaped, and waved before the LORD in priestly hands lifted up to heaven.

For just as surely as the whole harvest was seen in the firstfruits, so 'they that are Christ's'—having been counted as risen in his resurrection—must and shall rise again in due order 'at his coming' for the full harvest of all that are his own.

'Then cometh the end, when he shall have delivered up the kingdom to God, even the Father; when he shall have put down all rule and all authority and power', I Corinthians 15:24.

That is, following the resurrection—'*afterward* they that are Christ's at his coming'—'*then* cometh the end.' At this, Christ 'shall have delivered up the kingdom to God, even the Father', namely, delivered it up *as risen from the dead*.

Not only the *ecclesia*, but all the old testament saints, the Israel of God, all those who 'without us should not be made perfect', Hebrews 11:40. But now they are made perfect, perfect in one, perfect in the body of the resurrection, and so presented in perfection to God and the Father by the Son of his love.

This is called 'delivering up the kingdom', namely, the entire kingdom of the reign and dominion of Christ, called out from the foundation of the world to the end of it, brought to completion in the resurrection of the just.

And this is the consummation of the work of the Son throughout time, fulfilled in his incarnation, baptism, transfiguration, visitation, crucifixion, resurrection, ascension, and, at the last, in his coming again for his own.

'For the Lord himself shall descend from heaven with a shout, with the voice of the archangel, and with the trump of God: and the dead in Christ shall rise first: then we which are alive and remain shall be caught up together with them in the clouds, to meet the Lord in the air: and so shall we ever be with the Lord', I Thessalonians 4:16,17.

As to the use of the word 'kingdom', in 'when he shall have delivered up the kingdom to God, even the Father': whilst the subject is the resurrection of the *ecclesia*, nevertheless in that resurrection more is included, namely *all* 'they that are Christ's'.

This goes back to the foundation of the world, taking in the patriarchs and all the seed of promise, that is, all the old testament saints. These also are 'they that are Christ's', though they never saw the fulfilment of that in which they believed, nor experienced the constitution of the *ecclesia*, the body of Christ.

'These all died in faith, not having received the promises, but having seen them afar off, and were persuaded of them, and embraced them, and confessed that they were strangers and pilgrims on the earth', Hebrews 11:13.

What promises? Particularly, of the righteousness of faith through the death of the promised Messiah, and of the resurrection from the dead to an eternal inheritance. Then shall not these, equally with the *ecclesia*, at the coming of Christ and the resurrection of them that are his, be partakers of this better resurrection?

They shall indeed, for 'these all, having obtained a good report through faith, received not the promise: God having provided some better thing for us, that they without us should not be made perfect', Hebrews 11:39,40.

Openings in First Corinthians

Hence in the visions recorded in the Book of the Revelation there are seen twenty-four elders on thrones about the throne of God in heaven, symbolic of the twelve patriarchs and of the twelve apostles, and, if so, of the old and new testament saints whom they represent.

Likewise, though the names of the twelve apostles are in the foundations of the holy city, nevertheless the names of the twelve patriarchs are in the gates, signifying that in the resurrection at the coming of Christ for his own, *all* his own, from the foundation of the world, old and new testament saints alike, shall rise from the dead at the shout, at the voice of the archangel, and at the trump of God.

Hence ancient Job could say, 'For I know that my redeemer liveth, and that he shall stand at the latter day upon the earth: and though after my skin worms destroy this body, yet in my flesh shall I see God: whom I shall see for myself, and mine eyes shall behold, and not another; though my reins be consumed within me', Job 19:25-27.

Similarly David could cry in prophecy a thousand years before the coming of Christ, proclaiming his resurrection, 'Yet have I set my king upon my holy hill of Zion. I will declare the decree: the LORD hath said unto me, Thou art my Son; this day have I begotten thee', Psalm 2:6,7.

Moreover the prophet proclaimed to Israel, 'Behold, thy King cometh unto thee', Zechariah 9:9.

And again, Isaiah crieth unto Zion, 'Thy God reigneth!', Isaiah 52:7.

Now all these died in faith, looking for a kingdom, that is, an heavenly, and neither shall any of these heirs of faith be disappointed when Christ comes again for *all* that are his at the resurrection of the dead, for, with the *ecclesia*, they shall be raised to an everlasting kingdom and inheritance.

But this kingdom came not with observation, Luke 17:20, though they had thought to observe it at the coming of Christ.

However then – and even until now – it is interior and spiritual, so that of the inward present reign of Christ we read, 'the kingdom of God is not meat and drink; but righteousness, and peace, and joy in the Holy Ghost', Romans 14:17.

At present it is inward: but at the last it shall be outward. Hence Christ taught his disciples to pray, 'Thy kingdom *come*'. That is, 'come' with the resurrection and bringing in of the everlasting inheritance.

But – before Pentecost – these two things were what the apostles confounded, asking, 'Lord, wilt thou at this time restore again the kingdom to Israel?', Acts 1:6.

For they were yet blinded by Jewish prejudices: the kingdom was ordained and promised long before Israel, though Israel in turn looked for it: but it came not with observation, yet was inwardly established in the saints, though it shall not be seen in its glory till Christ comes again and delivers up the kingdom to the Father following the resurrection and after the destruction of all his enemies.

Of this, the dying thief had a better view than the apostles before Pentecost, for he cried out to the Saviour, 'Lord, remember me when thou comest into thy kingdom', Luke 23:42.

The kingdom therefore, in its manifestation and glory, pertains to the resurrection and the world to come.

In one way or another, however, whether as looked for, believed in, hoped after, or as inwardly received, spiritually entered, or experienced in union, from the beginning of the world to the end of it, 'they that are Christ's' shall surely hear the good word of God at the resurrection of the dead from the King in his beauty in the land that is very far off.

Openings in First Corinthians

'Then shall the King say unto them on his right hand, Come, ye blessed of my Father, inherit the kingdom prepared for you from the foundation of the world', Matthew 25:34.

And now from henceforth shall be brought to pass the saying that is written, 'The kingdoms of this world are become the kingdoms of our Lord, and of his Christ; and he shall reign for ever and ever', Revelation 11:15.

And again, 'And the angel said unto her, Fear not, Mary: for thou hast found favour with God. And, behold, thou shalt conceive in thy womb, and bring forth a son, and shalt call his name JESUS. He shall be great, and shall be called the Son of the Highest: and the Lord God shall give unto him the throne of his father David: and he shall reign over the house of Jacob for ever; and of his kingdom there shall be no end', Luke 1:30-33.

And this shall come to pass in its fulness when 'he shall have put down all rule and all authority and power', I Corinthians 15:24.

If so, the *present* rulers, and the *present* authorities, and the *present* powers, in this world and throughout time, *are not put down* on the one hand, but reign in authority and power under the heavens *against the kingdom and rule of the Son of God from the highest glory* on the other hand.

And these powers will *continue* their reign until he rises up from the throne of his Father who is Head over all, despite the adversaries in this present age, withal the enemies in their positions of vast authority, but, nevertheless, destined to be overthrown 'when he shall have put down all rule and all authority and power'.

'For he must reign'–that is, above all heavens, unseen and supreme, and, at that, despite the continued existence of the rule and authority and power at enmity far below–'he must reign, till he hath put all his enemies under his feet.

'The last enemy that shall be destroyed is death', I Corinthians 15:25,26.

If so, the earth, the world, the heavens, this present age, are all filled with and ruled by his *enemies*. In the beginning he appointed the lawfully ordained rule and authority and power, but, under the Adversary, these rebelled, and, from the Fall, brought down the darkness, and the reign of sin and death, upon the whole world.

In the midst of this, despite it all, the Son of God rules inwardly in the kingdom: 'The LORD said unto my Lord, Sit thou at my right hand, *until* I make thine enemies thy footstool.'

Meanwhile, from the ascension and throughout the age, 'the LORD shall send the rod of thy strength out of'—heavenly— 'Zion'—from the glory of the Highest into the heart of his people here below—*'rule thou in the midst of thine enemies'*, Psalm 110:1,2.

But these conditions will not prevail for ever: only *'until'*. That is what Paul is saying.

Thus the people of God have been strangers, pilgrims, and sojourners through this present evil world from the beginning, looking for the resurrection and the world to come.

So it was with Abel, Enoch, Noah, Abraham, Sarah, and all the seed of promise until the coming and ministry of the Messiah. And thus it was in the beginning with the *ecclesia*, and of all the remnant separated from the subsequent apostasy.

Hence it is said 'know ye not that the friendship of the world is enmity with God? whosoever therefore will be a friend of the world is the enemy of God', James 4:4.

And no wonder, for, 'The kings of the earth set themselves, and the rulers take counsel together, against the LORD, and against his anointed, saying, Let us break their bands asunder, and cast away their cords from us. He that sitteth in the heavens shall laugh: the Lord shall have them in derision', Psalm 2:2-4.

Thus the heathen rage, and so the people imagine a vain thing, Psalm 2:1, for the truth is, above on high in the heavenly glory, 'the Lord God omnipotent reigneth', Revelation 19:6, and, even now, far over all, he saith, 'Yet have I set my king upon my holy hill of Zion', declaring the decree, 'Thou art my Son; this day have I begotten thee', Psalm 2:6,7.

Nevertheless in the heavens below, and in the darkness of this world beneath, the god of this world, called the 'devil', and Satan, blinds the minds of them that believe not, II Corinthians 4:4.

But, since the cross, the words have come to pass, 'Now is the judgment of this world: now shall the prince of this world be cast out'—that is, from the heavenly glory, to fall to the earth and heavens below—John 12:31, Revelation 12:9-17.

Moreover it is very clear that the Holy Ghost, abiding in the *ecclesia*, will convince the whole world of judgment, namely, of judgment upon this present age.

Why? Because the Spirit dwells in the saints, but he does not, and he will not, dwell in the world, as it is written of both the whole world, and of the prince that rules over it, 'of judgment, because the prince of this world is judged', John 16:11.

Then this present fallen world 'is not of the Father, but is of the world', I John 2:16, and over it and its kingdoms the 'devil' rules, as he saith, showing Jesus all the kingdoms of the world and the glory of them, 'All this power will I give thee, and the glory of them: for that is delivered unto me; and to whomsoever I will I give it', Matthew 4:8, Luke 4:6.

But, saith Christ to his own, 'If the world hate you, ye know that it hated me before it hated you. If ye were of the world, the world would love his own: but because ye are not of the world, but I have chosen you out of the world, therefore the world hateth you', John 15:18,19.

Indeed, the Saviour 'gave himself for our sins, that he might deliver us from this present evil world, according to the will of God and our Father', Galatians 1:4.

Wherefore constantly we are employed in 'giving thanks unto the Father, which hath made us meet to be partakers of the inheritance of the saints in light: who hath delivered us from the power'—or authority—'of darkness, and hath translated us into the kingdom of his dear Son: in whom we have redemption through his blood, the forgiveness of sins', Colossians 1:12-14.

From all of which it is apparent that the whole world, begotten in the darkness and under the curse of the Fall, judged in itself and in its prince at the cross, is at enmity against God, and is the enemy of Christ.

If so, in that day, it shall fall beneath his feet. And so shall all his enemies, for, 'he must reign, till he hath put all enemies under his feet', I Corinthians 15:25.

'*All* enemies'? Who are these? Those over whom God hath raised him by the exceeding greatness of his power, according to the working of his mighty power, which he wrought in Christ when he raised him from the dead.

'And set him at his own right hand in the heavenly places, far above all principality, and power, and might, and dominion, and every name that is named, not only in this world, but also in that to come: and hath put all things under his feet', Ephesians 1:19-22.

As to us, inwardly in the kingdom of God, united with the King whom God hath set upon heavenly mount Zion, filled with the Spirit, but nevertheless still in this vile body and in the realm of this present evil world, consequently, 'we wrestle not against flesh and blood, but against principalities, against powers, against the rulers of the darkness of this world, against spiritual wickedness in heavenly places', Ephesians 6:12.

Here the enemies of Christ, whilst filling this present world, and encompassing it about – as 'the prince of the power of the air', Ephesians 2:2 – nevertheless ascend up from it in ranks of authority, even to 'heavenly places'.

This is the nature of 'this present evil world', Galatians 1:4, and indicates how vast, multiple, and varied are the spiritual and unseen enemies of Christ.

Nevertheless, high over all, in the heights of glory, he is seated on the throne of his Father, who 'must reign, till he hath put all' – mark that, *all* – 'enemies under his feet', I Corinthians 15:25.

Of all the books of the new testament, none opens so clearly or so vividly the ascension and reign of Christ in glory, and of his preserving the kingdom inwardly in his people below – despite this being in the midst of his enemies – nor of his final destruction of every one of those enemies, as does the Book of the Revelation.

However, these visions are couched in highly allegorical and figurative language, so that nothing is obvious and literal: everything is spiritual and mystical: nevertheless, for all this, *reality* is thus expressed.

Hence one may discern who are the enemies, how Christ brings them to judgment, and the manner of his bringing in the kingdom for God and the Father, world without end, Amen.

First appear the ecclesiastical enemies: more and more these fill and take over the outward profession of the *ecclesia*. But they will be judged, that judgment is pronounced, and destruction awaits them in the day of judgment. The meantime these hinder – by deceptive but fleshly duplication – and obscure the nature of the kingdom in this present evil age, in which they are so at home.

Next the Book of the Revelation depicts the worldly enemies of Christ and the people in whom he reigns, against whom the enmity and hatred of this world rages. But these shall be brought under, put down, and be judged in the day of his wrath.

Indeed, every one of the enemies – withal the affliction and tribulation caused by them to those of the kingdom of God throughout the age – shall be destroyed and brought into everlasting judgment and punishment at the coming of Christ to bring in the kingdom in glory, thus fulfilling the will, counsel, and purpose of God and the Father.

However with the close of Revelation chapter 11, the lower, earthly sphere is left behind: an entirely new elevation, a heavenly realm of vastly higher altitude, filled with serried ranks of ever ascending spiritual powers, comes into view.

But if brought to view, it is only to show that these are already defeated, and if left in their positions and states of authority, it is only in the permissive will of God, and for no longer time than that concluded by the last day in which the King of kings and Lord of lords arises from the throne in the highest, to overthrow and judge these enemies for ever.

In that day he shall dissolve the heavens and the earth in flaming fire, melting the very elements, creating a new heavens and a new earth wherein dwelleth righteousness, bringing in the kingdom in the resurrection world without end, Amen.

In the allegorical figures of the Book of the Revelation the great red dragon, that old serpent, called the 'devil' and Satan, together with all his powers and ranks of authority in heavenly places, as the first beast, the second beast, the false prophet, not to mention Babylon the whore, and Babylon the city, are all cast alive into the lake that burneth with fire and brimstone, there to suffer the judgment of everlasting punishment.

Nor are these all, for, together with them—as if they were living embodiments—follow what is called 'the last enemy', together with his consort: 'And death and *hadēs* were cast into the lake of fire. This is the second death', Revelation 20:14.

But that is exactly what the apostle Paul taught—not under figurative language, but in the words of clear doctrine—to the *ecclesia* of God which was at Corinth concerning this same momentous truth.

'The last enemy that shall be destroyed is death', I Corinthians 15:26.

Now, since death is that which occurs to *the body*—and cannot refer to the soul—then by what else shall the last enemy be destroyed than by the resurrection from the dead?

And this, in the creation, will, counsel, and purpose of God, is precisely what the apostle declares in I Corinthians 15:20-28 concerning the consummation of all things.

To achieve such a tremendous climax to the ages, to all time, to this present world, to every enemy, all things had been put in subjection beneath the feet of the Son of God in the ascension.

Nothing and no one—save he who committed all things to the Son, putting all things under him—I say, nothing either lives or has existence that Almighty God, even his Father, the Highest, has not put into subjection under him, that he might subdue all things unto himself.

That is, that he might subdue every enemy, bring this present evil age to a conclusion, command the fiery deluge, raise the very dead, create a new heavens and a new earth, bring in the world to come whereof we speak, and, finally, deliver up the kingdom to God and the Father.

So teaches the apostle: 'For he hath put all things under his feet. But when he saith all things are put under him, it is manifest that he is excepted, which did put all things under him', I Corinthians 15:27.

'And when all things shall be subdued unto him, then shall the Son also himself be subject unto him that put all things under him, that God may be all in all', I Corinthians 15:28.

The words 'And *when* all things shall be subdued unto him' are indicative of the end of the period commencing with the ascension and concluding with the descent of the Son at his second coming to judgment.

Then all things shall have been, and will be, subdued unto him.

This period began with the fulfilment of the prophecy, 'Sit thou at my right hand', and will finish with the consummation of the text *'until* I make thine enemies thy footstool', Psalm 110:1.

Of this Peter speaks on the day of Pentecost: 'Therefore being by the right hand of God exalted, and having received of the Father the promise of the Holy Ghost, he hath shed forth this, which ye now see and hear. For David is not ascended into the heavens: but he saith himself, The LORD said unto my Lord, Sit thou on my right hand, until I make thy foes thy footstool.

'Therefore let all the house of Israel know assuredly, that God hath made that same Jesus, whom ye have crucified, both Lord and Christ', Acts 2:33-36.

And so expounds the writer to the Hebrews, saying, 'Thou crownedst him with glory and honour, and didst set him over the works of thy hands: thou hast put all things in subjection under his feet. For in that he put all in subjection under him, he left nothing that is not put under him.'

But, if so, Why are all things as they are? Because there is a *period*, an *age*, between his being exalted, and his bringing his almighty power to bear upon his enemies:

'But now we see not *yet* all things put under him. But we see Jesus, who was made a little lower than the angels for the suffering of death, crowned with glory and honour', Hebrews 2:7-9.

During this his reign from the heights of glory *'until'* – at the last – he rises to put all things, vanquished, in subjection under himself at the last day, his authority is yet absolute: *even now* the *Father* hath put *all things* under his feet.

And so it must be, until he rises up in wrath and vengeance to make his enemies – *all* his enemies – his footstool for ever.

Still, even until that day, he reigns in glory in perfect patience, knowing, declaring, '*All things are delivered unto me of my Father*', Matthew 11:27, and, '*All* authority is given unto me *in heaven and in earth*', Matthew 28:18.

And, again, he saith unto the Father of himself, 'thou hast given him authority over all flesh', John 17:2.

Likewise the apostle teaches, 'he raised him from the dead, and set him at his own right hand in the heavenly places, *far above* all principality, and power, and might, and dominion, and every name that is named, not only in this world, but also in that which is to come:

'And *hath put all things under his feet*, and gave him to be the head *over all things* to the *ecclesia*, which is his body, the fulness of him that filleth all in all', Ephesians 1:20-23.

Hence, 'he hath put all things under his feet. But when he saith all things are put under him, it is manifest that he is excepted, which did put all things under him.

'And *when* all things shall be *subdued*' – not *put* only, but *subdued* actually, in the day of his wrath and vengeance – 'then shall the Son also himself be subject unto him that put all things under him, that God may be all in all', I Corinthians 15:27,28.

This answers to Revelation chapters 21 and 22; all the enemies destroyed, time being no more, the world to come having come to pass, the kingdom delivered up to the Father, the Son also himself being subject unto him that put all things under him, that God may be all in all.

The Son also himself? Subject? What is this? It is the Son *in terms of his humanity, the Son considered as head of the body, namely,* of that sonship in manhood which is conformed to his own image.

Head of the body, he is one with that body, in manhood after himself. New manhood: that *is* sonship, 'for we are members of his body, of his flesh, and of his bones'.

Just as Eve, taken out of the side of Adam, was of his flesh, and of his bones. This is a great mystery: but I speak concerning Christ and the *ecclesia*, Ephesians 5:30-32.

This signifies the second man, the last Adam, the quickening Spirit, one with his brethren, all alike in new manhood, he glorified in them, and they in him. In figure, thus was Adam glorified in Eve. But in Christ the reality transcends the figure higher than the heavens transcend the earth.

For it shall come to pass in truth that Christ shall glorify God in that unique risen manhood of sonship which at once declares him to be one with his brethren and one in and with the Father and with the Spirit.

Thus God shall be all in all, and seen to be all in all, filling the unity of that peerless humanity which stands for evermore in the oneness of sonship in Christ.

In manhood one with his own, in deity one with the Father and with the Spirit. Filled with the fulness of God.

All in all; Father, Son, and Holy Ghost, glorified to everlasting in the Son and his bride, of his body: flesh of his flesh, and bone of his bone. And if so, in the resurrection from the dead.

And, these things being given—and they *are* given—in heaven or in earth, in time or in eternity, in deity or in humanity, in life or in death, in this world or in the next, in counsel or in purpose, in the first creation or in the last: How, how, 'how say some among you that there is no resurrection of the dead?', I Corinthians 15:12.

FIFTH; THE ASSURANCE OF THE RESURRECTION THE MOTIVE FOR THE BAPTISM OF THOSE WHO CONFRONT DEATH; STAND IN JEOPARDY; DIE DAILY; AND FACE MARTYRDOM, PUTTING THE CORINTHIANS TO SHAME, I CORINTHIANS 15:29-34.

In this passage the apostle passes from 'they' to 'we' to 'I', all providing examples brought to bear on 'you'—the Corinthians—so as to shame them by these exemplary instances of the faith of God's elect, who show forth so evidently what it is to follow in the steps of Jesus, denying themselves, taking up their cross daily:

'For whosoever will save his life shall lose it; but whosoever shall lose his life for my sake and for the gospel's, the same shall save it', Mark 8:35.

Then what is this denying of the truth of the resurrection of the dead—essential and integral to the evangel—on the part of the Corinthians?

'Know ye not, that so many of us as were baptized into Jesus Christ were baptized into his death?', Romans 6:3.

'Now if we be dead with Christ, we believe that we shall also live with him', Romans 6:8.

This is the essence of the context of this entire passage, and of each example brought forward to enforce it, whether it were the 'they'–verse 29–the 'we'–verse 30–or the 'I'–verses 31 and 32.

'Else what shall *they* do'–whoever *they* are, they were not conspicuous amongst *you*, the Corinthians!–'which are baptized for the dead, if the dead rise not at all?'

If the dead rise not at all, then they who are baptized, were baptized for nothing: in which case what should their poor deluded lost souls do?

But they are *not* poor deluded lost souls: they are baptized into Christ's death indeed, nor shall they be disappointed in the issue. Were they to be, and the evangel–God forbid!–found to be untrue, 'Why are they then baptized for the dead?'.

Why? Because the evangel *is* true; because they *were* 'buried with him by baptism into death'; and because 'Now is Christ risen from the dead, and become the firstfruits of them that slept'.

Then, O ye Corinthians, *follow their example*, instead of *condoning those among you who denied it*, I Corinthians 15:29.

Surely it ought to be superfluous to state the obvious–if only from the context, let alone the absurdity–that 'Else what shall they do which are baptized for the dead?', I Corinthians 15:29, *cannot* refer to living persons being baptized on behalf of others who had died.

I feel no need to point out the use of the preposition ὑπὲρ in connection with the genitive plural of νεκρός, telling as is this usage when coupled with τῶν νεκρῶν, supporting the correct interpretation in context.

But why not? Because it is unnecessary to state the obvious, let alone buttress that statement with the niceties of Greek grammar.

The passage *must* refer to *oneself* being reckoned dead. 'He that believeth and is baptized shall be saved', Mark 16:16, can hardly refer to anything other than living believers being baptized for themselves. Nevertheless the figure of baptism shows that it was in view of their being dead.

Again, Jesus, commanding the eleven to teach all nations, baptizing them, scarcely supposes their going forth with spades, exhuming decomposed corpses, first reciting doctrine into the air over what was left of them, then, having soaked the grisly remains with water, returning the sodden corpses to the grave.

How much less can Jesus' commandment mean that each of the eleven was to go through the charade of doing the same thing one to another over the grave as if one of them could stand in for the buried corpse beneath their feet.

What! The holy apostles performing so ridiculous a ritual?

Yet, in effect, this is the monstrous perversity invented from I Corinthians 15:29 by those blasphemous heretics called 'Mormons', a deluded sect led to destruction by the insane ramblings of Joseph Smith.

And *these*, with *their* record, dare to call themselves 'The Church of Jesus Christ of Latter Day Saints'?

Such a synagogue of Satan may spruce up the outward man by a form of the law slyly incorporated into their appallingly sacrilegious fantasy called the 'Book of Mormon', hiding the blasphemies *really* held behind a chameleon-like appearance, but the discerning and spiritual know who gave them the 'kingdom' and 'glory of them' represented by their Salt Lake City prosperity.

Hence I repeat: the words 'What shall they do which are baptized for the dead?', neither wrench the larger context of I Corinthians chapter 15 nor the local context of verses 29-34, nor do they give the faintest warrant to those who reduce the passage to a perverse absurdity.

This is in fact a text wholly consistent with the teaching on baptism throughout the new testament.

It is unthinkable that the words 'They which are baptized for the dead' could refer to one being baptized for another who had died already. It *must* point to *oneself* being dead.

That is what one is baptized for: to show forth by that ordinance the being reckoned – and reckoning oneself – dead with Christ *already*.

Indeed, more: the being reckoned dead with Christ *when he died*. That is, before one's own decease *in practice*, so that *his* death is accounted of God *as one's own* even prior to what is called in scripture 'falling on sleep'.

And if so, this is equally true of his rising from the dead: 'For if' – by baptism – 'we have been planted together' – with him, in death – 'in the likeness of his death, *we shall be also in the likeness of his resurrection*', Romans 6:5.

If those who are thus baptized are not so raised, then everything will have proved to have been in vain: 'Else what shall they do which are baptized for the dead, if the dead rise not at all? why are they then baptized for the dead?', I Corinthians 15:29.

Why? Because just as their faith declared that by baptism they were dead and buried with Christ *already*, so the same faith showed that by rising up out of baptism they should arise from the dead at his coming: 'Christ the firstfruits; afterward they that are Christ's at his coming', I Corinthians 15:23.

'But now *is* Christ risen from the dead, and become the firstfruits of them that slept', I Corinthians 15:20.

That is what they shall do which are baptized for the dead, because the dead must *surely* rise after all; thus *that* is why they are baptized for the dead, because *after it* they shall rise again at the coming of the Lord for his own.

Evidently therefore those who are baptized for the dead are so baptized for two reasons.

One, their baptism *shows their present death and burial in the sight of God and in the inward witness of the Spirit*: 'Know ye not, that so many of us as were baptized into Jesus Christ were baptized *into his death*? Therefore we are buried with him by baptism *into death*', Romans 6:3,4.

Then, we are seen as *dead with him*, and, indeed, this is how we see ourselves: 'Likewise reckon ye also yourselves to be dead indeed unto sin, but alive unto God through Jesus Christ our Lord', Romans 6:11.

'Buried with him in baptism, wherein also ye are risen with him through the faith of the operation of God, who hath raised him from the dead', Colossians 2:12.

The second reason why those who are baptized for the dead are so baptized follows: it is in view of the death of *their own bodies*, when they fall asleep in Christ.

They believe that their death *does not count*. Why not? *Because it has already been counted.*

When? When they were baptized for the dead.

'Jesus said unto her, I am the resurrection, and the life: he that believeth in me, *though he were dead*, yet shall he live: and whosoever liveth and believeth in me *shall never die*. Believest thou this?', John 11:25,26.

We certainly do believe it, and so do they.

They? Who? Why, 'they', all of them, who are baptized for the dead. That was, and is, the reason for their being so baptized, *because* such a baptism *shows openly* what they believe.

The difficulty in I Corinthians 15:29 comes from the word 'for', as in 'baptized *for* the dead'. There is no English equivalent.

In fact, the Greek ὑπὲρ has virtually been transliterated into the English by the word 'hyper'. And what will you make of that?

In geometry, if one considers a cube, ὑπὲρ, *over*, would apply to the upper plane. But then one must consider in grammar whether it is with the accusative or genitive. And what will you make of that?

Not much, whoever you are: and the worst you can be is an academic know-all. The best, one who knows nothing save that Christ is our wisdom, and that the Spirit is truth.

Take the text as it stands and one *naturally* reads it the wrong way. But it is *essential* not to do so. Rather, one must gauge the nuance of the word 'for'—the nearest the translators could get to ὑπὲρ in this instance—from the context of both verse and passage.

Not to mention comparing both with *every other place* in which 'baptized' and 'baptism' occur.

Such places will always be consistent with each other. As God cannot deny himself, neither can scripture deny itself.

So then, they which are baptized for the dead are baptized *now* for when they are dead *afterwards*. Why? Because all their hope lies in the resurrection.

'If in this life only we have hope in Christ, we are of all men most miserable', verse 19.

But *now* we – and they – reckon ourselves dead, that is, to have died, so that *when* our bodies die in fact, all we can see is *resurrection*: 'Else what shall they do which are baptized for the dead, *if the dead rise not at all?* why are they *then* baptized for the dead?' Indeed, Why are they baptized at all?

In such a case they are baptized for nothing but a delusion! And not them only, but all of us. And not us only, but all who have fallen asleep in Christ before us: 'Then they also which are fallen asleep in Christ are perished', verse 18.

But they *hoped* not to perish. That was why they showed their faith and hope when they were baptized.

They were baptized for the dead, not for the perishing. 'Else what shall they do which are baptized for the dead, if the dead rise not at all? why are they then baptized for the dead?'

They – and we – were and are baptized by faith *now* for *when* they – and we – were and will be dead in fact.

They themselves – or we ourselves – were baptized 'for' *their own death, that it should be made manifest beforehand that they had died, and were dead, in and with Christ*. They are 'passed from death unto life', John 5:24, and shall neither see nor taste of death, John 8:51,52. Hence note that verse 29 is a question.

In fact it is *two* questions. And hypothetical questions at that. And *both* have death and resurrection in view.

Question *that*, and *then* where are they? Or we?

In truth, then they, or we, are perished. However, in reality, there *is* no question. Such questions are merely hypothetical and rhetorical. Not real at all. It is the *resurrection* that is real. And *that* is why they – and we – were baptized for the dead.

Baptized for the dead? But it was – and is – not *just* death that was – and is – in view. It is death *and resurrection*. But, evidently, one must die and join the dead before being raised. Then, one is baptized 'for the dead'.

The dead? Which dead? The dead as such. Then, being baptized, it is as if at the time one were standing over and above them that are buried, baptism being an acknowledgement not just that one will join them in their graves, but that in doing so it will be as *having died with Christ already*.

And Christ is 'the resurrection and the life'. Then, baptized for the dead? Yes, but as well call it 'death'. It is the being baptized with a view to death: to joining the dead, over which now one lives. But only till the grave claims our mortality.

So one is baptized by faith in Christ to show that one is baptized *facing one's dying and joining the dead*. Yes, baptized for the dead. But not with a view to *staying* dead: with a view to *rising from the dead*.

That is what one is declaring – *they* are declaring – by faith, and that is what Paul means by this difficult expression.

From which it follows that the reader is advised to read 'the dead' – as in 'baptized for the dead' – in terms of 'for when one is dead oneself'; for when one leaves the land of the living and joins 'the dead' in a collective sense.

That is it: 'for the dead' collectively. The word must be read as describing all those who have passed into the domain of death.

'The dead', I Corinthians 15:29, refers to *that state as such*, rather than one's own individual passage into it. 'The dead' in this verse is indicative of a certain realm – the realm of death – not one's actual decease and individual entrance into that realm.

It is the condition itself, not the individuals who have passed into it. One is baptized not for *them*, but for *it*.

It? Yes, the dominion under which all the dead lie, the domain into which every one of the deceased has passed. A state, that is, into which at the last *they* must pass – I Corinthians 15:29 – and *we* must pass. However, both *they* and *we* were and are baptized because we have confronted *it* before it confronts *us*.

And in that confrontation we have taken the shield of faith, believing that *already* we have died with Christ, and being assured that just as he who died for us rose again, so also we shall be partakers of his resurrection.

That is why they, and we, are 'baptized for the dead', I Corinthians 15:29.

By certain examples from his own continual experience, and that of others who suffered even unto death, or were suffering with the expectation of dying for the testimony which they held, the apostle shows how the faithful were to live: in the shadow of death, but in the hope of the resurrection.

'And why stand we in jeopardy every hour? I protest by your rejoicing which I have in Christ Jesus our Lord, I die daily.

'If after the manner of men I have fought with beasts at Ephesus, what advantageth it me, if the dead rise not? let us eat and drink; for tomorrow we die', I Corinthians 15:30-32.

Paul, and all the brethren with him, stood in jeopardy every hour. He was persecuted, men sought his destruction daily, false brethren went behind his back no sooner had they heard of yet another work being raised up under his ministry, or else some other person having been converted by his gospel.

So these fruitless, useless, worthless false brethren could not leave him alone, consumed with envy and fury, pursuing him as soon as he had departed, at his heels wherever he went, and in whatever country, stirring up the authorities also, even unto Caesar himself.

This was jeopardy indeed; here was persecution – according to the testimony of Jesus – of a truth.

And so it is with those sent of Christ, filled with the Spirit, running in the steps of the apostle, having received the same evangel, being blessed with like fruitfulness, even unto this day.

These also the false brethren hate, persecute, put out of the synagogue, and pursue with relentless energy.

As their fathers did to the psalmist, so these also heap iniquity upon the head of the servants of God, bearing false witness, purveying lies and evil tales which they and their sort invent and multiply from that day to this.

And who were these that so persecuted the servants of God, filled with the Spirit of Christ? Oh, they were the chief priests, elders, doctors of the law, rulers, scribes, Pharisees, Sadducees, and their hosts of followers after the flesh in Israel. But not in the Israel of God. These carry no weight there.

And so it is with their children even unto this present time in their 'churches' as they call them, with their 'evangelicalism' as they call it, persecuting the servants of God as their fathers before them persecuted Paul; the ministers of Christ; the psalmist; and, indeed, *all* the prophets and *every one* of the faithful in the land.

It does not worry these people that *they* are not persecuted.

No; supine and oblivious in self-righteousness, complacency, and pride, if one should point out that whereas *all* the godly were *always* persecuted, but that they are *never* persecuted, they would raise supercilious eyebrows and retire from such a madman as soon as decently possible.

Persecution? Foolish nonsense: What? *them* persecuted? with *their* 'Christ-like' spirit? with all the good *they* do in and to the world? Don't be ridiculous: Who would want to persecute *them*?

As to that so-called Servant of the Lord, and the people with him – not that there are many left; most we have managed to turn back – indeed, one expects they have all gone by now, leaving this wicked and deluded 'Servant' to his own devices: well, *he* ought to be persecuted, certainly.

He *should* stand in jeopardy every hour, besides any that are foolish enough to be with him, what with the volume of misinformation we have quite rightly spread abroad into all the earth beforehand, at present, after the event, and always behind the back.

Thus by the slander, lies, libel, and malicious gossip disseminated and recycled by these 'evangelicals' and their 'churches', all to stop Christ speaking by the mouth of his Servant, and to prejudice beforehand any would-be hearers or readers, they hope to have done God service, John 15:18,19; 16:1-3.

Hence like their father the devil, the father of lies, John 8:43-45, these set to with a will, showing themselves the children of the accuser of the brethren with a witness.

Wherefore, these who are *not* persecuted, *do* persecute. But we who *are* persecuted, do *not* persecute.

By this sure mark you can tell the difference. For as a sheep before his shearers is dumb, so we open not our mouths, going as a lamb to the slaughter, while these howl for our reputations, life, and, could they, even our blood, for all they are worth.

And that is all that they *are* worth. If not, 'why stand we in jeopardy every hour?', I Corinthians 15:30.

But we suffer it silently, because we look for a better resurrection. Then let the Corinthians—and all others—go and do likewise.

'I die daily', cried Paul, the Servant of Christ, I Corinthians 15:31. Yes, he died *daily*. Well, he expected that: it was why he had been baptized for the dead.

'Are they ministers of Christ? (I speak as a fool) I am more; in labours more abundant, in stripes above measure, in prisons more frequent, in deaths oft.

'Of the Jews five times received I forty stripes save one. Thrice was I beaten with rods, once was I stoned, thrice I suffered shipwreck, a night and a day I have been in the deep; in journeyings often,

'In perils of waters, in perils of robbers, in perils by mine own countrymen, in perils by the heathen, in perils in the city, in perils in the wilderness, in perils in the sea, in perils among false brethren;

'In weariness and painfulness, in watchings often, in hunger and thirst, in fastings often, in cold and nakedness.

'Besides those things that are without, that which cometh upon me daily, the care of all the churches. Who is weak, and I am not weak? who is offended, and I burn not? If I must needs glory, I will glory of the things which concern mine infirmities.

Openings in First Corinthians

'The God and Father of our Lord Jesus Christ, which is blessed for evermore, knoweth that I lie not.

'In Damascus the governor under Aretus the king kept the city of the Damascenes with a garrison, desirous to apprehend me: and through a window in a basket was I let down by the wall, and escaped his hands', II Corinthians 11:23-33.

O, Paul died daily. 'I protest by your rejoicing which I have in Christ Jesus our Lord, I die daily', I Corinthians 15:31.

'If after the manner of men I have fought with beasts at Ephesus, what advantageth it me, if the dead rise not? let us eat and drink; for tomorrow we die', I Corinthians 15:32.

There are no grounds for supposing that this analogy of Paul has anything to do with the uprising recorded in Acts 19:23-41.

Although the enmity of the silversmiths directed against the apostle by Demetrius of Ephesus began with a gathering of those of like trade addressed by him, the subsequent uproar that spread like wildfire to the confusion of the whole city was caused by the cry 'Great is Diana of the Ephesians', Acts 19:28, as though *this* notion were in jeopardy. By then, Paul was forgotten.

Indeed it was the two Macedonians, Gaius and Aristarchus, who were caught and rushed into the theatre, forthwith filled with crowds in a state of sheer confusion, conflicting in their opinion of why they were there at all:

'Some therefore cried one thing, and some another: for the assembly was confused; and the more part knew not wherefore they were come together', Acts 19:32.

Now it was the turn of Gaius and Aristarchus to be forgotten, for out of the mêlée they drew forth one Alexander, the Jews – of all people – putting him forth in the midst of the multitude.

'And Alexander beckoned with the hand, and would have made his defence unto the people.

'But when they knew that he was a Jew'—a Jew, mark; not a Christian: Demetrius' cause had been lost in the turmoil—'*a Jew*, all with one voice about the space of two hours cried out, Great is Diana of the Ephesians', Acts 19:34.

But what had that to do with the apostle Paul, who, by now, was far distant, and, in any event, never entered into the theatre? How can *this* be his 'fighting with beasts at Ephesus', as if Acts 19:23-41 were anything whatsoever to do with I Corinthians 15:32?

Note that Paul speaks in the first person: 'If after the manner of men *I* have fought': but he was not there on that occasion, and, if not, how could he have fought with beasts or anything else?

Again, those who *were* there—either the disappearing Gaius and Aristarchus or the gesturing Alexander—were at no stage remotely engaged in fighting: at the very most, they were no more than verbally on the defensive.

Furthermore it was the multitude that occupied the theatre: by the remotest stretch of the imagination not even the rudest and most ignorant of commentators could call that audience 'beasts'.

Finally, if ever man and beast *did* come together in such a place, it would be in the *arena*, not in the tiered seating of the theatre itself. It was the *latter* which would have been filled with and occupied by the *spectators*.

However in Acts 19 *Alexander*—certainly not Paul—*was* in the arena—by himself—seeking for two hours to make his defence before the audience of *men*, during not one single moment of which was the solitary occupant fighting against any wild animal, much less a plurality of beasts.

Besides all this – in any event – what have any of these affairs to do with the absent Paul, who, incidentally, writes in the *first person* in his analogy in I Corinthians 15:32?

These affairs had nothing at all to do with him, neither had the theatre when on that occasion it was so used.

Riots were not the purpose of the renowned theatre: *entertainment* was. Or, at least, what the people thought of as entertainment.

In which case gladiatorial combat, or men called out and chosen to fight against wild beasts, were the choice attractions. And it is to the latter of these that Paul alludes in his analogy.

But if so, how *did* men fight with beasts at Ephesus? By constraint. It was required of them: they were forced into it: the crowd loved it.

Failed or unpopular gladiators, persons fallen from grace with the authorities, recaptured runaway slaves, insubordinate soldiers, prisoners, condemned persons – any of these – perforce were armed, perhaps given a shield, and were condemned to enter the arena in the sight of the caged wild beasts under the high surrounding peripheral walls.

At a signal, the cage doors were drawn up, and the mortal combat began. Such rejected, disgraced, or condemned men were those who thus fought with beasts at Ephesus, who *must* do so, and would almost certainly be mauled to death in the event.

Knowing this, what was their language beforehand? 'Let us eat and drink; for tomorrow we die', I Corinthians 15:32.

But this, though language after the manner of men, was not the language of *every one* of those forcibly exposed to such slaughter. In the persecutions which had raged against the Christians, and would yet rage again, those who refused to deny Christ, or compromise the faith, faced the same death.

But with an entirely different attitude; with a wholly contrary utterance; and with an altogether distinct motive and prospect.

Nor did they fight, however vainly those fought—after the manner of men—who had eaten and drunken the night before. But these praised and prayed the night through.

They went defenceless to the same slaughter, carried mortally wounded and flailing in agony in the slavering jaws and beneath the lacerating claws of the beasts sent to execute so bloody and cruel a death upon them, to the delight of the multitude.

Whereas those that put up a fight braved it out the day before—'Let us eat and drink; for tomorrow we die'—these, as sheep delivered to the slaughter, opened not their mouths, unless it were in the singing of psalms, hymns, and spiritual songs, or the repetition of memorized scriptures.

Whence such fortitude? How come such an absolute contrast between the two classes facing the same death?

Because the one with reckless abandon laughed at death. But the other with faith in Christ believed in the resurrection of the dead.

Were not the resurrection the motive, their conduct would have been inexplicable.

Why be martyred? Why suffer? Why not compromise? Because 'if in this life only we have hope in Christ, we are of all men most miserable.' Hence they loved not their lives unto the death.

Why be thrown to the lions unless, after death, they believed that 'in Christ shall all be made alive'?

Likewise 'others were tortured, not accepting deliverance; that they might obtain a better resurrection: and others had trial of cruel mockings and scourgings, yea, moreover of bonds and imprisonment: they were stoned, they were sawn asunder, were tempted, were slain with the sword:

'They wandered about in sheepskins and goatskins; being destitute, afflicted, tormented; (of whom the world was not worthy:) they wandered in deserts, and in mountains, and in dens and caves of the earth', Hebrews 11:35-38.

Yes, and before Paul wrote, and after it, his constant expectation was to be a partaker of the same martyrdom – or one much like to it – so that hypothetically and in an analogy he could declare to the Corinthians concerning the stupendous prospect of the resurrection of the dead, 'If after the manner of men' – were it so: to die like them; yet so unlike them – 'I have fought with beasts at Ephesus, what advantageth it me, if the dead rise not?'

Why die for faith in Christ, if he rose not, and the dead rise not?

Or, if one *must* die, why not speak beforehand as did the reckless – 'let us eat and drink; for tomorrow we die'?

Why not? Because after death, we who have died with Christ, shall also live with him: 'for since by man came death, by man came also the resurrection of the dead', I Corinthians 15:21.

Now, who will the Corinthians follow? To the speech of which shall they listen? Let them beware of those to whom they gave ear, lest worldly wisdom or heathen recklessness corrupt their faith in Christ.

'Be not deceived: evil communications' – such as *'let us eat and drink, for tomorrow we die'*, taunted in self-mockery by rash and lawless men – 'evil communications corrupt good manners', I Corinthians 15:33.

'Awake to righteousness': keep yourselves pure, clean, holy, separate; shun worldliness, worldly talk, worldly company: *keep the resurrection from the dead in constant view.*

'Awake to righteousness, and sin not'; as you have sinned, denying the resurrection, or suffering those who do so, mingling their words with the words of God to which you should have been wholly given: *sin not!*

'For some have not the knowledge of God': else they would never have been reduced to such shameful corruption from the way of life and the truth of the evangel. 'I speak this to your shame', I Corinthians 15:34.

SIXTH; THE FOLLY OF QUESTIONING THE RESURRECTION OF THE DEAD SHOWN FROM CREATION; BY REVELATION; AND THROUGH THE OPENING OF A MYSTERY, I CORINTHIANS 15:35-58.

Because the folly of questioning the resurrection of the dead springs from the lawless rationalizing of intellectual presumption, the apostle anticipates the questionings which necessarily follow from 'some among you' who say 'that there is no resurrection of the dead'.

He expected this of such persons, despite all that he had taught up to this point, knowing full well the intractable nature of such arrogant rationalists and would-be intellectuals, who, exalting themselves above the most High, in effect at once argue the Creator out of the creation, and scoff at the very thought of his creating *anything further not yet in existence.*

Paul sets about deflating such swollen arrogance, piercing through its bloated conceit with the sword of the Spirit, which is the word of God.

He is determined to subdue such limiting of the Almighty to the confines of the carnal mind; to the boundaries of the things which can be seen; and to the imposition of precedents set by natural laws.

He goes to war against every form of intellectual rebellion, but not with fleshly weapons. For he did not war after the flesh.

Openings in First Corinthians

The weapons of his warfare were not carnal, but mighty through God to the pulling down of the strongholds of science falsely so-called, casting down reasonings, and bringing into captivity every thought to the obedience of Christ.

'But some one will say, How are the dead raised up? and with what body do they come?', I Corinthians 15:35.

If eye hath not seen, nor ear heard, neither hath it entered into the heart of man the things which God hath prepared for them that love him, I Corinthians 2:9, what kind of fool occupies himself with peering into the invisible; listening for the inaudible; and reasoning about the incomprehensible?

If such things lie beyond the senses, stretch past the imagination, exceed all known dimensions, confound every perceivable precedent, transcend all human understanding, and surpass anything ever dreamed of since man had existence, I repeat, What kind of fool goes about posing questions concerning superlative mysteries which lie altogether beyond this present world and visible creation?

Stupid questions! They are never answered. They cannot be answered.

How can anybody know what has never been envisaged? How can anyone comprehend what has not yet taken place? How can anything be explained that lies beyond human capacity to grasp?

The truth is, had these audacious questioners mortified their carnal minds and natural reasonings to submit to the confines of faith in the evangel, such folly would never have entered into their heads, much less passed through their lips.

But the fact that Paul anticipates such utterances shows to what depths of shame even some among the Corinthians could debase and drag down that evangel which once so earnestly they professed. What folly! 'Thou fool.'

Yet, nevertheless, bearing all things, believing all things, hoping all things, enduring all things, kindly condescending to lift up the fool out of his folly, the apostle brings that to bear upon him, which will greatly assist in his recovery, by causing him to see things on earth, in heaven, by revelation, and through a mystery, which are calculated at once to bring back to repentance and forward into faith.

First, things on earth, and things in heaven; that is, from creation: the apostle seems to bring forth three, but on examination in fact it must be four examples either of *change* or of *difference*.

The first example is that of seed that is sown; the second that of different kinds of flesh; thirdly, Paul points out the distinction in glory between heavenly and earthly bodies; finally, confining himself to the heavens, he points to the varying glories of the sun, moon, and the stars.

All these he cites as examples in the will, counsel, and power of God to cause changes and create differences in glory from a creation *already in existence*. Then why not of a creation *yet to come*?

In quoting verses 36-41 I use the interlinear translation from 'The Englishman's Greek New Testament', published by Samuel Bagster in 1877, this giving a very clear idea of the Greek, which, laid side by side with the Authorized, will prove helpful to the elucidation of the original.

'Fool; what thou sowest is not quickened unless it die. And what thou sowest, not the body that shall be thou sowest, but a bare grain, it may be of wheat, or of some one of the rest; and God to it gives a body according as he willed, and to each of the seeds its own body.

'Not every flesh is the same flesh, but one flesh of men, and another of beasts, and another of fishes, and another of birds.

'And bodies heavenly, and bodies earthly: but different is the glory of the heavenly, and different that of the earthly.

'One glory of the sun, and another glory of the moon, and another of the stars; star differing from star in glory', I Corinthians 15:36-41.

The first example in creation which hints at the resurrection is the longest, and certainly the most telling. It concerns not only *difference* but difference through *change*. Moreover, not only change, but a change *of the original thing*. Furthermore, a change of the original thing *effected through life from the dead*.

Now, this exemplifies the resurrection. And it does so in the present creation, year in and year out, before our very eyes. And what kind of a fool is he that ignores this staggering evidence? Answer: A blind fool.

Now, a sower sows the bare grain. He ploughs, scatters, harrows, so that the seed falls into the ground, and dies: 'Except a corn of wheat fall into the ground *and die*, it abideth alone', John 12:24. It abideth alone; that is, it retaineth its present state. *But that is not its destiny.*

Its destiny is to *die*. It was not brought forth to exist without change. It was not formed to abide in this present state. It was formed to fall into the ground and die.

And, dead, to be covered over by the earth, buried and left alone. By man. But not by God. Though dead, it shall–it must–rise again. But not in the same state: 'And that which thou sowest, thou *sowest not that body that shall be.*'

For a season, what was sown lay buried under the earth, but at the last, at the appointed time, out of the earth, up from the seed that died, rising again, a green blade, a shoot, a stalk, then the full ear.

But that was not what was sown.

No; for what was sown was *long ago* dead and buried. But what is risen is at last *that life – yea, that body – which must and shall rise from the dead.*

But it is *not the body which was sown.* It is *the body which rises from the dead.* For 'God giveth it' – in the resurrection from the dead – 'a body as it hath pleased him, and to every seed his own body', I Corinthians 15:38.

Again, 'All flesh is not the same flesh: but one kind of flesh is of men, and another flesh of beasts, another of fishes, and another of birds', verse 39. Yes, Paul, but what has *that* to do with the resurrection?

This is the apostle's second example, and it is given to illustrate *how differently God could, God did, and therefore God can, create utterly distinct kinds of living substances, each suited to its proper order.*

The flesh of man to rule over all; the flesh of beasts to graze in the field; the flesh of fishes to swim in the sea; and the flesh of birds to fly in the air.

Yes, but although flesh as such is common to each of the four, so diverse is the one from the other, each suited to its own kind of life and proper realm, formed each after its kind to multiply variously throughout the world for the duration of this present age, the whole combining to testify beyond all reasonable doubt that the LORD God not only *can* but *will* create that which is suited to the body of glory and immortality raised from the dead in the everlasting kingdom that pertains to the world to come.

And how much more is that *new* creation certain, considering – for all its wonderful diversity – the futility into which this present world has fallen, to groan and travail under pain, corruption, and death, so long as time shall last?

Who in their right mind can suppose that the Creator will rest with *that* state of affairs?

Only a fool could make such a supposition.

And only a fool could presume that he who made such suited diversity of flesh in *this* world, cannot again exert the same power in the last day suitably to clothe the body of resurrection in the world that is to come.

Thirdly, Paul compares heavenly bodies and earthly bodies; or, as the Authorized will have it, bodies celestial with bodies terrestrial. 'And bodies heavenly, and bodies earthly: but different is the glory of the heavenly, and different that of the earthly', 1 Corinthians 15:40.

Here are realms as different as time and eternity, with a glory peculiar to each, one that of the heavenly, the other that of the earthly. If so, why should not the Creator reserve a present glory for time, and a coming glory for eternity? For even now this suggests one glory, which passes, for this world; and another glory, which abides, for the world to come.

If there is a glory to the bodies that exist in the world, and this shines forth to show God's eternal power and Godhead in the things that are made upon the face of the earth, how diversely does that same power and Godhead appear in the creation of the things above in the heavens?

With what a distinct luminosity appears also the glory of the heavenly bodies, whether shining by day or by night? Compare the two, bodies terrestrial and bodies celestial, and what can one conclude?

The glory of God seen in the things which he has created and made is so wonderfully evident, yet so utterly different, that the heaven and the earth combine to declare and make manifest throughout time the new heavens and the new earth yet to come throughout everlasting glory.

Likewise, if the respective glory is so distinct from all that exists – whether terrestrial or celestial – in a world and age that is doomed to pass away, how much more glorious must be all that pertains to the new heavens and the new earth in an eternity which shall never pass away?

For it follows by a law of progression that just as there is a comparative glory between bodies heavenly and earthly in this age, there must also be one glory that pertains to the present creation, and another glory that pertains to that which is to come.

And if all this be true of heavenly and earthly bodies, whether in this world or the next, it most certainly must be true of the bodies of the saints in the resurrection of the dead.

Which is what Paul had set out to demonstrate in this third example of the things that differ, visible before the eyes of men, yet indicative of the resurrection yet to come, I Corinthians 15:40.

'There is one glory of the sun, and another glory of the moon, and another glory of the stars: for one star differeth from another star in glory', I Corinthians 15:41.

Here is the fourth and last example from creation given by the apostle Paul to lead the reflective mind to the witness of the Creator to the resurrection of the dead.

At first this might appear to be a continuation of the previous verse; however, but a moment's consideration shows that it cannot be so.

In the third example, verse 40, the apostle distinguishes between the glory of celestial – or heavenly – bodies and the glory of terrestrial – or earthly – bodies, making a comparison between the two.

But in verse 41 there is no such comparison.

In verse 40 the things peculiar to two distinct realms are compared, whereas in verse 41 only one of those realms is mentioned.

It is things unique to that–heavenly–realm alone that are contrasted. There is no reference to the terrestrial realm at all. Not a word concerning earthly bodies.

And if not, they do not enter into the equation. The comparison–in order to show the difference–is that of one heavenly body with another: the entire verse being concerned with the distinction between the glory of one heavenly body and that of another heavenly body: all the glory is in the heavens, the earth does not come into it.

In which case verse 41 is not only the fourth and last but it is equally a separate example from the three preceding instances.

The glory of the sun differs from the glory of the moon, differs from the glory of the stars, and the glory of one star differs from the glory of another star.

Well; but how does this exemplify the resurrection of the dead?

Because if there is such a multiplicity, variation, and complexity to the glory that shines in the heavens in that creation which waxeth old and is ready to vanish away, then, seeing that the LORD God Almighty has so great a glory to contrast, one form with another, in *this* creation, *how much more the everlasting glory of that which shall never decay, and cannot pass away, in the new creation of the world to come, whereof we speak?*

And, if so, in the resurrection from the dead.

Otherwise, why the *difference* in glory?

Because for all the differences in every glorious outshining throughout the heavens during the whole of time, put everything together, weigh the sum from the formation of the heavens till their dissolution, it is all no more than small dust in the balance compared to the glory that is yet to be revealed in the heavens that shall be created to suit the resurrection of the dead in glorious sonship.

But, at least, the difference—the astonishing difference—between one example of heavenly glory and another, must surely lead the mind to consider how much more an exceeding weight of glory pertains to that creation which still remains to be revealed, and that heaven which is yet to come.

And if yet to come, then in the resurrection of the dead.

Indeed, who but the most blinded fool can stand upon the earth, looking up into the heavens shining with glory, and not see what stares him in the face?

What? Then there is—and there *must be*—a resurrection from the dead for the world to come in consequence.

With such examples as these—as though he had enunciated no other doctrine!—well might Paul expostulate with the Corinthians from this cause alone 'Why should it be thought a thing incredible with you that God should raise the dead?', Acts 26:8.

Such examples themselves exclaim to them, Look up! Hearken!

For 'the heavens declare the glory of God; and the firmament showeth his handiwork. Day unto day uttereth speech, and night unto night showeth knowledge. There is no speech nor language, where their voice is not heard. Their line is gone out through all the earth, and their words to the end of the world', Psalm 19:1-4.

Surely this should have been their wisdom—over and above everything in Chapter 15 up to this point—that they should have looked up and seen – the witness being in their hearts – that in the resurrection from the dead 'they that be wise shall shine as the brightness of the firmament; and they that turn many to righteousness as the stars for ever and ever', Daniel 12:3.

For, 'Thou, Lord, in the beginning hast laid the foundation of the earth; and the heavens are the works of thine hands: they shall perish' – yea, and all the glory of them shall perish together – 'but thou remainest; and they shall all wax old as doth a garment; and as a vesture shalt thou fold them up, and they shall be changed: but thou art the same, and thy years shall not fail', Hebrews 1:10-12.

Then, these things being so, the first creation having waxed old and vanished away, how much more shall the Maker of heaven and earth magnify his resplendent glory beyond all that eye hath seen, ear heard, or hath entered into the heart of man to conceive, in that new creation, that new heaven and new earth – the first heaven and the first earth having passed away – waiting to greet the saints in the glorious resurrection from the dead, world without end. Amen.

The apostle now proceeds to the brightness of that revelation of which the four preceding examples from creation were a pale reflection: 'So also is the resurrection of the dead.

'It is sown in corruption; it is raised in incorruption: it is sown in dishonour; it is raised in glory: it is sown in weakness; it is raised in power: it is sown a natural body; it is raised a spiritual body. There is a natural body, and there is a spiritual body', I Corinthians 15:42-44.

Just as previously from creation there were four examples of the resurrection from the dead, so now by revelation there are four applications of those examples, followed by the necessary conclusion.

Four times over what is sown is contrasted with what is raised. The dead, whether sown in corruption, dishonour, weakness, or 'nature'—ψυχικόν, *psuchikon*—in the resurrection are raised in incorruption, glory, power, and spirituality, respectively.

And what is sown? Why, 'a body'. And what is raised? Why, 'a *body*', I Corinthians 15:44. Not a *spirit*.

It may be *spiritual*, but *what* is spiritual is not *a* spirit. What is raised is that which was sown, namely *a body*, albeit a *spiritual* body.

That is, like unto 'his glorious body', Philippians 3:21, in which, however spiritual, he ate, drank, was handled, seen, was of flesh and bones, yet, nevertheless, was raised a *body* for the glorious inheritance of the everlasting kingdom in the new heaven *and the new earth* of which—his people having been raised in his likeness—*he* is the heir.

As to the resurrection of that people, they are raised to an inexpressible glory far transcending anything either imagined or dreamed of—let alone experienced—whilst in this body and in the present world.

No matter *how* much that which was glorious had appeared to the saints below, the glory to come surpasses all with a far more exceeding, consummate and everlasting brightness, beyond all precedent, even as the apostle had taught from the comparisons in the previous verses: '*So also* is the resurrection of the dead', verse 42.

The resurrection of the dead was *sown*. Four times over Paul stresses this.

But, like the seed which fell into the ground and died, what shall be raised *is not the same thing*. Yet, a glory once did indwell that which was sown.

Nevertheless for all that glory, for all that which had been, for all the having been the temple of the Holy Ghost; for all the abiding in Christ, and Christ abiding in us; for all the Father himself indwelling our spirit; for all the heavenly treasure within; still, that which had so glorious a habitation in the days of our pilgrimage never abode in anything more permanent than a fragile clay vessel.

Never more than a clay vessel: of itself it was ever the body of sin and death destined for the grave.

The apostle, full of glory, still called that in which the glory dwelt 'this vile body'.

It was still that in which inbred sin remained, inexorably to bring down the body into the decay of age, disease, wasting, and death.

This is that which was sown: buried in the earth. Covered over out of sight.

It is what was sown in corruption, soon to be forgotten, out of mind beneath the soil. Of these decomposing remains, rotting and mouldering, Job saith: 'they shall lie down alike in the dust, and the worms shall cover them', Job 21:26.

And again, 'worms destroy this body': here is the sowing in corruption, Job 19:26.

Nevertheless, for all this, it is still the body that was sown. And if so, neither death, nor the grave, nor yet so ignominious a dissolution, can possibly prove to be the end. The end, that is, of the *body* that was sown.

As the body is sown in corruption, so in like manner it is sown in dishonour. Once comely, now corrupt; once had in honour, now sown in dishonour. No sooner the shadow of death passes over the features, but the cold hand of death closes over the corpse.

Now men avert their faces, who had once paid honour in the land of the living.

The soul having departed, how soon is comeliness turned to corruption, honour into dishonour.

How quickly the swiftly putrefying cadaver must be buried in the ground, the stink of death already tainting the air. This is to be sown in dishonour.

It is also to be sown in weakness. The life may have clung, held on with desperation, even to the very last. But loose its hold it must.

The strong, the mighty man, the valiant, all alike succumb to the king of terrors, and there is no escaping the inevitable departure of the soul from the body, no, not though one had in life the vigour of ten men.

When the grim reaper calls, the strength ebbs away, the life departs, the soul leaves the body, and nothing but the empty shell remains, so soon to turn to dust. This is called 'sown in weakness'.

It is to be sown a natural—*psuchikon*—body.

Natural? That is, shapen in iniquity; conceived in sin. Born in the man of sin and death. Belonging to the earth, earthy; under the curse, beneath the Fall. Of this present passing world. Doomed to decay and death.

That is what is 'natural' to man in the age that now is: the sentence already passed, the process of inbred sin and inherent dissolution at work even from conception, the passing of time inexorably sapping the life, until death parts soul and body: this is to be sown a natural body!

The degradation of this sowing under the ghastly hand of death is indicated by the grisly consequences of corruption, dishonour, weakness, and the immutable law of nature universally evident in all creation, namely–far from the theoretic fiction of evolution–the reality of decline and dissolution.

So soon! Martha knew this, and, when the Lord called for the grave of Lazarus to be opened, cried out in horror, 'Lord, by this time he stinketh: for he hath been dead four days', John 11:39.

But out of corruption, dishonour, weakness, and natural decay, Lazarus was chosen to show in a figure the raising to incorruption, the resurrection of glory, the rising again in power, and the certain promise of a spiritual body.

'Said I not unto thee, that, if thou wouldest believe, thou shouldest see the glory of God?', John 11:40.

Of this sowing in death, and raising to glory, through Christ the firstfruits, called, 'the Resurrection and the Life'–in whom, believing, though one were dead, yet shall one live–Peter speaks on the day of Pentecost, citing the case of David:

'Men and brethren, let me freely speak unto you of the patriarch David, that he is both dead and buried, and his sepulchre is with us unto this day.

'Therefore being a prophet, and knowing that God had sworn with an oath to him, that of the fruit of his loins, according to the flesh, he would raise up Christ to sit on his throne; he seeing this before spake of the resurrection of Christ, that *his* soul was not left in *hadēs*, neither *his* flesh did see corruption.

'This Jesus hath God raised up, whereof we all are witnesses', Acts 2:29-32.

Now, *here* is the Resurrection and the Life, even the firstfruits of them that slept.

Of this the apostle Paul speaks likewise, saying, 'David, after he had served his own generation by the will of God, fell on sleep, and was laid unto his fathers, and saw corruption: but he, whom God raised again, saw no corruption', Acts 13:36,37.

Yes, David saw corruption, together with all the saints which have been since the world began: their bodies, one and all, were sown in corruption.

But he whom God raised from the dead, Christ the firstfruits, saw no corruption, even as David prophesied some one thousand years before: 'For thou wilt not leave my soul in *sheol*; neither wilt thou suffer thine Holy One to see corruption', Psalm 16:10.

But *we* see corruption. Our body is sown in corruption; it is sown in dishonour; it is sown in weakness; it is sown a natural body.

A natural *dead* body.

Death cuts off all life, all honour, all strength, all that stands this side of the grave, shutting us up to revolting putrescence and decomposition, so soon to be forgotten in the darkness of the tomb, in which nothing is heard but the soft falling of decay.

If so, What a terrible enemy death proves to be: indeed, it is the last enemy.

When death strikes its mortal blow, it shall not strike again. The worst possible fears are realized, and the ultimate finality is foreclosed. Oh, death is the *last* enemy, with a witness.

But now is Christ risen from the dead, and become the first-fruits of them that slept.

As to the last enemy, 'the last enemy *that shall be destroyed* is death', I Corinthians 15:26. 'So also is the resurrection of the dead.

'It is sown in corruption; *it is raised in incorruption*: it is sown in dishonour; *it is raised in glory*: it is sown in weakness; *it is raised in power*: it is sown a natural body; *it is raised a spiritual body*', I Corinthians 15:42-44.

What then shall we say to these things? We shall echo with Paul, *'Death is swallowed up in victory'*, I Corinthians 15:54.

Wherefore observe that in each of the four instances, the very use of the word 'sown'—though what immediately precedes and for a season follows the sowing were never so ignominious—fills every soul in Christ with hope. Because sowing predicates hope. Hope of rising again. Of the *body* rising again.

And of that body which shall rise again—which was sown in death—the apostle declares in the first of four instances: '*It* is sown in corruption; *it* is raised in incorruption', I Corinthians 15:42.

Where that which was sown is the opposite in character to that which shall be raised.

What shall be raised is *incapable of decay*. If so, *it can never die again*: 'Christ being raised from the dead dieth no more'—and neither do those in Christ, who are raised in incorruption—'death hath no more dominion over him', Romans 6:9, and neither hath it over those in Christ, who are raised incorruptible.

Mark well that in this place—indeed in the whole of I Corinthians 15:42-44—Paul is not referring to the *soul*. It is not *that* that is 'sown'. It is the *body* that is 'sown'. The apostle refers to *the body*: '*It* is sown in corruption; *it* is raised in incorruption.'

Therefore in the resurrection there shall be an entire transformation. Nevertheless it is certain that—though radically transformed—*the body that shall be raised is the body that was sown.*

But raised 'incorruptible': '*it* is raised in incorruption', I Corinthians 15:42.

It is raised immortal, imperishable; it is raised with an inherent incapacity of decay; it is undying: in a word, it is raised 'incorruptible'.

To this end, whilst yet in the present corruption, the saints lived: and 'to them who by patient continuance in well doing' –despite all the weight and impediment of this corruptible body– 'seek for glory and honour and *immortality*'–this last being the same word in the Greek as that translated 'incorruption', I Corinthians 15:42–God, 'who will render to every man according to his deeds' will most assuredly render to all such saints 'eternal life', Romans 2:6,7.

Doubtless this entails the fight of faith, and at that against a veritable Goliath of an enemy, namely, the intrusive cloddishness of this heavy clay that so often weighs the soul down to earth with sighing and despondency.

Nevertheless the constant battle against carnal ease and indulgence is not much more than that which is required of athletes, who, to win the crown, must make consistent and painful sacrifices in the endeavour.

'Now they do it to obtain a corruptible crown; but we an *incorruptible*.

'I therefore so run, not as uncertainly; so fight I, not as one that beateth the air: but I keep under my body, and bring it into subjection', I Corinthians 9:25-27. 'If by any means I might attain unto the resurrection of the dead', Philippians 3:11.

And why not, seeing that we have been saved 'and called with an holy calling, not according to our works, but according to his own purpose and grace, which was given us in Christ Jesus before the world began, but is now made manifest by the appearing of our Saviour Jesus Christ, *who hath abolished death, and hath brought life and immortality*'–it is the same Greek word– '*to light through the gospel*', II Timothy 1:9,10.

This is the light of the heavenly vision that illuminates the heart of his people, every one of whom sets his countenance steadfastly towards Zion, looking for the resurrection of the body from the dead at the return of the Lord, to be raised in incorruption.

But for what, such an undying body, incapable of decay, save to live for ever, and to live for ever *in that body*.

To what end? To the end of 'an inheritance *incorruptible*, and undefiled, and that fadeth not away, reserved in heaven for you, who are kept by the power of God through faith unto salvation ready to be revealed in the last time', I Peter 1:4,5.

'Now unto the King eternal, *immortal*'– it is the same Greek word –'invisible, the only wise God, be honour and glory for ever and ever. Amen', I Timothy 1:17.

Secondly, 'It is sown in dishonour; it is raised in glory', I Corinthians 15:43. But though the body should be sown in dishonour, yet, Christ being in the saints, 'the body is dead because of sin; but the Spirit is life because of righteousness', Romans 8:10.

In this life they had reckoned themselves 'dead indeed unto sin, but alive unto God through Jesus Christ our Lord', Romans 6:11.

They had counted themselves 'crucified with Christ', Galatians 2:20. Hence therefore, despite this vile body, soon to be sown in dishonour, they had 'lived unto God', so that they passed the time of their sojourning here in fear, 'by patient continuance in well doing'– in *this* life –'seeking for *glory*'– in *that* life which is to come, Romans 2:7.

Nor shall they be disappointed: for though this vile body were 'sown in dishonour', beyond all question it shall be 'raised in glory' at the coming of Christ and the resurrection of the dead.

And what glory! 'For our conversation' – even now – 'is in heaven; from whence also we look for the Saviour, the Lord Jesus Christ: who shall *change* our vile body' – so dishonourable in its sowing: so inglorious – 'that it may be fashioned' – in the resurrection, when that which was sown is raised in glory – '*like unto his glorious body*', Philippians 3:20,21.

Like unto *his* glorious body? What likeness is that?

This was shown at the transfiguration, when 'he was transfigured before them: and his face did shine as the sun, and his raiment was white as the light', Matthew 17:2. Like that: his glorious body is like that; *and our body of glory will be like unto it*.

Again; 'He was transfigured before them. And his raiment became shining, exceeding white as snow; so as no fuller on earth can white them', Mark 9:2,3.

Like that: 'like unto *his* glorious body.'

Once more; 'And as he prayed, the fashion of his countenance was altered, and his raiment was white and glistering', Luke 9:29.

Altered, yes, as a foretaste of the glory that was to come; and we too, who are of his body, in Christ, likewise, 'we shall be changed' in the resurrection of the dead to everlasting glory.

What glory! 'And as he journeyed, he came near Damascus: and suddenly there shined round about him a light from heaven', Acts 9:3.

Whence the light? From a *person*. A glorified *person* in heaven. For the *person* gave forth the radiance: 'I am Jesus', came the voice of him who shone with such glory.

Again; 'And it came to pass, that, as I made my journey, and was come nigh unto Damascus about noon, suddenly there shone from heaven a great light round about me', Acts 22:6.

Openings in First Corinthians

This was the glory of the Lord, raised from the dead, ascended into heaven. Concerning which glory it is said of all those raised in his likeness, 'like unto'.

Once more; 'At midday, O king, I saw in the way a light from heaven, above the brightness of the sun, shining round about me', Acts 26:13. This was the light that shone so brightly from the glorified Son in heaven.

But in that day this light shall not only shine *round about* Paul: raised from the dead in the body of glory, the light shall shine *in* him, and *through* him, in glorious radiance, world without end.

And not Paul only, but likewise all those that love his appearing, as it is written, 'Christ the firstfruits; afterward they that are Christ's at his coming', I Corinthians 15:23.

And as is the firstfruits, so also shall be the harvest. Glorious. Glorified. Like that.

Though the body *was* sown in dishonour; *it is raised in glory*. *That* kind of glory: everlasting glory. The glory of the Son: 'like unto *his* glorious body, according to the working whereby he is able even to subdue all things unto himself', Philippians 3:21.

Thirdly: 'It is sown in weakness; it is raised in power', I Corinthians 15:43.

Observe the wording, 'sown in weakness'. There is nothing weaker than a dying man. None so weak as one on his death bed. No weakness like that of the last gasping breath, trailing into the expiry of the final dwindling sigh.

And then, what is weaker than the limp, lifeless, inert corpse, ready to be interred in the grave? That is to be sown in weakness indeed.

So weak! Then how wonderful it is that *this*—no matter how long the weakness of what was sown moulders beneath the earth—*this* is that which is to be 'raised in power'.

If so, there is no power, but absolutely no power, like that of the resurrection from the dead, 'When the Son of man shall come in his glory, and all the holy angels with him', Matthew 25:31. No wonder that 'with great power gave the apostles witness of the resurrection of the Lord Jesus', Acts 4:33.

Then how much more certainly of *all* the dead? 'Marvel not at this: for the hour is coming, in the which *all* that are in the graves shall hear his voice, and shall come forth; they that have done good, unto the resurrection of life; and they that have done evil, unto the resurrection of damnation', John 5:28,29.

It is not that the resurrection is anything other than a *proven, witnessed fact,* testified by the raising of Christ from the dead, and in the signs that followed:

'And the graves were opened; and many bodies'—mark that: bodies—'of the saints which slept arose, and came out of the graves after his resurrection, and went into the holy city, *and appeared unto many*', Matthew 27:52,53.

The Son does not raise *ghosts;* observe, it says *'many bodies'* were raised from the dead, '*and appeared unto many*'.

These *'many'* were contemporaries of Matthew: *he would never have written this without the certainty that none of the 'many' either would or could deny or ridicule the record of what they themselves had witnessed with their own eyes, and to which they had testified with their own mouths.*

Why should it be thought a thing incredible with you that God should raise the dead? He *did* raise the dead, and he *will* raise the dead. Even before his own resurrection Jesus heaped scorn upon those fools who scoffed *at so obvious and palpable a fact:*

'Do ye not therefore err, because ye know not the scriptures, neither the power of God?'–they were without excuse: they *had* the scriptures; they ought to have known them.

They *knew* of the power of God; they ought not to have limited that power, much less dismissed its exercise in relation to the resurrection at the last day–'For when they shall rise from the dead, they neither marry, nor are given in marriage; but are as the angels which are in heaven.

'And as touching the dead, that they rise: have ye not read in the book of Moses, how in the bush God spake unto him, saying, I am the God of Abraham, and the God of Isaac, and the God of Jacob? He is not the God of the dead, but the God of the living: ye therefore do greatly err', Mark 12:24-27.

Greatly err, because when God testified to Moses, *I am*–not *I was*–the God of Abraham, Isaac, and Jacob, he bore testimony to three men who had died *hundreds of years before*. But he was *still* their God: then their souls lived on, for it is certain that he is not the God of the dead, but of the living.

And if living at *that* time, when Jesus spoke, then, equally, their God *now also*, centuries and millennia making no difference to the God of glory, nor to the power of the living God.

And if he was the God of their living souls for so long a time, do you think that God by Jesus Christ will not raise them up in their bodies at the resurrection in the last day?

What, when Jesus testified 'Abraham'–note that name: *Abraham*, whose body had died millennia before–'Abraham rejoiced to see my day: and he saw it, and was glad.

'Then said the Jews unto him, Thou art not yet fifty years old, and hast thou seen Abraham? Jesus said unto them, Verily, verily, I say unto you, before Abraham was, I am', John 8:56-58.

Then do you suppose that Abraham shall not rise in the harvest at the end of the world, when Christ the firstfruits comes for his own?

What? not raise Abraham's body, and that of all the saints, when, just before raising Lazarus from the dead, in an open and public resurrection before multitudes – all of whom knew that Lazarus had been dead and buried, with putrefaction set in, these four days past – Jesus declared of himself what he was about to demonstrate to them all:

'I am the resurrection, and the life: he that believeth in me, *though he were dead*, yet shall he live: and whosoever liveth and believeth in me shall never die. Believest thou this?', John 11:25,26.

Believe? But they *saw* it: 'He cried with a loud voice, Lazarus, come forth. And he that was dead came forth, bound hand and foot with graveclothes: and his face was bound about with a napkin. Jesus said unto them, Loose him, and let him go', John 11:43,44.

This was the power of his resurrection, and every one of his saints shall experience its full magnitude, from the beginning of the world to the end of it, in the day of his coming to raise the dead.

Of this the Holy Ghost bears witness within, according to the scriptures and the power of God, even now fulfilling the prayers of the apostle Paul, as it is written,

'That the God of our Lord Jesus Christ, the Father of glory, may give unto you the spirit of wisdom and revelation in the knowledge of him: the eyes of your understanding being enlightened; that ye may know what is the hope of his calling, and what the riches of the glory of his inheritance in the saints,

'*And what the exceeding greatness of his power to usward who believe, according to the working of his mighty power, which he wrought in Christ, when he raised him from the dead, and set him at his own right hand in the heavenlies*', Ephesians 1:17-20.

Now, *that* is the power to raise what had been sown in weakness, a power *absolutely* certain in the resurrection of every one that believeth.

'Why should it be thought a thing incredible with you, that God should raise the dead?', Acts 26:8. What! In the teeth of the scriptures, and of the power of God?

'The hand of the LORD was upon me, and carried me out in the spirit of the LORD, and set me down in the midst of the valley which was full of bones, and caused me to pass by them round about:

'And, behold, there were very many in the open valley; and, lo, they were very dry.

'And he said unto me, Son of man, can these bones live? And I answered, O Lord GOD, thou knowest.

'Again he said unto me, Prophesy upon these bones, and say unto them, O ye dry bones, hear the word of the LORD. Thus saith the Lord GOD unto these bones; Behold, I will cause breath to enter into you, and ye shall live:

'And I will lay sinews upon you, and will bring up flesh upon you, and cover you with skin, and put breath in you, and ye shall live; and ye shall know that I am the LORD.

'So I prophesied as I was commanded: and as I prophesied, there was a noise, and behold a shaking, and the bones came together, bone to his bone.

'And when I beheld, lo, the sinews and the flesh came up upon them, and the skin covered them above: but there was no breath in them.

'Then said he unto me, Prophesy unto the wind, prophesy, son of man, and say to the wind, Thus saith the Lord God; Come from the four winds, O breath, and breathe upon these slain, that they may live.

'So I prophesied as he commanded me, and the breath came into them, and they lived, and stood up upon their feet, an exceeding great army', Ezekiel 37:1-10.

Yes, *'it is raised in power.'* Power to join bone to bone; power to fetch bones from the depths of the earth, from the bottom of the sea; from the utmost ends of the world.

Power to gather scattered dust, imperishable substance, indestructible matter, irreducible elements, from the bodies of all mankind since the foundation of the earth till the day of its dissolution: the *same* matter.

O, ye do greatly err, knowing neither the scriptures, nor the power of God.

'And I saw a great white throne, and him that sat on it, from whose face the earth and the heaven fled away; and there was found no place for them.

'And I saw the dead, small and great, stand before God; and the books were opened: and another book was opened, which is the book of life:

'And the dead were judged out of those things which were written in the books, according to their works.

'And *the sea gave up the dead which were in it; and death and hadēs delivered up the dead which were in them: and they were judged every man according to their works.*

'And death and *hadēs* were cast into the lake of fire. This is the second death. And whosoever was not found written in the book of life was cast into the lake of fire', Revelation 20:11-15.

Now, this is being sown in weakness but raised in power with a witness.

And how say some among you that there is no resurrection of the dead? Then, your faith is vain, and ye are yet in your sins. But now *is* Christ risen from the dead, and become the firstfruits of them that slept.

Fourthly, 'It is sown a natural body; it is raised a spiritual body', I Corinthians 15:44.

'It is sown a natural body.' This is that body which Paul calls 'our vile body'. It is conceived in sin, saith David, and shapen in iniquity. It is the body of sin, declares the apostle. It is born in sin, and hath the sentence of death in itself.

As with all natural things, it is subject to decay; is a seedbed of corruption; leads to groaning and travail; sickness and disease; and ends its meaningless existence in disillusioned vanity upon the death bed.

Thence, it is said to be 'sown'. That is, buried under the earth in death.

Yet what a glorious promise awaits all who 'fell asleep' in Christ. Though, like others, their body was sown a natural body, yet *their* existence here was not meaningless, neither were *their* years on earth spent in wasting and vanity.

By patient continuance in well doing they sought for glory and honour and immortality, confessing themselves to be strangers and pilgrims upon the earth, looking for a better resurrection, a heavenly country, and a city which hath foundations, whose builder and maker is God.

And thus seeking, so looking, they fell asleep in Christ, their souls departing to be with him for ever. But as to their bodies, each one, Paul declares, 'it is sown a natural body'.

Yes, but 'it' – mark that: *it* – 'it is raised a spiritual body.' Not 'it is raised a spirit', observe. God forbid! It – *it*, notice – 'it is raised a spiritual *body*.'

There is nothing ephemeral, nothing ghostly, about that: a spirit is a spirit is a spirit. What is spiritual is spiritual is spiritual. And a body is a body is a body. Then a spiritual body is a spiritual body is a spiritual *body*. And nothing less.

A *body* was sown, but having a certain nature. *That body shall be raised, having a different nature altogether*. But *still*, a body. Only, a body suited to the divine nature – for God is a Spirit, John 4:24 – namely, a spiritual body, raised to abide in him, and for his indwelling, with all saints, to the endless ages of everlasting glory.

But some man will say, A spiritual *body* is a contradiction in terms, and therefore, since it is spiritual, the resurrection cannot be of the *body*, much less that corpse which was buried in the grave.

Against such vain and godless theorizing, which, whilst boasting of itself as 'reason', actually intrudes into things which it has neither seen nor can see, having the temerity to speculate about dimensions beyond human capacity even to imagine, it is no wonder to discover that the apostle protests with withering scorn, 'Thou fool', I Corinthians 15:36.

A spiritual body a contradiction in terms? Then I will contradict the terms of such folly with the facts and evidence of the spiritual body, once having been sown in death – and at that, the ignominious death of the cross, where the Saviour, being made sin and bearing sins, was crucified under wrath and the curse – was thereafter raised from the dead by the glory of the Father, and 'was seen many days of them which came up with him from Galilee to Jerusalem, who are his witnesses unto the people', Acts 13:31.

That is, so seen many days after—mark that: *after*—'God raised him from the dead', Acts 13:30.

If such a fool should continue his palpable contradictions and say, But that was the Lord: whereas 'raised a spiritual body' refers to the saints, I Corinthians 15:44, I answer, Yes, the Corinthian text does refer to the saints; in that saidst thou truly.

Wherein thou liest, however, lurks hidden beneath the sly insinuation that *the resurrection of the body of the Lord, and that of his own, is different*. But the apostle declares, 'For if we have been planted together in the likeness of his death, we shall be also in the likeness of his resurrection', Romans 6:5.

And again, he 'shall *change*'—not *eliminate*; it says *change*—'our vile body, that it'—*it*, mark that, *it*—'may be fashioned'—*fashioned*, notice: Greek, *having the same form with*—'fashioned *like unto his glorious body*', Philippians 3:21.

Now where is the difference?

And where is your folly? Why, it is sunk like lead in the mired and dirty waters of your unbelief: 'The wicked are like the troubled sea, when it cannot rest, whose waters cast up mire and dirt. There is no peace, saith my God, to the wicked', Isaiah 57:20,21.

As to the spiritual body being, first, a *body* notwithstanding; and, second, answering to the resurrection—though changed—of *that body which was sown*: Consider:

Firstly, since *it*—the body—of the saints that is to be raised at his coming is in the likeness of *his* resurrection, and since it is fashioned *like unto* his glorious body, *it follows of necessity that it is a body notwithstanding, for all that it is a spiritual body.*

For its being *spiritual* does not, and cannot, nullify its being a *body*.

'And as they'—to whom the Lord had appeared, risen from the dead—'thus spake, Jesus himself stood in the midst of them.' He had appeared bodily to two of them; yet he had vanished out of their sight. Then *here* is a spiritual body; it belonged to and was capable of spiritual dimensions beyond understanding.

Thereupon the Lord appeared bodily to all of them, suddenly materializing in their midst: now this defies all imagination; but what *cannot* be denied is the *fact that in that spiritual body he did so, witness the testimony of the apostles.*

'Jesus himself'—*himself*, mark—'stood in the midst of them, and saith unto them, Peace be unto you.

'But they were terrified and affrighted, and supposed that they had seen a spirit'—that is, a ghost—'And he said unto them, Why are ye troubled? and why do thoughts arise in your hearts?

'Behold my hands and my feet, that it is *I myself: handle me, and see;* for a spirit *hath not flesh and bones, as ye see me have.*'

If so, his risen body, of flesh and bones, was for all that *a spiritual body*. But, despite that it was spiritual, *it was still corporeal and could be handled*. In a word, it *was* a body. And, recognizably, *his* body. Yet a *spiritual* body.

'And when he had thus spoken, he showed them his hands and his feet. And while they yet believed not for joy, and wondered, he said unto them, Have ye here any meat?

'And they gave him a piece of a broiled fish, and of an honeycomb. And he took it, and did eat before them.'

Then that is the end of all controversy. It was *him*. In *his body*. But raised *such a spiritual body that it had those distinct characteristics*. See Luke 24:36-43.

And as is the firstfruits, so shall be the harvest.

Secondly, carefully notice that – whether the Lord, or they that are his at his coming – it *is* that body which was sown. 'But Thomas, one of the twelve, called Didymus, was not with them when Jesus came. The other disciples therefore said unto him, We have seen the Lord.

'But he said unto them, Except I shall see in his hands the print of the nails, and put my finger into the print of the nails, and thrust my hand into his side, I will not believe.

'And after eight days again his disciples were within, and Thomas with them: then came Jesus, the doors being shut'—now, *that* manifestation was *spiritual*; yes: but it was *still his body*—'and stood in the midst, and said, Peace be unto you.

'Then saith he to Thomas, Reach hither thy finger, and behold my hands; and reach hither thy hand, and thrust it into my side: and be not faithless, but believing.

'And Thomas answered and said unto him, My Lord and my God.

'Jesus saith unto him, Thomas, because thou hast seen me, thou hast believed: blessed are they that have not seen, and yet have believed', John 20:24-29.

Now this spiritual body, materializing in their midst, was beyond any shadow of doubt *that in which he had been crucified*. That which was dead three days in the tomb. That which, raised from the dead by the glory of the Father, yet bore the print of the nails and the wound of the spear.

Then, as for us also, *it* is sown a natural body; yes, and *it* is raised a spiritual body.

'There is a natural body, and there is a spiritual body', I Corinthians 15:44.

The natural body is of the earth; it belongs to this world; it pertains to the present age; it is born, grows, withers, and dies, in a moment, a span of time; its generation is of the man of sin and death; it is in the Fall, under the curse, and of the flesh; it is rooted in Adam's transgression, and doomed to dissolution.

Yes, there is a natural body. But thanks be unto God, which giveth us the victory through our Lord Jesus Christ, *there is a spiritual body.*

The spiritual body is for the world to come; it is for the saints' rest; it is for the eternal inheritance; it belongs to the new heaven and the new earth; it pertains to the holy city, new Jerusalem, which comes down from God out of heaven; it is for everlasting bliss in the glorious inheritance promised in Christ before the world began, and entered into when the world is no more.

'There is a spiritual body.' It is for God, to abide in him, and he in us, in Father, Son, and Holy Ghost, world without end, manifesting forth his glory.

God is love; God is light; God is a Spirit. And, in that spiritual *body*, in the inheritance of *the world to come*, the light, life, and love of God shall radiate in and through that spiritual body, world without end. Amen.

'There is a spiritual body': it is divine, for God is a Spirit. It is heavenly, for we shall bear the image of the heavenly. It is glorious, for it is fashioned like unto his glorious body. It is everlasting, for evermore to radiate the indwelling of eternal life.

It is incorruptible, for it is not possible that it should decay. It is immortal, for it is incapable of dying. It is spiritual, for it is agreeable to the divine nature, for ever to worship in spirit and in truth.

O, mark well, all ye who are of the chosen generation, the heirs of promise, who are of faith, the sons of God, for to you the word is certain, and the promise is sure, world without end, as the Spirit and the truth bear witness: 'There *is* a spiritual body', I Corinthians 15:44.

The folly of questioning the resurrection of the dead has been shown from Creation, I Corinthians 15:35-41, followed by the revelation made manifest through the pen of the apostle, verses 42-44. This passage is the first part of the revelation. Paul now continues with the second and last part, verses 45-50.

'So also it has been written, The first man Adam became a living soul; the last Adam a quickening spirit. But not first the spiritual, but the natural, then the spiritual: the first man out of the earth, made of dust; the second man the Lord out of heaven.

'Such as he made of dust, such also those made of dust; and such as the heavenly [one], such also the heavenly [ones].

'And according as we bore the image of the [one] made of dust, we shall bear also the image of the heavenly [one]. But this I say, brethren, that flesh and blood cannot inherit [the] kingdom of God, nor does corruption inherit incorruption', I Corinthians 15:45-50.

As before, this rendering – which I consider far and away superior – is taken from 'The Greek-English New Testament', Bagster, 1877.

However, I refer the reader to the Authorized Version, only with the cautionary admonition to make a comparison with the passage quoted from Bagster – in order to ascertain the original – where this is necessary. 'And this will we do, if God permit', Hebrews 6:3.

'And so it is written, The first man Adam was made a living soul; the last Adam was made a quickening spirit.' So the Authorized Version.

The alternative interlinear reading, literally translating the same – and peerless – Received Greek Text, renders this verse: 'So also it has been written, The first man Adam became a living soul; the last Adam a quickening spirit', I Corinthians 15:45.

From which we are to observe that all that is begotten after the flesh – man, woman, and child: born, begetting, dying – springs from one single progenitor, Adam.

But for all the appearances in the world, he is not the *only* Adam, nor is he the *only* progenitor, in the mind, will, counsel, and purpose of God.

Though every living soul – in every dying body – may be all that is visible on earth, populating the world, *more exists that pertains to the world to come than is visible to earthly sight.*

That is, there is a *first* Adam, yes, *but there is also a last Adam.*

And these two are essentially, radically, and absolutely different the one from the other. Furthermore, what Paul is about to reveal is this: *so also are their respective posterities.*

One Adam, the first, begat after himself. Such living souls– having the sentence of death in themselves – constitute all that is to be seen of mankind throughout the whole world, in every generation, and among all nations.

This is visible humanity, the sum of all living souls begotten after the flesh by natural generation. But – as is evident from the first Adam – such living souls, together with those that begat them, and every one begotten by them, spend their fleeting days in corruptible bodies, destined for death and the grave.

Despite the appearance of vigour and growth this sentence of death is just as true at conception, birth, growth, and in youth.

All descend from the first Adam, who was made a living soul from the dust of the ground by the breath of the Lord God, as it is written, 'And the Lord God formed man of the dust of the ground, and breathed into his nostrils the breath of life; and man became a living soul', Genesis 2:7.

Thus Adam was made a living soul by God, but he became the man of sin and death by himself.

And after himself he begat his posterity, which, according to the flesh, has multiplied and does multiply, generation after generation from the beginning until now, being that humanity, the only humanity, dying humanity – the living soul descending after death into *sheol* or *hadēs* – seen upon earth.

But it is not the only humanity, nor is the first Adam the only Adam, seen before God in heaven.

Because there is *another* Adam, the *last* Adam, called 'a quickening spirit', seated in the glory of heaven, who, with *his* posterity, is heir of the world to come by the resurrection from the dead.

The former is that to which Paul referred when he said, 'The first man Adam became a living soul'; even as he had declared before, 'For as in Adam all die', I Corinthians 15:22.

The latter is that to which the apostle points when he says, 'the last Adam a quickening spirit', which finds its responsive expression in I Corinthians 15:22 with the words 'even so in Christ shall all be made alive'.

'The last Adam a quickening spirit': observe that the Holy Ghost sets 'the last Adam' over against – and in contrast with – 'the first Adam'.

Many unspiritual, uninspired, and ignorant persons – not to mention so-called Hymn writers – misrepresent Christ by calling him 'the second Adam'. Not so the apostle Paul. He is definitive: the Son of God is 'the last Adam', not the second; *the last*.

There is not another: after the *last* there can be no other. There is no such thing as 'a second Adam'.

The *last* Adam, in terms of his being 'a quickening spirit', is the consummation of the purpose of God, the fulfilment of all things, the beginning of *everlasting* glory.

The Holy Ghost reveals him as the last Adam, and as the second man, in contrast with the first Adam, the first man.

If 'the last *Adam*', then Headship is postulated.

If the first man Adam is reckoned as the head and progenitor of that seed which—subsequent to his transgression and becoming the man of sin and death—issued forth from him, *then this is equally true of the last Adam, the head of that progeny—he having wrought righteousness and ascended on high—begotten in him*. Hence the first man Adam is referred to as 'the figure of him that was to come', Romans 5:14.

But who was to come? Why, the last Adam, a quickening spirit.

Romans 5:12-21 contrasts the two men; their two acts; the judgment of God upon those acts; the consequences of that judgment; and the effect of this upon the two seeds respectively.

This doctrine is stated in order to reveal the truth of the Reconciliation, or, as it ought to have been translated, the Substitution.

However, whilst taking up the truth of the first Adam and the last, I Corinthians 15:45 does so in relation to the resurrection of the dead.

Nevertheless Headship, which appears in Adam consequent to the bringing in of sin and death after the Fall, proceeds in Christ subsequent to his death and resurrection from the ascension.

Then, '*the last Adam, a quickening spirit*', refers to the Son of God in glory following the completion and vindication of his work on earth.

And if the Son is the last Adam from the glorious ascension, then he is so above the heavens, whence all the favour of God that proceeds from him, namely, his work; the judgment of God upon that work; the consequences of that judgment; with the assured fulfilment in grace of every promise, appears established and secure to all his seed.

What favour exactly? What consequences precisely? Those of 'a quickening spirit'.

Note that he is 'a quickening spirit' in terms of being the last Adam, a unique name, and one exclusive to the context of I Corinthians 15. If so, of the resurrection of the dead in Christ.

The meaning is obvious: the last Adam quickens, and he quickens spiritually, a conclusion inherent in the title 'a quickening spirit'. But who and what does he quicken? The answer is contextually indisputable: he quickens his saints, and he quickens their dead bodies.

This quickening begins inwardly in his people on earth. Such an interior work is expounded and enlarged under the title 'Quickening' in my book 'Saving Faith', which the reader would do well to ponder with diligence.

However, in I Corinthians 15:45, quickening is in the context of *the dead bodies of the saints*, and is that which is to be wrought in virtue of the office of the Son of God as The Last Adam: *thus* he is 'a quickening spirit' in the resurrection of the mortal remains of every one of his own people, as it is written, 'Blessed are the dead which die in the Lord from henceforth', Revelation 14:13.

The word 'quickening' – *zōopoieō* – occurs some twelve times in the new testament, and the majority of these occurrences refers to the Son of God quickening *the buried bodies* of his own people in the resurrection from the dead.

For example, 'As in Adam all die, even so in Christ shall all' – the dead in Christ – 'be made alive', I Corinthians 15:22, where 'made alive' is *zōopoieō*, 'quicken', or, grammatically, in this case, 'be quickened'.

Again, 'For as the Father raiseth up *the dead*, and *quickeneth them*; even so the Son *quickeneth* whom he will', John 5:21.

Once more, 'God' – is he – 'who *quickeneth* the dead, and calleth those things which be not as though they were', Romans 4:17. What things? Why, the bodies of the saints in the coming resurrection of the dead.

Certainly, this is a thing which 'is not'; and yet God speaks about it 'as though it were': 'For the vision is for an appointed time, but at the end it shall speak, and not lie: though it tarry, wait for it; because it will surely come, it will not tarry', Habakkuk 2:3.

Another example: 'But if the Spirit of him that raised up Jesus from the dead dwell in you, he that raised up Christ from *the dead* shall also *quicken* your *mortal bodies* by his Spirit that dwelleth in you', Romans 8:11.

Quicken your mortal bodies? Yes, for 'this mortal must put on immortality', I Corinthians 15:53.

Does anyone doubt this? 'Thou fool, that which thou sowest is not *quickened*, except it die', I Corinthians 15:36.

Openings in First Corinthians

'Marvel not at this: for the hour is coming, in the which *all that are in the graves shall*—shall, shall—'*hear his voice, and shall come forth; they that have done good, unto the resurrection of life*', John 5:28,29.

'Jesus said unto her, I'—the last Adam, a quickening spirit—'am the resurrection and the life: he that believeth in me, *though he were dead*, yet shall he live', John 11:25.

Live? Yes, live again *in the body*, in the resurrection of the dead, which the raising of Lazarus, who had believed on him, yet had died, and lain four days in the grave, proved infallibly, demonstrating in a figure the coming resurrection of the dead.

Now this is the certain destiny, and it will be the sure accomplishment, of 'the last Adam, a quickening spirit', I Corinthians 15:45; whence, therefore, the name, the office, and the description.

'Howbeit that was not first which is spiritual, but that which is natural; and afterward that which is spiritual', I Corinthians 15:46, Authorized Version.

Translating the same Received Text—the *only* safe Greek Text, largely ignored by and since the Revised Version, 1881, when the fallacious Westcott and Hort text became the basis for modern translations—the thoroughly sound interlinear—and literal—translation of 'The Englishman's Greek-English New Testament', 1877, renders this verse as follows: 'But not first the spiritual, but the natural, then the spiritual.'

Not first the spiritual? No. Adam came first, and hence the natural man is called 'the first man Adam', who was made a living soul.

Afterwards came Christ, a life-giving spirit, declared to be the Son of God with power, according to the Spirit of holiness, by the resurrection from the dead, Romans 1:4.

Hence, 'afterward that which is spiritual.'

The Authorized Version continues, 'the first man is of the earth, earthy: the second man is the Lord from heaven', verse 47, but this does not at all translate the Greek: it confounds the Greek.

'The Englishman's Greek-English New Testament' of 1877 is different: it clarifies the Greek. Quote: 'The first man out of the earth, made of dust; the second man the Lord out of heaven.'

The Authorized states 'of the earth, earthy' but the Greek is composed of quite different words: first, γῆς, *gēs*, the appropriate grammatical form of γῆ, *gē*, earth. The next word *in the Greek text* is χοϊκός, *choikos*, meaning – in this grammatical form – 'of the dust'.

Two entirely distinct Greek words, rendered – in effect, so as to hide the difference from the reader – by one and the same English word in the Authorized Version.

But the difference between the two Greek words is distinguished precisely by the Greek-English New Testament of 1877, namely, quote: 'of the *earth*, made of *dust*.' For Adam, of the earth, *was* made of dust. And so are we. For unto fallen Adam the LORD God said, Genesis 3:19, 'dust thou art, and unto dust shalt thou return'. And so shall we. This came first.

'The second man the Lord out of heaven.' He came down from heaven: 'I came down from heaven', John 6:38. 'And no man hath ascended up to heaven, but he that came down from heaven', John 3:13.

'Ye are from beneath; I am from above: ye are of this world; I am not of this world', John 8:23.

He ascended up to heaven: 'So then after the Lord had spoken unto them, he was received up into heaven', Mark 16:19.

'He was parted from them, and carried up into heaven', Luke 24:51. 'I ascend unto my Father, and your Father; and to my God, and your God', John 20:17.

He is in heaven, and is the heavenly man: the second man. 'The second man the Lord out of heaven', I Corinthians 15:47.

'And sat on the right hand of God', Mark 16:19.

'What and if ye shall see the Son of man ascend up where he was before?', John 6:62.

'Sat down on the right hand of the Majesty on high', Hebrews 1:3.

'The LORD said unto my Lord, Sit thou on my right hand, until I make thy foes thy footstool', Acts 2:34,35.

This is the heavenly man, a life-giving spirit, who is the firstfruits of them that slept. And as is the firstfruits, so will be the harvest.

'As is the earthy, such are they also that are earthy: and as is the heavenly, such are they also that are heavenly', I Corinthians 15:48.

But the translators repeat the same grievous and wholly unnecessary error, as will appear by comparison with the following interlinear literal translation: 'Such as he made of dust'–the Greek is *choikos*, not *gēs*; compare verse 47–'such also those made of dust; and such as the heavenly [one], such also the heavenly [ones].'

Where the seed springing from the Head and progenitor, bears the nature and image of him from whom their descent is counted, either the first, made of dust; or the second, come out of heaven.

'And as we have borne the image of the earthy, we shall also bear the image of the heavenly', I Corinthians 15:49.

'The Englishman's Greek-English New Testament', Bagster, 1877, reads: 'And according as we bore the image of the [one] made of dust, we shall bear also the image of the heavenly [one]', I Corinthians 15:49.

'As *we* bore'? '*We* shall bear also'? But who is *we*? It is those who first bore the image of the one made of dust. This is the image of the man who transgressed, the first man Adam, the man who brought in the Fall, the man of sin and death, formed from the earth, made of dust, cursed to return to dust. '*We*' bore that image.

We were born in and of that image, shapen in iniquity, conceived in sin: that was our nativity and our genealogy. We were sons of disobedience: that is, disobedience begat us, and disobedient we were.

There was no difference between us and others: *any* others.

We were the children of wrath, even as others: then, if so, wrath hung over the children of men; it overshadowed their conception; they were the children of it; the wrath of God in the curse preceded, anticipated, and accompanied their generation: 'children of wrath, even as others.'

It was by one man's disobedience, upon which came the curse, wrath, and judgment; by one man's disobedience we were made sinners: the whole generation, the entire seed, of that man of disobedience, appeared in the image of their progenitor, and, in him, passed under the judgment justly brought upon that man and his issue.

Having borne the image of the one made of dust, dust we were, dust we are, and unto dust shall we return. Namely, we shall return to dust by way of death and the grave; by way of corruption; of dishonour; of weakness; and of the flesh; of that decay and dissolution which is the inevitable end of all who bore the image of the one formed from the earth, made of dust, the first man Adam.

And *we* shall bear *also*? When all alike bore the image of the one made of dust? Then who are '*we*'? We are those of whom it is written, 'according as we bore the image of the [one] made of dust, *we* shall also bear the image of the heavenly [one]'.

Who are these? Not *all* who bore – or bear – the image of the one made of dust, but a people chosen out to be of the heavenly man, the second man, the last Adam.

If so, those brought under the power of the potter: 'Hath not the potter power over the clay, of the same lump to make one vessel unto honour, and another unto dishonour?

'What if God, willing to show his wrath, and to make his power known, endured with much longsuffering the vessels of wrath fitted to destruction: and that he might make known the riches of his glory on the vessels of mercy, which he hath afore prepared unto glory, even us, whom he hath called, not of the Jews only, but also of the Gentiles?', Romans 9:21-24.

Here is the 'we' of I Corinthians 15:49.

'For he saith to Moses, I will have mercy on whom I will have mercy, and I will have compassion on whom I will have compassion. So then it is not of him that willeth, nor of him that runneth, but of God that showeth mercy', Romans 9:15,16.

And again: 'Therefore hath he mercy on whom he will have mercy, and whom he will he hardeneth', Romans 9:18.

And who are these, the 'we', who, having first borne the image of the one made of dust, thereafter, called by grace, shall also bear the image of the heavenly one?

These are those spoken of in a certain place, saying, 'Blessed be the God and Father of our Lord Jesus Christ, who hath blessed us with all spiritual blessings in heavenly places in Christ: according as he hath chosen us in him before the foundation of the world, that we should be holy and without blame before him in love: having predestinated us unto the place of sonship by Jesus Christ to himself, according to the good pleasure of his will, to the praise of the glory of his grace, wherein he hath made us accepted in the beloved', Ephesians 1:3-6.

It is these, and none other, who 'shall bear the image of the heavenly one'.

Jesus spake of them, known of the Father before ever the heavens or the earth were formed, even from everlasting; given to the Son in the will, counsel, and purpose of God, so that they were seen in him before the world was created or Adam was fashioned from the dust of the ground.

'I have manifested thy name'–the name of Father–'unto the men which thou gavest me out of the world: thine they were, and thou gavest them me; and they have kept thy word', John 17:6.

'I pray for them: I pray not for the world, but for them which thou hast given me; for they are thine. And all mine are thine, and thine are mine; and I am glorified in them', John 17:9,10.

All these are of the heavenly one, hence he says, 'They are not of the world'–no, not in the will, counsel, and purpose of God; and now, called by grace, not in the man of dust either– 'even as I am not of the world', John 17:16.

'For whom he did foreknow, he also did predestinate to be conformed to the image of his Son, that he might be the firstborn among many brethren. Moreover whom he did predestinate, them he also called: and whom he called, them he also justified: and whom he justified, them he also glorified', Romans 8:29,30.

This is the 'we', and thus shall 'we' bear the image of the heavenly one.

These are the Father's; they are also the Son's: for all those who are the Father's are the Son's; and all those who are the Son's are the Father's.

Hence of them he saith, 'My Father, which gave them me, is greater than all; and no man is able to pluck them out of my Father's hand', John 10:29.

'All that the Father giveth me shall come to me', saith Jesus, 'and him that cometh to me I will in no wise cast out', John 6:37.

No, for 'I came down from heaven, not to do mine own will, but the will of him that sent me', John 6:38.

What will is this? 'This is the Father's will which hath sent me'– from heaven–'that of all which he hath given me I should lose nothing, but should raise it up again at the last day', John 6:39.

This 'raising up again' will appear in the image of the heavenly one, namely, of him that came down from heaven to do his Father's will.

As to those that come to him, this coming is not of blood, nor of the will of the flesh, nor of the will of man–how could it be? man is of the earth, made of dust–but it is out of heaven from God and the Father that these come to the Son.

Hence it shall and must follow, 'they shall be all taught of God. Every man therefore that hath heard, and hath learned of the Father'–saith the Son–'cometh unto me', John 6:45.

And to what end, but that every one of them shall 'bear the image of the heavenly one', being raised up at the last day.

'Now this I say, brethren, that flesh and blood cannot inherit the kingdom of God; neither doth corruption inherit incorruption', I Corinthians 15:50.

No. It does not, and it cannot. But yet we *are* in a body of flesh and blood, subject to corruption: what of this?

What of it? this has already been shown: *it must die first, then it shall rise to inherit.*

For, 'it is sown in corruption; it is raised in incorruption: it is sown in dishonour; it is raised in glory: it is sown in weakness; it is raised in power: it is sown a natural body; it is raised a spiritual body', I Corinthians 15:42,43.

Then that flesh and blood, called 'this vile body', though it cannot inherit the kingdom of God, nevertheless *can* still *be sown*. And that is precisely what takes place: 'it *is* sown.' It can still *die*. And that is exactly what is written: '*it* is sown' in death.

Likewise, what happens to the body in the grave precludes the inheritance of the kingdom of God by its very state: 'neither doth corruption inherit incorruption.'

But though the grave claim the dead body, though corruption rot the corpse, *it is not that that is raised.*

Not that? No; what is *changed* is raised. And so it is written, 'It is sown in corruption; *it is raised in incorruption.*'

Moreover it is certain beyond all doubt that what is raised in incorruption; in glory; in power; and as a spiritual body, cannot fail to inherit the kingdom of God.

How shall this be? Through him who loved us, and gave himself for us: through Christ the firstfruits, 'who shall *change* our vile body, that it may be fashioned like unto his glorious body, according to the working whereby he is able even to subdue all things unto himself', Philippians 3:21.

Openings in First Corinthians

Thus through Jesus Christ our Lord, the last Adam, a quickening spirit; through the second man, the Lord from heaven: though flesh and blood cannot, *we* can, and we *shall* inherit the kingdom of God; and though corruption cannot, *incorruption* can, and incorruption *shall* inherit the kingdom of God, to the praise of the glory of his grace, world without end. Amen.

The apostle had shown the folly of questioning the resurrection of the dead – and of asking presumptuous questions about it – first from the evidence manifest in creation, I Corinthians 15:35-41.

Next he proceeded to demonstrate the same thing by revelation, I Corinthians 15:42-50.

Finally he crowns this overwhelming body of inspired truth with the opening of a mystery, followed by a closing word of comfortable admonition, I Corinthians 15:51-58.

'Behold, I show you a mystery; We shall not all sleep, but we shall all be changed, in a moment, in the twinkling of an eye, at the last trump: for the trumpet shall sound, and the dead shall be raised incorruptible, and we shall be changed', I Corinthians 15:51,52.

Paul alerts the reader to what he is about to say: 'Behold'; directing the focus of their attention, and sharpening the concentration of their minds by this peremptory and anticipatory watchword.

To what? To the fact that he is about to unfold a mystery, so as to show them things hitherto veiled from their sight and comprehension: 'Behold!' here is a mystery, and he is about to show them what is in the will, mind, counsel, and purpose of God concerning things to come.

It cannot be overstressed that mysteries can never be understood: they can be shown, in the sense that the Seer can describe the vision uniquely unveiled to him. That is, he can make known what he has seen, whether by speech or in writing, to those to whom he is sent.

Nevertheless, despite any such speech or writing, God reserves his divine prerogative, because for all the description, *it requires the Spirit to make the thing described an interior reality to the reader and hearer.*

Furthermore, regarding the fact that the apostle is to show them a mystery, here is no appeal whatsoever to the intellect, to human reason, or to anything that man is capable of understanding mentally: it is solely an appeal to *faith.*

Mysteries, revealed or shown to the apostolic administration, or to the prophetic ministry in consequence, are *believed.* Not understood. Faith acts upon them. But understanding founders upon them.

This mystery—afore seen in vision and revelation by the apostle—which now is to be shown to the *ecclesia* at Corinth, concerns *what happens to the bodies of the quick and the dead; the living and the buried; of all who ever were, are, or shall be in Christ, when the last trumpet shall sound.*

This unfolds in two parts: What happens to the quick, or living bodies; and what happens to the dead, or buried bodies, respectively.

I Corinthians 15:51 tells you *that* we shall all be changed, whether it be all the dead, or all the living. In a word, *all* in Christ shall be changed, from the beginning of the world to the end of it.

But, next, I Corinthians 15:52 tells you *when* we shall all be changed, and how quickly, no matter that it be the dead out of every generation to the ends of the earth and from the depths of the sea, or whether it be the faithful remnant of the saints still living upon the earth in the instant that the great and last trumpet awakens the dead.

Notwithstanding, in each case, either *that* we shall all be changed; or *when* we shall all be changed, *the change referred to in the mystery is that of the body*.

First consider *that* we shall all be changed. It must be so, since, I Corinthians 15:50, 'flesh and blood cannot inherit the kingdom of God; neither doth corruption inherit incorruption'. Then it follows, because we *do* inherit the kingdom of God, and we *shall* inherit incorruption, that *'we shall* all be changed'.

To be precise, our *bodies*, of flesh and blood, shall be changed; and *our corruption*, mouldering in the grave, shall be changed. And in this change, there is a difference between the quick and the dead.

Why? Because 'we shall not all sleep', I Corinthians 15:51.

That is, our *bodies* shall not all sleep. Some shall *never die*: they shall be changed, as was Christ in the transfiguration, *whilst still alive in this present* – but dissolving – *world*.

No, we shall not all sleep, some shall be alive at his coming; nevertheless, we *shall* all be changed.

When? Ponder well *when* we shall all be changed, and how *quickly*, whether it be the dead, or the living:

'In a moment, in the twinkling of an eye, at the last trump: for the trumpet shall sound, and the dead shall be raised incorruptible' – *this* is first; fast as the twinkling eye blinks to a close – 'and *we* shall be changed' – *that* is next; swift as the twinkling eye flashes open. I Corinthians 15:52.

Neither are the 'sleeping' dead bodies of all that ever died in the faith, nor the living bodies of the believing remnant alive in the dying moments of time, *all* that shall be 'changed': Greek ἀλλαγησόμεθα, *from* ἀλλάσσω, *allassō, to make other; alter*.

Openings in First Corinthians

For not only they, but at the last trump the heavens and the earth also shall be subject to the same 'change':

'And, Thou, Lord, in the beginning hast laid the foundation of the earth; and the heavens are the works of thine hands: they shall perish; but thou remainest; and they all shall wax old as doth a garment; and as a vesture shalt thou fold them up, *and they shall be changed*', Hebrews 1:10-12.

Where 'shall be changed' answers to the Greek ἀλλαγησόνται – apart from the slight difference in grammar at the ending, exactly the same word as in I Corinthians 15:51 and 52 – *from* ἀλλάσσω, *allassō, to make other; alter.*

As to *how* so stupendous a change shall take place in the very heavens and earth, and *how* so astounding a mystery as that of the resurrection of the dead in bodies of glory, and, at the blink of an eye, the transformation and transfiguration of the bodies of the living saints shall take place: why, it is by the word of the Lord.

'Who shall *change*' – μετασχηματίσει *from* μετασχηματίζω, *metaschēmatizō, transform; to make of another form* – 'our vile body, that it may be fashioned like unto his glorious body, according to the working whereby *he is able even to subdue all things unto himself*', Philippians 3:21.

'But of that day and hour knoweth no man, no, not the angels of heaven, but my Father only', Matthew 24:36. 'For when they shall say, Peace and safety; then sudden destruction cometh upon them, as travail upon a woman with child; and they shall not escape', I Thessalonians 5:3. 'And what I say unto you I say unto all, Watch', Mark 13:37.

'Watch therefore, for ye know neither the day nor the hour wherein the Son of man cometh', Matthew 25:13.

'But the day of the Lord will come as a thief in the night; in which the heavens shall pass away with a great noise, and the elements shall melt with fervent heat, the earth also and the works that are therein shall be burned up.

'Seeing then that all these things shall be dissolved, what manner of persons ought ye to be in all holy conversation and godliness, looking for and hasting unto the coming of the day of God, wherein the heavens being on fire shall be dissolved, and the elements shall melt with fervent heat?

'Nevertheless we, according to his promise, look for new heavens and a new earth, wherein dwelleth righteousness', II Peter 3:10-13.

'For yourselves know perfectly that the day of the Lord so cometh as a thief in the night', I Thessalonians 5:2.

In that day, the trumpet shall be blown, even the last trump, as it is written, 'He shall send his angels with a great sound of a trumpet, and they shall'—mark, *they* shall: that is, to bear up the *bodies* of the risen saints—'gather together his elect from the four winds, from one end of heaven to the other', Matthew 24:31.

It is not that—in a figure—trumpets had not sounded before—six times, metaphorically, they had sounded before.

'And I saw the seven angels which stood before God; and to them were given seven trumpets.' 'And the seven angels which had the seven trumpets prepared themselves to sound', Revelation 8:2,6.

And they did sound. In an allegory the first four angels sounded, but the world heard nothing, and saw nothing, neither did the inhabitants of the earth understand anything.

Thereafter, in the figure, the severity increases:

'And I beheld, and heard an angel flying through the midst of heaven, saying with a loud voice, Woe, woe, woe, to the inhabiters of the earth by reason of the other voices of the trumpet of the three angels, which are yet to sound!', Revelation 8:13.

And, in the vivid imagery of the Book of the Revelation, 'The fifth angel sounded', Revelation 9:1; 'And the sixth angel sounded', Revelation 9:13.

Then, one remained: the last, seventh angel. One trumpet was yet to sound, that is, the last trump.

And sound it shall, not only in prophecy in the Revelation; but in reality, at the last day: 'And the seventh angel sounded', Revelation 11:15. To apprehend the sound thereof, read my book 'The Revelation of Jesus Christ', which I neither received of man, neither was I taught it, but by the revelation of Jesus Christ, Galatians 1:12.

Thenceforth, at the sounding of this seventh, last, trump, that also is brought to pass which is written: 'We shall not all sleep, but we shall all be changed, in a moment, in the twinkling of an eye, at the last trump: for the trumpet shall sound, and the dead' – which are in Christ – 'shall be raised incorruptible, and we shall be changed', I Corinthians 15:51,52.

This is that by which the apostle Paul consoles those whose brethren or sisters had died, for, in his comfortable words to them, he calls their dying 'falling asleep', saying:

'But I would not have you to be ignorant, brethren, concerning them which are asleep, that ye sorrow not, even as others which have no hope. For if we believe that Jesus died and rose again, even so them also which sleep in Jesus will God bring with him.

'For this we say unto you by the word of the Lord, that we which are alive and remain unto the coming of the Lord' – for we shall not *all* sleep – 'shall not prevent' – that is, anticipate, or come before – 'them which are asleep.'

No: for the trumpet shall sound, and *the dead* shall be raised incorruptible. *Then*, in the twinkling of an eye, *we* – which are alive and remain – *shall be changed.*

'For the Lord himself shall descend from heaven with a shout.' Mark that: first, a shout. This is the last word. It is the omega. The ending. This is the hour that is to come in which all that are in the graves *shall hear his voice.* In a shout. *And shall come forth*; they that have done good, unto the resurrection of life.

'With the voice of the archangel.' This is the angels, sent forth of the archangel, to minister for them that are the heirs of salvation, carrying their changed, transformed, transfigured bodies to meet the Lord in his coming.

It is his 'sending forth his angels with a great sound of a trumpet, and they shall gather together his elect from the four winds, from one end of heaven to the other.'

'And with the trump of God.' This is the 'great sound of a trumpet.' It is the sounding of the seventh angel with the last trump.

'For the trumpet shall sound, and the dead shall be raised incorruptible, and we shall be changed.'

Oh, mark well how it shall be in that day, in that hour: 'the Lord himself' – note that emphasis: *himself* – 'shall *descend from heaven*' – then, *that* is where he has been, *all this time*, ever since the ascension: but no more – 'descend from heaven with a shout, with the voice of the archangel, and with the trump of God: *and the dead in Christ shall rise first.*'

The dead in Christ shall rise *first*. Not that *all* of us shall have slept, or shall sleep. Some shall not. But *all* shall be changed.

In a moment, in the twinkling of an eye, at the last trump: for the trumpet shall sound, and the dead shall be raised incorruptible, and *we* shall be changed.

We shall be changed?

Yes, in the twinkling of an eye, as the dead are raised, the living saints shall be changed also: 'Then we which are alive and remain shall be caught up together with them in the clouds, to meet the Lord in the air: and so shall we ever be with the Lord. Wherefore comfort one another with these words', I Thessalonians 4:13-18.

'For this corruptible must put on incorruption, and this mortal must put on immortality. So when this corruptible shall have put on incorruption, and this mortal shall have put on immortality, then shall be brought to pass the saying that is written, Death is swallowed up in victory', I Corinthians 15:53,54.

Observe, 'This corruptible *must* put on incorruption, and this mortal *must* put on immortality.'

But why *must* it? Because of the truth enunciated earlier, 'Now this I say, brethren, that flesh and blood *cannot* inherit the kingdom of God; *neither* doth corruption inherit incorruption', I Corinthians 15:50.

Now, if *we* are to inherit the kingdom of God, but flesh and blood *cannot* inherit the kingdom of God, it follows that such an inheritance must require that we put off flesh and blood.

How? By death and the grave. Then this mortal *body* must, of necessity, be put off, the soul meanwhile being with the Lord.

'Not for that we would be unclothed'–that is, our soul unclothed from our body–'*but clothed upon*'–with what was sown in mortality, but raised in immortality–'*that mortality might be swallowed up of life*', II Corinthians 5:4.

If so, this mortal body—whether in the resurrection of the dead, or the transformation of the living, at the last trump—*must*, in the resurrection, put on immortality *in the body*, so that we, ourselves, may inherit the kingdom of God.

Then shall be brought to pass the saying that is written, 'Come, ye blessed of my Father, inherit the kingdom prepared for you from the foundation of the world', Matthew 25:34.

For this to take place, flesh and blood, the natural body, *must* be put off; and the resurrection of the dead, the transformation, the spiritual body, *must* be put on. And so Paul says, 'this mortal *must* put on immortality.'

Likewise 'neither doth corruption'—this corruptible body inhabited in this life, and corrupting in the grave thereafter, *cannot* inherit the kingdom, *not in that state*—hence, 'neither doth corruption inherit incorruption', I Corinthians 15:50.

Wherefore it follows of necessity, 'this corruptible'—body—'must put on incorruption'—in the body raised from the dead. For, 'it is sown in corruption; it is raised in incorruption', where the *it* refers to *the body*, whether sown or raised.

Then, 'incorruption' refers to the body of glory, raised from the dead. '*It* is sown in dishonour; *it* is raised in glory: *it* is sown in weakness; *it* is raised in power: *it* is sown a natural body; *it* is raised a spiritual body', I Corinthians 15:42-44.

Wherefore he saith, 'neither doth corruption inherit incorruption', I Corinthians 15:50; concluding, 'For this corruptible *must* put on incorruption', I Corinthians 15:53.

'So when this corruptible shall have put on incorruption, and this mortal shall have put on immortality'—When? When we shall all be changed: in a moment, in the twinkling of an eye, at the last trump:

'For the trumpet shall sound, and the dead shall be raised incorruptible, and we shall be changed'–'then shall be brought to pass the saying that is written, Death is swallowed up in victory', I Corinthians 15:54.

Death can no more be seen. It is swallowed up. It is as if death had never been: victory has swallowed up death and its effects wholly and utterly, so as to abolish it entirely. Who did this? Who wrought this victory? When and how was the last enemy annihilated to the uttermost?

It was determined of God when he sent his Son:

'Who hath saved us, and called us with an holy calling, not according to our works, but according to his own purpose and grace, which was given us in Christ Jesus before the world began, but is now made manifest by the appearing of our Saviour Jesus Christ,

'Who *hath*' – hath; hath; past tense – hath '*abolished death*' – swallowing it up in victory – '*and hath brought life and immortality to light through the evangel*', II Timothy 1:9,10.

Wherefore he saith, 'I am the resurrection, and the life: he that believeth in me, though he were dead, yet shall he live: and whosoever liveth and believeth in me shall never die', John 11:25,26. 'Christ the firstfruits; afterward they that are Christ's at his coming', I Corinthians 15:23.

And if so, and it is so, we may say, and that truly, 'O death, where is thy sting? O *hadēs*' – it is not *grave*: this is another blunder, and a shocking one, on the part of the translators – 'O *hadēs*, where is thy victory?', I Corinthians 15:55.

What more apt comment upon these words can there be, than that made by the apostle on another occasion, when triumphing in the victory won by Christ on behalf of all his people:

'What shall we then say to these things? If God be for us, who can be against us? He that spared not his own Son, but delivered him up for us all, how shall he not with him also freely give us all things? Who shall lay anything to the charge of God's elect? It is God that justifieth. Who is he that condemneth?

'It is Christ that died, yea rather, that is risen again, who is even at the right hand of God, who also maketh intercession for us.

'Who shall separate us from the love of Christ? shall tribulation, or distress, or persecution, or famine, or nakedness, or peril, or sword? As it is written, For thy sake we are killed all the day long; we are accounted as sheep for the slaughter.

'Nay, in all these things we are more than conquerors through him that loved us.

'For I am persuaded, that neither death, nor life, nor angels, nor principalities, nor powers, nor things present, nor things to come, nor height, nor depth, nor any other creature, shall be able to separate us from the love of God, which is in Christ Jesus our Lord', Romans 8:31-39.

As to death, 'he hath abolished death, and hath brought life and immortality to light through the evangel.' As to *hadēs*, 'What is it but that he also descended first into the lower parts of the earth?'

And then? Then, victorious over death and *hadēs*, he ascended up far above all heavens, *with every one of his elect seen in himself.* 'Wherefore he saith, When he ascended up on high, he led captivity captive, and gave gifts unto men', Ephesians 4:8.

'And without controversy great is the mystery of godliness: God was manifest in the flesh, justified in the Spirit, seen of angels, preached unto the Gentiles, believed on in the world, received up into glory', I Timothy 3:16.

Christ's victory over *hadēs* on behalf of all his people from the beginning of the world to the end of it has been opened at length in these pages under the heading 'The Body of Christ and the Gifts', I Corinthians 12:14-13:13, also published separately as a paperback.

Besides this, the tract 'The Mystery of Godliness' expounds the triumphant victory proclaimed in I Timothy 3:16, so that it is superfluous to reiterate the same wonderful truths in this place.

Suffice it to repeat with Paul his praise to the mighty Conqueror from the verses in context: 'Death is swallowed up in victory. O death, where is thy sting? O *hadēs*, where is thy victory?'

'The sting of death is sin; and the strength' – it is δύναμις, *dunamis*, power – 'the *power* of sin is the law', I Corinthians 15:56. Now, what does *that* mean?

One thing is certain: no legalists either will or can explain the meaning of these words, for their content lies altogether beyond their experience.

But first, 'The sting of death is sin.' But since sin brings forth death – 'for the wages of sin *is* death' – it follows that sin precedes death.

If so, one might expect this place to read, 'The sting of *sin* is death.'

But one would be wrong, for it does not so speak. Then here is yet another instance of the necessity of being led by the Spirit, so that scripture speaks for itself, as opposed to men speaking for scripture.

Then how is it that 'The sting of *death* is sin'? It is certain that the sting is in the tail, Revelation 9:10, and hence it is *after* death, by which the deceased have been stung, that the discovery is made as to the cause of the sting.

Sin, yes; but not *before* death, otherwise it could not be said, 'The sting *of death* is sin.'

Then, *after* death the sting is plunged into the terrified soul awakened to its unending and ever-conscious existence beyond the grave and for eternity.

In this life the vast majority refused to face two overwhelming criteria, towering above all others. The first is sin. The second, death.

But in the life to come, from the very moment of death, immediately the soul is brought face to face with these burning issues: first, that *their sin*, which they had ignored, *caused their death.*

And next, just a split second the other side of death, the sting strikes: *one must, but one cannot, pay the price of sin; neither can one find an atonement for it: it is too late.*

'And as it is appointed unto men once to die'–*then* comes the sting–'*but after this* the judgment', Hebrews 9:27. After this? After what? After death.

Then what? Then the judgment.

Judgment of what? Of all the vast accumulation of unpaid, unatoned sins against the law of God, and against the righteousness of God.

Then, *after death* comes the sting: *the sins ignored throughout life, and even unto death, pierce the soul through and through with a thousand barbs, for now the consciousness of one's being is wide awake to the reality that the debt incurred can never, no, never, be paid by the undying soul, world without end.*

This is the judgment of God on sin, realized too late after death, being the sting of death. And it is both final and irrevocable.

But this is not so of those found in Christ, for the Redeemer drew the sting on behalf of all the elect. 'Who his own self bare our sins in his own body on the tree', I Peter 2:24. 'So Christ was once offered to bear the sins of many', Hebrews 9:28.

'For this is my blood of the new testament, which is shed for many for the remission of sins', Matthew 26:28. 'Christ died for our sins according to the scriptures', I Corinthians 15:3. Then, there is neither death, nor sting, for the children of God.

'And the strength of sin is the law', I Corinthians 15:56. This is that law which those whited sepulchres, the blind Pharisees who call themselves 'reformed', tell us is the Christian's rule of life.

Well, Paul calls it the sentence of death; the rule of condemnation; a killing letter; a dreadful yoke; and assures us that far from directing us to righteousness and life it curses us, sin finding its strength and power in its very rule and commandment: 'the strength of sin *is the law.*'

But the strength of Christ is deliverance from the law.

'But now we are delivered from the law, that being dead wherein we were held', Romans 7:6. 'For I through the law am dead to the law, that I might live unto God', Galatians 2:19. 'For Christ is the end of the law for righteousness to every one that believeth', Romans 10:4.

'God sent forth his Son, made of a woman, made under the law, to redeem them that were under the law, that we might receive the place of sons', Galatians 4:4,5.

'For sin' – whose strength is *the law* – 'shall not have dominion over you: for ye are not under the law, but under grace', Romans 6:14.

Then, for the elect, the power of sin, which is the law, is broken, because 'ye also are become *dead to the law* by the body of Christ', Romans 7:4; where, by his death, *and our death in him*, we are for ever beyond the reach of the law and the realm of legal jurisdiction.

If so, 'Thanks be to God, which giveth us the victory, through our Lord Jesus Christ.'

'Therefore, my beloved brethren, be ye steadfast, unmoveable, always abounding in the work of the Lord, forasmuch as ye know that your labour is not in vain in the Lord', I Corinthians 15:58.

The Conclusion: I Corinthians 16:1-24

On the collection for the saints at Jerusalem, verses 1-4

Consider the first matter raised by the apostle in these concluding remarks: 'Now concerning the collection for the saints, as I have given order to the churches of Galatia, even so do ye. Upon the first day of the week let every one of you lay by him in store, as God hath prospered him, that there be no gatherings when I come.

'And when I come, whomsoever ye shall approve by your letters, them will I send to bring your liberality unto Jerusalem. And if it be meet that I go also, they shall go with me', I Corinthians 16:1-4.

It is just as well that the reader should have and compare the literal translation: 'Now concerning the collection which [is] for the saints, as I directed the assemblies of Galatia, so also ye do. Every first [day] of the week each of you by him let put, treasuring up whatever he may be prospered in, that not when I come collections there should be.

Openings in First Corinthians

'And when I shall have arrived, whomsoever ye may approve by epistles these I will send to carry your bounty to Jerusalem: and if it be suitable for me also to go, with me they shall go', I Corinthians 16:1-4.

This passage contains the only two references in the new testament to 'collections' and 'gatherings'–not surprisingly, since the original Greek λογία occurs but twice, both in this same place. Then shall such a cult of bad manners, ill breeding, and vile practice be drawn from such meagre origins?

Yes it shall, since it is the covetousness of sacramental and evangelical deceit that takes occasion from so minute, irrelevant, and obscure an origin.

Yet, behold, so tiny a seed has grown into a vast mustard tree, in which the carrion birds flock by multitudes to take their ease. How is this?

Well, dare if you will to ignore the two formidable figures at each end of the aisle, as the open plate is passed from one captive to another under the eagle-eyed gaze of these warders. Or else consider the furtive and hasty opening of the closed fist of the helpless victims beneath the vigilant scrutiny of the berobed vergers transfixed upon the passage of the ornate box between one hand and another.

And would you thus humiliate guests in your *own* house?

But come to the epitome of hypocrisy and observe the traditions of the Brethren, as, the bread and wine yet stuck in their gullet, the clink of coins or louder crisping of notes anticipates the passing of Judas' velvet bag one to another with peremptory gusto.

Yet this display of sanctimonious hypocrisy all these, one with another, justify from I Corinthians 16:1-4?

But I Corinthians 16:1-4 was nothing to do with *the assembly*. It was altogether to do with *each one at home*. It was nothing to do with *money*. It was altogether to do with *goods*. It was nothing to do with *their affairs*. It was altogether to do with *the saints at far-distant Jerusalem*.

And into what contorted deformity have they wrested I Corinthians 16:1-4, to pay—under duress of embarrassment—for their *own* affairs, and, at that *when they assemble*? What? Pay the 'salary' of the pastor, the 'stipend' of the minister, the 'maintenance' of the 'church'?

What? set their croupiers to rake the share of the extortion to support their *own* exclusive sectarian proselytizing under the name of *their* denominational 'missionary' society? Yes, and a portion also for this cancerous growth, or that tumefied exhibition, *all nothing but a vile travesty of I Corinthians 16:1-4, and an apostate denial of the one body*.

But the 'gathering' of goods, on the part of single individuals, upon the first day of the week, stored at each separate household, accrued week by week, would be parcelled together as a whole when anticipation of the arrival of the apostle was imminent.

Then, with their own brethren having letters from the *ecclesia*, together with brethren accompanying the apostle, the whole would be conveyed as their gift of bounty to the saints at Jerusalem.

On ministering to the saints at Corinth, verses 5-14

But when would the apostle come? In labours more abundant, withal the care of all the *ecclesiai*, that was the question, and, as best he might determine at the time of writing, the apostle Paul now addresses himself to it in their favour, I Corinthians 16:5-9.

Yet—as may be seen from the second epistle—even this frankness in making known the possibilities open to him, consistent with the varied calls upon his ministry, became yet another twisted occasion for criticism of the apostle by the multitude of his traducers. See II Corinthians 1:15-17,23-24; 2:1,12-13.

From this kind of smear by the swarming busybodies seething with envy of the apostle, Paul did his utmost to shield Timothy, I Corinthians 16:10-11.

As to Apollos, Paul would have encouraged him to enter fully into the fellowship of brethren labouring with the apostle, but he would not, preferring that independence which stood in 'his will was not at all to come at this time', verse 12.

How this self-will contrasted with the united will of Paul's fellowlabourers and fellow-workers, all one with him in the mind of the Spirit and the will of God. Not to say subjection to the apostle in the ministry. What a difference between 'as I have given order to the churches of Galatia, so do ye', and 'I greatly desired' Apollos 'to come unto you with the brethren: but *his* will was not at all to come at this time'.

The more spiritual will see the wisdom and aptness of the exhortation which the apostle interjects at this very point, though immediately afterwards he returns to the subject of the obedient brethren who ministered among them and to others.

Note the words which straightway follow verse 12, and be not unwise concerning their connection with what had just been stated: 'Watch ye, stand fast in the faith, quit you like men, be strong.' Withal, 'Let all your things be done with charity', I Corinthians 16:13,14.

Any amount of individuality in eloquence or personal gift, however mighty in the scriptures, in and of itself will never result in anything more than the gathering of mute but admiring hearers.

Openings in First Corinthians

Far from resulting in that 'more excellent way' in which the love of God in Father, Son, and Holy Ghost manifests itself in the entire body as one and in mutuality throughout the *ecclesia*, the effect will be to 'draw disciples after them'.

Mere knowledge, gift and eloquence: these are things that 'puff up' the individual, and invite schism in admiring followers. That is unless one die daily, take up the cross constantly, and humble oneself in a broken heart and contrite spirit continually.

The outcome of the exercise of gift merely as such—especially if exceptional—will always exalt individualism, unless meekly tempered to the sanctification of the saints, the work of the ministry, and the edification of the body of Christ, according to I Corinthians 13.

At the last, the exercise of such gift is either a question of subjection to Christ as *indwelling the brethren in the ecclesia to the profit of the whole body*, or else of creating admiring followers about oneself, the very opposite to that sought of God, wrought of Christ, and effected by the Spirit.

The latter was that so earnestly pursued by the apostle Paul, to which all that he had been given in grace was yielded in submission, that, being jealous over them all—from the least to the greatest—he had espoused them—*them*, mark it: them; *as one body*—to one husband, that he might present them as a chaste virgin to Christ, II Corinthians 11:2.

Ministry concerning Stephanas, Fortunatus, and Achaicus, verses 15-18

Paul now continues with his concluding remarks, concerning Stephanas, Fortunatus, and Achaicus. 'I beseech you, brethren'—that is it: they were his *brethren*—'ye know the *house*'—mark that: the *house*—'of Stephanas'—so he *opened his house*—'that it is the firstfruits of Achaia', I Corinthians 16:15.

Firstfruits? Yes: further to Crispus and Gaius, 'I baptized also the *household* of Stephanas', I Corinthians 1:16. Here are firstfruits.

So that when a place was needed, a house, Stephanas and his household fully and freely opened their home.

Now the translators confuse us once again, adding the words 'and that they have addicted themselves to the ministry of the saints', I Corinthians 16:15.

But this is as inaccurate as it is misleading, implying that—in the manner of modern addicts to the—so-called—'ministry', these likewise thrust themselves into the work.

But this ignores the Greek, the context, and the natural flow of the wording. Observe the literal translation: 'Ye know the *house* of Stephanas, that *it* is Achaia's first-fruit, and for *service to the saints they*'—plural: the *whole household*—'they appointed *themselves*'—plural; that is, their entire house was open to the saints.

So that Stephanas and his household fully opened their home 'for διακονίαν'—*service*, or ministry, *in that way*—so that *to this end* 'to the saints they appointed themselves', I Corinthians 16:15.

Not 'addicted' themselves: they were not addicts. They 'arranged', they 'set themselves'—Greek, ἔταξαν—to open their home from the first, in order to 'serve' the saints *in that manner*, for the exercise of the gifts of the Spirit in the unity of one body.

The last thing that is intended is that they thrust themselves into the 'ministry', as the past and present generation exemplify, and as the Authorized translators seem to suggest by the wording 'addicted *themselves* to the ministry'.

In the translators' case, doubtless, implying the Anglican 'priesthood', but others would read in their respective caveat, whether Baptist, Brethren, Presbyterian, Evangelist, Methodist,

'Free Church', or I know not what other so-called 'ministry' just as it pleases them to turn the scripture to justify their multitudinous malpractices, as opposed to being called of God, sent by Christ, and empowered through the Spirit, in the unity of one body.

What the household of Stephanas *actually did*, was to give up their own home to serve the saints by the provision of a place to meet – and thus for brethren to minister among themselves – being the first household to be called in Achaia.

And this service they freely and gladly rendered, that the work might grow, the apostle and his ministers might have a place to preach, and, in consequence, that every member of the body, suitably gifted, might assemble to the profit and edification of all.

The Authorized Version – and, I would add, the Englishman's Greek New Testament – places virtually the whole of verse 15 in parenthesis: so that what concerns the household of Stephanas is to be read as an aside.

Therefore the words 'I beseech you, brethren', verse 15, should be followed immediately in one's reading by the continuation 'that ye submit yourselves unto such, and to every one that helpeth with us, and laboureth', verse 16.

That is, the wording in the parenthesis, or brackets – concerning Stephanas – should be taken as a diversion, and, in order to maintain the continuity of the sense, at first ignored completely. Thus one should read up to the opening bracket in verse 15, and then, for the time being, disregard the enclosed wording concluded by the closing bracket of that verse.

It is *verse 16* that declares the subject about which Paul beseeches the brethren before the parenthesis of verse 15, namely, submission 'to such' *as those mentioned and implied before that – bracketed – aside*.

If so, this refers to being subject to the apostle, and to those who ministered with him, sent to the *ecclesiai* for the sanctification of the saints, and edification of the body.

'I beseech you, brethren, that ye submit yourselves unto *such*, and to *every one* that helpeth *with us*, and laboureth.' Whether in fact that included Stephanas or not being beside the point as to the exposition of the phraseology used in this place.

Paul—who was in the regions of Philippi—was glad of the coming of the messengers sent from the *ecclesia* at Corinth, namely, of Stephanas, Fortunatus, and Achaicus: they supplied what was lacking on the part of the Corinthian brethren.

There is no need to suppose that this was material, although it may have been. What was most lacking was *spiritual*, and the intelligence to convey to the apostle the dire need of his ministry in consequence.

That lack—whatever else—these messengers supplied, and, as laying out the matter before the Lord, and making intercession to God, besides gendering the inspiration for this epistle, refreshed Paul's spirit and theirs.

Then, the Corinthians were their debtors indeed, and ought to credit such invaluable service, I Corinthians 16:17,18.

SALUTATIONS; AN ADMONITION; THE BLESSING,
I CORINTHIANS 16:19-24.

The closing salutations are touching and vital: there is nothing formal or cold about them. They spring from the abiding love of God in Father, Son, and Holy Ghost, experimentally indwelling the one body, so that hearts in Asia, filled with the Spirit, embrace the hearts of those indwelt by the same one Spirit in the *ecclesia* at Corinth.

Thus, one body was a *reality*, spanning time and space, distance and location, this world and age, coming down from God out of heaven to unite in everlasting bonds the body and bride of Christ in the most immediate, intimate, and experimental of unions.

'The churches'– ἐκκλησίαι –'of Asia'– that vast sub-continent, yet, wherever, all as one joined in fervent love for the *ecclesia* at Corinth, known and read of all men –'salute you', I Corinthians 16:19.

Likewise the warmth of the salutation that follows: 'Aquila and Priscilla salute you much in the Lord, with the *ecclesia* that is in their house', I Corinthians 16:19. The fervour of this salutation originated from the very first beginnings at Corinth, in which Aquila and Priscilla shared so intimately with Paul.

On his first arrival in the city of Corinth, Paul 'found a certain Jew named Aquila, born in Pontus, lately come from Italy, with his wife Priscilla; (because that Claudius had commanded all Jews to depart from Rome:) and came unto them.

'And because he was of the same craft, he abode with them, and wrought: for by their occupation they were tentmakers.' Being a Jew, Aquila would have attended the synagogue. Going to the Jew first, Paul would have accompanied him. 'And he reasoned in the synagogue every sabbath, and persuaded the Jews and Greeks', Acts 18:2-4.

But when matters came to a head – for, under the apostolic ministry and power of the Holy Ghost, they must come to a head – Paul shook his raiment at the disobedient and gainsaying Jews, declared their blood to be on their own heads, his hands being clean, and that henceforth he would go to the Gentiles.

At that he departed, entering into a certain man's house, named Justus, one that worshipped God, whose house joined hard by the synagogue. Some days before Silas and Timotheus had joined Paul, Acts 16:5, yet it does not appear that Aquila and Priscilla left their original lodging to join the apostle at Justus' house, although without doubt–together with all the believing Jews–they separated themselves to stand with Paul for the truth of the evangel.

However the record does not state that any but Paul himself entered Justus' house, nor that the brethren met there. From elsewhere it is clear that such a meeting was much more likely from the beginning to have been with the household of Stephanas, Acts 18:7, compare I Corinthians 16:15.

En passant I would observe that Stephanas, whose household–and therefore home–is stated to have been in Corinth, and who, indeed, was of the very first to have been baptized–and at that, by Paul himself–at Corinth, is called 'the firstfruits of Achaia'.

However, elsewhere a brother, Epaenetus, is also called 'the firstfruits of Achaia unto Christ', Romans 16:5. But, on the one hand, Paul refers to 'the *house* of Stephanas, that *it* is the firstfruits of Achaia', I Corinthians 16:15, where the whole *household* is the firstfruits, and, at that, specifically *in* Corinth, I Corinthians 1:16.

Whereas on the other hand it is not to an entire household but to an *individual* that Paul points when he says, 'Salute my wellbeloved Epaenetus, who is the firstfruits of Achaia unto Christ', Romans 16:5. So that because the 'firstfruits' in the one case is that of an entire household, and in the other that of one particular brother, these must not be seen as contradictory references.

Besides this, whilst Corinth was the capital of Achaia, a *part* of Greece, just because Stephanas' household was in the city of Corinth, does not mean–say on Paul's approaching journey; or attending Paul from outside the city–that Epaenetus was any less of Achaia for not being a citizen of the capital. In any event, colloquially Achaia was not infrequently a euphemism loosely employed by some to denote the whole of Greece.

But it is to the warmth and intimacy of the salutations that attention is to be drawn: the more especially since Aquila and Priscilla had been with the Corinthians – yea, had quit the synagogue – from the very beginning. Then, how *close* their relationship, and, if so, affectionate the greeting.

And not only so, but 'with the *ecclesia* that is in their house'. Then, they were no longer at Corinth, but had moved elsewhere, and, at that, with much increase and fruitfulness. Nor were they behind in their praise of the work of God which they had witnessed at Corinth, so that the entire congregation in their house insisted on joining the salutation with rejoicing and gladness, their hearts being knit together in love, Colossians 2:2.

Indeed, 'All'–*all*–'the brethren greet you.' With the next verse the King James' translators, in their often incomprehensibly weird vagaries, suddenly change the rendering of exactly the same Greek word from 'salute' to 'greet'. So that consonant with 'salute', I Corinthians 16:19, what *should* follow reads 'All the brethren salute you. Salute ye one another with a holy kiss', I Corinthians 16:20.

When Paul embraces all the brethren in the warmth of this salutation, it is no extravagant hyperbole: it is a sober reality. This reflects the unity in one body of all the children of God, and, if children of God, then brethren to one another by virtue of that heavenly birth. These were one: all knew of and embraced each other, to the ends of the earth.

That was the nature of the unity which was in the beginning, in the love of it: 'All the brethren salute you.'

'Salute ye one another with a holy kiss.' Yes, but what does this mean precisely? In context – mark that: *context* – since 'All the *brethren*'–not *sisters*–'salute *you*', immediately precedes the injunction, 'Salute *ye* one another', by implication this refers to the *brethren*; the context itself supplying the order of persons embraced by the pronoun 'ye'–'ye one another with an holy kiss.'

Not that sisters would not do likewise to their sisters, as 'even nature itself' would 'teach you', I Corinthians 11:14, the sisters showing their respect to their elderly women with a holy kiss, their affection one to the other with like sisterly modesty, and their joy in the children of the saints with an affectionate embrace. On the other hand, 'ye'–*brethren*–'salute *one another* with an holy kiss', I Corinthians 16:20.

Besides all this, the Greek φίλημα–from φίλος, *philos*, or, as we transliterate it into English, *philanthropy*–in this case, between brethren, the embrace of *holy* philanthropy, is by no means to be taken for granted as if it were the same thing as biased–and would-be–interpretations of the word 'kiss'.

So that all this promiscuous hugging and kissing of men and women, youths and not-so-likely maidens, which we see in the loose and disorderly conduct of certain sects and denominations is far, far wide of the restraint implied in this verse. A restraint *more* than supported *by the consistent tenor of the new testament governing modesty of deportment and propriety of behaviour between the sexes, whether in the teaching of the Lord Jesus, or of his holy apostles.*

Outside of such unrestrained cults, the 'holy kiss' has degenerated into the meaningless customs still remaining by tradition in a now defunct Christendom, once divided into 'Orthodox', Roman Catholic, and Protestant nations. The Roman Catholic practice was–and meaningless tradition, followed as a national custom, still keeps up the form–of a peck on each cheek, male and female alike. Protestant countries–naturally a more reserved tradition: anyway, it *had* to be different–preferred the handshake, but the origins were and are equally indiscriminate and national.

However, *brethren*, separate from the world, citizens of an heavenly country, knowing themselves and each other beloved and elect of God, 'Salute one another with an holy kiss', and, doubtless, respectively, so do sisters. And none other: this belongs to the love of God, in Father, Son, and Holy Ghost, indwelling the *ecclesia*, as walking in due order, in the doctrine, discipline, and ordinances of the apostles.

'The salutation of me, Paul, with mine own hand', I Corinthians 16:21. Here the apostle seals all that he has written – or that has been written by transcription on his behalf – with this unmistakable signature. There was no doubting his own distinctive writing, and it appears as a kind of seal to the epistle, saluting the brethren, and standing bold and large with that unique handwriting of the apostle in and of his own name. No one could copy that: it was Paul's own salutation by his choice and peculiar signature. And what could be more personal, or what of more comfort than that?

Perhaps I should add in closing that from this place there is neither profit nor warrant to enter into speculation about Paul's eyesight, I Corinthians 16:21.

'If any man love not the Lord Jesus Christ, let him be Anathema Maranatha.' One is not greatly enlightened by the reading from Bagster's 1877 Interlinear Greek English New Testament – so helpful elsewhere – in this mysterious passage: 'If anyone love not the Lord Jesus Christ, let him be accursed: Maran Atha', I Corinthians 16:22.

As to the word ἀνάθεμα, *anathema*, this is derived from a Greek compound, and is used elsewhere in the new testament, where, characteristically, it has been translated 'cursed' or 'accursed'. So that the apostle is saying that, after all that he had written through sixteen chapters, if anyone *still* contends, then *that person does not love the Lord Jesus Christ, because he slights his word*, as his continued and obstinate contention abundantly demonstrates.

Then let him be accursed: cut off and excommunicated from the *ecclesia*, his sins retained unto him, and abominated by all the brethren. Just so one who preached another gospel: 'let him be accursed', Galatians 1:8; and, as if that were not enough, so strong is the apostle's indignation, he repeats the words again: 'let him be accursed', Galatians 1:9.

And, in a manner, but a different manner, Paul's holy zeal moves him to repetition in I Corinthians 16:22 also. For some inexplicable reason the translators failed to render the Greek ἀνάθεμα 'accursed', or 'cursed', as—correctly—was the case in Galatians 1:8,9. Here in Corinthians, however, some inexplicable fancy moved them to *transliterate* the Greek word 'anathema'.

But—as in Galatians—he is not content with one curse: he multiplies the curse. Here, however, not by repetition, but by adding the Syriac or Aramaic tongue, a language few but the Jews among them would have understood. But there is no doubting Paul's vehemence, language or no language.

There is no point in attempting to explain the word transliterated into Greek, '*Maranatha*'. The truth is, no one—lexicographer or not—*really* knows what it means, any more than the Gentile Corinthians would have known: but the apostle's vehement indignation and zeal for the Lord leave no doubt whatever as to the intent of this word, added to 'accursed!' where *loving the Lord Jesus Christ* is synonymous with *obeying the apostolic evangel from the heart and throughout the life with meekness of submission.*

But the believing Jews knew the Aramaic expression, and could—as if the tone and context were not enough!—soon explain it to the Gentile saints. However, the explanation most necessary is this: Why Aramaic? This is not the language of the new testament.

It is the language of those who had awaited the coming of the new testament. Yet who—as a people—missed and rejected it when it came to them.

Does it mean 'the LORD comes'? No one *really* knows. But it *is* anticipatory of the coming of Messiah, even by its very tongue.

Then what was the problem, since they supposed that they knew so much about tongues? Well, what did *this* tongue tell them?

It had been the language of the Jews awaiting the Lord's *first* coming. Not his second coming. If so, it was language which the remnant according to the election of grace, that is, the believing Jews *had seen fulfilled*, and had *confessed as being fulfilled*. That is, they cried out aloud in triumph, '*Jesus Christ is come in the flesh*', I John 4:2.

And *that* said, as I Corinthians 15:1-8 clarifies, *all* is said. For whosoever confesses with the mouth, and believes from the heart, the precious and crucial doctrine of Paul's opening verses concerning the coming resurrection of the dead, at once exults and rejoices that 'Jesus Christ is come in the flesh', thereby confessing *the entire apostolic doctrine, especially as it pertained to this epistle*, and *thereby* demonstrating *unfeigned* love of the Lord Jesus Christ.

If any–but *any*–man could not, would not, or did not do so, then let that man be *accursed: Maranatha*. For Christ had come, and we who love the Lord Jesus Christ–his title from the *ascension*, note–thereby own all the truth of his deity; his eternal sonship; and his manhood; besides all that the faith embraces from his incarnation to his ascension. This is to love him.

For this is the witness of God, which he hath witnessed of his Son. This is that eternal life, which was with the Father, and was manifested to the apostles. Truly their fellowship was with the Father, and with his Son Jesus Christ. And so was– and is–theirs, who love the Lord Jesus Christ in sincerity and truth.

This is he that came by water and by blood, even Jesus Christ: not by water only, but by water and blood. And it is the Spirit that beareth witness, because the Spirit is truth. And, worshipping the Father in Spirit and truth, we love the Lord Jesus Christ. Who does not, let him be accursed: *maranatha!*

Openings in First Corinthians

As to the saints of God, the believing brethren, the *ecclesia*, with one heart, one voice, one accord, it is said of them concerning the Lord Jesus Christ, 'whom having not seen, ye love; in whom, though now ye see him not, yet believing, ye rejoice with joy unspeakable and full of glory.'

This shows the Spirit of Christ. But if any man have not the Spirit of Christ, he is none of his, Rom. 8:9. Anathema Maranatha.

'The grace of our Lord Jesus Christ be with you', I Corinthians 16:23. Again, the Lord's title from the ascended glory. Thence, by the grace of God, flows down all the favour of his work on earth, ratified by the Father of glory, and sealed by the Holy Ghost from heaven, assured in the evangel by faith without the works of the law to all at Corinth, gathered in the unity of one body.

This grace, ever proceeding from the Son, assuredly extends to all the brethren, and that, being ministered continually by the Holy Spirit of promise below, in the *ecclesia* unitedly awaiting the coming of the Lord from heaven, to the glory of God and the Father, world without end. Amen.

'My love be with you all in Christ Jesus', I Corinthians 16:24. With you *all*. My *love*. Read of it again in I Corinthians 13. Experience it again throughout the epistle. It is with you *all*.

In Christ Jesus. Then, not without the cost of a suffering, though anointed pathway: *his* pathway, fulfilled anew in his persecuted and afflicted servant for *their* sakes.

But still, to see the fruitfulness of this love, to the apostle Paul, no suffering, but absolutely *no* suffering, could be counted too great a price to pay. Amen.

JOHN METCALFE

INDEX

TO OTHER PUBLICATIONS

Psalms, Hymns, and Spiritual Songs	iii
The 'Apostolic Foundation' Series	ix
Lectures from Church House, Westminster	xix
Other Titles	xxv
'Tract for the Times' Series	xxxix
Evangelical Tracts	xliii
Ecclesia Tracts	xlvii
Foundation Tracts	li
Tape Ministry Information	lv
Magazine	lvi
Magazine Order Form	lvii
Book Order Form	lix
Tract Order Form	lxi
Tract Order Form	lxiii

PSALMS, HYMNS AND SPIRITUAL SONGS

Thoroughly revised second edition

THE PSALMS

OF THE

OLD TESTAMENT

The Psalms of the Old Testament, the result of years of painstaking labour, is an original translation into verse from the Authorized Version, which seeks to present the Psalms in the purest scriptural form possible for singing. Here, for the first time, divine names are rendered as and when they occur in the scripture, the distinction between Lord and Lord has been preserved, and every essential point of doctrine and experience appears with unique perception and fidelity.

The Psalms of the Old Testament is the first part of a trilogy written by John Metcalfe, the second part of which is entitled *Spiritual Songs from the Gospels*, and the last, *The Hymns of the New Testament*. These titles provide unique and accurate metrical versions of passages from the psalms, the gospels and the new testament epistles respectively, and are intended to be used together in the worship of God.

Price £2.50 (*postage extra*)
(hard-case binding, dust-jacket)
Printed, sewn and bound
by the John Metcalfe Publishing Trust
ISBN 1 870039 75 0

SPIRITUAL SONGS
FROM
THE GOSPELS

The *Spiritual Songs from the Gospels*, the result of years of painstaking labour, is an original translation into verse from the Authorized Version, which seeks to present essential parts of the gospels in the purest scriptural form possible for singing. The careful selection from Matthew, Mark, Luke, and John, set forth in metrical verse of the highest integrity, enables the singer to sing 'the word of Christ' as if from the scripture itself, 'richly and in all wisdom'; and, above all, in a way that facilitates worship in song of unprecedented fidelity.

The *Spiritual Songs from the Gospels* is the central part of a trilogy written by John Metcalfe, the first part of which is entitled *The Psalms of the Old Testament*, and the last, *The Hymns of the New Testament*. These titles provide unique and accurate metrical versions of passages from the psalms, the gospels and the new testament epistles respectively, and are intended to be used together in the worship of God.

Price £2.50 *(postage extra)*
(hard-case binding, dust-jacket)
Printed, sewn and bound
by the John Metcalfe Publishing Trust
ISBN 0 9506366 8 1

THE HYMNS
OF THE
NEW TESTAMENT

The Hymns of the New Testament, the result of years of painstaking labour, is an original translation into verse from the Authorized Version, which presents essential parts of the new testament epistles in the purest scriptural form possible for singing. The careful selection from the book of Acts to that of Revelation, set forth in metrical verse of the highest integrity, enables the singer to sing 'the word of Christ' as if from the scripture itself, 'richly and in all wisdom'; and, above all, in a way that facilitates worship in song of unprecedented fidelity.

The Hymns of the New Testament is the last part of a trilogy written by John Metcalfe, the first part of which is entitled *The Psalms of the Old Testament*, and the next, *Spiritual Songs from the Gospels*. These titles provide unique and accurate metrical versions of passages from the psalms, the gospels and the new testament epistles respectively, and are intended to be used together in the worship of God.

Price £2.50 (*postage extra*)
(hard-case binding, dust-jacket)
Printed, sewn and bound
by the John Metcalfe Publishing Trust
ISBN 0 9506366 9 X

'THE APOSTOLIC FOUNDATION OF THE CHRISTIAN CHURCH' SERIES

Third Printing

FOUNDATIONS UNCOVERED

THE APOSTOLIC FOUNDATION
OF THE
CHRISTIAN CHURCH

Volume I

Foundations Uncovered is the introduction to the major series: 'The Apostolic Foundation of the Christian Church'.

Rich in truth, the Introduction deals comprehensively with the foundation of the apostolic faith under the descriptive titles: The Word, The Doctrine, The Truth, The Gospel, The Faith, The New Testament, and The Foundation.

The contents of the book reveal: The Fact of the Foundation; The Foundation Uncovered; What the Foundation is not; How the Foundation is Described; and, Being Built upon the Foundation.

'This book comes with the freshness of a new Reformation.'

Price 75p *(postage extra)*
Paperback 110 pages (Laminated cover)
Printed, sewn and bound
by the John Metcalfe Publishing Trust
ISBN 0 9506366 5 7

Thoroughly revised and extensively rewritten second edition

Third Printing

THE BIRTH OF JESUS CHRIST

THE APOSTOLIC FOUNDATION OF THE CHRISTIAN CHURCH

Volume II

'The very spirit of adoration and worship rings through the pages of *The Birth of Jesus Christ*.

'The author expresses with great clarity the truths revealed to him in his study of holy scriptures at depth. We are presented here with a totally lofty view of the Incarnation.

'John Metcalfe is to be classed amongst the foremost expositors of our age; and his writings have about them that quality of timelessness that makes me sure they will one day take their place among the heritage of truly great Christian works.'

From a review by Rev. David Catterson.

'Uncompromisingly faithful to scripture ... has much to offer which is worth serious consideration ... deeply moving.'

The Expository Times.

Price 95p *(postage extra)*
Paperback 160 pages (Laminated cover)
Printed, sewn and bound
by the John Metcalfe Publishing Trust
ISBN 1 870039 48 3

*Thoroughly revised and extensively rewritten
second edition (Hardback)*

Third Printing

THE MESSIAH

THE APOSTOLIC FOUNDATION
OF THE
CHRISTIAN CHURCH

Volume III

The Messiah is a spiritually penetrating and entirely original exposition of Matthew chapter one to chapter seven from the trenchant pen of John Metcalfe.

Matthew Chapters One to Seven

GENEALOGY · BIRTH · STAR OF BETHLEHEM
HEROD · FLIGHT TO EGYPT · NAZARETH
JOHN THE BAPTIST · THE BAPTIST'S MINISTRY
JESUS' BAPTISM · ALL RIGHTEOUSNESS FULFILLED
HEAVEN OPENED · THE SPIRIT'S DESCENT
THE TEMPTATION OF JESUS IN THE WILDERNESS
JESUS' MANIFESTATION · THE CALLING · THE TRUE DISCIPLES
THE BEATITUDES · THE SERMON ON THE MOUNT

'Something of the fire of the ancient Hebrew prophet ...... Metcalfe has spiritual and expository potentials of a high order.'
The Life of Faith.

Price £7.75 *(postage extra)*
Hardback 420 pages
Laminated bookjacket
Printed, sewn and bound
by the John Metcalfe Publishing Trust
ISBN 1 870039 51 3

Second Edition (Hardback)

THE SON OF GOD AND SEED OF DAVID

THE APOSTOLIC FOUNDATION OF THE CHRISTIAN CHURCH

Volume IV

The Son of God and Seed of David is the fourth volume in the major work entitled 'The Apostolic Foundation of the Christian Church'.

'The Author proceeds to open and allege that Jesus Christ is and ever was *The Son of God*. This greatest of subjects, this most profound of all mysteries, is handled with reverence and with outstanding perception.

'The second part considers *The Seed of David*. What is meant precisely by 'the seed'? And why 'of David'? With prophetic insight the author expounds these essential verities.

Price £6.95 *(postage extra)*
Hardback 250 pages
Laminated bookjacket
Printed, sewn and bound
by the John Metcalfe Publishing Trust
ISBN 1 870039 16 5

CHRIST CRUCIFIED

THE APOSTOLIC FOUNDATION
OF THE
CHRISTIAN CHURCH

Volume V

Christ Crucified, the definitive work on the crucifixion, the blood, and the cross of Jesus Christ.

The crucifixion of Jesus Christ witnessed in the Gospels: the gospel according to Matthew; Mark; Luke; John.

The blood of Jesus Christ declared in the Epistles: the shed blood; the blood of purchase; redemption through his blood; the blood of sprinkling; the blood of the covenant.

The doctrine of the cross revealed in the apostolic foundation of the Christian church: the doctrine of the cross; the cross and the body of sin; the cross and the carnal mind; the cross and the law; the offence of the cross; the cross of our Lord Jesus Christ.

Price £6.95 (*postage extra*)
Hardback 300 pages
Laminated bookjacket
Printed, sewn and bound
by the John Metcalfe Publishing Trust
ISBN 1 870039 08 4

JUSTIFICATION BY FAITH

THE APOSTOLIC FOUNDATION
OF THE
CHRISTIAN CHURCH

Volume VI

THE HEART OF THE GOSPEL · THE FOUNDATION OF THE CHURCH
THE ISSUE OF ETERNITY
CLEARLY, ORIGINALLY AND POWERFULLY OPENED

The basis · The righteousness of the law
The righteousness of God · The atonement · Justification
Traditional views considered · Righteousness imputed to faith
Faith counted for righteousness · Justification by Faith

'And it came to pass, when Jesus had ended these sayings, the people were astonished at his doctrine: for he taught them as one having authority, and not as the scribes', Matthew 7:28,29.

Price £7.50 (postage extra)
Hardback 375 pages
Laminated bookjacket
Printed, sewn and bound
by the John Metcalfe Publishing Trust
ISBN 1 870039 11 4

THE CHURCH: WHAT IS IT?

THE APOSTOLIC FOUNDATION OF THE CHRISTIAN CHURCH

Volume VII

The answer to this question proceeds first from the lips of Jesus himself, Mt. 16:18, later to be expounded by the words of the apostles whom he sent.

Neither fear of man nor favour from the world remotely affect the answer.

Here is the truth, the whole truth, and nothing but the truth.

The complete originality, the vast range, and the total fearlessness of this book command the attention in a way that is unique.

Read this book: you will never read another like it.

Outspokenly devastating yet devastatingly constructive.

Price £7.75 *(postage extra)*
Hardback 400 pages
Laminated bookjacket
Printed, sewn and bound
by the John Metcalfe Publishing Trust
ISBN 1 870039 23 8

THE REVELATION OF JESUS CHRIST

THE APOSTOLIC FOUNDATION OF THE CHRISTIAN CHURCH

Volume VIII

Uniquely perceptive and original, the result of decades alone in the secret place of the most High, abiding under the shadow of the Almighty, this peerless work on the Revelation of Jesus Christ will stand the test of time and eternity for its heavenly, spiritual, and divine opening into the last book of the last apostle of the new testament, for all who have an ear to hear what the Spirit saith unto the churches.

Here is the transcript of the series of addresses delivered over some eighteen months during 1997 and 1998, in the Assembly Hall, Church House, Westminster, London, by John Metcalfe.

The famed Assembly Hall is used as the Synod Chamber of the Church of England as occasion requires.

Price £9.25 (*postage extra*)
Hardback 640 pages
Laminated bookjacket
Printed, sewn and bound
by the John Metcalfe Publishing Trust
ISBN 1 870039 77 7

LECTURES FROM CHURCH HOUSE, WESTMINSTER

COLOSSIANS

This concise and unique revelation of the Epistle to the Colossians has the hallmark of spiritual originality and insight peculiar to the ministry of John Metcalfe. It is as if a diamond, inert and lifeless in itself, has been divinely cut at great cost, so that every way in which it is turned, the light from above is enhanced and magnified to break forth with divine radiance showing colour and depth hitherto unsuspected.

Price 95p *(postage extra)*
Paperback 135 pages (Laminated cover)
Printed, sewn and bound
by the John Metcalfe Publishing Trust
ISBN 1 870039 55 6

MATTHEW

This concise revelation of the essence and structure of the Gospel according to Matthew, the culmination of years of prayer and devotion, retreat and study, opens the mind of the Spirit in the unique vision of Jesus Christ, the son of David, the son of Abraham, recorded in the first gospel.

Price 95p *(postage extra)*
Paperback 135 pages (Laminated cover)
Printed, sewn and bound
by the John Metcalfe Publishing Trust
ISBN 1 870039 61 0

PHILIPPIANS

The Epistle of Paul the Apostle to the Philippians is opened by this work from the pen of John Metcalfe with that lucid thoroughness which one has come to expect from a ministry received 'not of men, neither by man, but by the revelation of Jesus Christ'.

The work of God at Philippi is traced 'from the first day' until the time at which the epistle was written. Never was Lydia or the Philippian jailor drawn with more lively insight. The epistle itself is revealed in order, with passages–such as 'the mind that was in Christ Jesus'–that evidence the work of no less than a divine for our own times.

Price £1.90 *(postage extra)*
Paperback 185 pages (Laminated cover)
Printed, sewn and bound
by the John Metcalfe Publishing Trust
ISBN 1 870039 56 4

PHILEMON

This penetrating revelation of the Epistle to Philemon opens the substance of four consecutive lectures given by John Metcalfe in The Hoare Memorial Hall, Church House, Westminster, London.

Price £1.90 *(postage extra)*
Paperback 190 pages (Laminated cover)
Printed, sewn and bound
by the John Metcalfe Publishing Trust
ISBN 1 870039 66 1

FIRST TIMOTHY

This penetrating revelation of the First Epistle to Timothy opens the substance of five consecutive lectures given by John Metcalfe in The Hoare Memorial Hall, Church House, Westminster, London.

Price £2.00 (*postage extra*)
Paperback 220 pages (Laminated cover)
Printed, sewn and bound
by the John Metcalfe Publishing Trust
ISBN 1 870039 67 X

Third Printing

CREATION

Genesis 1:1, 'In the beginning God created the heaven and the earth.'

This spiritually penetrating and outstandingly original revelation of the Creation from Genesis chapters 1 and 2 opens the substance of five consecutive lectures given by John Metcalfe, commencing in the Hoare Memorial Hall and later moving to the central Assembly Hall, Church House, Westminster, London.

The Hoare Memorial Hall was used as the House of Commons at various times during the Second World War. Many of Sir Winston Churchill's renowned war time speeches were delivered in this Hall. The famed Assembly Hall is used as the Synod Chamber of the Church of England as occasion requires.

Price £2.00 (*postage extra*)
Paperback 230 pages (Laminated cover)
Printed, sewn and bound
by the John Metcalfe Publishing Trust
ISBN 1 870039 71 8

MARK

This penetrating revelation of the Gospel according to Mark opens the substance of seven consecutive lectures given by John Metcalfe in The Hoare Memorial Hall, Church House, Westminster, London.

Price £2.35 (*postage extra*)
Paperback 290 pages (Laminated cover)
Printed, sewn and bound
by the John Metcalfe Publishing Trust
ISBN 1 870039 70 X

THE FIRST EPISTLE OF JOHN

Deeply spiritual and of the very essence, it is as if one heard the apostle himself taking and opening the book in a way that is unprecedented.

> THE BEGINNING . THE MESSAGE . THE COMMANDMENTS
> THE LITTLE CHILDREN . THE ABIDING
> THE WITNESS . THE CONCLUSION

Price £9.25 (*postage extra*)
Hardback 585 pages
Laminated bookjacket
Printed, sewn and bound
by the John Metcalfe Publishing Trust
ISBN 1 870039 78 5

OTHER TITLES

Second Edition
Fourth Printing

NOAH AND THE FLOOD

Noah and the Flood expounds with vital urgency the man and the message that heralded the end of the old world. The description of the flood itself is vividly realistic. The whole work has an unmistakable ring of authority, and speaks as 'Thus saith the Lord'.

'Mr. Metcalfe makes a skilful use of persuasive eloquence as he challenges the reality of one's profession of faith ... he gives a rousing call to a searching self-examination and evaluation of one's spiritual experience.'

The Monthly Record of the Free Church of Scotland.

Price £1.90 *(postage extra)*
Paperback 155 pages (Laminated cover)
Printed, sewn and bound
by the John Metcalfe Publishing Trust
ISBN 1 870039 22 X

DIVINE FOOTSTEPS

Divine Footsteps traces the pathway of the feet of the Son of man from the very beginning in the prophetic figures of the true in the old testament through the reality in the new; doing so in a way of experimental spirituality. At the last a glimpse of the coming glory is beheld as his feet are viewed as standing at the latter day upon the earth.

Price 95p *(postage extra)*
Paperback 120 pages (Laminated cover)
Printed, sewn and bound by
the John Metcalfe Publishing Trust
ISBN 1 870039 21 1

THE RED HEIFER

The Red Heifer was the name given to a sacrifice used by the children of Israel in the Old Testament – as recorded in Numbers 19 – in which a heifer was slain and burned. Cedar wood, hyssop and scarlet were cast into the burning, and the ashes were mingled with running water and put in a vessel. It was kept for the children of Israel for a water of separation: it was a purification for sin.

In this unusual book the sacrifice is brought up to date and its relevance to the church today is shown.

Price 75p *(postage extra)*
Paperback 100 pages
ISBN 0 9502515 4 2

OF GOD OR MAN?

LIGHT FROM GALATIANS

The Epistle to the Galatians contends for deliverance from the law and from carnal ministry.

The Apostle opens his matter in two ways:

Firstly, Paul vindicates himself and his ministry against those that came not from God above, but from Jerusalem below.

Secondly, he defends the Gospel and evangelical liberty against legal perversions and bondage to the flesh.

Price £1.45 *(postage extra)*
Paperback 190 pages (Laminated cover)
ISBN 0 9506366 3 0

THE BOOK OF RUTH

The Book of Ruth is set against the farming background of old testament Israel at the time of the Judges, the narrative—unfolding the work of God in redemption—being marked by a series of agricultural events.

These events—the famine; the barley harvest; the wheat harvest; the winnowing—possessed a hidden spiritual significance to that community, but, much more, they speak in figure directly to our own times, as the book reveals.

Equally contemporary appear the characters of Ruth, Naomi, Boaz, and the first kinsman, drawn with spiritual perception greatly to the profit of the reader.

Price £4.95 (*postage extra*)
Hardback 200 pages
Laminated bookjacket
Printed, sewn and bound
by the John Metcalfe Publishing Trust
ISBN 1 870039 17 3

A QUESTION FOR POPE JOHN PAUL II

As a consequence of his many years spent apart in prayer, lonely vigil, and painstaking study of the scripture, John Metcalfe asks a question and looks for an answer from Pope John Paul II.

Price £1.25 (*postage extra*)
Paperback 105 pages (Laminated cover)
ISBN 0 9506366 4 9

DIVINE MEDITATIONS
OF
WILLIAM HUNTINGTON

Originally published by Mr. Huntington as a series of letters to J. Jenkins, under the title of 'Contemplations on the God of Israel', the spiritual content of this correspondence has been skilfully and sympathetically edited, abridged, and arranged so as to form a series of meditations, suitable for daily readings.

Mr. Huntington's own text is thereby adapted to speak directly to the reader in a way much more suited to his ministering immediately to ourselves, in our own circumstances and times.

It is greatly hoped that many today will benefit from this adaption which carefully retains both the spirit and the letter of the text. If any prefer the original format, this is readily available from several sources and many libraries.

Nevertheless, the publishers believe the much more readable form into which Mr. Huntington's very words have been adapted will appeal to a far wider audience, for whose comfort and consolation this carefully edited work has been published.

Price £2.35 (*postage extra*)
Paperback 300 pages (Laminated cover)
Printed, sewn and bound
by the John Metcalfe Publishing Trust
ISBN 1 870039 24 6

Second Edition
Third Printing

THE WELLS OF SALVATION

The Wells of Salvation is written from a series of seven powerful addresses preached at Tylers Green. It is a forthright and experimental exposition of Isaiah 12:3, 'Therefore with joy shall ye draw water out of the wells of salvation.'

John Metcalfe is acknowledged to be perhaps the most gifted expositor and powerful preacher of our day and this is to be seen clearly in The Wells of Salvation.

Price £2.35 *(postage extra)*
Paperback 285 pages (Laminated cover)
Printed, sewn and bound
by the John Metcalfe Publishing Trust
ISBN 1 870039 72 6

Second Printing

SAVING FAITH

The sevenfold work of the Holy Ghost in bringing a sinner to saving faith in Christ opened and enlarged.

True faith is the work of God. False faith is the presumption of man. But where is the difference? *Saving Faith* shows the difference.

Price £2.25 *(postage extra)*
Paperback 250 pages (Laminated cover)
Printed, sewn and bound
by the John Metcalfe Publishing Trust
ISBN 1 870039 40 8

DELIVERANCE FROM THE LAW
THE WESTMINSTER CONFESSION EXPLODED

Deliverance from the Law. A devastating vindication of the gospel of Christ against the traditions of man.

Price £1.90 (*postage extra*)
Paperback 160 pages (Laminated cover)
Printed, sewn and bound
by the John Metcalfe Publishing Trust
ISBN 1 870039 41 6

PRESENT-DAY CONVERSIONS
OF THE NEW TESTAMENT KIND

FROM THE MINISTRY OF
JOHN METCALFE

The outstandingly striking presentation of this fascinating paperback will surely catch the eye, as its title and contents will certainly captivate the mind: here is a unique publication.

Woven into a gripping narrative, over twenty-one short life stories, all centred on conversions that simply could not have happened had not God broken in, and had not Christ been revealed, the book presents a tremendous challenge, at once moving and thrilling to the reader.

Price £2.25 (*postage extra*)
Paperback 240 pages (Laminated cover)
Printed, sewn and bound
by the John Metcalfe Publishing Trust
ISBN 1 870039 31 9

THE BEATITUDES

A unique insight destined to be the classic opening of this wonderful sequence of utterances from the lips of Jesus.

The reader will discover a penetration of the spiritual heights and divine depths of these peerless words in a way ever fresh and always rewarding though read time and time again.

Price £1.90 (*postage extra*)
Paperback 185 pages (Laminated cover)
Printed, sewn and bound
by the John Metcalfe Publishing Trust
ISBN 1 870039 45 9

PASTORAL LETTERS TO THE FAR EAST

Feeling the abiding spiritual value of letters written by John Metcalfe in his absence from the Far East, Miss Sie Siok Hui cherished the correspondence to her, and at the same time was moved to seek for similar writings to some of her closest sisters in Christ.

Gathering these letters together, it was her earnest desire that such an enduring testimony should be made available to all the faithful remnant in our own day. The result of her prayers and spiritual exercise appears in the publication 'Pastoral Letters to the Far East'.

Price £2.00 (*postage extra*)
Paperback 240 pages (Laminated cover)
Printed, sewn and bound
by the John Metcalfe Publishing Trust
ISBN 1 870039 74 2

LAW AND GRACE CONTRASTED

A SERIES OF ADDRESSES

BY

WILLIAM HUNTINGTON

The Child of Liberty in Legal Bondage · The Bondchild brought to the Test · The Modern Plasterer Detected Not under Law · The Law a Rule of Life?

Mr. Huntington's own text is adapted to speak directly to the reader in a way much more suited to his ministering immediately to ourselves, in our own circumstances and times.

It is greatly hoped that many today will benefit from this adaption which carefully retains both the spirit and the letter of the text. If any prefer the original format, this is readily available from several sources and many libraries.

Nevertheless, the publishers believe the much more readable form into which Mr. Huntington's very words have been adapted will appeal to a far wider audience, for whose comfort and consolation this carefully edited work has been published.

Price £2.35 (*postage extra*)
Paperback 265 pages (Laminated cover)
Printed, sewn and bound
by the John Metcalfe Publishing Trust
ISBN 1 870039 76 9

TWO NEWLY PUBLISHED TITLES

THE GIFTS AND BAPTISM OF THE SPIRIT

For so long confusion has reigned in respect of THE GIFTS AND BAPTISM OF THE SPIRIT. Here at last is that spiritual, sound, and balanced opening of the Holy Scripture from I Corinthians 12:1-13.

This gives the unmistakable ring of apostolic authority, puts the matter beyond the realm of speculation or experiment, past all doubt bringing the text into the light of revelation of Jesus Christ.

Price 95p (*postage extra*)
Paperback 128 pages (Laminated cover)
Printed, sewn and bound
by the John Metcalfe Publishing Trust
ISBN 1 870039 80 7

THE BODY OF CHRIST AND THE GIFTS

For so long confusion has reigned in respect of THE BODY OF CHRIST AND THE GIFTS. Here at last is that spiritual, sound, and balanced opening of the Holy Scripture from I Corinthians 12:14-13:13.

This gives the unmistakable ring of apostolic authority, puts the matter beyond the realm of speculation or experiment, past all doubt bringing the text into the light of revelation of Jesus Christ.

Price 95p (*postage extra*)
Paperback 140 pages (Laminated cover)
Printed, sewn and bound
by the John Metcalfe Publishing Trust
ISBN 1 870039 82 3

TWO NEWLY PUBLISHED TITLES

THE COMING RESURRECTION OF THE DEAD

For so long confusion has reigned in respect of THE COMING RESURRECTION OF THE DEAD. Here at last is that spiritual, sound, and balanced opening of the Holy Scripture from I Corinthians 15.

This gives the unmistakable ring of apostolic authority, puts the matter beyond the realm of speculation or prejudice, past all doubt bringing the text into the light of revelation of Jesus Christ.

Price 95p (*postage extra*)
Paperback 145 pages (Laminated cover)
Printed, sewn and bound
by the John Metcalfe Publishing Trust
ISBN 1 870039 85 8

THE GIFTS OF TONGUES AND OF PROPHECY

For so long confusion has reigned in respect of THE GIFTS OF TONGUES AND OF PROPHECY. Here at last is that spiritual, sound, and balanced opening of the Holy Scripture from I Corinthians 14.

This gives the unmistakable ring of apostolic authority, puts the matter beyond the realm of speculation or experiment, past all doubt bringing the text into the light of revelation of Jesus Christ.

Price 95p (*postage extra*)
Paperback 90 pages (Laminated cover)
Printed, sewn and bound
by the John Metcalfe Publishing Trust
ISBN 1 870039 86 6

NEWLY PUBLISHED

OPENINGS IN FIRST CORINTHIANS

The Beginning · The Vision
The Opening: The Testimony of Christ

Judgment concerning the Testimony:

Judgment concerning divisions; Judgment concerning the wicked; Judgment pertaining to the saints; Judgment concerning questions of marriage; Judgment concerning meats offered to idols; Judgment concerning headship.

Judgment concerning assembling together:

The Lord's Supper; The Unity of the Spirit in the Body of Christ; The manifestation of the Gifts in the Assembly; The Evangelical Truth of the Resurrection of the Dead.

The Conclusion

Price £9.25 (*postage extra*)
Hardback 495 pages
Laminated bookjacket
Printed, sewn and bound
by the John Metcalfe Publishing Trust
ISBN 1 870039 84 X

'TRACT FOR THE TIMES' SERIES

'TRACT FOR THE TIMES' SERIES

The Gospel of God by John Metcalfe. No. 1 in the Series. Laminated cover, price 25p.

The Strait Gate by John Metcalfe. No. 2 in the Series. Laminated cover, price 25p.

Eternal Sonship and Taylor Brethren by John Metcalfe. No. 3 in the Series. Laminated cover, price 25p.

Marks of the New Testament Church by John Metcalfe. No. 4 in the Series. Laminated cover, price 25p.

The Charismatic Delusion by John Metcalfe. No. 5 in the Series. Laminated cover, price 25p.

Premillennialism Exposed by John Metcalfe. No. 6 in the Series. Laminated cover, price 25p.

Justification and Peace by John Metcalfe. No. 7 in the Series. Laminated cover, price 25p.

Faith or Presumption? by John Metcalfe. No. 8 in the Series. Laminated cover, price 25p.

The Elect Undeceived by John Metcalfe. No. 9 in the Series. Laminated cover, price 25p.

Justifying Righteousness by John Metcalfe. No. 10 in the Series. Laminated cover, price 25p.

Righteousness Imputed by John Metcalfe. No. 11 in the Series. Laminated cover, price 25p.

The Great Deception by John Metcalfe. No. 12 in the Series. Laminated cover, price 25p.

A Famine in the Land by John Metcalfe. No. 13 in the Series. Laminated cover, price 25p.

Blood and Water by John Metcalfe. No. 14 in the Series. Laminated cover, price 25p.

Women Bishops? by John Metcalfe. No. 15 in the Series. Laminated cover, price 25p.

The Heavenly Vision by John Metcalfe. No. 16 in the Series. Laminated cover, price 25p.

The Mystery of Godliness by John Metcalfe. No. 17 in the Series. Laminated cover, price 25p.

EVANGELICAL TRACTS

EVANGELICAL TRACTS

1. **The Two Prayers of Elijah.** Light green card cover, price 10p.

2. **Wounded for our Transgressions.** Gold card cover, price 10p.

3. **The Blood of Sprinkling.** Red card cover, price 10p.

4. **The Grace of God that brings Salvation.** Blue card cover, price 10p.

5. **The Name of Jesus.** Rose card cover, price 10p.

6. **The Ministry of the New Testament.** Purple card cover, price 10p.

7. **The Death of the Righteous** (*The closing days of J.B. Stoney*) by A.M.S. (his daughter). Ivory card cover, price 10p.

8. **Repentance.** Sky blue card cover, price 10p.

9. **Legal Deceivers Exposed.** Crimson card cover, price 10p.

10. **Unconditional Salvation.** Green card cover, price 10p.

11. **Religious Merchandise.** Brown card cover, price 10p.

12. **Comfort.** Pink card cover, price 10p.

13. **Peace.** Grey card cover, price 10p.

14. **Eternal Life.** Cobalt card cover, price 10p.

15. **The Handwriting of Ordinances.** Fawn card cover, price 10p.

16. **'Lord, Lord!'.** Emerald card cover, price 10p.

17. **Conversion.** Wedgewood card cover, price 10p.

ECCLESIA TRACTS

ECCLESIA TRACTS

The Beginning of the Ecclesia by John Metcalfe. No. 1 in the Series, Sand grain cover, price 10p.

Churches and the Church by J.N. Darby. Edited. No. 2 in the Series, Sand grain cover, price 10p.

The Ministers of Christ by John Metcalfe. No. 3 in the Series, Sand grain cover, price 10p.

The Inward Witness by George Fox. Edited. No. 4 in the Series, Sand grain cover, price 10p.

The Notion of a Clergyman by J.N. Darby. Edited. No. 5 in the Series, Sand grain cover, price 10p.

The Servant of the Lord by William Huntington. Edited and Abridged. No. 6 in the Series, Sand grain cover, price 10p.

One Spirit by William Kelly. Edited. No. 7 in the Series, Sand grain cover, price 10p.

The Funeral of Arminianism by William Huntington. Edited and Abridged. No. 8 in the Series, Sand grain cover, price 10p.

One Body by William Kelly. Edited. No. 9 in the Series, Sand grain cover, price 10p.

False Churches and True by John Metcalfe. No. 10 in the Series, Sand grain cover, price 10p.

Separation from Evil by J.N. Darby. Edited. No. 11 in the Series, Sand grain cover, price 10p.

The Remnant by J.B. Stoney. Edited. No. 12 in the Series, Sand grain cover, price 10p.

The Arminian Skeleton by William Huntington. Edited and Abridged. No. 13 in the Series, Sand grain cover, price 10p.

FOUNDATION TRACTS

FOUNDATION TRACTS

1. **Female Priests?** by John Metcalfe. Oatmeal cover, price 25p.

2. **The Bondage of the Will** by Martin Luther. Translated and Abridged. Oatmeal cover, price 25p.

3. **Of the Popish Mass** by John Calvin. Translated and Abridged. Oatmeal cover, price 25p.

4. **The Adversary** by John Metcalfe. Oatmeal cover, price 25p.

5. **The Advance of Popery** by J.C. Philpot. Oatmeal cover, price 25p.

6. **Enemies in the Land** by John Metcalfe. Oatmeal cover, price 25p.

7. **An Admonition Concerning Relics** by John Calvin. Oatmeal cover, price 25p.

8. **John Metcalfe's Testimony Against Falsity in Worship** by John Metcalfe. Oatmeal cover, price 25p.

9. **Brethrenism Exposed** by John Metcalfe. Oatmeal cover, price 25p.

10. **John Metcalfe's Testimony Against The Social Gospel** by John Metcalfe. Oatmeal cover, price 25p.

MINISTRY BY JOHN METCALFE

TAPE MINISTRY BY JOHN METCALFE
FROM THE U.K. AND THE FAR EAST
IS AVAILABLE

In order to obtain this free recorded ministry, please send your blank cassette (C.90) and the cost of the return postage, including your name and address in block capitals, to the John Metcalfe Publishing Trust, Church Road, Tylers Green, Penn, Bucks, HP10 8LN. Tapelists are available on request.

Owing to the increased demand for the tape ministry, we are unable to supply more than two tapes per order, except in the case of meetings for the hearing of tapes, where a special arrangement can be made.

THE MINISTRY OF THE NEW TESTAMENT

The purpose of this substantial A4 gloss paper magazine is to provide spiritual and experimental ministry with sound doctrine which rightly and prophetically divides the word of truth.

Readers of our books will already know the high standards of our publications. They can be confident that these pages will maintain that quality, by giving access to enduring ministry from the past, much of which is derived from sources that are virtually unobtainable today, and publishing a living ministry from the present. Selected articles from the following writers have already been included:

Eli Ashdown · John Berridge · Abraham Booth
John Bradford · John Bunyan · John Burgon
John Calvin · Donald Cargill · John Cennick · J.N. Darby
George Fox · John Foxe · William Gadsby · John Guthrie
William Guthrie · Grey Hazlerigg · William Huntington
William Kelly · John Kennedy · John Kershaw
John Keyt · Hanserd Knollys · John Knox · James Lewis
Martin Luther · Robert Murray McCheyne · John Metcalfe
Brownlow North · Thomas Oxenham · Alexander–Sandy–Peden
J.C. Philpot · J.K. Popham · James Renwick · J.B. Stoney
Henry Tanner · Arthur Triggs · John Vinall · John Warburton
John Welwood · George Whitefield · J.A. Wylie

Price £1.75 (*postage included*)
Issued Spring, Summer, Autumn, Winter.

Magazine Order Form

Name and address (in block capitals)

....

....

....

Please send me ...... current copy/copies of The Ministry of the New Testament.

Please send me ...... year/s subscription.

I enclose a cheque/postal order for £......

(Price: including postage, U.K. £1.75; Overseas £1.90)
(One year's subscription: including postage, U.K. £7.00; Overseas £7.60)

Cheques should be made payable to The John Metcalfe Publishing Trust, and for overseas subscribers should be in pounds sterling drawn on a London Bank.

10 or more copies to one address will qualify for a 10% discount.

Some back numbers from Spring 1986 available.

Please send to The John Metcalfe Publishing Trust, Church Road, Tylers Green, Penn, Bucks, HP10 8LN.

All publications of the Trust are subsidised by the Publishers

Book Order Form

Please send to the address below:

	Price	Quantity
A Question for Pope John Paul II	£1.25	......
Of God or Man?	£1.45	......
Noah and the Flood	£1.90	......
Divine Footsteps	£0.95	......
The Red Heifer	£0.75	......
The Wells of Salvation	£2.35	......
The Book of Ruth (Hardback edition)	£4.95	......
Divine Meditations of William Huntington	£2.35	......
Present-Day Conversions of the New Testament Kind	£2.25	......
Saving Faith	£2.25	......
Deliverance from the Law	£1.90	......
The Beatitudes	£1.90	......
Pastoral Letters to the Far East	£2.00	......
Law and Grace Contrasted by William Huntington	£2.35	......
The Gifts and Baptism of the Spirit	£0.95	......
The Body of Christ and the Gifts	£0.95	......
The Coming Resurrection of the Dead	£0.95	......
The Gifts of Tongues and of Prophecy	£0.95	......
Openings in First Corinthians (Hardback edition)	£9.25	......

Lectures from Church House, Westminster

	Price	Quantity
Colossians	£0.95	......
Philippians	£1.90	......
Matthew	£0.95	......
Philemon	£1.90	......
First Timothy	£2.00	......
Mark	£2.35	......
Creation	£2.00	......
The First Epistle of John (Hardback edition)	£9.25	......

Psalms, Hymns & Spiritual Songs (Hardback edition)

	Price	Quantity
The Psalms of the Old Testament	£2.50	......
Spiritual Songs from the Gospels	£2.50	......
The Hymns of the New Testament	£2.50	......

'Apostolic Foundation of the Christian Church' series

		Price	Quantity
Foundations Uncovered	Vol. I	£0.75	......
The Birth of Jesus Christ	Vol. II	£0.95	......
The Messiah (Hardback edition)	Vol. III	£7.75	......
The Son of God and Seed of David (Hardback edition)	Vol. IV	£6.95	......
Christ Crucified (Hardback edition)	Vol. V	£6.95	......
Justification by Faith (Hardback edition)	Vol. VI	£7.50	......
The Church: What is it? (Hardback edition)	Vol. VII	£7.75	......
The Revelation of Jesus Christ (Hardback edition)	Vol. VIII	£9.25	......

Name and address (in block capitals)

....

....

....

If money is sent with order please allow for postage. Please address to:- The John Metcalfe Publishing Trust, Church Road, Tylers Green, Penn, Bucks, HP10 8LN.

cut here

Tract Order Form

Please send to the address below:

                                                                            Price   Quantity

Evangelical Tracts

Title	Price	Quantity
The Two Prayers of Elijah	£0.10	......
Wounded for our Transgressions	£0.10	......
The Blood of Sprinkling	£0.10	......
The Grace of God that brings Salvation	£0.10	......
The Name of Jesus	£0.10	......
The Ministry of the New Testament	£0.10	......
The Death of the Righteous by A.M.S.	£0.10	......
Repentance	£0.10	......
Legal Deceivers Exposed	£0.10	......
Unconditional Salvation	£0.10	......
Religious Merchandise	£0.10	......
Comfort	£0.10	......
Peace	£0.10	......
Eternal Life	£0.10	......
The Handwriting of Ordinances	£0.10	......
'Lord, Lord!'	£0.10	......
Conversion	£0.10	......

'Tract for the Times' series

Title	No.	Price	Quantity
The Gospel of God	No. 1	£0.25	......
The Strait Gate	No. 2	£0.25	......
Eternal Sonship and Taylor Brethren	No. 3	£0.25	......
Marks of the New Testament Church	No. 4	£0.25	......
The Charismatic Delusion	No. 5	£0.25	......
Premillennialism Exposed	No. 6	£0.25	......
Justification and Peace	No. 7	£0.25	......
Faith or Presumption?	No. 8	£0.25	......
The Elect Undeceived	No. 9	£0.25	......
Justifying Righteousness	No.10	£0.25	......
Righteousness Imputed	No.11	£0.25	......
The Great Deception	No.12	£0.25	......
A Famine in the Land	No.13	£0.25	......
Blood and Water	No.14	£0.25	......
Women Bishops?	No.15	£0.25	......
The Heavenly Vision	No.16	£0.25	......
The Mystery of Godliness	No.17	£0.25	......

Name and address (in block capitals)

....

....

....

If money is sent with order please allow for postage. Please address to:- The John Metcalfe Publishing Trust, Church Road, Tylers Green, Penn, Bucks, HP10 8LN.

cut here

Tract Order Form

Please send to the address below:

	Price	Quantity
Ecclesia Tracts		
The Beginning of the Ecclesia	No. 1 £0.10	......
Churches and the Church (J.N.D.)	No. 2 £0.10	......
The Ministers of Christ	No. 3 £0.10	......
The Inward Witness (G.F.)	No. 4 £0.10	......
The Notion of a Clergyman (J.N.D.)	No. 5 £0.10	......
The Servant of the Lord (W.H.)	No. 6 £0.10	......
One Spirit (W.K.)	No. 7 £0.10	......
The Funeral of Arminianism (W.H.)	No. 8 £0.10	......
One Body (W.K.)	No. 9 £0.10	......
False Churches and True	No.10 £0.10	......
Separation from Evil (J.N.D.)	No.11 £0.10	......
The Remnant (J.B.S.)	No.12 £0.10	......
The Arminian Skeleton (W.H.)	No.13 £0.10	......
Foundation Tracts		
Female Priests?	No. 1 £0.25	......
The Bondage of the Will (Martin Luther)	No. 2 £0.25	......
Of the Popish Mass (John Calvin)	No. 3 £0.25	......
The Adversary	No. 4 £0.25	......
The Advance of Popery (J.C. Philpot)	No. 5 £0.25	......
Enemies in the Land	No. 6 £0.25	......
An Admonition Concerning Relics (John Calvin)	No. 7 £0.25	......
John Metcalfe's Testimony Against Falsity in Worship	No. 8 £0.25	......
Brethrenism Exposed	No. 9 £0.25	......
John Metcalfe's Testimony Against The Social Gospel	No.10 £0.25	......

cut here

Name and address (in block capitals)

....

....

....

If money is sent with order please allow for postage. Please address to:- The John Metcalfe Publishing Trust, Church Road, Tylers Green, Penn, Bucks, HP10 8LN.